FISHES

A Field and Laboratory Manual on Their Structure, Identification, and Natural History

GREGOR M. CAILLIET
Moss Landing Marine Laboratories

MILTON S. LOVE
Occidental College

ALFRED W. EBELING
University of California, Santa Barbara

Wadsworth Publishing Company
Belmont, California
A Division of Wadsworth, Inc.

Biology Editor: Jack Carey

Editorial Assistant: Ruth Singer

Production Editor: Sandra Craig

Cover Designer: Paula Shuhert

Print Buyer: Ruth Cole

Art Editor: Marta Kongsle

Text Designer: Perry Smith

Copy Editor: L. Jay Stewart

Technical Illustrator: Lynn McMasters

Compositor: Graphic Typesetting Service

Printed in the United States of America

1 2 3 4 5 6 7 8 9 10—90 89 88 87 86

ISBN 0-534-05556-7

Library of Congress Cataloging in Publication Data

Cailliet, Gregor M., 1943–
    Fishes: a field and laboratory manual on their structure, identification, and natural history.

    Bibliography: p.
    Includes index.
    1. Fishes—Anatomy—Laboratory manuals. 2. Fishes—Identification. 3. Fishes. I. Love, Milton S., 1947 – II. Ebeling, Alfred W., 1931–   III. Title.
QL639.C218   1986   598   85-20218
ISBN 0-534-05556-7

CONTENTS

PREFACE

During our collective fifty years of teaching ichthyology and fishery biology, we have used many excellent textbooks but have had to devise our own laboratory exercises and associated handouts. It is no wonder, then, that more teaching assistants than we care to remember have suggested that we gather this array of teaching material and organize it into a manual. Following this suggestion, we realized, might allow the copy machine to cool down and would also obviate endless collation and distribution. In addition, students would have all their materials in one place, and the more ambitious of these class participants could prepare ahead.

We have also observed that students often have difficulty bridging the gap between theory as presented in textbooks and in lectures, and empiricism as practiced in both the laboratory and the field. This manual is designed to help students construct that bridge. We run the risk of duplicating some information commonly found in textbooks in order to provide discussions and explanations to introduce the exercises, thus helping students to formulate the connections between general principles and specific inquiries. This approach works to guide students through the maze of parts to gain the whole, helping them to transform memorized facts into concepts that stimulate explorations to discover relationships and understanding.

The discourse and exercises in *Fishes: A Field and Laboratory Manual* evolved over time. They were conceived originally for courses in general ichthyology, primarily covering the functional morphology and systematics of fishes. However, as we changed our perception of ichthyology as a subject, we added numerous laboratory and field exercises on the general biology of fishes. We also extended the subject material and exercises associated with each topic to be applicable to fisheries science and aquaculture subjects. The result is a manual that is suitable for students in a range of subjects, including ichthyology, fish biology, fishery biology, and aquaculture. It will also serve professionals as an accessible reference on many subjects of fish biology.

The manual is divided into three sections. Section One provides detailed information on the morphology of fishes, which we believe is the basic prerequisite to an understanding of both the systematics and the biology of fishes. This section contains information on the most readily observable characters, thus leading naturally into the study of systematics, the manifestation of evolutionary processes, in Section Two, Taxonomic Characters in Identification, Variation, and Classification. Both Sections One and Two provide exercises that allow students to further explore the various morphological structures of fishes and how they function, thus allowing fishes to become remarkably successful throughout the world.

In Section Three, Natural History of Fishes, we go into the field to collect fishes and study them in their natural habitats. This section includes chapters on collection and survey techniques, age and growth, feeding, reproduction, and parasites of fishes (for those who have just discovered sushi bars and sashimi). Each chapter introduces readers to techniques that are useful in basic biological studies of fishes, many of which are directly applicable to fishery biology, aquaculture, and conservation.

The creation of this manual has benefited greatly from interactions with our instructors and colleagues. We are very grateful to all who provided guidance. Numerous individuals reviewed and provided comments on various drafts and sections of the manual. We especially thank M. Eric Anderson, George Arita, Richard Bray, Frank Henry, Richard Ibara, Ralph Larson, Robert Lea, Susan E. Smith, Richard A. Tubb, and the Wadsworth reviewers: Martin R. Brittan, California State University, Sacramento; Michael H. Horn, California State University, Fullerton; Peter B. Moyle,

University of California, Davis; Jack Musick, Virginia Institute of Marine Science; and Theodore W. Pietsch, University of Washington. In addition, Cynthia Annett, Mark Carr, Gary Grossman, Kevin Lohman, Gary McDonald, Donald Nelson, David Noakes, Dan Reed, and Bernd Wursig offered valuable suggestions for various exercises. We especially appreciate permission to use the original artwork of Margaret Bradbury, Bonnie Hall, Dan Miller, and Susan E. Smith, and we thank those authors and artists who allowed us to base our illustrations on their work. Lynn McMasters did a wonderful job of depicting fish morphology and in producing the fine original illustrations for this manual.

Having been both students and instructors during our careers, we recognize the importance of student input in creating a more effective exchange of knowledge in both the classroom and the field. We therefore thank all of our students for their enthusiastic and valuable help in organizing, using, and reviewing the work contained in this manual. We dedicate the book to them.

GREGOR M. CAILLIET

MILTON S. LOVE

ALFRED W. EBELING

SECTION ONE
MORPHOLOGY OF FISHES: FORM AND FUNCTION

To understand how a fish functions, we must know how it is assembled. It is extremely valuable for the taxonomist, physiologist, or ecologist to have a strong background in morphology. In the following sections, we describe how fishes are constructed.

First, we present details of external morphology, which are valuable in taxonomic (descriptive) studies. Included is a description of the general anatomy of fishes, along with descriptions of other, often specialized, structures such as scales, barbels, cirri, dentition, photophores, and electric organs. Second, we provide a general description of the internal morphology of fishes. This serves as a general guide to the structure and arrangement of the internal organs, including the alimentary canal, liver, spleen, pancreas, kidney, gonads, swimbladder, and the circulatory and nervous systems. Later chapters give more detailed coverage of several of these functional systems.

Knowledge of the skeletal system and its organization is essential to a complete understanding of the functional operation of the fish body. In addition, the characteristic kinds and shapes of the various body components are important taxonomically and phylogenetically. Therefore, we dedicated a separate chapter to the osteology of fishes (chap. 3). Here the laboratory exercises are designed to aid in completely disassembling and correctly reassembling a fish, a feat that yields a more complete understanding of its structure. Several other more specialized techniques, useful in analyzing skeletal anatomy, are also included.

The muscle system of fishes, coupled closely with the skeletal system, is described in chapter 4. The functional relations between the more important muscles and associated bones are described and explained for a better understanding of how a fish moves such structures as its trunk, tail, and paired and median fins and how it opens and closes its mouth and operculum.

Chapter 5 deals with some of the more interesting categories of fish function by presenting specific laboratory exercises in functional morphology, behavior, and physiology. Several exercises cover sensory mechanisms used by fishes, including laboratory sessions on vision, chemoreception, mechanoreception, and electroreception. The next set of exercises centers on fish respiration and feeding, including dissections of gill apparati, behavioral and morphological studies of respiration and feeding, and exercises demonstrating how closely linked respiratory and feeding movements are. The following portion of chapter 5 presents exercises on fish swimming, including studies of morphology, behavior, and muscle physiology. The next exercises cover the swimbladder and how it is structured, how its volume is adjusted, and how to measure gases that are concentrated there. Finally, the last portion of chapter 5 contains exercises on the various ways in which fishes reproduce, including a survey of reproductive modes and their associated morphology.

These five chapters, we believe, will allow a fish biologist to experience a wide variety of dissections, demonstrations, exercises, and experiments that cover, at least partially, the form and function of fishes.

Chapter 1
Basic Anatomy: External

Although the three main living groups of fishes[1] (jawless, cartilaginous, and bony) share certain external features, they differ considerably in several ways (Wake 1979). All, for example, have external gill openings, median "fins," external nostrils, a muscular trunk and tail, and a mouth. However, the shape, structure, and numbers of these structures differ among individuals of these three groups. Using specimens available to you during laboratory sessions, locate the morphological features described in the following paragraphs.

JAWLESS FISHES

The jawless fishes (Agnatha), which include both lampreys and hagfishes, have a suctorial mouth; hence they are often called **cyclostomes** ("round mouth"). The hagfishes have several thick, fingerlike whiskers (**barbels**) around the mouth and nostril, and the mouth has horny plates with

1. The plural word *fishes* emphasizes more than one species, while the plural word *fish* simply means more than one individual, no matter what species. For example, one would do a taxonomic analysis of the *fishes* of California but would ask how many fish were caught on a party boat.

rows of sharp, broadly triangular teeth (fig. 1.1). These fishes are blind, and the normal site for the eyes is often marked with small light-colored areas. They are usually scavengers. The lampreys, on the other hand, are usually parasitic; therefore, they have a mouth and **oral disk** with rasping teeth, with which they attach themselves to fish hosts to suck out their bodily fluids (fig. 1.2).

In addition to the suctorial mouth, these fishes have a variable number of gill slits: lampreys have 7 and hagfishes have from 1 to as many as 16, depending on the species. Neither of these fishes possesses paired fins, but some have median structures called **finfolds** and a **caudal fin**. In the lamprey, the finfolds have cartilaginous rodlike supports, but in the hagfish, they do not. Two additional features that unite these two kinds of fishes and serve to distinguish them externally from other fishes are their single median nostril and their lack of scales.

CARTILAGINOUS FISHES

The four groups of cartilaginous fishes (Chondrichthyes) have several distinguishing features; we give descriptions of

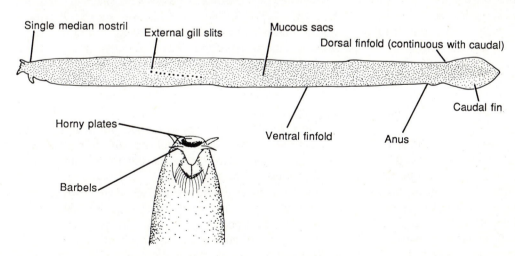

Figure 1.1 The external anatomy of the Pacific hagfish (*Eptatretus stoutii*) with details of the suctorial mouth. (Miller and Lea 1972)

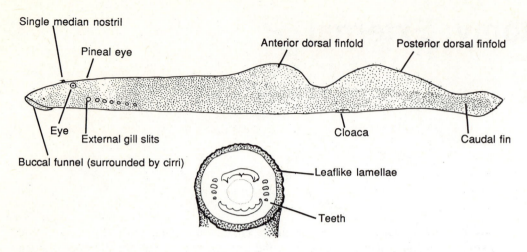

Figure 1.2 The external anatomy of the Pacific lamprey (*Lampetra tridentata*) with details of the suctorial mouth. (Miller and Lea 1972)

each. We begin by listing those characteristics that occur in all members of this group and then describe how these features differ from the jawless and bony fishes. The major difference is the existence in the Chondrichthyes of a well-developed lower jaw. In addition, the presence of true bony teeth on both jaws and the beginning of calcification within the vertebrae serve to distinguish cartilaginous from jawless fishes. In the chimaeroids, the upper jaw is permanently fused to the cranium, while in the sharks, skates, and rays, it is separate. Other morphological features that distinguish chondrichthyans from agnathans are paired fins, gills with individual openings, often a pair of **spiracles** on the top of the head, and a pair of elongate **claspers** on the inner edge of the ventral fins in mature males. They use these in internal fertilization. Also in contrast to agnathans, the cartilaginous fishes have scales (fig. 1.3). These **placoid** scales are developmentally and histologically similar to teeth.

The sharks will be represented in our description and dissections by *Squalus acanthias*, the spiny dogfish, since it is ubiquitous and abundant. Sharks have five to seven gill clefts on each side of the head and a free eyelid on the upper portion of the eye. The body is divided into the head, trunk, and tail regions, and sharks have two sets of paired fins, distinct dorsal fins, often a median ventral fin, and a **heterocercal** caudal fin with the dorsal lobe larger than the ventral lobe (fig. 1.4).

Skates and rays differ from other elasmobranchs in several external features, the most distinct being the greatly enlarged pectoral fins attached to the sides of the head and the gills located in front of and below these fins. Skates and rays often take water in through the spiracles on top of the head (these are modified residual gill openings) instead of through the mouth because they live on the bottom and their gills are oriented ventrally. In addition, they lack a free upper eyelid. There are several families of skates and rays that differ mostly in the placement of the dorsal fins, the

shape of the body, and the structure of the jaws and teeth. One quite distinct species is the electric ray, *Torpedo californica* (fig. 1.5), which besides having characteristics typical of this group, has two dorsal electric organs. These paired electric organs are modified muscle tissue, apparently used to immobilize their prey. Other raylike fishes (group Batoidei) are not pictured here. These are the devil rays (Mobulidae), bat rays (Myliobatidae), stingrays (Dasyatidae), and guitarfishes (Rhinobatidae). Another family included in the group Batoidei is the sawfishes (Pristidae), which have gills on the underside of the pectoral fins and a very noticeable double-edged saw-toothed sword attached to the nose.

Skates are members of the family Rajidae and morphologically differ from rays primarily by having a widely expanded pair of pectoral wings extending forward around the head as a thin, shelflike plate. In some species, a prominent wedge of rostral cartilage gives the skate an elongated nose (fig. 1.6a). Specialized structures such as **scapular spines, malar** and **alar hooks** on males, ventral pore patterns, and the shape of the rostrum are often used to distinguish skate species (fig. 1.6a). The tail of skates is usually slender and often short, and it has two small dorsal fins on it. The mouth and adjacent nostrils and the five paired gill openings are on the ventral surface (fig. 1.6b).

The final group included in the Chondrichthyes is the Holocephali, often called chimaeras or ratfishes. These fishes have characteristics that appear to be intermediate between those of the sharks, skates, and rays on one hand and the bony fishes on the other. They have a cartilaginous skeleton and lay eggs in horny capsules, and the males have paired claspers used for internal fertilization—all characteristics typical of elasmobranchs. Some features unique to the Holocephali include the single opening to the four pairs of gills on each side of the head, which is covered by a dermal opercle, and an anal opening that does not empty

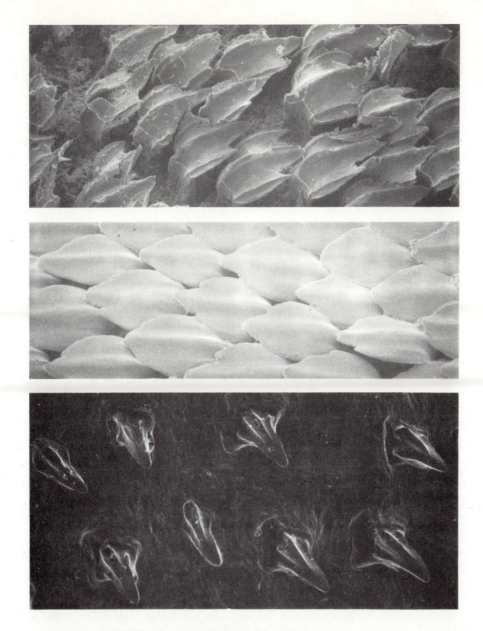

Figure 1.3 Surface view of placoid scales as found in elasmobranchs. (Scanning electron micrographs by Signe Lundstrom, Moss Landing Marine Laboratories)

into a **cloaca** but opens individually just anterior to the **urogenital opening**. Also, their upper jaw is immovably fused to the cranium, which is why they are referred to as Holocephali or "whole heads." They also have sexually dimorphic features such as the clasper just in front of the eyes on the head of the male (see fig. 1.7) and they have electroreceptive canals on the surface of the head.

BONY FISHES

The bony fishes (Osteichthyes) are an incredibly diverse group, and it is impossible to present all the morphological variations found in these fishes. There are certain external features typical of bony fishes, however, and we present these first. Then we describe specialized structures found on many bony fishes, such as cirri, spines, and snouts.

The bony fishes are often represented by species like the yellow perch, *Perca flavescens*, which is quite abundant and is available for study through commercial supply houses. The main external features, such as the dorsal, anal, and caudal median fins, the pectoral and pelvic paired fins, the bony gill cover (**operculum**), the mouth with its bony jaw structures and flexibility, and the lateral line, are all relatively common among bony fishes (fig. 1.8).

Not all fishes have bodies shaped like the hypothetical fish in fig. 1.8, which is usually referred to as elongate, basslike, or **fusiform** (fig. 1.9a). Other common body

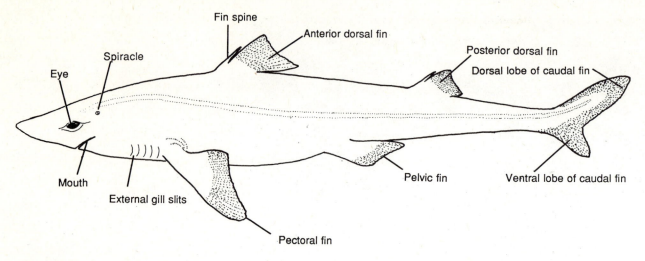

Figure 1.4 External features of the spiny dogfish, *Squalus acanthias*. The existence of fin spines is not typical of all sharks, but the remaining characters are representative. (Miller and Lea 1972)

shapes are eellike or **elongated** (fig. 1.9b) and **ovate** or **truncated** (fig. 1.9c). When describing the shape of a fish body, the perch would be considered **compressed**, thin, or narrow (fig. 1.9d). Other possible shapes are **depressed** or flattened (fig. 1.9e) and **subcircular** or hemispherical (fig. 1.9f). A further definition of body shapes is presented by Bond (1979), in which the lateral view, combined with the cross-sectional view, results in such terms as compressiform (fig. 1.9d), depressiform (fig. 1.9e), anguilliform (fig. 1.9b), filiform (an extreme elongation such as in the snipe eel), taeniform (an eellike body that is laterally compressed as in gunnels), and globiform (fig. 1.9f).

The placement of the pelvic fins also varies considerably among bony fishes and provides information about its phylogenetic position and maneuverability of the body. The perch has its pelvic fins in a **thoracic** position, directly under the pectoral fins and connected internally to the pectoral girdle (fig. 1.10b). In more primitive bony fishes, such

as herrings, the pelvic is located **abdominally** (fig. 1.10a), while in more advanced bony fishes, it is thoracic or **jugular**, well in advance of the pectoral girdle (fig. 1.10b). An extreme case is one in which the pelvic fin is actually under the chin or eye, and this condition is termed **mental** (fig. 1.10b).

Caudal fin shape and structure have many variations among the bony fishes, ranging from **naked**, without rays on the tip, to **forked, indented,** and **rounded** (fig. 1.11). The shape and structure of the caudal fin is related to its function. Fishes, for example, with narrow **caudal peduncles** and forked caudal fins often are continuous fast-swimming types, while those with undifferentiated caudals are less active in their swimming activities, and some occupy small crevices in near-shore rocky environments.

Two other structures associated with caudal fins should be mentioned. In some primitive fishes an **adipose fin**, a median dorsal fin with no bony elements, lies near the caudal fin (fig. 1.12b). In fast-swimming fishes, such as tunas, there often is a series of little median fins (called **finlets**) dorsally and ventrally immediately in front of the narrow caudal peduncle (fig. 1.12a). These fins supposedly reduce drag created by water flowing over the fish's body during swimming movements. Often a lateral protruberance called a **keel** occurs on the caudal peduncle of such fishes and probably serves as a stabilizing factor in these fast fishes.

Bony fishes occupy many kinds of habitats and consume a wide variety of food, so they have evolved a vast array of mouth and snout forms. The perch has a typical mouth shape that is usually referred to as **terminal**, located directly at the front of the body (fig. 1.13e). Other shapes include overhanging or **inferior** mouths, such as in anchovies (fig. 1.13c); projecting lower jaws or **superior**

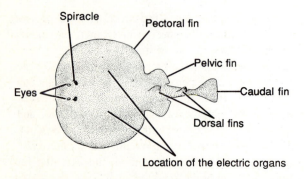

Figure 1.5 External features of the electric ray, *Torpedo californica*, a member of the family Torpedinidae. (Miller and Lea 1972)

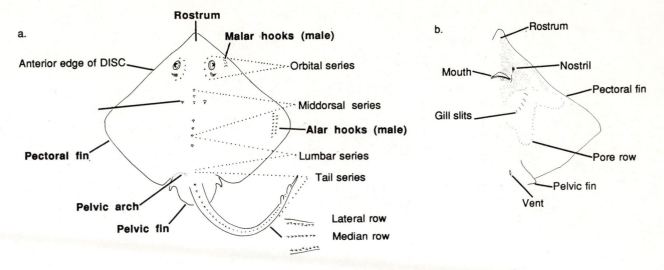

Figure 1.6 External features and terminology of dorsal spines, morphometric characters, and pore patterns of skates (family Rajidae): (a) dorsal view; (b) ventral view, showing the pore pattern of the big skate, *Raja binoculata.* (After Miller and Lea 1972)

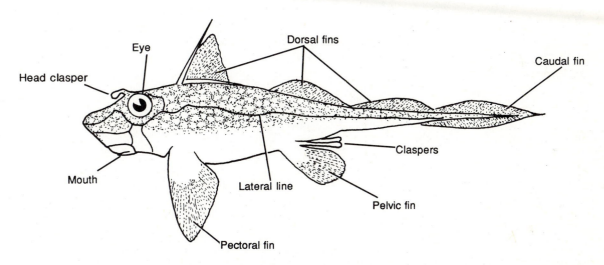

Figure 1.7 External features of a male ratfish, *Hydrolagus colliei.*

mouths, as in barracudas (fig. 1.13a); tubular snouts with the jaws at the tip, as in many small, picker-type feeding reef fishes (fig. 1.13b); and prolonged upper jaws, as in swordfishes (fig. 1.13d). The words *terminal, inferior, superior,* and *extended* can also be applied to the position of the lips (see fig. 1.13e,f).

Some fishes have specialized structures associated with the head (fig. 1.14). These include spines on the preopercle bone, on the skull above the eye, and in front of the nostrils and cirri, or flaplike organs attached to the skin of the head and along the body. These structures, along with the **suborbital stay**—a posteriorly directed subdermal bone associated with the circumorbital series—characterize fishes in the order Scorpaeniformes, which includes, among others,

the temperate rockfishes and tropical scorpionfishes (family Scorpaenidae), sculpins (family Cottidae), and greenlings (family Hexagrammidae). Chondrosteans (bowfins and reedfishes) have **gular plates**, occurring either singly or in pairs between the sides of the lower jaw (Lagler et al. 1977). Some bottom-feeding fishes such as catfishes (numerous families in the Siluriformes) have barbels situated around the mouth (fig. 1.8), which are used in chemoreception or mechanoreception (Moyle and Cech 1982).

Ventrally, the floor of the fish head includes a membrane that encloses the gill cavity and is supported by a series of bones called **branchiostegal rays** (fig. 1.14). These gill membranes can be categorized as **free**, not joined to the

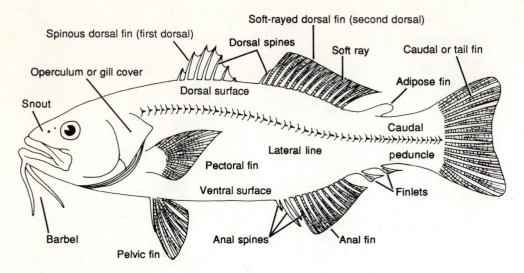

Figure 1.8 Hypothetical bony fish, a composite to show most of the common external features.   (Drawn by Susan E. Smith, from Squire and Smith 1977)

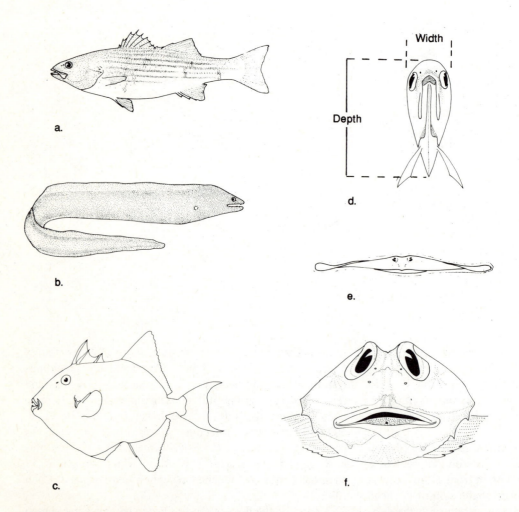

Figure 1.9 Classification of body forms in fishes: (a) elongate, fusiform, or basslike; (b) anguilliform, eellike, greatly elongated, or attenuated; (c) ovate or truncated; (d) compressed, compressiform, thin, narrow, deep, or perchlike; (e) depressed, depressiform, or flattened; and (f) globiform, subcircular, or hemispherical. (Miller and Lea 1972)

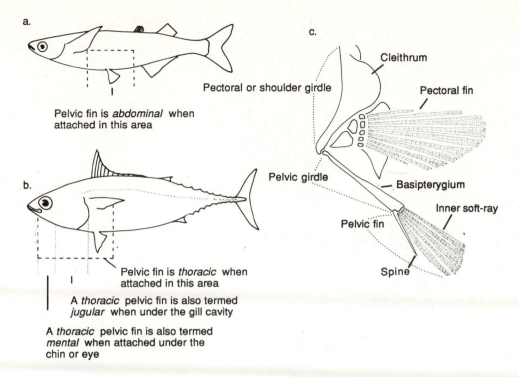

Figure 1.10 Abdominal and thoracic fin placement and construction (a) and (b), with a diagram of the pectoral and pelvic girdles of a fish with thoracic pelvic fins, that is, joined to the pectoral girdle (c). (Miller and Lea 1972)

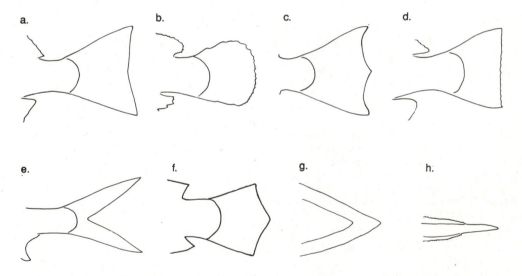

Figure 1.11 The various shapes of the caudal fins of bony fishes: (a) indented; (b) rounded; (c) double truncate; (d) square, truncate, or straight; (e) forked; (f) pointed with fin present; (g) pointed with fin not differentiated; and (h) naked, without rays on tip. (Miller and Lea 1972)

isthmus or to each other (fig. 1.15a), **united,** joined to each other but not joined to the isthmus (fig. 1.15b), or **joined** to the isthmus (fig. 1.15c). The number of branchiostegal rays may distinguish different taxa.

Inside the gill cavity of most bony fishes are four **gill arches,** each bearing **gill filaments** on the posterior edge of its upper and lower limbs and toothlike structures called **rakers** on its anterior or leading edge (fig. 1.16). We will discuss the structure and function of these filaments and rakers later. Often the shape, location, and number of gill rakers are used taxonomically.

Teeth occur mostly in the mouth: usually on the lower

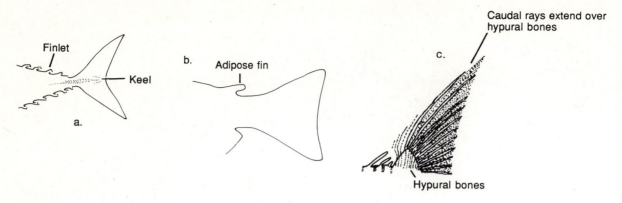

Figure 1.12 Additional structures asssociated with the tails of bony fishes: (a) the tail of a tuna, family Scombridae; (b) the tail of a salmon, showing the adipose fin; and (c) caudal rays extending over the hypural bones. (Miller and Lea 1972)

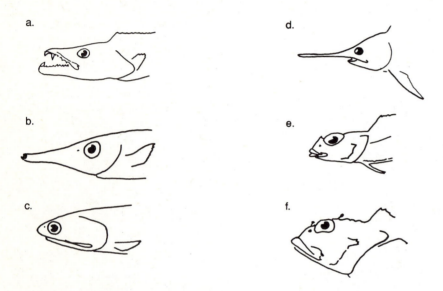

Figure 1.13 Terminology of the various mouth and snout forms: (a) the lower jaw projecting beyond the upper jaw, as in the Sphyraenidae; (b) a tubular snout with jaws at the tip, as found in the Macrorhamphosidae; (c) a snout that is overhanging or projecting beyond the mouth, so the mouth is termed inferior, as in the Engraulidae; (d) a prolonged upper jaw that forms a swordlike beak, as found in the Istiophoridae; (e) jaws (and lips) that are terminal (i.e., at the end of the body), as in the Cottidae; and (f) an extended upper jaw with the lower lip inferior or included, as found in the Blenniidae. (Miller and Lea 1972)

jaw bone (**mandible**) and free margin (**gape**) of the upper jaw (**premaxilla** and sometimes **maxilla**) (fig. 1.17). In more primitive fishes, both the premaxilla and maxilla bear teeth, although more advanced bony fishes have the maxilla excluded from the gape, and therefore it is toothless. Several kinds of teeth occur in fishes. These can be categorized as **caniniform**, **incisoriform**, or **molariform** (fig. 1.17c,d,e). The kinds differ in general morphology, with caniniform teeth having an elongated, narrow appearance, incisors having a sharp cutting edge, and molariform being blunt and stout for grinding and crushing.

Other head bones that may bear teeth include the vomer, palatine, basibranchials, and gill arches. Even the tongue of some fish carry teeth (fig. 1.17).

Several other external structures deserve attention since they are also useful in fish taxonomy and interpreting adaptations. One such is scales. The placoid scale of elasmobranch fishes has already been described (see fig. 1.3). Relatively primitive bony fishes, such as gars and sturgeons, have **ganoid** scales, which are rhombic in shape and differ from the scales of more advanced fishes in that they have an outer layer of ganoine, a hard inorganic sub-

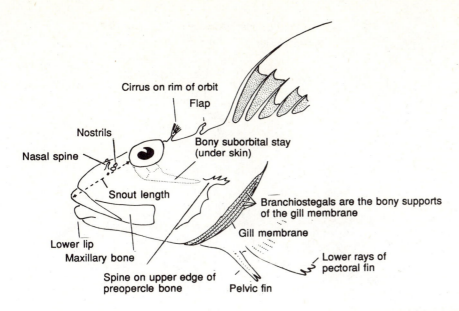

Figure 1.14 A diagram of a hypothetical sculpin showing some head and fin structures. (After Miller and Lea 1972)

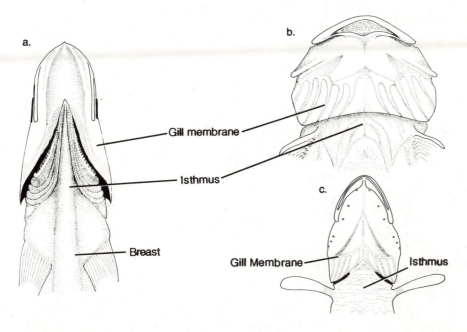

Figure 1.15 The three ways that gill membranes are attached in different fishes: (a) gill membranes that are free, not joined to the isthmus or to each other, as in the Osmeridae; (b) gill membranes that are joined to each other or united, but not joined to the isthmus, such as in the Cottidae; and (c) gill membranes that are joined to the isthmus, as in the Stichaeidae. (Miller and Lea 1972)

stance (fig. 1.18a). Scales typical of more advanced fishes can be **cycloid** or **ctenoid** (fig. 1.18b,c), and they are generally referred to as bony-ridge scales. Specimens of fish scales of all types can be obtained directly from biological supply houses.

Studies on scale morphology (lepidology) have revealed many interesting characteristics of taxonomic use (Batts 1964, Delamater and Courtenay 1974). Microscopically, the scale surface is covered by a complexity of ridges and spines (fig. 1.19). Each scale has dorsal and ventral edges and anterior and posterior edges, with each of these edges indicating four fields (basal, apical, and two exposed fields). These fields have further minute structures, which are often distinct enough to distinguish one fish species from another (Batts 1964). However, it should be noted that not all scales appear exactly as in fig. 1.19a. Directly over the lateral line,

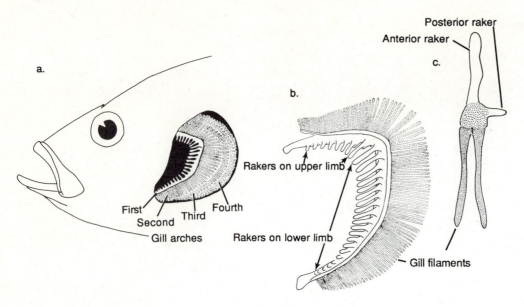

Figure 1.16 The arrangement and structure of gill rakers and gill arches of a bony fish: (a) the position of gill arches inside the gill cavity of a bony fish with the gill cover or operculum removed; (b) a side view of the first gill arch (a raker in the angle between the upper and lower limbs is counted with the lower rakers); (c) a top view of a cross section of the first gill arch. (Miller and Lea 1972)

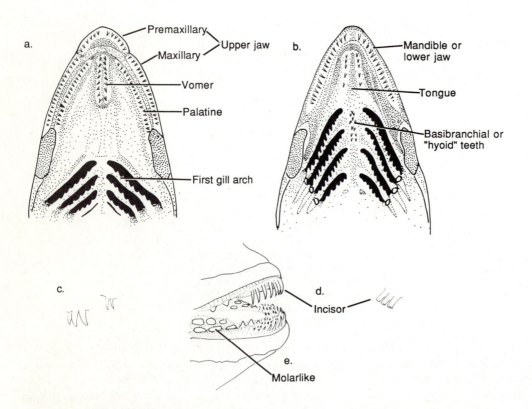

Figure 1.17 Diagram of the bones inside the mouth or buccal cavity that may bear teeth in bony fishes, with pictures of the different kinds of teeth existing in the heads of fishes: (a) the roof of the mouth showing bones with teeth; (b) the floor of the mouth showing bones with teeth and tongue; (c) caniniform teeth; (d) incisors; (e) molarlike teeth. (Miller and Lea 1972)

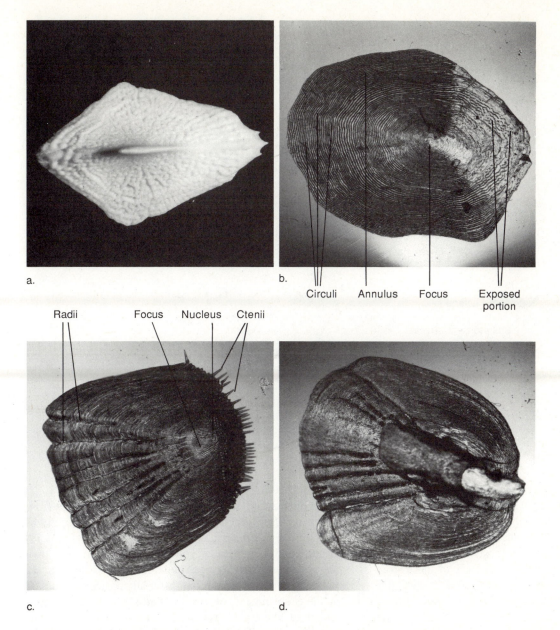

Figure 1.18 The four kinds of scales found on bony fishes: (a) ganoid scale (scute) from a sturgeon; (b) cycloid scale; (c) ctenoid scale; (d) lateral-line scale. (Prepared and photographed by Jim Brennan, Moss Landing Marine Laboratories)

scales have canals in them that allow water to flow through to the lateral-line sensory system (fig. 1.19c). Therefore, some of the structures near the center of the scale (focus) are different in these scales. Fish, especially ones with thin, deciduous scales, occasionally lose them. Lost scales are replaced by regenerated scales, which lack central detail because they quickly fill up the vacant space. Such a scale adds growth rings only after the space is filled and the fish grows larger (fig. 1.19d). These scales, therefore, look different from nonregenerated ones and are not useful for aging.

SCALE MORPHOLOGY EXERCISE

It is relatively easy to observe the microanatomy of teleost scales. Simply remove a scale—preferably taken from a preserved fish—from the area dorsal to the lateral line and place it on a microscope slide, either directly or indirectly by using double-side transparent tape. Since attached epidermal tissue makes observation of fine detail difficult, the scale should be carefully cleaned using fine forceps, brushes, and water or isopropyl alcohol. Once the scale is cleaned, place either a cover slip or another slide on top of

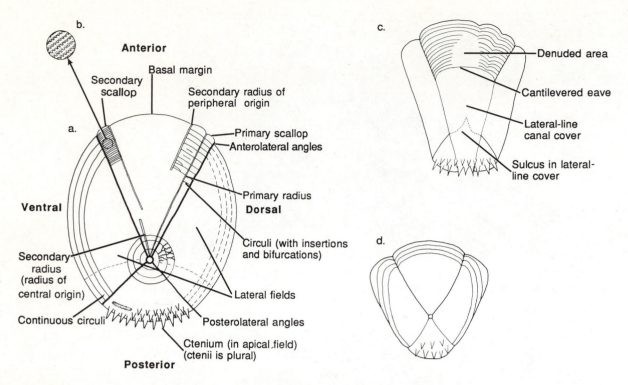

Figure 1.19 Detailed anatomy of a typical teleost ctenoid scale: (a) morphological terminology of a normal scale following Batts 1964 and Delameter and Courtenay 1974 ; (b) close-up drawn using a scanning electron microscope of the teeth occurring along the crests of the circuli; (c) a lateral-line scale, showing the canal cover with its cantilevered eave over the anterior canal opening; (d) a regenerated scale.

the scale and observe it directly through a dissecting scope, using both transmitted and reflected light. Under relatively high power, most fine details shown in fig. 1.19 should become obvious. A dab of alizarin stain, applied locally with a fine brush, often helps delineate some of these structures. Should a scanning electron microscope be available, follow the procedures outlined by Delamater and Courtenay (1974) to resolve some of the more minute structures. After you have studied a normal scale from your specimen, remove scales from the lateral line and from other areas along the body to compare their shapes, structures, and other details.

Since it has been shown by Batts (1964) that Pacific flatfish species have distinctly different scale morphology,

another interesting study would be to remove scales from individuals of several different species in a local family of fishes. Using the descriptive anatomy shown in fig. 1.19, and perhaps other features you might notice on your own scale specimens, try to determine if these characters are good ones to use in keying out different species of fishes. If you have specimens of Pacific flatfishes, remove scales from these and try to use the key that Batts (1964) constructed to identify flatfishes by their scale morphology. Obviously, such scale characteristics would be useful to someone conducting a feeding-habit analysis by studying the stomach contents of a piscivorous fish, in which scales are common remains of the prey ingested.

Chapter 2
Basic Anatomy: Internal

It is not our objective, nor is it possible in a general manual, to describe in minute detail the internal anatomy of fishes. This kind of treatment, if desired, is available in a vertebrate (Wake 1979) or comparative anatomy text that deals with such commonly available fish as the spiny dogfish or the yellow perch. We feel that a general introduction to the internal soft anatomy of fishes will provide ichthyology and fishery biologists the opportunity to become familiar with the general anatomy of a fish, thus allowing the biologist to infer how a fish functions from its structure. For this reason, our anatomical approach will be a general and functional one.

JAWLESS FISHES

Since the lamprey acts both as parasite and predator, its internal anatomy is highly specialized. Lampreys and hagfishes have similar internal morphologies, with the exception of mouth structures and feeding modes, so only the lamprey is treated here. For further information on the internal anatomy of jawless fishes, see references such as Brogal and Fänge (1963), Hardisty and Potter (1972), Wischnitzer (1972), and Wessells and Center (1975).

The alimentary morphology of the lamprey may be seen best in a longitudinal (or sagittal) section showing the well-developed cartilage and muscle systems associated with the feeding apparatus: the mouth region and continuing through the coelomic cavity to the cloaca (fig. 2.1). The mouth region is dominated by the horny teeth on the tongue, the lingual cartilage used to move this rasping tongue, and the well-developed musculature and cartilaginous structure required by this fish for its existence. The buccal funnel is surrounded by a circular muscle (**annularis**), which helps maintain suction on the prey. This funnel is supported by a ring of cartilage.

Since the lamprey is usually attached and feeding while breathing, its head is modified so that both functions can occur simultaneously, whereas in free-living hagfishes, the systems are not separated. For example, an anteriorly

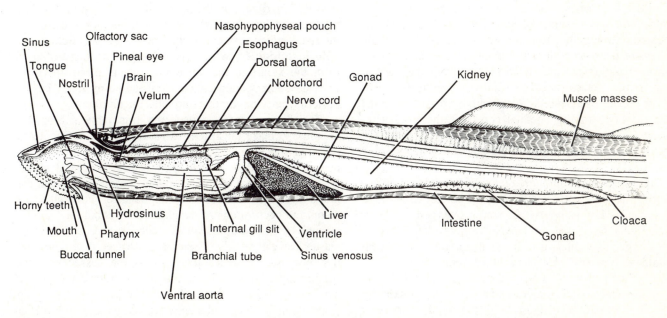

Figure 2.1 A longitudinal cross section of the Pacific lamprey from the head to the cloaca. (After Wessells and Center 1975)

projecting cavity (**hydrosinus**) separates feeding and respiration. At the rear of the **pharynx**, anteriorly pointing tentacles attach to the **velum**, a structure preventing back flow of water from the gills. Continuing ventrally from the pharynx is a **branchial tube**, which ends blindly underneath the **esophagus**. The opening to this tube contains the curtainlike velum, and the walls of the tube contain seven internal gill slits on each side. This tube is also called the **respiratory tube**, since its gill slits lead into gill pouches. Larval and nonparasitic lampreys breathe through their mouths, whereas adult, parasitic individuals have water flow only through their branchial sacs (Hardisty and Potter 1972).

The lamprey has no true stomach; the esophagus directly becomes intestine at a junction distinguished by a valve. Surface area on inner walls of the intestine is increased by a longitudinal fold called the **typhlosole**. The heart, liver, kidney, and gonads fill the remainder of the coelom. The heart is simple: It has only three chambers without a **medial septum**. The first chamber is the thin-walled **sinus venosus**, which receives blood from the venous system. Blood passes through an opening to the thin-walled **atrium** and then through another opening to be pumped out by the **ventricle** into the **ventral aorta**, where it is transported to the gills for oxygenation.

• Why does the lamprey not need a medially divided heart such as those of birds and mammals?

The liver is located just behind the heart and is usually a yellowish color. Above and behind the liver is the kidney, which lies along each side of the dorsal visceral wall. Tubules of this kidney, termed **opisthonephric**, pass wastes into the **archinephric ducts**, which extend posteriorly in the tissue between the kidney and visceral cavity. The archinephric ducts unite to form the **urogenital sinus**, which empties into the cloaca. Adult lampreys have a single gonad that occupies most of the remaining coelomic cavity. This gonad is connected by mesentery from the median dorsal portion of the visceral cavity. Its products, either eggs or sperm, are released directly into the body cavity and leave the body through genital pores via the **urogenital papilla**. The testis can be distinguished by its reticulated appearance, while the ovary usually contains many small eggs.

Thus, the lamprey, though a relatively simple and primitive fish, has several specializations for its unique mode of life. It can feed on its host while pumping oxygenated water over its gills, and it has a relatively well developed kidney with a large glomerular surface area that allows a great deal of fluid to pass from blood to the excretory system. The lamprey can live in both seawater and freshwater. In the sea, it prevents osmotic water loss by having tough skin, by using its salt-secreting cells in the gills to rid the fish of salt absorbed in the gut, and by using circulation through the kidney to prevent excessive water loss. In freshwater, the lamprey's glomeruli and nephrons excrete large amounts of excess water while retaining essential proteins and salts.

CARTILAGINOUS FISHES

In this section, we briefly describe the internal anatomy of elasmobranch fishes, using the common spiny dogfish, *Squalus acanthias*, as our example. We then describe the digestive, respiratory, urogenital, circulatory, and sensory systems of elasmobranchs more thoroughly so that these systems can then be compared with those in jawless and bony fishes. Again we omit minute detail, which is adequately represented in several manuals of shark anatomy (Wischnitzer 1972, Gilbert 1973, Wessells and Center 1975, Ashley 1976, and Gans and Parsons 1981) and in recent textbooks on ichthyology (Lagler et al. 1977 and Bond 1979).

Since sharks, skates, and rays are free living and generally eat other mobile organisms, they have evolved muscular mouths well adapted for grasping, holding, and biting prey by using an impressive array of teeth. Elasmobranch mouths and teeth vary considerably among species of sharks, skates, and rays. Tooth form ranges from the grinding platelike structures on the jaw of bat rays (Myliobatidae) to the sharp, incisorlike teeth of the more piscivorous sharks (i.e., family Carcharhinidae). However, the alimentary canal of the spiny dogfish is generally representative of all elasmobranchs (fig. 2.2). A buccal cavity with an immobile tongue leads to the pharynx, where gill openings admit water to the branchial cavity. Leading to the stomach, the esophagus or gullet has walls covered with papillae. The stomach is divided into two portions: the anterior (**cardiac**) and the posterior (**pyloric**) portions. The cardiac part has many **rugae,** or longitudinal folds, on its internal surface to increase the digestive area. Behind the **pyloric sphincter**, which controls the movement of food from the stomach, the small intestine is made up of an anterior, short section called the **duodenum** and a larger, posterior portion with thicker walls, the **ileum**.

The ileum has interconnected transverse sheets that combine to make the **spiral valve**, a structure analogous to rugae in that it increases the absorptive area. Behind the ileum is the **colon**, which ends where the **rectal gland** begins. The rectal gland excretes excess salts from the blood to help maintain osmotic balance. Following the colon, the **rectum** enters the **cloaca**, the common chamber through which the intestinal, rectal gland, and urinary wastes leave the body. The cloaca also serves a reproductive purpose: In males it serves as the passageway for sperm, while in females it acts as the birth canal, where newborn young are delivered or, in the case of egg-bearing elasmobranchs, where the eggs are passed to the ocean for further development.

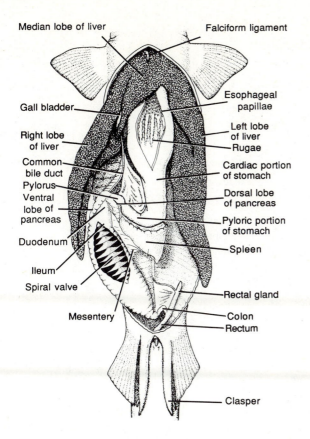

Median lobe of liver

Falciform ligament

Gall bladder

Esophageal papillae

Right lobe of liver

Left lobe of liver

Rugae

Common bile duct

Cardiac portion of stomach

Pylorus

Ventral lobe of pancreas

Dorsal lobe of pancreas

Duodenum

Pyloric portion of stomach

Ileum

Spleen

Spiral valve

Mesentery

Rectal gland

Colon

Rectum

Clasper

Figure 2.2 A detailed diagram from a ventral view detailing the internal anatomy of the spiny dogfish and showing the alimentary system. This specimen is male, as evidenced by the claspers shown at the bottom. (After Wischnitzer 1972)

Among the organs in the remainder of the shark's coelomic cavity, the large, oily, trilobed liver produces bile that is drained via hepatic ducts toward the gall bladder (fig. 2.1), a structure that is often embedded in the liver tissue. The liver contains a hydrocarbon called squalene that has a low specific gravity. Thus when relatively large, the liver can provide a considerable amount of buoyancy to reduce the energy costs of swimming. The liver also converts nutrients into usable forms and stores them for later use. Another obvious organ is the pancreas, which is larger and more prominent in elasmobranchs than in lampreys and hagfishes. The pancreas, which lies in the **mesentery** near the pyloric stomach and the duodenum (fig. 2.2), produces enzymes that break down proteins, carbohydrates, and fats. The dark triangular spleen near the end of the pylorus produces, stores, and eliminates blood cells.

The other easily observed organs in the coelomic cavity are the kidney and gonads, collectively called the urogenital system (fig. 2.3). Although these two organs have entirely different functions, they are associated morphologically and functionally. In males, modified portions of the kidney tubules and ducts also transport sperm and so can have

either excretory or reproductive functions. In females, however, the two organs are separated structurally and functionally. Unmodified ducts drain female kidneys, and ovaries release their eggs into oviducts lying near the posterior portion of the kidney. Further detail indicates how the urogenital system of elasmobranchs functions. In males, the testes are paired, elongated oval structures at the front of the body cavity (fig. 2.3). Modified kidney tubules called **efferent ductules** transport sperm to the **archinephric duct**. At the posterior end of each archinephric duct, **seminal vesicles** connect to the sperm sac and contribute secretions to make up the seminal fluid, which helps transport sperm. The sperm sac and seminal vesicle join to form the urogenital sinus, a cavity within the urogenital papilla. The dark, elongated kidneys, located near the middorsal line, contain large masses of tubules, which provide large surface areas and a renal countercurrent system (Lacy et al. 1985) for filtering the blood, and drain into the archinephric ducts. The cloaca receives exiting products from all three systems: feces, urine, and sperm. Finally, males have modified pelvic fins called **claspers**, which are used as copulatory organs. Males have sacs that secrete fluid to lubricate the medial groove in the clasper to facilitate sperm transportation. In some specialized elasmobranchs, such as skates, the claspers have spring-loaded hooks, to secure the female during copulation.

In females, the ovaries are ovals located at the anterior end of the body cavity and suspended from the kidneys by the **mesovarium** membrane. The oviducts unite anteriorly to form the **ostium**, an opening receiving the eggs; then they continue backward to open into the cloaca on each side of the urinary papilla. The oviduct includes an **oviducal (nidamental** or **shell) gland**, which secretes a shell around the eggs. The oviducts end at the uterus, an enlarged portion housing the developing embryo. In contrast to the male duct, the female archinephric duct is not convoluted and is less prominent. Like males, females have a urinary papilla and a cloaca receiving excretory and reproductive products, although in reproduction the female cloaca serves as the birth canal. Eggs develop in the ovaries and, during ovulation, burst through the ovarian walls into the coelom near the ostium. There the eggs begin to descend into the oviducts, which are highly elastic. Eggs are fertilized in the oviduct before the shell gland provides them a thin membranous covering, which later breaks down and disappears. Embryos then gestate for a long time (around two years for *Squalus*), nourished by the yolk suspended in a sac from the ventral side of the embryo. Although this external yolk sac is usually used up fully at birth, a smaller internal yolk sac remains within the newborn shark's body cavity to provide more sustenance. This process is not exactly the same in all species of elasmobranchs. In some forms, the females lay eggs containing a large amount of yolk encased in a horny shell that then develop outside the mother. In other forms, the nutrition for the developing embryos does not come

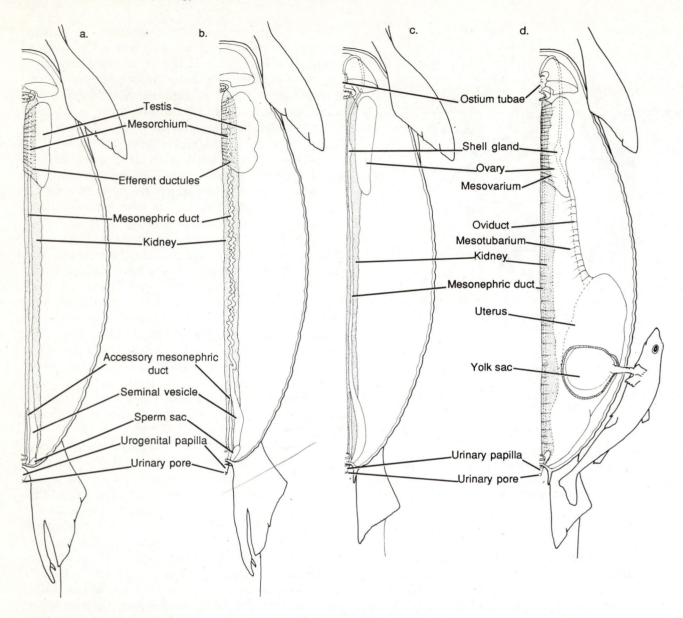

Figure 2.3 Ventral cutout views showing the urogenital systems from immature (a,c) and mature (b,d) individuals of both sexes of the spiny dogfish, *Squalus acanthias.*   (After Wischnitzer 1972)

from a yolk sac but rather is derived directly from placental papillae (**trophonemata**) lining the uterine wall.

The respiratory apparatus of elasmobranchs resembles that of bony fishes, with some differences. Water is taken in through the mouth and **spiracle** (an aperture above the five internal gill slits) and is pumped back and then out through five or more pairs of internal gills (the dogfish has five). The gills are arranged differently in sharks from those in bony fishes in that the water leaves each gill via an individual external gill slit instead of through a single opercular opening (fig. 2.4). The gill arches—a series of cartilaginous rings with skeletal elements—provide support for the individual gill respiratory structures (fig. 2.5a). Extending forward and inward from the gills, gill rakers contain, trap,

and direct the food toward the esophagus (fig. 2.5b). Gill filaments are arranged on the arches' gill rays to ensure maximum diffusion of gases between the water flowing out the gill slit and the blood flowing within. Crossing the filaments, the tiny foldlike gill lamellae contain blood capillaries and are the actual site of diffusion of oxygen into and carbon dioxide out of the blood. Gills actually have two halves, together called a **holobranch** and each of the pair a **demibranch** (fig. 2.5b). In sharks a hyoidean demibranch on the skull wall of the first gill pocket contains a few rudimentary gill lamellae. This **pseudobranch**, however, is probably not respiratory, and it may secrete hormones.

The circulatory system of sharks is a primitive closed

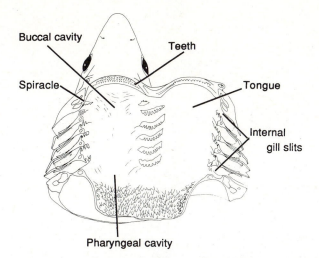

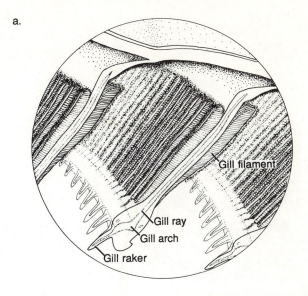

Figure 2.4 A ventral cutaway of the respiratory area in the spiny dogfish, *Squalus acanthias*, showing the relationship between the gill area and the external gill slits. (After Wischnitzer 1972)

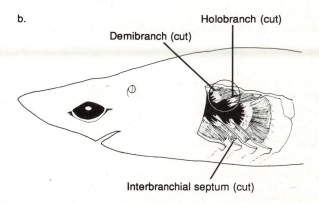

Figure 2.5 A lateral cutaway of the respiratory area in the spiny dogfish, *Squalus acanthias*, showing the direction that the water and food particles are directed: (a) a portion of one gill arch dissected out to show relative positions of the different structures; (b) the left side of the head showing the respiratory area. (After Wischnitzer 1972)

system in which the heart pumps oxygen-poor blood from the systemic veins to the gills. The four-chambered heart passes blood from the dorsal chamber (sinus venosus) to the atrium and ventrally into the ventricle, whose muscular pump forces it through the **conus arteriosus** to the ventral aorta and on toward the gills. The section in this chapter on bony fishes describes further details on circulation common to the two fish groups.

Although we will not detail the central nervous system of elasmobranchs extensively, we single out several particularly interesting elements of their sensory system for a brief description. A very detailed description can be found in Smeets, Nieuwenhuys, and Roberts (1983). Sharks have a well-developed lateral-line system located in the skin of the head region. Water-filled canals of this system contact the external environment through lines of pores, allowing water motion to stimulate sensory **neuromast** cells that are located within the canals. Thus the neuromasts and underlying nerves are used to detect differences in small water movements around the fish, as might be caused by friend or enemy. Similar disturbances can also be detected in a different way. A set of pits comprise the electroreceptive system called the **ampullae of Lorenzini**. These are canals in the skin filled with a gelatinlike material that also contain sensory cells. Movements or disturbances near the shark change the voltage drop along the canals, which allows the fish to sense other organisms nearby.

Along with these mechanoreceptors and electroreceptors, the shark's head is covered with numerous chemoreceptors, or tiny sensory pockets between the placoid scales. These allow the shark to recognize certain chemicals in the water, such as those from food, and enable them to avoid noxious materials. Elasmobranchs also have very sensitive nostrils, but the actual mechanism for olfac-

tion is virtually the same as that found in other vertebrates. Each receptor is a nerve cell sensitive to some molecular property when in contact. The nerve impulse is transmitted toward the olfactory bulb of the brain.

Externally the nostrils consist of two olfactory sacs, which contain many skin folds sensitive to chemicals. These sacs have two openings, a different setup than in bony fishes, whose olfactory bulbs connect with the pharynx internally. Since the two shark nostrils are usually located on extreme sides of the head, the fish can receive directional information, and an individual can locate the source of a smell by comparing the intensity of input between the two nostrils.

The eyes of elasmobranchs are constructed in much the same way as the eyes of bony fishes and so serve their sub-

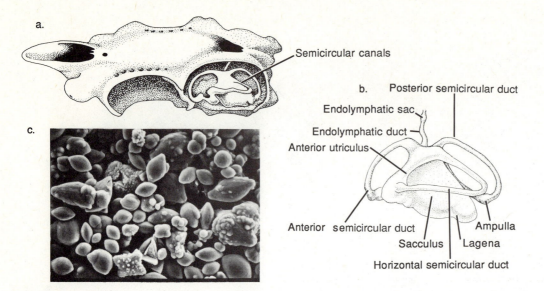

Figure 2.6 The position, shape, and structure of the semicircular canals of the inner ear of the spiny dogfish, *Squalus acanthias*: (a) placement within the neurocranium; (b) a lateral view of the left ear; (c) a scanning electron micrograph of statoconia from the leopard shark (*Triakis semifasciata*). (Parts a and b after Wischnitzer 1972; part c prepared and photographed by Guillermo Moreno and Kevin Hill, Moss Landing Marine Laboratories)

jects just as well in visually locating potential prey and predators. We cover details of ocular anatomy in the section on bony fishes.

The inner ears of sharks also resemble those of bony fishes, especially in that each ear contains three semicircular canals occupying three different planes and three membranous sacs (the **sacculus, utriculus,** and **lagena**) (fig. 2.6). These canals and sacs are filled with **endolymph** fluid but are surrounded by a fluid called **perilymph**. Lining the semicircular canals are hairlike cilia, sensitive to movements of endolymph, which responds to the motion of the fish's body and head. Two endolymphatic ducts, which open into pores on the surface of the head, provide a fluid-filled channel to the inner ear. One main difference between the inner ear of sharks and bony fishes is that in newborn sharks, these ducts allow mineral crystals or grains of sand (sometimes called **statoconia**) to enter the three sacs of the inner ear; the grains act as **otoliths** to help detect gravity. Whether or not these are formed endogenously is still a question (Lowenstam 1981). True otoliths of bony fishes are large, calcareous structures secreted by the fish, and they are species-specific in size and shape. Since their inner ear is constructed in three planes, sharks can assess acceleration, deceleration, and their position with respect to gravity. In addition, they may also use the inner ear, particularly the lagena, for hearing.

Although we have described the external and internal anatomy of elasmobranchs, using *Squalus acanthias* as our representative, other chondrichthyan groups, such as that of holocephalans or chimaeras and even other species of elas-

mobranchs, have quite different morphologies (see Stahl 1978, Raikow 1978). For example, the chimaera *Hydrolagus colliei* differs considerably in having only a single gill opening covered by a soft operculum (Raikow 1978). Additional references given at the end of section 1 compare the different groups and species.

BONY FISHES

With several exceptions, organs similar in structure to those of elasmobranchs fill the visceral cavity of bony fishes. These include the digestive tract and its accessory organs, the liver and pancreas, the spleen, the gonads, and the kidneys (fig. 2.7). A new structure, the gas-filled swimbladder—used mainly for bouyancy—occurs in about half the species of bony fishes. Bony fishes, and teleosts in particular, are a highly diverse group, and their internal anatomy reflects this. Most of the following descriptions of structures and their organization will apply to typical teleosts, such as the yellow perch (*Perca flavescens*), the teleostean stereotype of several manuals on vertebrate morphology. Yet other species are equally good subjects for class study. Moreover, variations from the stereotype demonstrate the kinds and amount of adaptation that, metaphorically, have made teleosts the "insects of the vertebrates" in both their relative diversity and abundance.

From mouth to anus, the first cavity in the alimentary tract—the oral or buccal cavity—is between the mouth and first row of gill rakers. Behind this oral cavity, the pharynx

Trout

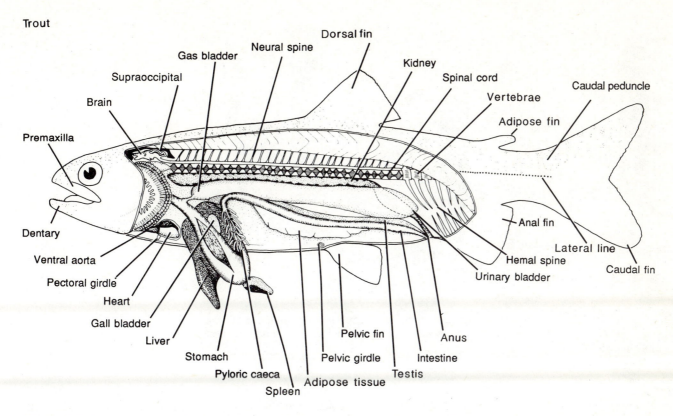

Figure 2.7 A lateral view of the internal anatomical features in a typical bony fish.

contains the branchial complex of hyoid apparatus and gill arches. Often, **pharyngeal teeth** are present both on the roof and floor of the pharynx (see chap. 1 on external morphology). These help hold prey before they are swallowed and perhaps help grind prey for easier digestion. The pharyngeal wall is interrupted by five pairs of gill slits, which allow water to enter the gill cavity from the mouth. Beyond the pharynx, the esophagus—a short straight tube—leads to the stomach, which is often divided into two portions: one anterior (the **cardiac**) and the other posterior (**pyloric**).

Where the stomach narrows into **duodenum, pyloric caeca**—fingerlike extensions of the gut—presumably function to increase digestive surface area. Some teleosts, usually multivores, lack a differentiated stomach. At this level of the alimentary canal, the massive liver usually lies just anterior and dorsal to the stomach and covers much of the anterior body cavity. The liver drains, through a series of tubules, into the gall bladder, which enters the duodenum via the bile ducts near the site where the pyloric caeca, if present, are located. Next, the intestine, which varies in length and form among different species, ends in the anus. Under the intestine, the pancreas is exposed in some fishes but embedded in the liver and very hard to discern in others. Lying on the posterior dorsal surface of the stomach is the spleen, an elongated structure that, as in elasmobranchs, helps produce and maintain blood cells.

The gonads, kidneys, and often the swimbladder occupy space in the coelom above the intestine and behind the stomach (figs. 2.7, 2.8). As in elasmobranchs, the reproductive organs and kidneys are closely interrelated and form the urogenital system. The kidneys are paired, elongated organs fixed to the dorsal body wall (figs. 2.7, 2.8). They are comprised of many tubules and ducts that expand anteriorly into a head kidney consisting primarily of blood sinuses. Here clumps of capillaries filter out waste particles. At the posterior end of the kidneys, these tubules descend to unite as long ducts (**Wolffian ducts**), which drain the kid-

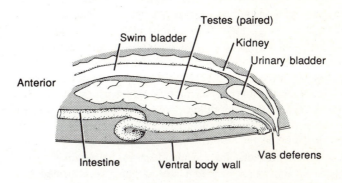

Figure 2.8 A diagrammatic scheme showing the arrangement of the kidneys and urogenital organs, viewed laterally, from the left side of a representative bony fish.

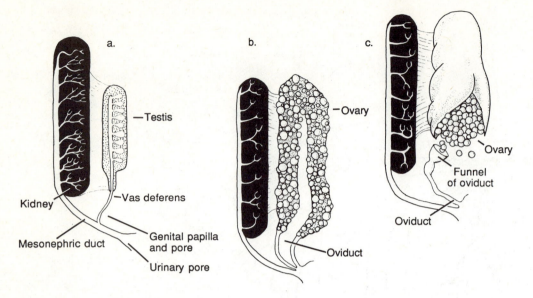

Figure 2.9 Arrangement of the kidneys and gonads in the urogenital systems of both male (a) and female (b) bony fishes. The female system with an open funnel to the oviduct (c) occurs in salmonids. (After Hoar 1955)

ney into the urinary bladder in males or into the urogenital sinus in females. Thus in males the urinary bladder is a discrete structure located dorsal to the alimentary tract, while in females it becomes part of the oviducts and forms the urogenital sinus. In males, the external projection of the urinary bladder is called the urinary papilla, and waste products are eliminated through it. Waste materials are excreted through a urogenital pore in females.

The reproductive system of male bony fishes includes paired testes located behind the stomach and duodenum, below the swimbladder, and just above the intestine (fig. 2.8). The testes are lobulated and have longitudinal folds along their main axis. Within these folds, the tubular **vas deferens** lead to the exterior between the urinary papilla and the anus. In all fishes except salmonids, the vas deferens exit through the body wall at the genital pore. They are not a part of the kidney as they are in elasmobranchs. In females, the ovaries are usually paired egg sacs located in the same position as the testes in males (fig. 2.9). Some fish (e.g., the yellow perch) have a single unpaired ovary. The oviducts, which—except in salmonids—are continuous with the ovaries, receive either ripe or fertilized eggs. Eggs are usually expelled through an abdominal pore just behind the anus. Thus the oviduct forms a viaduct from the ovary to the abdominal pore. The system is variously modified to allow live-bearing in viviparous females (see Hoar 1969).

When present, the swimbladder—a balloonlike organ used in most fishes to regulate buoyancy—is located between the intestinal tract and the gonad and kidney (figs. 2.7, 2.8, 2.10). **Physostomous** fishes have a tubular connection between swimbladder and alimentary canal.

Physoclistous fishes have a closed bladder with no such connection; they have specialized vascularization and glandular tissue to regulate the gas volume. The more advanced teleosts have physoclistous swimbladders, with a **rete mirabile** ("wonderful network") consisting of many parallel capillaries shaped and assembled to concentrate gases from the blood in the gas gland on the surface of the swimbladder (fig. 2.10). This is accomplished in an intricate countercurrent exchange mechanism whereby arterial blood flows inward to the swimbladder, makes a turn outward at the gas gland, releases more oxygen and other gases that back-diffuse into the adjacent inward flow, and finally flows outward into the venous system. Thus gases are concentrated at relatively high pressures in the gas gland to diffuse into the swimbladder. To remove gases from the bladder, many fishes also have an **oval body** where gas can diffuse out of the swimbladder into the blood. The swimbladder has at least three distinct layers of tissue that provide it elasticity while making it gas tight. A more detailed description of swimbladders can be found in chapter 5, pages 73–74.

We will describe the circulatory system of bony fishes in enough detail to convey the process of respiration. Generally, the circulatory system has four main components: the heart, the branchial system, the visceral circulation, and the somatic blood supply (see fig. 2.11).

In the heart, blood passes forward through four chambers: the sinus venosus, atrium, ventricle, and **bulbus arteriosus** (figs. 2.11, 2.12). The sinus venosus delivers blood from the **common cardinal veins** (ducts of Cuvier) directly into the atrium, which is a single, large chamber anterior to the sinus venosus. No valve is apparent between these two chambers, but there is a valve between the atrium

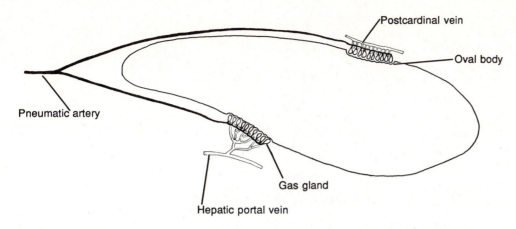

Figure 2.10 Diagram showing a swimbladder in a teleost with its circulatory system and associated filling and emptying mechanisms. (After Chiasson 1974)

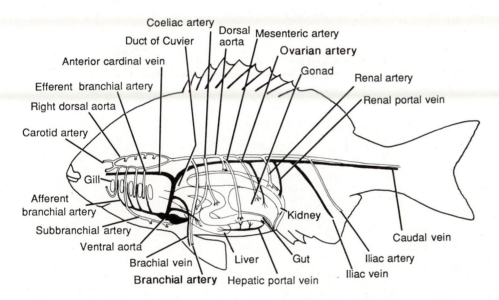

Figure 2.11 Diagram of the blood circulation in a bony fish, showing the major blood vessels and the portion of the body they serve. (After Bond 1979)

and the ventricle. The ventricle is a thick, muscular structure that pumps blood into the bulbus arteriosus, the enlarged base of the ventral aorta.

Once the blood has been pumped forward from the heart, it flows via the ventral aorta to the gills and gill capillaries, where oxygen diffuses into it from the water. From there it is distributed throughout the systemic circulation. Three pairs of vessels deliver blood from the ventral aorta to the gills: The first and second afferent arches branch directly, but the third and fourth leave the aorta as a single vessel and branch from this common trunk (fig. 2.11). These **afferent branchial arteries** cross the gill arch and send capillary branches around the margins of the gill filaments, where they join branches to the **efferent branchial arteries** throughout the length of the filament in

cross capillaries or blood spaces called **secondary lamellae** (figs. 2.11, 2.13). It is through the epithelium of these lamellae that respiratory gas exchange occurs—oxygen for carbon dioxide—between the deoxygenated blood and oxygenated water crossing the gill's surface. The efferent branchial arteries parallel the afferent arteries, with each receiving a branch from the filaments for every branch sent to the filament from the afferent arteries. Thus oxygenated blood flows out of the gills to be collected by the paired **dorsal aortas.**

The dorsal aorta transports oxygenated blood to the rest of the body—including the visceral circulation where blood is supplied to the intestinal system, the swimbladder, the liver, the pancreas, the kidneys, and the gonads—and to the somatic circulation where blood is transported to the fins

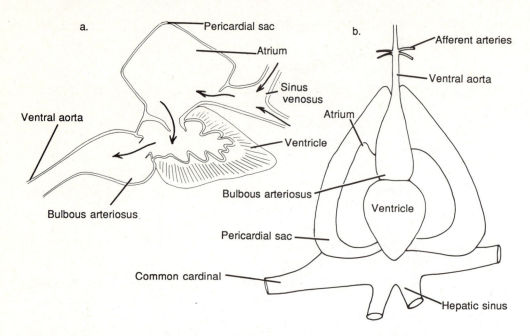

Figure 2.12 Two views of the heart in a bony fish: (a) lateral view of a section of the heart, showing the direction of blood flow; (b) ventral view of the heart, showing the relative positions of the various chambers. (After Chiasson 1974)

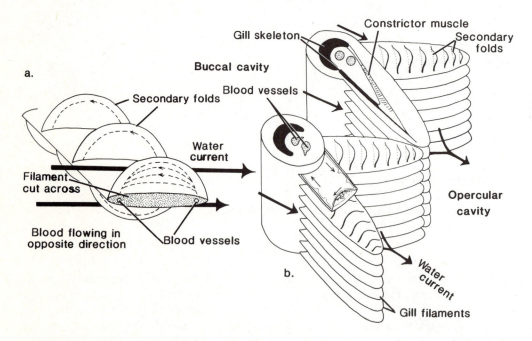

Figure 2.13 Diagram of (a) the circulation of blood in the gills and how it is situated (b) within the gill-arch structures. Water flow is indicated by large arrows; note how blood and water flow in opposite directions. (After Hughes 1966, 1980)

and trunk of the fish (fig. 2.11). The venous system generally parallels the arterial system and drains the blood, which is now deoxygenated and carries metabolic products, such as carbon dioxide, back to the gills for another round.

If you would like more information on how the circulation of blood through the gills in a fish operates relative to

the flow of oxygenated water, see the section Respiration and Feeding in chapter 5 (pp. 62–68). Several exercises there are designed to help clarify this phenomenon.

The nervous system of bony fishes is typical of vertebrates. There are four main parts: the central nervous system; the peripheral nervous system, the autonomic ner-

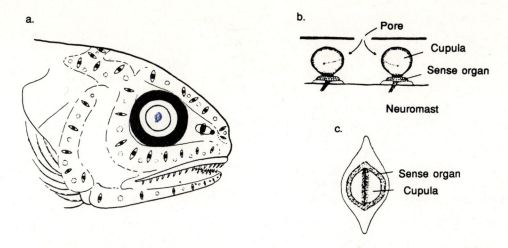

Figure 2.14 Diagram showing the head of a fish with an elaborate cephalic lateral line network (a), along with a lateral view of the cross section of a lateral line (b), and a view from the skin surface (c). (Marshall 1969)

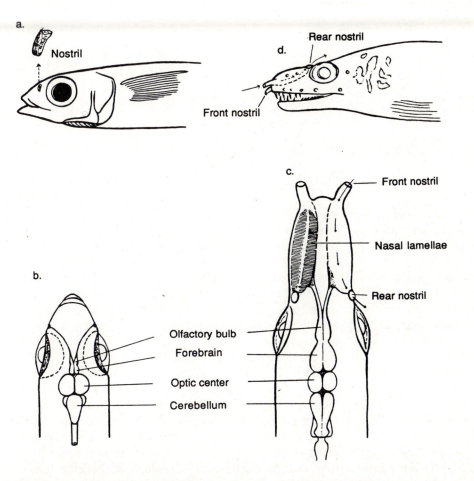

Figure 2.15 Diagrams of the olfactory organs and their relationship to the brain in two teleost fishes: (a) side view and (b) top view of the head of a flying fish, with reduced development of these organs; (c) top view and (d) side view of the well-developed olfactory organs of a moray eel. (Marshall 1969)

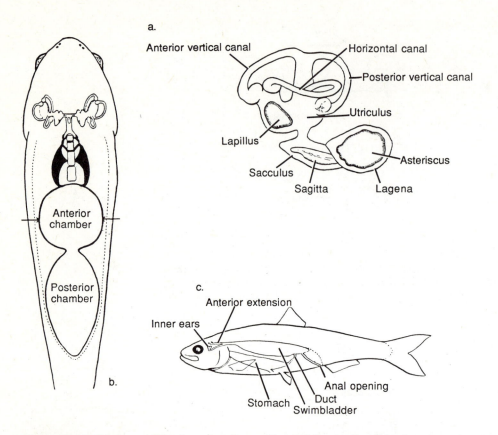

Figure 2.16 Diagram of the inner ear in carplike and herringlike fish. In most teleosts, however, the asteriscus is smaller and the sagitta is the largest otolith. (a) The semicircular canal system of a minnow, showing the three canals, three chambers, and three otoliths contained in these chambers; (b) a dorsal view of the inner ear and its relation to weberian ossicles and the swimbladder of an Ostariophysan fish; (c) the anterior portion of the swimbladder in a herring, which is shaped like a Y so that the air-filled bladder comes in close proximity to the inner ear. (Marshall 1966)

vous system, and the special sense organs. Since courses in general zoology cover the first three systems, we shall not deal with them here (except in the exercises in chapter 5, under Sensory Mechanisms, pp. 52–62). Rather, we shall emphasize the main sense organs: the lateral line (acoustico-lateralis), the nose, the ear, and the eye. All of these sense organs connect to the central nervous system; the details of these connections are covered in many texts, such as Bond (1979), Chiasson's (1974) manual on the yellow perch, and Bone and Marshall (1982).

The lateral line system in bony fishes is a superficial series of interconnected canals in the bone, scales, and skin on the head (cephalic part) and usually along the midlateral region of the flanks (hence the name **acoustico-lateralis**), but it is often above and below the midlateral region as well (fig. 2.14). These canals open to the exterior through pores in the scales (see the description in chap. 1 of external morphology). Inside the canals, a series of ciliated sensory cells usually support caplike structures (**cupulas**) that move in response to water movement. In some fishes, however, the sensory cells—called **neuromasts**—do not bear cupulas;

they respond directly to the water movement in the canals. Thus a canal is full of "weather vanes" that are sensitive to hydrodynamic pressure changes transmitted from outside the fish. The neuromasts are innervated by the lateral line branch of the **vagus nerve** on the trunk region and by the **facial** and **glossopharyngeal** nerves on the head.

In bony fishes, water circulates through each nostril via two openings (see fig. 2.15a,d). Water enters the anterior opening, passes over the olfactory epithelium, which lines the nasal compartments, and exits through the posterior opening. The olfactory epithelium contains many sensory cells per unit of surface area in its complex folds, which increases the surface area over which chemicals in the ambient water are sensed (fig. 2.15b,c). Of course, development of the olfactory sense varies with the ecological needs of the fish. Fishes that live in turbid waters tend to have well-developed nostrils, while those that inhabit more sunlit waters have a strong visual sense and tend to have poorly developed olfactory organs.

The inner ear of bony fishes is very complex, and hence its total function is not entirely known. As in elasmo-

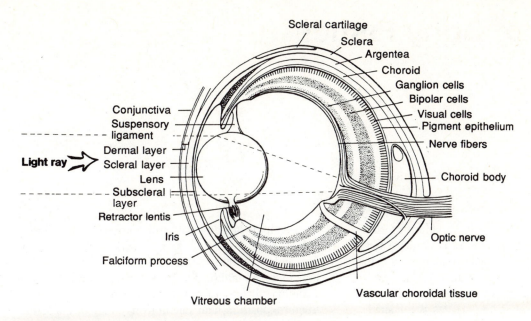

Light ray

- Conjunctiva
- Suspensory ligament
- Dermal layer
- Scleral layer
- Lens
- Subscleral layer
- Retractor lentis
- Iris
- Falciform process
- Vitreous chamber

- Scleral cartilage
- Sclera
- Argentea
- Choroid
- Ganglion cells
- Bipolar cells
- Visual cells
- Pigment epithelium
- Nerve fibers
- Choroid body
- Optic nerve
- Vascular choroidal tissue

Figure 2.17 Diagrammatic vertical section of a teleost eye, showing relative positioning of its component parts. Note how the ray of light is bent by the lens so that it focuses on the retina. (Bond 1979)

branchs, the three semicircular canals are arranged in three planes (fig. 2.16; see exercise on the labyrinth, chapter 5, pp. 60–61). The **horizontal** and **posterior vertical canals** are embedded in the posterior braincase (**neurocranium**), specifically in the **prootic**, **opisthotic**, and **epiotic** bones (*-otic* refers to hearing), while the **anterior vertical canal** and the remaining chambers—**utriculus** and larger **sacculus**—are within the cranial cavity of the braincase. The inner ear can also be divided into the **pars superior** (including the semicircular canals and utriculus) and the **pars inferior** (the sacculus and **lagena**).

At the base of each canal, an enlargement or ampulla lined with neuromasts opens into a chamber. The first chamber is the utriculus, which is just beneath and posterior to the ampullae of the anterior vertical and horizontal semicircular canals. A posterior extension from the utriculus connects the posterior ampullae of the semicircular canals. The sacculus is a large chamber beneath and behind the utriculus, and a third chamber, the lagena, is located near the end of the sacculus. Each of these three chambers contains an **otolith** (earstone), which responds to gravitational forces and changes in orientation of the fish as well as to sound-wave vibrations.

The largest otolith, called the **sagitta**, is in the sacculus; the other two otoliths are the **lapillus** in the utriculus and the **asteriscus** in the lagena. The specific functions of each otolith are not well understood, but current thought is that the lapillus responds to gravitational stimulus (impinges on neuromasts), and the sagitta and asteriscus respond to inertial stimuli such as lateral tilting and fore-aft movements, respectively (Lowenstein 1971). Most likely the sagitta and lagena respond to sound and contribute to hearing.

Although the eye of bony fishes is variable in structure, it generally resembles the vertebrate eye. The optic nerve serves the retina, which receives light rays focused into images through the lens after being transmitted unbent through the cornea (fig. 2.17). The aspect and shape of the eye are controlled by a series of complex retractor and lenticular muscles, in contrast to the extrinsic muscles in the eyes of agnaths and elasmobranchs (Wischnitzer 1972, Wessells and Center 1975). Various specializations distinguish the eyes of many bony-fish species. Some have more than one lens; others have oblong eyeballs. Fish that live in dark waters have mostly rodlike cells containing special pigments in the retina for sensitive black-and-white vision in dim light. Others have many conelike cells for acute color vision in well-lighted waters. We cover some of these specializations in chapter 5.

Chapter 3
Osteology of Bony Fishes

In this chapter we introduce you to the structure of the skeleton in bony fishes, a subject of utmost importance for several reasons. First, you cannot understand how a fish swims, maneuvers, feeds, and breathes without knowing the mechanics of associated bones and muscles. Second, the adaptive variation in bone form among species is reflected in important taxonomic characters for identifying and classifying fish, whether at the species, family, or higher levels. Some of the skeletal characteristics of bony fishes help explain the impressive and rapid adaptive radiation of these fishes, enabling them to occupy an amazing variety of habitats in all aquatic environments. These characteristics include vertebral number, structure of the jaws, pelvic fin formula (relative number of soft and spiny rays), position of the pectoral and pelvic fins, and caudal fin composition.

To facilitate understanding, we treat the skeleton of fishes much as one would a mechanical device such as an automobile, bicycle, or watch. In order to comprehend their functions, one must thoroughly understand the basic structure of the bones and how they are arranged. To gain this familiarity with fish osteology, you must first actually dismantle a fish piece by piece, while carefully studying the construction, and then, after cleaning all the parts, reassemble the skeleton so that all of the bones are properly connected. Though this is painstaking work, it demonstrates essential relationships between structure and function, and it makes comprehension easier in the long run. During the dismantling process, you must carefully note the separate parts and their relative positions. Drawing and labeling individual parts make reassembly easier.

Therefore our objectives in this section are:

1. To describe the major steps in dismantling a fish, that is, how to separate the skull from the axial skeleton, remove the pectoral and pelvic girdles, and remove the various remaining portions of the head (operculum, hyoid arch, hyomandibular series, and gills) from the neurocranium. For additional instruction, refer to Konnerth (1965) and Hildebrand (1968).
2. To describe the preparation and cleaning of each major portion of the skeleton, giving explicit instructions and providing clear diagrams to follow. We will describe the osteology of bony fishes in a general way, so that biologists using different species will be able to recognize and note bones that vary somewhat in shape. Remember that although a bone's specific structure may be slightly different from species to species, its general structure, position, and function may remain the same. For this reason, a detailed diagram showing the osteology of a generalized teleost will serve well to describe most bony fishes.
3. To provide an annotated list of the names of bones, following the classic reviews by Regan (1910), Goodrich (1930), Starks (1930), Gregory (1933), Stokely (1952), Harrington (1955), Norden (1963), and Mujib (1967). This list includes what we feel to be the most commonly used recent names for particular bones (see also Lagler et al. 1977 and Bond 1979).
4. To provide additional directions for osteological study of specimens by clearing and staining, whereby the bones are differentially stained and the muscle tissues are made transparent.

Then in chapter 4, we describe how the major muscles interact with these bones, especially in the head region, the fins, and along the lateral musculature.

HOW TO DISMANTLE A FISH: THE START

First, remove the head from the body. Several junctions need severing in order to do this. The top of the **pectoral girdle** on both sides attaches to the skull by the **posttemporal** bone (see figs. 3.1, 3.4, 3.5, 3.8). Clear away the skin and muscle from the dorsal part of the pectoral girdle where it meets the skull. Once this area is relatively clean, move the pectoral girdle left to right and back in order to find the location of its connection with the skull. Be careful not to cut them, but carefully move the two bones and cut between them. Repeat this process on the opposite side.

The ventral attachment of the pectoral girdle is where the two **cleithra** meet the **urohyal**, a single bone lying medially between the two opercular series of bones (fig.

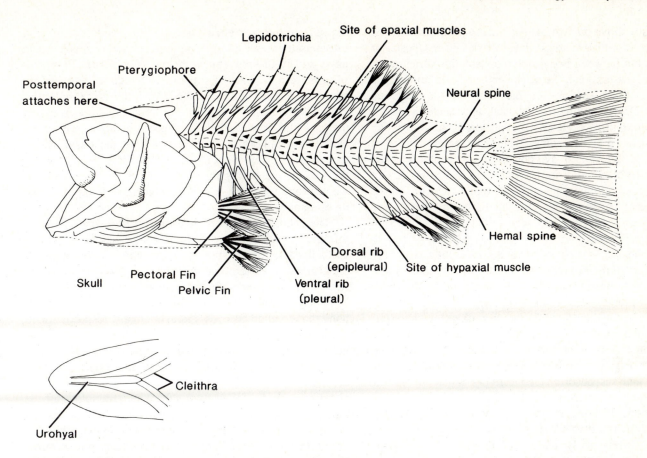

Figure 3.1 Diagram of the lateral view of the entire skeleton of a bony fish, showing its organization. Note the location of the posttemporal bone, one site of attachment of the pectoral girdle to the skull. Also note, in the lower left-hand insert, where the lower portion of the pectoral girdle, the cleithra, attaches to the urohyal.

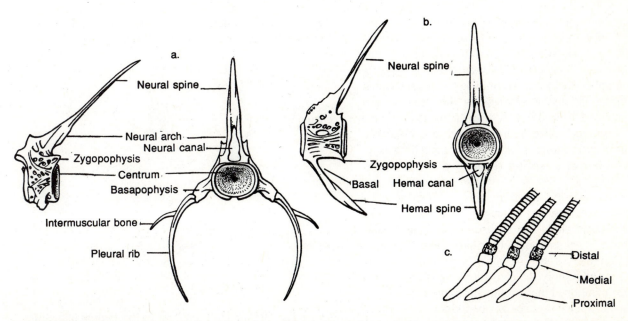

Figure 3.2 The two kinds of vertebrae found in teleosts: (a) abdominal; (b) caudal. (c) A lateral view of the pterygiophores of the median fins. Note that the three portions are shown separately; in most teleosts they are fused.
(a and b: Bond 1979, p. 72)

3.1). Again, move the two parts in order to find this junction and sever it with a sharp scalpel. To detach the posterior skeleton, cut between two of the most anterior vertebrae or in front of the first one, the **atlas vertebra**, and remove the remaining three sections of the fish: (1) the vertebral column, (2) median fins (dorsal, anal, and caudal), and (3) the **appendicular** skeleton (the pectoral and the pelvic girdles) (fig. 3.1). In some fishes, the pelvic girdle is attached at the ventral symphysis of the pectoral girdle ventrally (thoracic position), while in others it is located well behind (abdominal position). In either case, this girdle can be easily removed by severing tissue in front of the joined girdle bones, collectively called the **basipterygia** (fig. 3.4).

From here it is best to begin disarticulating relatively simple parts of the skeleton and then to proceed to the more complex and layered. Therefore, the following sections will cover in order: (1) the **axial skeleton**, excluding the skull but including median fins; (2) the **appendicular skeleton**; and (3) the skull and branchial arches, including the **suspensorium**, hyoid arch, branchial arches, and finally the braincase or **neurocranium**. The neurocranium supports the jaws and suspensorium, collectively called the **splan-chocranium**. Diagrams that can be made into overlays best represent the layering of the head bones and reveal the spatial relations between various bones and their neighbors (see fig. 3.8 repeatedly during this dismantling and reconstructing exercise).

THE AXIAL SKELETON (WITHOUT THE SKULL)

Similarly structured elements are repeated along the main trunk or axis of the fish. First, remove the tissue surrounding the skeleton, primarily the **epaxial** (dorsolateral) and **hypaxial** (ventrolateral) muscle masses (see fig. 3.1). By repeatedly dipping the fish body into hot or warm water, you will soften the tissue surrounding the skeleton just enough to remove it easily. This saves considerable time and effort during the entire dismantling process. However, keep in mind that too long in the hot dip results in a mysterious pile of bones, a hopeless assembly problem for any beginner.

Be careful to preserve the many ribs and intermuscular bones extending sideways from the vertebral column. Reconstructing the whole fish skeleton takes considerable time but creates a valuable model for later study. If you do not reconstruct the whole fish, make sure you seek out, draw, and carefully study the construction and location of the structures mentioned in the following paragraphs.

The teleostean axial skeleton has two kinds of vertebrae. In the abdominal region, **precaudal vertebrae** bear ribs and intermuscular bones; they have neural spines but no haemal spines (fig. 3.2a). More posteriorly in the caudal or trunk region, **caudal vertebrae** bear no ribs and few, if any, intermuscular bones; they have prominent neural spines and have added haemal spines below (fig. 3.2b). **Pterygiophores** form the base of support for the dorsal and anal fin rays (fig. 3.2c). They are embedded in the dorsal musculature and are usually comprised of three fused bones, called the proximal, medial, and distal pterygiophores. On top of each pterygiophore, a small hemisphere, the **basal**, forms part of the fin-ray support. Several delicate muscles along the axis of the pterygiophores move fin rays laterally as well as longitudinally, providing considerable flexibility of fin orientation.

The caudal skeleton of teleosts, an important character for study of relationships and phylogeny, has become quite specialized in many species. It is made up of modified preterminal and terminal vertebrae, which support and strengthen the caudal fin for use in propulsion (fig. 3.3). Modified neural spines and neural arches form splints and bony plates called **epurals** and **uroneurals**, respectively. In advanced teleosts, the last two caudal vertebrae (the first ural and first preural centra, ural number two being lost) are fused into a single element called the **urostyle**. Below the urostyle four to six haemal arches are usually modified into platelike supports called **hypurals**. The terminology of the most posterior vertebrae can be confusing, but usually the last vertebra is the **ultimate** or **preural vertebra**, while the one immediately preceding is the **penultimate** or **preural II vertebra**. The term **antepenultimate** refers to the vertebra anterior to the penultimate.

THE APPENDICULAR SKELETON

The pectoral girdle and its associated fins are basically a series of linearly connected bones forming a circle around

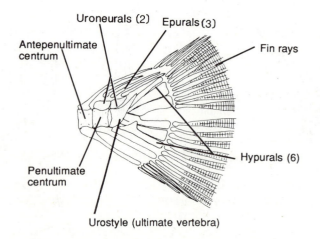

Figure 3.3 Generalized diagram of the caudal skeleton of teleosts. In more advanced teleosts, especially those that swim continually, fusion of various elements, such as the hypurals and preural vertebrae, occurs often.

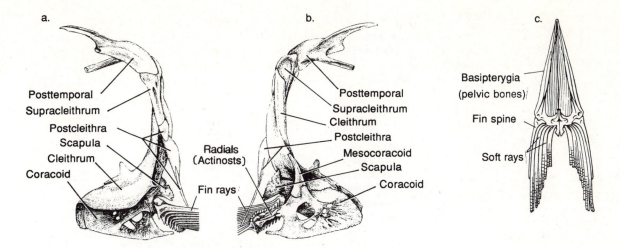

Figure 3.4 Diagram of the appendicular skeleton of the teleost *Pomolobus mediocris:* (a) outer view of left pectoral girdle; (b) inner view of left pectoral girdle; (c) ventral view of the pelvic girdle of *R. saxatilis.* (Parts a and b drawn by Margaret G. Bradbury, from Mead and Bradbury 1963; part c from Bond 1979)

the trunk of the fish just behind the opercular opening (fig. 3.4). The bones of this sequence begin with the posttemporal, which connects the pectoral girdle and neurocranium at attachment points on the **epiotic** and **opisthotic** bones (see figs. 3.5, 3.7, 3.8). Following the posttemporal, the girdle has, in order, the **supracleithrum, post-cleithrum,** and **cleithrum** bones. Attached to the base of this semicircular series are the **scapula** and **coracoid**, which support the pectoral fin rays via a series of smaller bones called **radials** or **actinosts**. In more primitive fishes, like the salmonids, there is also a bone called the **mesocoracoid**, which acts as a brace between the cleithra (above) and the coracoids and scapulae (below). This series of bones, along with the muscles that move them, has made advanced teleosts more maneuverable in spatially complex environments, such as reef areas.

The simpler pelvic girdle has also increased bony fish maneuverability by enlarging and moving forward to insert under the pectoral fins. It consists primarily of a paired set of plates called **basipterygia**, to which the fin rays are directly attached (fig. 3.4). In most advanced teleostean fishes, the pelvic fin consists of a spine followed by several soft rays.

THE SKULL AND ITS ASSOCIATED BONES

Once you have prepared the posterior axial and appendicular skeletons, prepare to disassemble the skull and its associated bones. Before beginning, you should learn a few general techniques (see Konnerth 1965). Do not disarticulate the head bones too quickly or thoroughly since the main benefit is step-by-step observation of how the parts fit together and function as a whole. Use hot water sparingly

to help soften tissues, but do not immerse the head so it disintegrates, leaving a confused pile of bones that cannot be easily reassembled. It is also best to dissect only one side of the head at a time. As you remove bones from one side, those on the other side remain intact as a guide for reassembly. For the same reason, it is best to keep the jaw complex with its suspension intact, as well as the hyoid with branchial apparatus. A good way to do this is to wrap sections in cheesecloth or rags and dip each carefully.

In a strict sense, the skull is part of the axial system, but here you will prepare the skeleton of the head region as a separate unit. Start with the superficial bones—the circumorbital series and the part of the branchiocranium associated with the opercular covering. Then prepare the splanchnocranium (oromandibular region), which includes the upper and lower jaws and suspensorium, consisting of the **palatine**, pterygoid series, **symplectic**, **quadrate**, and **hyomandibular** bones. Continue posteriorly with the bones of the hyoid apparatus and those partially supporting the branchial bones. After this second layer is removed, cleaned, and diagramed (fig. 3.5), carefully dissect out the tiny numerous bones comprising the branchial region and supporting the gills (fig. 3.6b,c). Once these superficial bones are removed from the head, you will find the bones that comprise the neurocranium, which is classified into **endodermal** (ethmoid, orbital, otic series) and **dermal** (nasal, frontal, parietal, and so on) parts.

GUIDELINES FOR PREPARING STUDY SKULLS

This section roughly follows Nelson (1963) and Konnerth (1965).

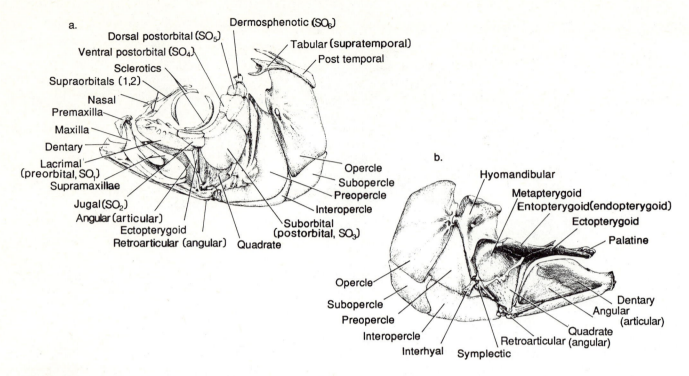

Figure 3.5 Superficial face bones and suspensorium of *Pomolobus mediocris*: (a) lateral view of the left side of the head, underlying bones of the neurocranium not shown; (b) inner view of the left suspensorium, lower jaw, and opercular series. (Drawn by Margaret G. Bradbury, from Mead and Bradbury 1963)

1. Remove the skin and as much tissue as possible from the head.
2. Remove both eyes and their associated muscular and nervous tissue.
3. Locate the **circumorbital series** and remove the left side by inserting a sharp scalpel underneath it and undercutting in a circular fashion. Should you have a scorpaeniform fish as a specimen, cut carefully in the posterioventral region about the retrorse suborbital stay. Keep the circumorbital series connected until you are ready to completely dissect out all tissue. Once each small bone is removed, mark it or tape it in its natural position onto a nearby piece of paper to use as a guide for reassembly.
4. Slice between the right and left halves of the upper and lower jaws. This will allow you to separate both sides of the head anteriorly.
5. Disarticulate the jaw assembly from the rest of the head bones by cutting between the lower jaw at the symplectic or hyomandibular bone and the small bone to the gill apparatus, the **interhyal**. Then swing the entire jaw apparatus laterally away from the skull while noting where it articulates. At the point where the hyomandibular attaches dorsally at the sphenotic bone, slice through connective tissue and remove the entire side of the jaw (see figs. 3.5, 3.7, and 3.8).
6. To remove the hyoid and branchial complex from the remaining head region, disarticulate the interhyal from

inside the hyomandibular series on the opposite side and cut around the bones of the gills at the roof of the mouth (the upper pharyngeal bones) that are usually fused and closely attached to the base of skull (see figs. 3.5, 3.6, and 3.8). Then, to further clean the bones of the gill arches and their supporting bones, proceed carefully to tease and pick at the tissue holding the bones together. Disassembly of the anteriolateral bones, the hyoid series—from the glossohyal to interhyal—does not require special care because the linkages are fairly easy to reconstruct. However, the branchial apparatus is difficult to clean and reassemble completely. You may want to keep it intact while simply locating the position of each tiny component under the connective tissue. Simply dry the entire branchial apparatus for several days before returning it to its proper anatomical place. Unfortunately, it often shrivels up or twists so that it may not fit properly.

7. Now return to the splanchnocranium and remove the most exterior series of bones, which are the opercular bones, from the jaw assembly (figs. 3.5, 3.8). The opercular series can be separated on each side from the jaws by carefully cutting between the interopercle and the preopercle bones from the posterior ends of the preopercle forward. Next detach the anterior end of the interopercle from the mandible and clean the four remaining bones.
8. Clean the suspensorium and the jaw bones (figs. 3.5,

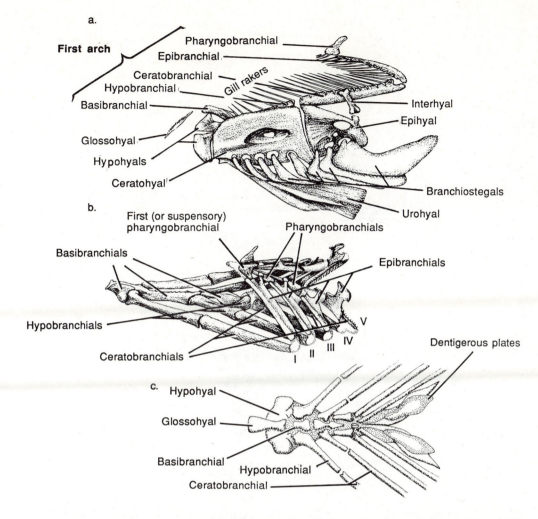

a.

First arch

Pharyngobranchial
Epibranchial
Ceratobranchial
Gill rakers
Hypobranchial
Basibranchial
Glossohyal
Hypohyals
Ceratohyal

Interhyal
Epihyal
Branchiostegals
Urohyal

b.

First (or suspensory)
pharyngobranchial
Pharyngobranchials
Basibranchials
Epibranchials
Hypobranchials
Ceratobranchials
V
IV
III
II
I

Dentigerous plates

c.

Hypohyal
Glossohyal
Basibranchial
Hypobranchial
Ceratobranchial

Figure 3.6 Hyoid arch in a branchial basket of *Pomolobus mediocris:* (a) lateral view of left hyoid arch with associated branchiostegal rays and first branchial arch; (b) three-quarter view of branchial arches; (c) dorsal view of the base of the same structure for the rockfish *Sebastes.* (Parts a and b drawn by Margaret G. Bradbury, from Mead and Bradbury 1963; part c after Morganroth and Morganroth 1969)

3.8). Retain the connections among these bones for orientation; limit the cleaning process to dipping them into hot water for short periods, then scraping and picking with scalpel and forceps.

9. Finally you can clean the neurocranium by more severe soaking and picking since most of the skull bones are securely sutured together. Cleaning and degreasing the skull and all associated bones (and softening the connective tissues) can be accomplished by any of several procedures and chemical treatments. Restricted dipping in hot water to soften tissues and then scraping or picking the tissues away are the best techniques when you want to keep structures intact. However, once cleaned, most bones must still be degreased and perhaps bleached. Simply soaking in hot water removes small amounts of oil, but detergents that contain enzymes or "presoakers" (Ossian 1970) are particularly effective;

for stubborn jobs, soak in 5 percent bleach for 15 to 60 minutes. Acetone is a less effective substitute for detergents. Degrease your specimen with care, however; it would be a shame to disarticulate your hard work at this late stage by too strong a final cleaning. A technique that works quickly on both fresh-frozen and preserved specimens using trypsin or pancreatin is described by Mayden and Wiley (1984).

10. Once your skull or skeleton has been dissected, cleaned, and degreased, assemble the various bones by gluing them back together with common model airplane glue (or, even better, a glue gun). To keep certain bones oriented correctly during the drying phase, use a malleable clay to temporarily secure joints until the glue dries. The skull or entire skeleton can then be mounted on a stand that holds the specimen through the **foramen magnum** of the skull.

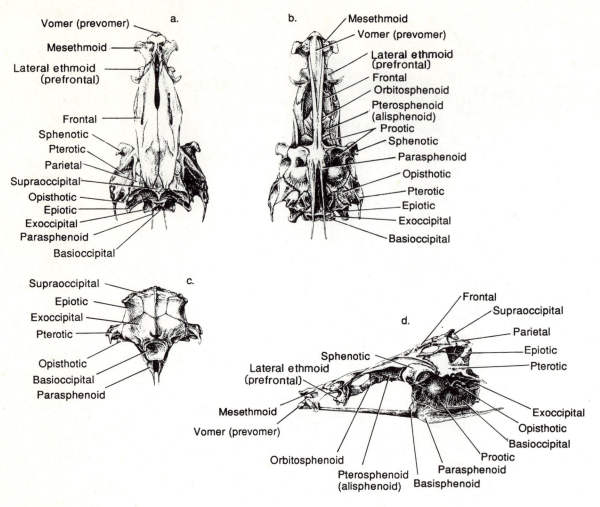

Figure 3.7 Neurocranium of *Pomolobus mediocris:* (a) dorsal view; (b) ventral view; (c) posterior view; (d) lateral view. (Drawn by Margaret G. Bradbury, from Mead and Bradbury 1963)

Now you can study the completed skeleton. You should carefully study the following figures (previously referred to in this guide) with specimen in hand. Note how your fish skeleton differs from the figures of generalized configurations of bones. Continuously ask yourself what functional reasons explain the differences in your specimen from those pictured.

ANNOTATED AND DESCRIPTIVE LIST OF TELEOST BONES

The following complete list of teleostean bones is extracted from several review references on fish osteology (Harrington 1955, Norden 1963, Mujib 1967, and Bond 1979). This is not intended to be the final word on bone terminology, but rather it provides synonyms for bone names taken from different authors so that researchers who know the same bones by different names can communicate. The latest or most widely accepted name precedes its synonyms.

I. Axial skeleton
  A. Skull
    1. Neurocranium
      a. Olfactory region
        Mesethmoid (Ethmoid, Hypethmoid): a medial bone lying between nasal capsules.
        Lateral Ethmoids (Prefrontals): a pair of bones in the ethmoid region, which separate the olfactory capsule from the orbit.
        Vomer (Prevomer): a median bone, usually bearing teeth, at the anterior extremity of the roof of the mouth.
        Preethmoids: paired bones in the floor of the nasal capsules.

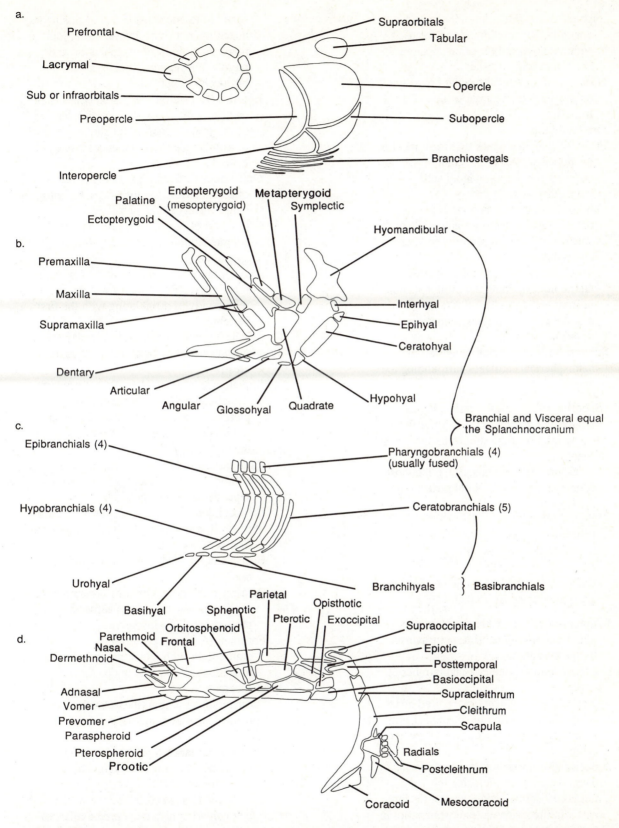

Figure 3.8 Diagrammatic layering showing the bones of the teleost skull: (a) the superficial suspensorium; (b) the facial suspensorium; (c) the internal branchial apparatus on the hyoid arch; (d) the neurocranium and the pectoral girdle. Superimpose these layers in order to visualize which systems are interconnected. If you have access to transparency copiers, copy the three superficial layers and superimpose them on each other, layer by layer. (Modified from Harder 1975)

Supraethmoids (Mesethmoids): paired bones dorsal to the mesethmoid (ethmoid).

Kinethmoid (Rostral): median unpaired bone in cyprinoid fishes.

Nasals: a pair of small tubular bones lying on the sides of the anterior tips of the frontals.

b. Orbital region

Frontals: a pair of bones that form most of the dorsal surface of the cranium, covering the orbitosphenoid and pterosphenoids.

Orbitosphenoid: median bone between orbits, forming the floor and walls of the anterior end of cranial cavity (in *Salmo* and *Cyprinus*).

Pterosphenoids (Alisphenoids): paired lateral bones joining the orbitosphenoid in front and the sphenotics (auto-sphenotics) and prootics behind (in *Salmo*).

Sclerotics (Sclerotic cartilage): pair of hemispherical cartilages surrounding the eyeballs.

"Suborbitals": a series of paired bones around the margin of the orbit; usually six or less; bear the suborbital lateral line canal.

Lachrymal (Preorbitals, SO_1): the most anterior bone in suborbital series; often the largest.

Jugal (SO_2)

Postorbital (SO_3)

Fourth Suborbital (SO_4)

Fifth Suborbital (SO_5)

Dermosphenotic (SO_6): the last four are also called the postorbitals.

"Supraorbitals": paired bones along the upper margin of the orbit; not traversed by the lateral line.

Supraorbitals (number 1 and number 2)

c. Otic region

Sphenotics (Autosphenotics): paired bones lying beneath the dermosphenotics and forming the lateral processes behind the orbit.

Pterotics (Autopterotics, Autopalatines): paired bones each enclosing the horizontal semicircular canal of the inner ear; join the sphenotic (autosphenotic) in front, the prootic below, and the epiotic and exoccipital behind; covered by posttemporal.

Prootics: paired bones each forming the base of the otic capsule and enclosing the utriculus in a ventrolateral bulla; join pterosphenoid in front, sphenotic and pterotic above, and exoccipital and basioccipital behind.

Epiotics (Epioccipitals): paired bones each enclosing the posterior semicircular canal; join supraoccipital above, pterotic in front, and exoccipital beneath and behind.

Opisthotics (Intercalary): paired bones, often excluded from otic capsule, lying beneath and behind pterotic; cover junction of pterotic, epiotic, and supraoccipitals, and perhaps the sphenotic.

Exoccipitals: paired bones at back of skull; form the sides of the foramen magnum, with condyles articulating with the first vertebra.

Supraoccipital: median bone forming posterior roof of skull; often bears a crest.

Supratemporals (Tabulars, Extrascapulars, Scalebones): paired bones covering the pterotic; contain part of lateral line and articulate with the posttemporal bone of the pectoral girdle.

Parietals: paired bones on roof of skull behind the frontals and partly or wholly separated by supraoccipital.

Basioccipital: bone forming posterior base of skull, articulating with centrum of the first vertebra.

Basisphenoid: small, median, Y-shaped bone in rear of orbit.

Parasphenoid: long, unpaired bone running midline below the orbits; between prevomer and basioccipital.

Foramen Magnum: posterior opening in cranium through which the spinal cord passes as it leaves the brain.

2. Branchiocranium

a. Oromandibular region (the Splanchnocranium equals the jaws and palate)

(1) Upper jaw

Premaxillaries (Premaxilla): paired bones forming front of gape; toothed.

Maxillaries (Maxilla): paired bones behind or above the premaxillaries.

Supramaxillaries (Supramaxilla): one or two pairs of bones above the maxil-laries; in primitive teleosts only.

(2) Lower jaw

Angulars (Anguloarticulars with next bones in more advanced teleosts): paired bones occupying part of posterior end of lower jaw.

Retroarticulars (Angulars, Retro-angulars): paired bones each at the lower posterior corner of the angular.

Dentaries: large paired bones forming the front of the lower jaw and fused at the front with the ossified tip of the sesamoid angular (Meckel's cartilage).

Sesamoid Angular (Meckel's cartilage, Coronomeckelian): paired bones each inside of angular bone of lower jaw and involved in attachment of mandibular adductor muscle.

(3) Suspensorium (Palatines, Pterygoids, Hyomandibulars)

Palatines (Autopalatines): paired bones forming the most anterior component of the pterygoquadrate arch.

Entopterygoids (Endopterygoids): paired, articulating with palatine in front and joining metapterygoid behind.

Metapterygoids: paired bones, each joining the entopterygoid in front and articulating with hyomandibular behind.

Ectopterygoids (Pterygoids): paired bones, each joining the entopterygoid above and the quadrate behind; between palatine and quadrate.

Quadrates: paired bones, each joining the ectopterygoid in front, the entopterygoid above, and articulating beneath with the angular of the lower jaw.

Hyomandibulars: paired bones each articulating above with the otic capsule and the symplectic below.

Symplectics: small paired bones each at the lower tip of the hyomandibular.

4. Opercular series (Operculum)

Opercles (Operculars): flat paired bones comprising most of the gill cover.

Preopercles (Preoperculars): paired bones ahead of opercle, partially cover hyomandibular and carry a branch of lateral line canal; lie just behind suspensorium of lower jaw.

Interopercles (Interoperculars): paired bones lying below preopercles, separating them from the subopercles.

Subopercles (Suboperculars): paired bones lying below opercles and overlapping the branchiostegal rays.

Subtemporals (Suprapreopercles): one or more small paired dermal tube bones carrying the lateral line canal across the gap between the preopercle and supratemporal (tabulars); often absent.

b. Hyoid region

Interhyals: small paired cartilage bones, each connecting the epihyal beneath to the symplectic or hyomandibular above.

Epihyals: paired bones each joining the ceratohyal beneath; bear three pairs of branchiostegal rays.

Ceratohyals: paired bones joining the hypohyals in front and bearing branchiostegal rays below.

Hypohyals (upper and lower): paired set of bones joining ceratohyal behind and joining with the glossohyal medially.

Glossohyal (Basihyal): unpaired bone lying just above the junction of the lower hypohyals with front end free; forms base of tongue.

Urohyal: unpaired bone behind and beneath the glossohyal; it arises in a septum between the longitudinal throat muscles.

Branchiostegal Rays (Branchiostegals): from 6 to 34 pairs of rays arising from the ceratohyal or epihyal and forming the floor of the branchial chamber.

c. Branchial region

Pharyngobranchials (Dorsal Pharyngeal Plate, Infrapharyngobranchials): paired bones forming upper members of the first (usually) four branchial arches; the fourth sometimes bear teeth.

Pharyngeal Plate: three pairs of small, toothed dermal plates that are found in gills; the first pair born on the third pharyngobranchials, the second pair on the fourth pharyngobranchials, and the third pair on the fifth pharyngobranchials.

Epibranchials: paired cartilage bones beneath pharyngobranchials of the first (usually) four arches; articulate with ceratobranchials below.

Ceratobranchials: paired bones beneath epibranchials on (usually) all five arches; the fifth sometimes bears the lower pharyngobranchial teeth; articulate below with hypobranchials.

Hypobranchials: paired bones beneath ceratobranchials of the (usually) first four arches; sometimes covered dorsally by tooth-bearing plates; in salmonids, they are on each of the first three gill arches.

Basibranchials: usually three unpaired bones lying in midline, articulating end-to-end with each other and with the glossohyal in front and grasped by the paired hypobranchials.

  B. Vertebral column
    1. Vertebrae
    Abdominal Vertebrae (Precaudal Vertebrae)
    Caudal Vertebrae
    Atlas Vertebra
    Ultimate Vertebra (Preural Vertebra)
    Penultimate Vertebra (Preural II Vertebra)
    Epineurals

II. Appendicular skeleton
  A. Median fins
    1. Caudal fin

Epurals: two or three median bones that lie dorsal of uroneurals; detached; believed to be modified neural spines.

Uroneurals: three pairs of bony plates that lie over the last three upturned vertebrae and the urostyle; believed to be remnants of neural arches; the larger, more anterior pair is sometimes called the caudal bony plate.

Urostyle (Ural Vertebra): the cartilaginous termination of the vertebral column; in salmonids it curves dorsad behind the last three upturned vertebrae.

Hypurals: series of (usually) six expanded haemal spines that lie ventrally of the three upturned vertebrae and the urostyle; often fused in advanced fishes.

Parhypural: the last haemal spine (see Bond 1979).

    2. Dorsal fin and anal fins

Pterygiophores: a series of three endoskeletal rods that support the dorsal and anal fins; have three segments, including (1) round distal bone, (2) short, horizontal middle bone, and (3) long, pointed proximal bone.

Fin rays: dermal bony rays of two kinds: (1) soft and articulated fin rays, and (2) spiny, nonarticulated fin rays.

Interneurals: a series of median supporting rods that lie in the muscle, anterior of dorsal fin, between the bifurcated neural spines.

Interhaemals: similar series of median sup-

porting rods as interneurals, but lie in the muscle, anterior of anal fin between the bifurcated haemal spines.

  B. Paired fins
    1. Pelvic fins

Basipterygium (Pelvic Bone): a triangular endochondral bone that, in pairs, forms the pelvic girdle; collectively called basipterygia.

Pelvic fin rays

    2. Pectoral fins

Posttemporals: a pair of forked dermal bones that connect the pectoral girdle to the epiotic and opisthotic bones of the cranium.

Supracleithrum (plural: Supracleithra): a pair of curved dermal bones located in the pectoral girdle that connect the cleithra with the posttemporals.

Postcleithrum (plural: Postcleithra): usually three pairs of small, scalelike dermal bones that lie in a vertical series posterior to the cleithra; occur in all salmonids; in some fishes these bones act as a brace for the pectoral girdle.

Cleithrum (plural: Cleithra): a pair of large, curved intramembranous bones that form most of the pectoral girdle.

Scapula (plural: Scapulae): a pair of flat bones located in the pectoral girdle; articulate anteriorly with coracoids and posteriorly with the cleithra.

Coracoid (plural: Coracoids): a pair of triangular bones of the pectoral girdle; articulates with the cleithra and the scapulae.

Mesocoracoid (plural: Mesocoracoids): a pair of curved bones that act as braces between cleithra (above) and coracoids and scapulae (below); in primitive fishes like salmonids.

Radials (Actinosts): small endochondral bones of each pectoral girdle that articulate proximally with scapulae and distally with the fin rays.

Pectoral fin rays

METHODS FOR CLEARING AND STAINING FISHES

Over the years, several techniques have been developed so that it is unnecessary, at least for small fish or small portions of large fish, to dissect out all the bones to study osteology. In these techniques, the general approach is to stain the entire fish with a noticeable dye (such as alizarin red) and then to clear the external tissue so that only the bones retain the stain. These specimens can then be studied by a dissecting microscope to decipher their bony structures with the fish specimen intact. In more recent advances, both cartilage and bone are stained differentially on the same specimen (Dingerkus and Ohler 1977). The following guide to clearing and staining is a modified version of several published methods (Hollister 1934, Taylor 1967a and 1976b, Simons and Van Horn 1970/71 and 1971, Dingerkus and Ohler 1977, Dingerkus 1981, Brubaker and Angus 1984, and Mayden and Wiley 1984).

It has long been known that methylene blue and toluidine blue are good stains to use on cartilage, and alizarin red S is very good at staining bone. Usually potassium hydroxide is used for clearing the tissues so that the stained bones and cartilage can be seen. A paper by Simons and Van Horn (1970/71) proposed, in addition, alcian blue for staining cartilage, especially on fresh material. It produces superior results when compared to either methylene or toluidine blue. However, in general this dye produces poor results in fishes preserved in either formalin or alcohol, primarily due to difficulty in removing the excess alcian blue from the flesh. More recently, however, biologists have been using enzyme solutions to clear the flesh, either instead of potassium hydroxide or in conjunction with it; this enables the researcher to obtain results that are far more reliable and useful, in which the cartilage remains a deep blue color. The resulting specimens have intense blue cartilage, dark red bones, and clear, transparent flesh, without being torn apart by the procedures used. In addition, these specimens can be preserved, and they still produce high quality results, even those that have been in formalin or alcohol for many years.

The following materials are needed for this procedure:

1. Alizarin red S powder
2. Potassium hydroxide (KOH)
3. Distilled water
4. Borax or sodium borate powder
5. Glycerine
6. Trypsin or pancreatin powder
7. Thymol crystals
8. 40% formaldehyde solution
9. 3% hydrogen peroxide (H_2O_2)
10. Xylene
11. Alcohol, either 95% ethanol or 99% isopropyl
12. Alcian blue 8GN
13. Glacial acetic acid

(Note: Items 10 and 11 are used if the fish is fatty or you plan to embed it in plastic.)

The stock solutions are prepared as follows:

1. Stock potassium hydroxide: Mix 100 grams of potassium hydroxide in 900 ml of distilled water to make a 10% solution (100g/liter).
2. 2% potassium hydroxide: Mix two parts 10% KOH solution (solution #1) to eight parts distilled water to make a 2% solution.
3. 10% formalin: Mix one part 40% formaldehyde to three parts distilled water.
4. Bleaching solution: Mix two to three parts 3% hydrogen peroxide with seven to eight parts 2% potassium hydroxide (solution #2).
5. Saturated sodium borate solution: Mix sodium borate in distilled water to make a saturated solution; allow to settle until clear.
6. Enzyme buffer: Mix three parts saturated sodium borate (solution #5) with seven parts distilled water.
7. Stock stain solution:
   a. Mix the following:
      5 ml 50% glacial acetic acid
      10 ml glycerine
      60 ml 1% chloral hydrate
   b. Saturate with alizarin red S stain.
8. Stain solution: Mix 1 ml of stock stain solution (solution #7) in 100 ml 2% KOH (solution #2).
9. Alcian blue stain: Mix 10 mg alcian blue 8GN with 80 ml 95% ethyl alcohol and 20 ml glacial acetic acid (50%). This solution must be made fresh.
10. Glycerine solutions: Prepare the three solutions for use in sequence:
    a. 30% glycerine in 2% KOH
    b. 60% glycerine in 2% KOH
    c. 90% glycerine in 2% KOH

Methods for preparing, staining, and clearing fish specimens:

1. Fix specimens in 10% formalin (solution #3). Allow specimens to remain in this solution for three to four days. For specimens already in formalin or alcohol, ignore this step and proceed to step #2.
2. Soak specimens in water until the formalin is removed. If the specimen is not to be cleared immediately, store it in 40% isopropyl alcohol.
3. Scale and eviscerate the specimen as far as possible here. Remove the eyes. In delicate specimens, scaling should be done after the staining.
4. Bleach the specimen in a solution of 2% KOH and hydrogen peroxide (solution #4) until most dark pigments are gone. The specimens should appear yellowish. This step should take five to seven days.
5. Place the specimen directly into the alcian blue stain solution (solution #9) for 24 to 48 hours.
6. Transfer the specimen to distilled water for two to three hours, or until it sinks.
7. Place specimen in enzyme buffer (solution #6). Make the volume of this solution about 10–40 times the volume of the specimen. Mix 1/4 tsp. trypsin or pancreatin powder to each 400 ml of enzyme buffer. Change this solution once a week. Leave the fish in enzyme solution

until most of the vertebral column can be seen and the caudal peduncle is clear. For small specimens this process should take several days to a week; for large ones it may take several weeks or even months.

8. Place the fish in stain solution (solution #8) for several hours or until the fin rays are deep red. Be careful not to overstain the tissue.

9. Place the specimen in 2% KOH (solution #2) until the excess stain is leached out. Several changes of the solution may be needed. Small fish usually destain in one to two days, while larger specimens may take longer. If dark yellowish areas still remain in the tissue, return the fish to the enzyme solution until they disappear.

10. Place specimen in 30% glycerine in 2% KOH for 24 hours.

11. Place specimen in 60% glycerine in 2% KOH for 24 hours.

12. Place specimen in 90% glycerine in 2% KOH for 24 hours.

13. Store specimen in pure glycerine to which a few crystals of thymol have been added to prevent mold and bacteria from growing.

Some notes regarding potential problems and difficulties with this technique follow:

1. Fishes with especially thick connective tissue or excessive fat deposits will require special treatment such as longer soak times in the clearing solutions. You will have to experiment with various modifications in order to satisfy the requirements of your particular group of fishes.

2. Some fish, after clearing, will have a dark brownish substance along the haemal arch. Soaking the fish in 2% KOH for several days will usually remove this coloration.

3. The fin rays of certain fish, especially some flatfish, seem to be damaged by 2% KOH. The tip of the rays begins to split and fray after several days in this solution. If possible, watch your specimen carefully each day and remove it from the KOH as soon as you notice any damage. If excess stain still remains in the tissue, the specimen should be returned to the enzyme solution until destained. The bones of fish destained in enzyme solution will be lighter in color than those destained in 2% KOH. However, destaining is faster in the enzyme solution.

4. For extremely old specimens that have been stored in formalin for a long time, this technique might not be successful.

Chapter 4
Muscular Morphology of Bony Fishes

INTRODUCTION

Now that you are familiar with the osteology of bony fishes, a more complete understanding of how the various bones function requires basic knowledge about the morphology of the muscles associated with them. As stated in a review of bony fish myology by Winterbottom (1974, p. 226), "Muscles have been described under an incredible variety of names in the descriptive literature." Therefore, this subject can be confusing. For consistency, we follow Winterbottom's terminology, and we restrict this discussion to muscles both obvious and of primary importance. We start with the muscles of the head, which are extremely important for feeding and respiration; then we briefly describe the main muscles along the body, which are primarily responsible for locomotion in fishes; and we finish with both median and paired fin musculature.

Before we detail the muscular anatomy of these functional parts, a few basic definitions and concepts are in order. Muscles can be classified by their action or their position. The action of **flexion** is lateral bending away from the midline of the frontal plane of the fish, while **extension** is the opposite action, a return to the midline. A flexing muscle is termed a **flexor**; an extending muscle is an **extensor**. Generally, the flexors of one side are the extensors of the other. Muscles that elevate a structure are usually called **levators** or **erectors**; those that lower a structure are called **depressors**. Another scheme classifies muscles into **abductors**, which pull a structure away from the median caudal line in the sagittal plane, and **adductors**, which do the opposite by pulling it back toward the body. A muscle that pulls a structure to the side is often called an **inclinator**; one that can spread fin rays apart is an **arrector**. **Rotation** refers to the movement of a single fin ray about its longitudinal axis. Finally, when a fin ray passes through a circle, this is termed **circumduction**, a combination of flexion, adduction, rotation, abduction, and extension.

Muscles classified by their position can also be classified and named by their **origin** or **insertion**. A muscle's origin refers to the stationary, or relatively most stable, site of attachment (Winterbottom 1974). Its insertion is the site of attachment on the structure that moves when the muscle contracts. Usually these sites of attachment are bones, but they can also be tendons or masses of fibers. Often a muscle is named after its origin and insertion sites. In this case, the prefix will refer to its origin and the suffix to its insertion. For example, the sternohyoideus muscle originates on the sternum (the cleithrum and coracoid) and inserts on the hyoid arch (the urohyal), which moves when the muscle contracts. A second term often describes a muscle's position relative to another muscle of the same name. **Superficialis, medius,** and **profundus** refer to the other muscles more shallow, intermediate, or deeper in position, respectively. Finally, flexible structures in a fish body may have different degrees of freedom of relative movement. Usually, one degree of freedom refers to one pair of antagonistic muscles moving a muscle in one plane—back and forth. For example, a pair of levator and depressor muscles will pull a fin away from and/or back toward the body.

HEAD MUSCULATURE

It has often been stated that the evolutionary success of teleosts is due to the rapid diversification of their feeding and respiratory mechanisms. Indeed, in his classic study of the pharyngeal jaws of cichlid fishes, Liem (1973) stated that the "evolutionary success [of cichlids] seems to be due to the perfection of [these] adaptations." The muscles in the head of a teleost fish illustrate such perfection, and the importance of the head in fishes is reason enough to familiarize oneself with its musculature. Lauder (1981, 1983a, 1983b, 1983c), and Motta (1984) have further studied functional feeding repertoires in fishes.

The head or **cranial** musculature is conveniently divided into four structural and functional groups: the jaw muscles, the muscles of the suspensorium, the opercular muscles, and the ventral head muscles.

Jaw Muscles

The muscles of the jaw and cheek region are somewhat superficial, and most are visible after simply peeling the skin

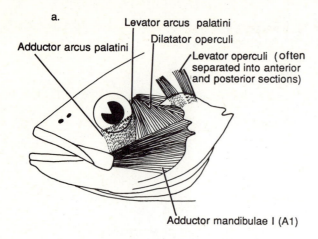

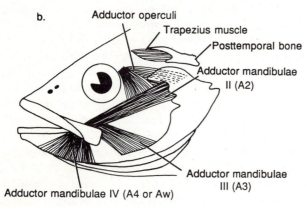

Figure 4.1 The jaw, suspensorium, and opercular musculature of a representative teleost: (a) with the superficial tissue and skin removed; (b) with some of the larger superficial muscles removed, such as A1 and the levator operculi and part of the opercle cut away. (Modified from Winterbottom 1974)

away. Although their structure, position, and number differ from species to species, those we describe here are found in most teleost fishes. The most obvious is the **adductor mandibulae,** which acts primarily to close the mouth (fig. 4.1). It is often subdivided into several parts (usually four), denoted by separate numbers or letters (Winterbottom 1974). These parts (also called sections) may have somewhat different functions and sites of origin and insertion. The most obvious section, usually distal to all the others, is the **adductor mandibulae 1 (A 1),** which inserts on the maxilla and, depending upon the species, originates on any of several bones: the quadrate, symplectic, preopercle, hyomandibular, one or more of the three pterygoid bones, and even other nearby bones. This muscle is primarily involved in feeding. It holds the maxilla in place during jaw protrusion and helps close the jaws afterward.

The **adductor mandibulae 2 (A 2)** is ventral and medial to A 1 and may insert on the posterior part of the dentary bone of the mandible on a ligament between the maxilla and mandible or on both sites (fig. 4.1). It originates on the

quadrate, symplectic, mesopterygoid, metapterygoid, hyomandibula, or preopercle. To expose this muscle, bisect the adductor mandibulae 1 and either open it sideways or remove it entirely. When the adductor mandibulae 2 contracts, it closes the mouth and helps adduct the suspensorium. Thus, it is active during feeding and the expiration phase of respiration.

The **adductor mandibulae 3 (A 3)** is medial to the other two and inserts on the dentary and/or the ligament between the maxilla and mandible. It originates on the lateral parts of the quadrate, symplectic, metapterygoid, and often the hyomandibula bones. This muscle has much the same function as A 2 in that it helps adduct the suspensorium and closes the mouth.

The fourth muscle in the adductor mandibulae series lies anterior to the other three and inserts on the medial face of the dentary. To expose this muscle, you must remove part of the dentary bone. The **adductor mandibulae 4 (A 4 or A w)** originates on the medial face of the quadrate and, in some fishes, the preopercle. It lies medial to the intermandibularis (a muscle described later in the ventral head muscle section). The A w (also referred to as the **intramandibularis**) is not involved in respiration but acts to close the jaws during feeding. To make sure you understand how each of these jaw muscles works, pull gently on each with a pair of forceps and watch the resulting action.

Suspensorium Muscles

A small group of muscles controls the lateral expansion of the suspensory complex (comprised of the palatine, ectopterygoid, metapterygoid, sympletic, preopercle, hyomandibula, quadrate, and entopterygoid bones); these muscles control the size of the buccal cavity. Expose these by removing the skin on the head above the cheek area and jaw musculature (fig. 4.1). One large relatively superficial muscle, the **levator arcus palatini,** abducts the suspensory complex to enlarge the buccal cavity. Opposing muscles, usually two, adduct the complex to reverse this action. All three muscles originate somewhere on the skull and insert on the hyomandibular bone. Specifically, the levator arcus palatini, which is easily visible superficially above the adductor mandibulae series and anterior to the dilatator operculi, inserts on the lateral side of the hyomandibula and originates on the skull, usually at the posterior circumorbital and sphenotic bones. One of the opposing muscles, the **adductor arcus palatini,** which actually lies inside the suspensorium underneath the neurocranium and can be viewed through the orbit once the tissue is removed, inserts medially on the hyomandibula and usually originates on the parasphenoid and prootic bones.

In some fishes, an extra muscle, called the **adductor hyomandibulae,** occurs either behind the adductor arcus palatini or before the adductor operculi (described later), and it seems to act like the adductor arcus palatini. It inserts medially on the hyomandibula and originates on the posterior process of the prootic and ventral portion of the pterotic. Often these two muscles appear fused and cannot be easily separated. Again, manipulate these muscles to observe their actions.

Opercular Muscles

A set of muscles connecting the postorbital portion of the skull to the operculum controls the size of the opercular cavity, and it also influences the expansion of the buccal cavity, the opening of the mouth, and the protrusion of the jaws. The most obvious and superficial muscle in this series is the **dilatator operculi**, which inserts medially on the dorsal part of the operculum and originates at the skull on the sphenotic, frontal, hyomandibula, and pterotic bones (fig. 4.1). It lies just behind or beneath the levator arcus palatini and often appears to be part of it, but the two muscles can be teased apart. Indeed the two act together to abduct the operculum. Through various connections among these bones, contraction of the dilatator operculi also enlarges the buccal cavity and helps protrude the mouth. Once you have completed this section on muscles and reviewed the section on osteology, you will be able to trace these interconnections and their actions.

The **levator operculi**, a muscle often divided into anterior and posterior parts, is located behind and somewhat underneath the adductor mandibulae and dilatator operculi (fig. 4.1). It inserts medially on the opercular surface and originates at the skull near the attachment of the posttemporal and pterotic bones. The levator operculi, which may simply be an extension of adductor arcus palatini or the adductor operculi muscles (Winterbottom 1974), helps protrude the mouth, and it also depresses the lower jaw.

Inserting below the insertion of the levator operculi on the medial surface of the operculum and just behind the hyomandibula, the **adductor operculi** muscle originates at the skull on any of several bones such as the exoccipital and pterotic (fig. 4.1). This deep muscle, which may also simply be a continuation of the adductor arcus palatini anteriorly and the levator operculi posteriorly, connects the inside of the operculum to the top of the skull. It adducts the operculum and therefore helps to compress the opercular cavity during expiration.

The **adductor hyomandibulae**, which is also indistinct because it may just continue the adductor arcus palatini posteriorly and the adductor operculi anteriorly, occurs only in certain fishes. Therefore, we exclude it from our generalized diagram of the head muscles (fig. 4.1). It inserts on the back of the hyomandibula and usually originates on the prootic and pterotic, or cleithrum, bones.

Finally, the **trapezius** helps position the pectoral girdle and therefore moves the branchiostegal rays and the lower jaw (fig. 4.1). It inserts on the posttemporal and the dorsal tip of the cleithrum and originates at the skull on the pterotic and epiotic bones. To determine this muscle's main function, pull it and note the results.

Ventral Head Muscles

When you turn a fish on its back, you can see that several muscle masses make up the floor of the mouth and connect variously to the jaws, the hyoid arch, the inside of the operculum, and the branchiostegal rays. To expose some of these muscles, first peel the skin from the ventral surface of the head between the gills. Starting at the symphysis of the lower jaws, using a scalpel and forceps, peel the skin posteriorly to the end of the hyoid apparatus. Do this carefully near the branchiostegal rays since these muscles are often quite small, diffuse, and difficult to distinguish.

Myologists disagree on the identification, recognition, nomenclature, and function of many ventral head muscles. These muscles may vary considerably among families of teleosts and even among similar species from the same family. Therefore, we only describe the more obvious and common ones. For further detail on structure and nomenclature, consult Winterbottom (1974), and for information on electromyographical functional analysis, see Osse (1969) and Lauder (1981, 1983b, 1983c).

The most anterior muscle in this group is the **intermandibularis**, which connects the two dentaries of the lower jaw (fig. 4.2). To reveal this muscle, you may have to

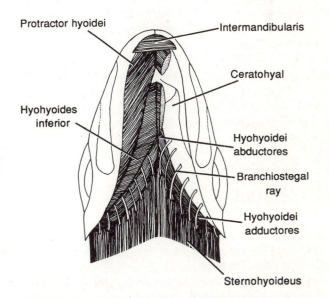

Figure 4.2 Diagram of the ventral head muscles of a teleost fish. In order to see some of the connections with bones, the protractor hyoidei and hyohyoides inferior on the left side are removed. (Modified and generalized from Winterbottom 1974)

spread or cut the protractor hyoidei (described in the next paragraph). The intermandibularis draws the jaws together during expiration by compressing the buccal cavity.

The **protractor hyoidei (geniohyoideus)** is a compound muscle that connects the hyoid arch to the lower jaw (fig. 4.2). Attaching anteriorly to the medial face of the dentary, its fibers spread posteriorly, often as far as the end of the angular. Its variable posterior site of attachment is usually on lateral parts of the hyoid arch, often including the first few branchiostegal rays and the interopercle. Because its anterior part contracts during expiration and its posterior part contracts during inspiration, this muscle probably aids in moving water through the oral and buccal cavities (Osse 1969).

Not occurring in all teleosts, the next three muscles are poorly understood as to their sites of attachment, specific configurations, and functions. The **hyohyoides inferioris** arises from the ventral midline, usually on the urohyal, and spreads up and out to attach onto the hyoid arch, usually at the ceratohyal, under the first few branchiostegal rays (fig. 4.2). Judging from its sites of attachment, this muscle apparently keeps tension on the hyoid arch, and it may aid the posterior portion of the protractor hyoidei during inspiration. The complex of **hyohyoidei abductores** muscles connects, by means of tendons, the most anterior branchiostegal ray to the ventral part of the hyoid arch, usually the ventral hypohyal or ceratohyal bones. This set of muscles is often quite difficult to distinguish from other muscular tissue about the branchiostegal rays and the hyoid arch. Since the hyohyoidei abductores attach to the most anterior branchiostegal ray, they probably spread the rays apart. The **hyohyoidei adductores**, on the other hand, lie between the more posterior branchiostegal rays and usually attach dorsally to the medial faces of opercular bones, such as the opercle and subopercle. These fibers pass laterally and posteriorly from ray to ray, and together with other fibers they form a continuous sheet on the medial side of the branchiostegal rays. Judging by their configuration and sites of attachment, these muscles close the rays. To see how these muscles function individually, tease the separate strands apart and pull them back and forth.

Other Muscles

Another muscle in the region of the ventral head muscles but not integrally involved with them is the **sternohyoideus** (fig. 4.2). Located behind the hyoid arch, it inserts on the urohyal and originates on the lower anterior edge of the cleithrum and coracoid bones. Posteriorly it merges with the hypaxial musculature. The sternohyoideus pulls the hyoid arch backward, thus depressing the lower jaw. Several other minor muscles associated with the ventral part of the head,

pectoral girdle, and branchial arches are not considered here, but they are detailed by Winterbottom (1974: 248–271).

BODY MUSCULATURE

The main mass of a fish is in its body musculature, which gives the fish its shape and main source of locomotion. Yet this mass is comprised of only a few different kinds of muscles arranged to maximize power output in a very intricate and often perplexing way. Skin the fish to observe the general arrangement of the body musculature. Slice the skin vertically behind the head and horizontally just along and beneath the dorsal fin. Then pull the skin away carefully by using scalpel, fingers, and forceps to circumvent the muscles underneath.

By removing the skin, you have exposed muscle tissue that is covered by zigzag, segmentally arranged **myotomes** (embryologically, **myomeres**), which are separated from each other by **myosepta (myocommata)** (fig. 4.3). These myotomes are divided into three portions: the dorsal mass, called the **epaxialis** or **epaxial muscle mass**; the ventral mass of muscles, which lies below the lateral septum and is called the **hypaxialis** or **hypaxial muscle mass**; and usually a lateral mass, called the **lateralis superficialis**, which occurs at the midline of the body overlying the ventral position of the epaxialis, the dorsal portion of the hypaxialis, and the lateral septum. The lateralis superficialis is shallow, red, with very thin fibers used mostly for sustained swimming (see the exercise on swimming morphology and function in chap. 5).

In advanced teleosts, the hypaxialis may divide in two near the trunk. The more dorsal **obliquus superioris** has fibers that pass posteroventrally across the myotome; the more ventral **obliquus inferioris** has fibers passing posterodorsally. Because this is difficult to visualize, we suggest that you refer to Alexander (1969) for a comprehensive description of this arrangement. It is also helpful to look carefully at the arrangement of the fibers in the myotomes of the fish you are dissecting. Attempt to trace single fibers from their superficial "origin" on an anterior myoseptum through the muscle mass in the myotome to their deeper posterior "insertion" on the following myoseptum. Finding the exact point where the obliquus superioris becomes the obliquus inferioris is almost impossible.

The terms *origin* and *insertion* as applied to epaxialis and hypaxialis muscles are used somewhat arbitrarily since it is difficult to trace the meanderings of single myotomes or single muscle fibers. The epaxialis, as a muscle mass, extends anteriorly to attach to the skull and often to the dorsal part of the pectoral girdle. The myotomes then follow a tilted V- or crescent-shaped path to the lateral septum. Therefore, as a whole, the epaxialis probably originates on

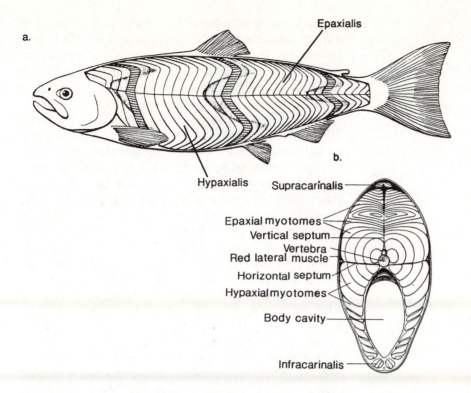

Figure 4.3 Lateral view (a) and cross-sectional view (b) of the teleost body musculature. The gray portion diagrammed in (a) shows the pattern that the whole myomere (shown as hatched) displays as it traverses medially toward the vertebral column and the midline of the body. The cross section (b) is taken through the fish approximately at the insertion of the dorsal fin. (Bond 1979)

the vertebral centra, neural arches, and spines and inserts on the lateral bases of the dorsal fin rays, even though the individual muscle fibers may attach quite differently, as described above.

The hypaxialis has a similar orientation, except that it lies below the lateral septum, has the coelom to circumvent anteriorly, and so has myotomes that may extend in any of three directions: posteroventrally, anteroventrally, and back again. As mentioned, the most dorsal muscle mass, extending posteroventrally is the **obliquus superioris**. Some of its fibers extend anteriorly (and dorsally) to attach to the neurocranium, usually at the otic region, and its more lateral fibers often attach to the cleithrum. Ventrally, these fibers usually extend to the ends of the pleural ribs farthest from the ventral midline. At the posterior end of the trunk, these fibers insert on the bases of the caudal fin rays.

The **obliquus inferioris** lies below the obliquus superioris where its fibers proceed posterodorsally. Anteriorly, they often attach to the cleithrum and coracoid; ventrally, they merge with the sternohyoideus muscle; and posteriorly, they connect the ribs under the obliquus superioris.

The way all these muscle masses work to cause the sinusoidal body waves that propel the fish forward is perceptually difficult to comprehend; this requires considerable thought mixed with abundant anatomical study. It will help you to consult the works of authors who have presented the most likely models (Nursall 1956, Willemse 1959, Alexander 1969, Lagler et al. 1962 and 1977, and Chiasson 1974). Knowing that the epaxial and hypaxial muscle bundles originate at the midline on the vertebral centra and insert at the dorsal and ventral edge of the body, you may not see why they should bend the fish's body laterally when they contract. But recall that these muscles have radical bends in them and are segmentally arranged. Thus when these muscles contract, they must pull at the midline in a convoluted way that creates a posterior wave of lateral bending as well as the propulsive force forward.

The best way to perceive this process is to inspect the arrangement of the myotomes in your specimen. First, using your fingers or a probe, follow one inward by separating two at the myoseptum between them. This is best done either in the hypaxial or epaxial muscle mass near the fish's tail. Another way to see this arrangement is to cut a cross section of a fish and locate the "cones of myomeres" that mark the posterior flexures of more anterior myotomes. A third, perhaps more difficult, way is to make a horizontal (frontal) section to clarify the relationship of the myotomes to the midline (i.e., the vertebral column; see fig. 4.4).

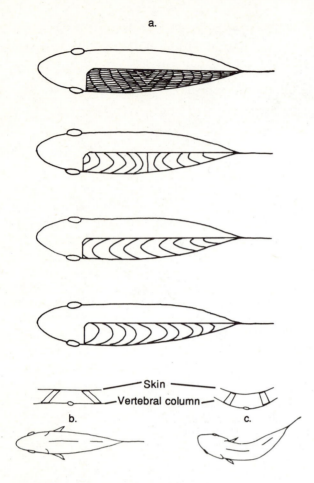

Figure 4.4 (a) Several examples of myomere patterns that result from horizontal (longitudinal) sections of the epaxial musculature of a teleost. The differences are due mainly to the distance above the midline and the angle at which the sections were taken. Can you duplicate these sections? (b) A theoretical diagram showing the flexure shape of a myomere in which the muscle fibers are relaxed. (c) Another diagram showing the theoretical shape of a myomere in which the muscle fibers, which parallel the midline, are contracted. See the text for further explanation. (Part a redrawn from Willemse 1959; parts b and c redrawn from Nursall 1956)

Depending upon the angle of your incision and the depth you choose to cut into the fish's dorsal body, you can obtain several different patterns. The pattern most often used to illustrate the orientation of the myotomal flexures is shown in figure 4.4a.

Another consideration in understanding the mechanism of body flexures is the orientation of individual muscle fibers and the direction in which they exert pressure on the myosepta, the vertebral column, and the skin of the fish. Carefully observe the orientation of fibers in your fish. Recall that the fibers run parallel to the fish's axis, originating near the vertebral column and inserting near the ventral or dorsal midlines, often at the anal or dorsal fins.

Convince yourself of this by seeing how these fibers traverse their myotomes in particular and the fish body in general.

Now let us see how a series of muscle contractions can cause the sinusoidal side-to-side movements of the fish's tail that propel it forward. At rest, the individual myotomes assume a rhomboidal shape when viewed in a horizontal (or frontal) cross section (see fig. 4.4a,b). Then, when they contract, the individual muscle fibers, which run parallel to the midline, shorten by approximately half their length while maintaining their volume or mass so that the rhomboid becomes more rectangular (see fig. 4.4c). Consequently, the myotome and its associated myosepta orient more perpendicularly to the midline to push it aside and bend the fish laterally. When the muscles at one point on one side contract, the muscles opposite those on the other side must relax and actually stretch a bit. Thus sequential waves of contractions and relaxations proceed posteriorly along the fish's tail creating a net force forward (see Nursall 1956, Willemse 1959, Alexander 1969, Chiasson 1974, and the section on swimming in chapter 5 for further elaboration).

Median and paired fins of fishes perform a variety of functions. They may stabilize or alter the fish's forward motion. Or, in lieu of body contractions, they may provide the main propulsive force themselves. Obviously, then, their muscle-mediated movements are complex. Knowing their muscles gives you a basis for understanding the functions of these fins. First, we shall describe the musculature of the median fins (caudal, dorsal, and anal) and then the muscles of the paired fins (pelvic and pectoral).

FIN MUSCULATURE

Median Fins

Caudal Fin

Reflecting the variety of caudal fin types in fishes, the associated musculature varies considerably in development and arrangement. Nevertheless, basic components exist, including a flexor dorsalis, a flexor ventralis, a hypochordal longitudinalis, and an interradialis. We restrict the following description to these muscles and omit many of the modifications that have occurred in teleosts. The specimen you dissect should be perch- or basslike with general fusiform shape, moderate lateral compression, relatively thick caudal peduncle, and moderate aspect ratio (height to breadth) of caudal fin. However, if you have a highly streamlined carangiform or scombriform fish, be sure to notice that their slender peduncle and lunate caudal fin complex have their caudal muscles reduced or lost altogether.

Begin dissecting the caudal region by skinning all the way past where the caudal fin rays meet the last vertebral

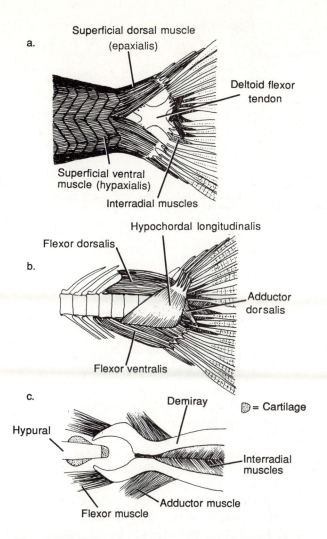

Figure 4.5 Diagram showing main caudal muscles of a generalized teleost: (a) the superficial muscles with only the skin removed; (b) the deeper layers with the epaxial and hypaxial muscles removed; (c) a horizontal (frontal) section of the tail, showing muscle attachments. (Parts a and b after Winterbottom 1974; part c after Nursall 1963)

elements. Among the fin rays, usually fairly close to their base, you will find numerous bundles of muscle fibers interconnecting the rays (fig. 4.5a). These **interradialis** muscles usually lie between adjacent rays, but sometimes they pass over more than one. They pull its caudal fin rays together. Also visible superficially are the plain-looking **deltoid flexor tendon** and the continuation of epaxial and hypaxial muscle masses, which tend to merge here.

Now cut away these superficial muscle masses, being careful not to damage any of the underlying muscles. In this deeper caudal layer, a muscle originates mostly on the lower hypurals and passes posterodorsally to insert on three or four of the more dorsal fin rays in the upper half of the caudal fin (fig. 4.5b). This **hypochordal longitudinalis** muscle draws the dorsal fin rays together, presumably act-

ing in opposition to the interradialis muscles. Also in this layer, a bundle of muscle tissue originates on the last few neural spines, their centra, and the upper hypurals; it inserts on the dorsal caudal fin rays. This **flexor dorsalis** muscle, which may consist of several different bundles, causes lateral bending or movement away from the midline in the frontal plane of the fish.

Ventrally, another muscle mass resembles the flexor dorsalis and has similar sites of insertion and origin. This **flexor ventralis** is also complex and originates on the lateral faces of the haemal spines and arches of the last few vertebrae, the parhypural, and the lower hypurals; it inserts on the lateral bases of the ventral branched rays of the caudal fin. This muscle is the flexor in figure 4.5c of a frontal section in the ventral region of the tail. In only a few families of teleosts, an additional muscle—the **adductor dorsalis** (fig. 4.5b)—originates laterally from the upper hypurals and urostyle and inserts posteroventrally on the uppermost of the central caudal fin rays. Presumably, this muscle can spread the ventral caudal fin rays by opposing parts of the interradialis muscles. As its position in figure 4.5c indicates, it can move individual rays laterally. Demonstrate this by pulling the muscle.

• Does it move any other part of the caudal fin?

(For a more detailed functional analysis of caudal fin action, see Lauder 1982.)

Dorsal and Anal Fins

Both dorsal and anal fins have three similar sets of muscles (erector, depressor, and inclinator) that control the movements of the fins and their individual fin rays. For brevity we shall describe only the sets associated with the dorsal fin; you should realize that similar muscles with similar names work the anal fin. For example, the erectores dorsales has a counterpart in the anal fin called the erectores anales (see fig. 4.6). Besides these three sets of muscles, a series of medial carinal muscles called the **supracarinalis** and **infracarinalis** are paired and cordlike. These muscles lie along the dorsal and ventral midlines and connect the bases of both median and paired fins (fig. 4.7).

In the dorsal fin, the **erectores dorsales** usually originate on the fronts of basal pterygiophores (see fig. 4.6c) and insert, usually via tendons, at the bases of the fin rays. These muscles erect the fin rays in an anterior direction (see fig. 4.6a). On top of these erector muscles, the **depressores dorsales** originate on the backs of the basal pterygiophores and insert on the back and at the base of the fin ray involved. They oppose the erectors by pulling the fin ray backward and toward the body. The **inclinatores dorsales**, which are usually shorter and more superficial than the erectors or depressors, originate on the fascia between the skin and epaxialis, and they insert on the side of the base on

a.

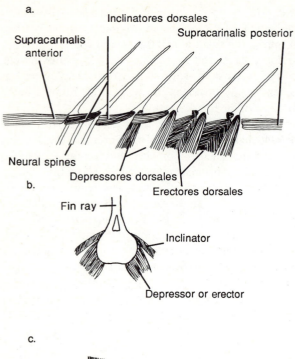

Supracarinalis anterior

Inclinatores dorsales

Supracarinalis posterior

Neural spines

Depressores dorsales

Erectores dorsales

b.

Fin ray

Inclinator

Depressor or erector

c.

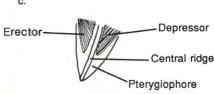

Erector

Depressor

Central ridge

Pterygiophore

Figure 4.6 Diagram showing muscles of the dorsal fins in a generalized teleost: (a) the three muscle systems with the epaxial muscle mass removed (also, for the third and fourth ray, the inclinatores dorsales have been removed so the erectores dorsales can be seen, and for the fifth and sixth ray, the depressores dorsales have been removed); (b) a diagrammatic cross section of a fin ray, showing attachment of muscles; (c) a diagram showing the general pattern of attachment of depressors and erectors to a pterygiophore. A similar arrangement exists for the anal fin. (Modified from Winterbottom 1974)

the particular spine or fin ray. The inclinators, which move the fin rays back and forth laterally, are well developed in fishes that primarily use fin motions in swimming.

Paired Fins

Pelvic Fins

To find this relatively simple set of muscles, peel away the skin and associated scales at the base of the pelvic fins. See the relatively long, triangularly shaped muscles with the apex directed anteriorly. The six major bundles of muscles lie along the basipterygia (pelvis) of the pelvic girdle, three on the ventral part and three on the dorsal part of each half of the pelvis (see fig. 4.8a).

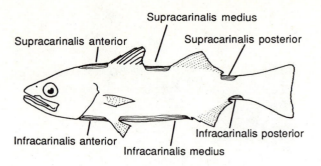

Supracarinalis anterior

Supracarinalis medius

Supracarinalis posterior

Infracarinalis anterior

Infracarinalis medius

Infracarinalis posterior

Figure 4.7 Generalized teleost fish with dark bars indicating the relative positions of the carinal muscles. (After Winterbottom 1974)

To reveal the positions, shapes, and connections of the pelvic muscles—especially those lying dorsal to the pelvis—remove the entire pelvis and carefully slice away extraneous tissue, leaving all muscles to be studied intact (see fig. 4.8 for orientation).

First, examine the pelvic girdle from the ventral aspect (see fig. 4.8b). The most prominent surface muscle, the **abductor superficialis pelvicus**, originates on the ventral portions of the pelvis and inserts via tendons on the more anterior rays of the pelvic fin. As its name implies, this muscle pulls the pelvic fin away from the body. Just below this superficial muscle lies the **abductor profundus pelvicus**, also with similar sites of origin and insertion and so with similar function as its superficial counterpart. In order to see this muscle, cut through the abductor superficialis pelvicus. Then you can demonstrate the actions of these muscles by firmly grasping one end of the cut muscle with a pair of forceps and gently pulling it back and forth to observe the movements of the pelvic fin and some of its individual rays. More laterally (see fig. 4.8b), the **arrector ventralis pelvicus** muscle, which originates ventrolaterally on the pelvis and inserts on the ventral base of the first pelvic rays, pulls the pelvic fin rays apart and away from the body.

Now turn the pelvic girdle over to examine its most prominent muscle, the **adductor superficialis pelvicus** (fig. 4.8c). Often this muscle lies below the **extensor proprius**, a muscle originating on the dorsal surface of the pelvis front and inserting posteromedially on several inner pelvic fin rays. Although not universally present in teleosts (so not included in fig. 4.8), the extensor proprius can be located by its origin and insertion if present.

• If you find it in your specimen, what do you think its function is?

Like the adductor profundus pelvicus, the adductor superficialis pelvicus pulls the pelvic fin back toward the body in a posterior motion. When present, it originates on

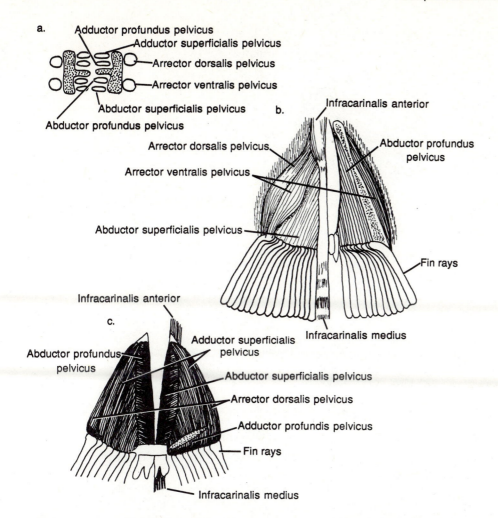

Figure 4.8 Diagrams showing the musculature of a generalized teleost pelvic girdle: (a) cross section of pelvis, showing general location of the muscle masses; (b) ventral view of the pelvic muscle, girdle, and fin rays, with the left infracardinalis anterior and medius, arrector ventralis pelvicus, and abductor superficialis removed so that the underlying muscles can be seen better; (c) dorsal view, with hypaxialis, left adductor superficialis pelvicus, abductor superficialis pelvicus, and infracarinales anterior and medius removed. (After Winterbottom 1974)

the dorsal surface of the pelvis and inserts, either via tendons or directly, on all the fin rays and the pelvic spine. Finally, the **arrector dorsalis pelvicus** lies lateral to the adductors, originates on the dorsal side of the pelvis, and inserts on the top of the inner half of the first fin ray or spine. As with the arrector ventralis, this muscle spreads and curves fin rays to apply stabilizing hydrodynamic forces while the fish is swimming.

• Can you verify this action?
• Knowing that more advanced teleosts often occupy heterogeneous environments, must be highly manueverable, and have their pelvic fins located far forward, often before their pectorals, describe how you think their pelvic musculature is arranged.

Pectoral Fins

The pectoral fins have muscles that basically act like the pelvic muscles, although they are more diverse in both form and function. In more advanced teleosts, the pectoral fins are located farther up the fish's side and so are more useful in stabilizing and maneuvering their bodies. In order to do this effectively, the muscles that move the fin rays must abduct, adduct, bend, straighten, and even, perhaps, circumduct or rotate. As you study these muscles, you should determine how they combine to perform these different actions.

To reveal the pectoral fin muscles, carefully remove the skin on the body near the fin, both laterally and medially (inside the axilla). The muscles that move the fin comprise two opposing masses: the lateral (or dorsal) mass consists

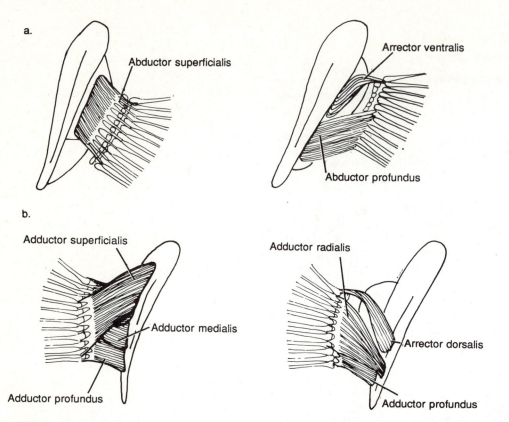

Figure 4.9 Diagram showing the left pectoral fin musculature of a generalized teleost fish: (a) the muscles from a lateral view (left) with the fin close to the body—the deeper view (right) has the abductor superficialis removed; (b) the muscles from a medial view (left) with the pectoral fin oriented away from the body—the deeper view (right) has the adductor superficialis and adductor medialis removed.

of abductors, or extensors, and the medial (or ventral) mass of adductors, or flexors. Most of these muscles originate on the cleithrum or two associated bones, the coracoid and scapula, and insert on one of the four **radials (actinosts)** or on the ends of the fin rays themselves. Again it is often valuable and informative to cut through one of the meatier superficial muscles to see the deeper ones beneath. While doing this, be sure to pull the muscles various ways to see their actions on the pectoral fin or fin rays.

First, locate the **abductor superficialis** (fig. 4.9), a large muscle on the lateral (ventral) surface of the pectoral fin that pulls the fin away from the body forward and downward. It originates on the lateral surface of the cleithrum and inserts diffusely or via tendons to the outer, anterior bases of the fin rays. Cutting this muscle in half and spreading the two halves to each side with pins, you will see the **abductor profundus**, which originates primarily on the lateral surface of the coracoid and secondarily on the cleithrum and scapula; it inserts via tendons on the medial tips of the fin rays. In addition, the **arrector ventralis** spreads the fin rays and draws the first ray forward and downward (fig. 4.9a). It originates mostly on the cleithrum and inserts via tendons medially on the base of the inside half of the first fin ray.

By pulling the pectoral fin away from the body to expose its medial musculature, three salient muscles are revealed. The **adductor superficialis** is the most dorsal and is usually distinguishable from the other two (fig. 4.9a). It primarily originates on the top and inside of the cleithrum but secondarily on the scapula, coracoid, and even mesocoracoid of some fishes. It inserts through tendons attaching to the medial surfaces of the ends of fin rays, usually beyond their bases. It draws the fin upward and backward against the body. In some fishes, a muscle directly underneath the adductor superficialis called the **adductor medialis** (fig. 4.9b) also originates on the cleithrum and inserts mainly on the middle fin rays via tendons. The deepest of the three adductors, the **adductor profundus**, usually originates on the coracoid and the cleithrum and inserts via tendons on the rear bases of all the fin rays except the first. As with all the adductors, it helps pull the pectoral fin back toward the body, but by pulling downward as well.

By cutting the adductor muscles and either removing or pinning them to the side, you can see the deeper muscles of the medial surface of the pectoral fin (fig. 4.9b). The most dorsal is the **arrector dorsalis**, which originates on the cleithrum and coracoid—and sometimes on a part of the scapula—and inserts via tendons on the base of the medial half of the first ray. Therefore, it presumably helps spread the rays of the pectoral fin by drawing the first ray upward and backward. Its medial counterpart, the **lateral arrector ventralis**, works in consort to rotate the fin about its axis. In many teleosts, another deeper muscle, the **coracoradialis**, originates from the coracoid and inserts on the ventral face of the fourth radial. It presumably pulls the radial downward and backward, permitting the pectoral fin to be "double-jointed." Finally, the **adductor radialis**, which connects the radials and often the coracoid to the most ventral fin rays, draws the fin upward and backward, much in the same manner as the arrector dorsalis.

Chapter 5
Exercises in Functional Morphology

INTRODUCTION

Now we can look in more detail at the diverse ways fishes have adapted their morphologies to survive in their watery habitats. Of the huge number of systems and adaptations to choose from, we have selected some of the more interesting morphological and functional adaptations for laboratory exercises. Pick and choose among them as your interests and available facilities dictate. We have made each exercise as short as possible and have provided references for further study and answering questions.

Since many of the exercises require either live, fresh, or preserved specimens of a variety of fishes, we suggest ways to obtain specimens. Use local sources if possible. We have tried to design these exercises as generally as possible to take advantage of the kinds of fish available to any individual in any given location. Therefore, a collection of local fishes benefits any exercise in ichthyology because it provides not only voucher specimens but also extras for dissection and manipulation as we describe. Collect fishes from nearby waters or from local fish markets or aquarium stores. Often, you can even eat the results of your experiments. Otherwise, prepared specimens and demonstrations can be purchased through the various commercial biological supply houses. For demonstration and sometimes dissections, specimens from museums of natural history may also be available for loan.

Should you assemble a study collection, we suggest the following procedures: Gather specimens of as many types (families and species) of fishes as possible. Try to obtain fishes from a variety of habitats, such as smooth bottom and rough bottom near-shore areas, offshore waters, sand and mud habitats, epipelagic regions of a lake or the ocean, rivers and streams, estuaries, tidal creeks, and perhaps even the deep sea, should facilities provide. These specimens should represent different lifestyles or habits: schooling fishes, sedentary fishes that await their prey, fishes that pick at their prey or filter it from the plankton in the water column, and nocturnal fishes. Since a fish's habits and habitats influence the evolution of its morphology, such a diverse collection allows comparative studies of adaptation. In addition, try to obtain specimens of fish other than

teleosts: for example, hagfish, lampreys, elasmobranchs, and the more primitive bony fishes. Also examine young as well as adults. Chapters 10 and 11 (sect. 3) provide suggestions on how to sample fishes in different environments. You may also want to peruse the literature on the natural history of fishes in your particular area.

Some of the specimens you collect should be preserved for later use (see chap. 11 in sect. 3). Some of the following exercises work better if the subjects are fresh and not preserved in a fixative; others work better using preserved fish. If possible, keep some of the hardier fishes alive in aquaria so that you can see them in action.

In this chapter, we present study exercises in how fishes sense their surrounding environment; how they feed and respire; how they swim; how they fill, empty, and utilize their swimbladders; and how they reproduce. Throughout these exercises, we emphasize how natural selection has adapted fish morphologies to function most efficiently and effectively to maximize the chances of the fish's survival. For an interesting history of this functional approach to morphology, see Russell (1982).

SENSORY MECHANISMS

Imagine that you are a fish and so must understand what is going on around you in your aquatic home in order to survive: the ambient physical, chemical, and biological events. The first thing to know is that certain events appear quite differently in water. Light appears less intense, and colors are not so bright. The surrounding medium feels denser than air. You would find it difficult to detect scents, let alone determine their direction of origin. You perceive sounds differently than you are used to, sometimes sharply and at other times dully, as though your ears are plugged. Again, as with scents, you have difficulty determining the direction of source. You start to get uncomfortable because you feel that you cannot perceive possible threats or know where to find food and shelter. Moreover, you cannot communicate with other fishes to ask. These are just a few of the problems a "novice" fish must face. Obviously, evolution, through natural selection, has adapted fishes to overcome these challenges. The following exercises will help you understand how.

Thus far, you have located most of the organs that a fish might use to sense its environment and have some idea of how they are generally constructed. Now you need to view these organs as an integrated system to understand how a particular fish perceives its surroundings. Then you can compare other kinds of fishes to see how they differ in their sensory adaptations and how these adaptations reflect their different ways of life.

Exercise 1: Survey of the Sensory Adaptations of Fishes

Select a fish from the collection available, preferably a different kind from that of other people involved in this exercise so you can compare a variety of kinds. In examining your specimen, consider the following questions:

1. Read the following list of main types of stimuli:

temperature	light
pressure	colors
touch	images and shapes
gravity	movement of objects
sound	electromagnetic fields
electric fields	salinity
chemicals	

   • What types should this fish respond to? Can you think of any stimuli that are not on this list? Try to group these stimuli into broader categories.

2. From several ichthyology textbooks, we compiled the following list of kinds of sense organs commonly found on fishes:

taste buds	barbels
epidermal nerve endings	eyes
temperature receptors	nostrils
lateral-line organs	ampullae of Lorenzini
cephalic lateral-line organs	semicircular canals
cirri	(inner ear)

   • Does your specimen have all of these kinds? If not, which does it have and which are missing?

For those it has, answer the following questions:

   • How many individual organs of each particular kind can you find?
   • Where are they located?
   • How large are they? (For example, are the organs large or small relative to those in another species of fish?)

   • What is the organ's basic structure and how does it work?
   • Is there anything unusual about any of the sense organs on your fish? If so, what? Is something larger? Does it orient in a different way? Are there sense organs that you cannot find yet which would seem to be essential? If they are absent, how can your fish compensate?
   • Are there any sense organs on your fish that appear unnecessarily well developed? For example, does it have an elaborate pair of eyes (perhaps with a larger diameter, many cones or dense rods, or special absorptive pigments; see, for example Munk 1964a and 1964b, Northmore et al. 1978, McFarland et al. 1979, Lythgoe 1980, and Allen et al. 1982) and yet live in a dark environment? How do you explain this? (Hint: Perhaps the fish also has photophores, which are light-producing organs, so it needs well-developed eyes to detect the weak light from these organs on other individuals, such as members of the opposite sex.)

Taste buds and lateral-line organs are small structures often widely distributed in the epidermis and best examined histologically (see reviews by Flock 1971 and Hara 1971). Generally, lateral-line organs occur along the flanks and across the head. Taste buds occur not only in the mouth but also in the gill cavity, on the gill arches, or on appendages such as fins and barbels.

One way around a time-consuming histological study is to pinpoint their locations at the ends of nerves that serve them. These sensory structures are innervated by cranial nerves VII, VIII, IX, and X. To examine the distribution of the tiny organs, therefore, it is necessary to stain these nerves using a technique devised by Freihofer (1966) and Freihofer et al. (1977). Like clearing and staining bones, this involves serial staining and destaining until nerves stand out from surrounding tissues that have been cleared. Since even this procedure is quite lengthy and too detailed for presentation in this manual, we refer you to the generalized structure and arrangement of the cranial nerves (see fig. 8 in Bernstein 1970, p. 55) and to the original references of Freihofer (1966), Fraser and Freihofer (1971), and Freihofer et al. (1977), which describe in detail the methodology necessary to decipher the peripheral nerves and their associated sense organs. If you have the facilities to do such nerve staining, it would be interesting to compare those fishes that have an impressive array of taste buds (perhaps cyprinids, ictalurids, mullids, or mugilids) with those that do not (perhaps small, schooling planktivores such as atherinids or engraulids). For further information, consult Bernstein (1970), Hara (1971), Chiasson (1974), and Lagler et al. (1977).

3. When you think you understand, at least from a morphological point of view, the sensory systems on your fish, suggest how the fish uses this combination of or-

gans to get along in its particular habitat. You may have to consult references, either relating to your species or to comparative studies of sensory mechanisms (see, for example, Hoar and Randall 1971, Oakley and Schafer 1978, Ali 1980, and Northcutt and Davis 1983). Then consider the following questions:

- Does your fish use sensory cues mostly to stay in "comfortable" conditions, to find food, to avoid predators, to seek shelter, or to find mates?
- Which of these sensory organs do you think are the most important to your fish? Why?
- Are these also the most elaborate or best developed on your specimen?
- By looking at one specimen, do you now have a comprehensive view of the sensory modalities used by the entire species? (Hint: How might structures change during ontogeny or vary between sexes?)
- Do you find any apparent effect of obviously well-developed sense organs on the state of development of other sensory systems? (Hint: Do catfish with their elaborate olfactory sense organs also have well-developed eyes?)

4. In order to put all this into perspective, share your results with others who are also studying this aspect. Then, from a comparative viewpoint, consider the following:

- Are some sense organs restricted to particular higher taxa? (Hint: Do you find electroreceptive organs only in elasmobranch fishes?)
- Do all members of smaller taxa—for example, families—tend to share a similar array of sensory modalities? Why?
- Do sensory mechanisms mostly relate to the habitats in which the fish live or to the fish's particular behaviors? Suggest other relations. (Hint: Do you tend to find less lateral-line development in constantly swimming, schooling fishes than in fishes that quietly occupy crevices in tidepools or occupy burrows in mudflats?)
- Is there a strong relationship between the fish's sensory apparatus and its general shape or morphology? (Hint: Do laterally compressed fishes tend to have better developed eyes and more poorly developed olfactory organs than do truncate or dorsoventrally depressed fishes?)

5. If possible, study several different kinds of individual fish from the same species: for example, juveniles, subadults, and adults or males and females.

- Is there any indication that ontogenetic stage influences the kind of sensory array characteristic of a species? Explain (see, for example, Allen et al. 1982 and Pankhurst and Lythgoe 1983).
- Is there any indication that sex influences relative development of the sensory organs? (Hint: Some lanternfishes have sexually dimorphic luminescent or-

gans, located both ventrally and dorsally on the caudal peduncle. What would this suggest?)

Exercise 2: Brain Morphology as It Relates to Sensory Mechanisms

The sensory organs transmit their information (that is, input) to the central nervous system where it is processed in the appropriate part of the brain for a response (output). To understand this basic sequence of sensory input-output relations, an introduction to brain morphology is essential. More specifically, it is important to compare portions of the brain responsible for different outputs to see if they vary in their relative states of development. Because the brain is enclosed in a relatively hard, bony protective structure, the neurocranium, it is difficult to dissect. You have a chance here to put your knowledge of skull morphology to good use.

Carefully dissect the brains of several species of fishes, preferably those with different primary senses (e.g., those that rely primarily on vision or on olfaction or on hearing). Compare the general arrangement of their brains, but pay particular attention to enlargement of certain parts relative to others.

1. Review the general structure of the neurocranium (sect. 1, chap. 3, pp. 31–34), noting the location of the brain with its olfactory, optic, and otic portions. Remember that the names of the bones relate to their functions. For example, *otic* (as in spenotic) refers to hearing. Also, before you dissect your fish, think about how its skull differs, if it does, from the usual skull so that you will have less trouble finding the brain.

2. Pick a specimen that either tends to specialize in one sensory mechanism or tends to generalize and use several. Perhaps others you work with will have surveyed several kinds: fish that use primarily vision, olfaction, or hearing as well as fish that rely on all three.

- Do other fishes rely primarily on their lateral line or taste senses? If so, which part of the brain would be involved?

3. Shave the skin from the top of the fish's head, noting as you expose the skull where the brain is most likely to be housed. Once you have removed the skin and connective tissues, you may see portions of the brain. If not, continue to shave carefully in a horizontal (frontal) plane until you reach the brain cavity. This may be difficult and time consuming, especially in a large specimen with a thickly covered skull. Be patient and also careful not to pierce the last layer of skull, which could overlie delicate brain tissue. When you see the first bit of brain, carefully remove skull tissue from all

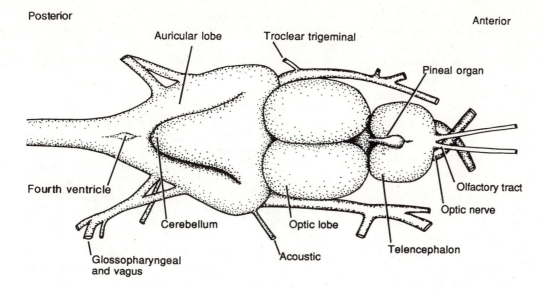

Posterior   Anterior

Auricular lobe   Troclear trigeminal   Pineal organ

Olfactory tract

Optic nerve

Fourth ventricle

Cerebellum   Optic lobe   Telencephalon

Glossopharyngeal   Acoustic
and vagus

Figure 5.1 A generalized version of a dorsal view of the teleost brain. (After Chiasson 1974)

around it to expose the whole brain. Take care not to disturb the brain tissue itself.

4. After you have cleared away most bony and connective tissues from around the brain, you can do the following: Draw the general structure of the brain from a dorsal view, noting the different lobes, their relative proportions, other associated structures, and as many of the nerve connections as you can locate (fig. 5.1).

   You can find more detailed information on brain structure in Bernstein (1970), Lagler et al. (1977), and Northcutt and Davis (1983). Next carefully dissect the brain out of the neurocranium to expose the ventral surface. From dorsal and ventral views, you can then decide which portions of the brain are best developed. You can assess relative size of the major parts by estimating the area as seen from top or bottom, although such projections can be misleading because they ignore curvature of the brain. Or, as suggested by Bauchot et al. (1976 and 1977), you can separate the major parts, dry them for a specified time, weigh each, and determine relative size of each as its portion of total brain or body weight.

5. Once you have completed your dissection and compiled your results, consider the following questions:

   • Does your fish appear to have one part enlarged as though one sense is expanded over others? If so, which sense? (Hint: Be careful here because the optic lobe is almost always larger than the olfactory lobe. Why?)
   • Does the largest portion of the brain correspond to the largest sense organ previously determined?
   • Does your specimen have any parts noticeably smaller than you expected? If so, what parts and why?
   • What other considerations should you make before arriving at major conclusions from this morphological

study? (Hint: Were your methods without error? Are lobe volume and lobe density the same thing, and do they relate equally to each sensory mechanism?)

6. Now compare the results from your fish to those of other species—especially relative size, weight, or volume of the different portions of the brain and how these values relate to the fish's principal mechanism(s).

Exercise 3: Functional Morphology of Olfactory Organs

In an excellent review article, Hara (1971, p. 79) concluded, "Chemoreception plays an important and indispensable role in the behavior of fishes. It is involved in the procurement of food, recognition of sex, discrimination between individuals of the same or different species, in defense against predators, in parental behavior, in orientation, and in so many other ways." He then described the various approaches to studying chemosensory organs and classified such organs by their structure, location, and central innervation: olfaction or smell, gustation or taste, and "common" or general chemical senses (for a similar approach, see Appelbaum and Schemmel 1983). This exercise exemplifies chemoreception in fishes by stressing the olfactory organs; a later exercise will concern the taste-bud system.

As briefly described in chapter 2, the main olfactory organ is the bulb-shaped nasal rosette, which is housed within a canal water flows through; this organ is innervated by the first cranial nerve. Fishes are **macrosmotic** if they have well-developed olfactory organs and **microsmotic** if their olfactory sense is poorly developed. The shape of the nasal rosettes can also differ considerably. Burne (1909) recognized three kinds: oval, found in most fishes; round, in predatory fast-moving fishes; and elongate, in more sedentary fishes such as eels. Often the shape of these rosettes relates to the configuration, position, and length of their enclosing canal. That is, fishes with short, narrow canals must have small, usually roundish, nasal rosettes, whereas fishes with extremely long canals can accommodate larger, more elongate rosettes and therefore more sensory surface.

Again, use the comparative approach to see these different adaptations. Select several specimens with noticeably different olfactory structures: perhaps one elasmobranch and teleosts with both eyes and nostrils well-developed or eyes more developed than nostrils or nostrils better developed than eyes. Generalized teleosts like minnows, smelt, anchovies, and herring often fit the first category; more predatory visual feeders like pike or bass fit the second; bottom or crevice-dwelling organisms, like eels, burbots, and catfish, fit the third. After you choose your fish, consider the following questions:

1. Find the olfactory structures and note how many there are.
2. Describe their general structure and orientation.

   • How many openings do they have?
   • Where are they located and how far apart?
   • What causes water to move through these openings and across the olfactory sensory tissue?

3. Cut through the canal to study the nasal rosette.

   • Is the olfactory tissue macrosmotic or microsmotic?
   • Devise a way to estimate the total surface area on which scents (molecules) might impinge. Do surface irregularities increase such area? How does this complicate your method of estimation? How would you standardize your method to make your results comparable with others from perhaps larger or smaller fishes? (Hint: Hara's 1971 article suggests a method.)
   • Does the rosette in your specimen typify any of the shape categories already mentioned?
   • Does its shape relate to the shape and length of its canal?
   • Does its shape relate to the lifestyle of the species exemplified by your fish?

4. Now consider how the olfactory organ functions. With live fish, how would you determine the following:

   • The path that water takes in flowing through the nasal canal.
   • The rate at which water flows from the incurrent to the excurrent opening.
   • What influences this rate.
   • How much water is transported through the nostrils and past the sensory tissue.

   • How this flow is influenced by the habits of the fish, such as swimming and eating.

5. Again, compare your findings with those from other species.

   • Does the structure or arrangement of the olfactory organ relate to the phylogenetic position of the fishes studied? Does the olfactory structure of elasmobranchs differ much from that of teleosts?
   • Does the olfactory structure relate to the lifestyle, swimming mode, or feeding habits of the fishes studied?
   • In fishes with a strong visual sense, do you also find well-developed olfactory organs or poorly developed ones? That is, do the two senses supplement or complement one another?
   • How important do you think olfaction is to most fishes? Is the structure of the olfactory organs flexible in the sense that it varies noticeably among fishes in general?

Exercise 4: Behavioral Responses to Chemosensory Cues

Many fishes use chemosensory cues to help them procure food, defend themselves, orient to specific locations, or relate to other organisms (Brett and Groot 1963, Bardach et al. 1967, Kleerekoper 1969, and Sutterlin 1975). These chemical cues are received by both gustatory organs (taste buds) and olfactory sense organs (nasal rosettes), and they can give the fish information about where and when and how much of a chemical exists in the surrounding water. The fish's response will be influenced by the kind and amount of chemical substance in the water, its distance from the fish, and the movement of water in which it is dissolved. Many chemicals stimulate behavioral reactions in fishes (see Sutterlin 1975 for a review). It is the objective of this simple exercise in chemoreception to explore the ways fishes detect chemicals in their surroundings, the typical responses they exhibit to such chemicals, and the factors determining the amount and kind of response to chemical stimuli.

There are two basic behavioral ways to measure a response to a stimulus in fishes. One is to perform choice experiments, in which a fish is given two stimuli and is expected (or trained) to respond to one in preference to the other. These are commonly performed as Y-tube experiments in aquaria, with the source of the chemical stimulus coming through one fork of the Y-tube and the predicted response being the movement of the target fish toward or through that fork. The other method is to describe the range of "typical" behavioral responses to a chemical stimulus and to measure the intensity with which fish respond to different substances or different concentrations of a specific substance. The exercise here takes this second approach.

In some sophisticated studies on the chemosensory responses of bullhead catfish (genus *Ictalurus*), Bardach et al. (1967) distinguished the sense organs the fish actually used by modifying individual fish. To eliminate vision, they blinded the catfish with phemerol. To eliminate olfactory systems, they severed the tracts or cauterized the nares. To eliminate the taste buds on barbels, they amputated these organs or, in some, severed portions of the seventh cranial nerve. In this way, the investigators could monitor the reaction of fishes to the chemical cue being administered with one, two, or three of their senses intact.

For these experiments, we will not be so sophisticated since that would require both considerable experience and training in caring for captive fishes and dissection techniques and a good deal of time. You can learn a sufficient amount by simply observing the overall reaction of individual fishes to various chemical stimuli.

Suggestions Regarding Design of Aquaria, Choice of Fish and Stimuli, and Design of Experiments

Many species of fishes respond readily to chemical cues in their surroundings. To ensure success of this laboratory project, you should attempt to choose fish that will respond predictably. One excellent choice would be fish in the genus *Ictalurus*, which have olfactory organs as well as extremely well-developed taste buds distributed all over the head, on the sides of the fish, and on the fins and barbels (Bardach et al. 1967). Other potential fish subjects include the salmon (Brett and Groot 1963), flatfishes, killifishes (*Fundulus*), or silversides (*Menidia*) (Sutterlin 1975). Still other fishes can be chosen from those available at a tropical aquarium store.

Since behavioral responses to chemical stimuli can be varied and somewhat difficult to quantify, we suggest studying only general responses to them, and we also recommend ways to evaluate the roles that dose, distance, water movement, and other factors play in determining the amount and kind of behavioral response in your study fish. Bardach and fellow researchers (1967) devised an ingenious setup to study their catfish. Fish were kept individually in an aquarium prior to their studies. For the experiments, fish were placed in large, flat tanks (2 by 3 m) with 600 liters of water, 10 cm deep. Water could be made to flow into this aquarium at variable speeds and current patterns, which were ascertained using fluorescent and dye compounds. A remotely controlled camera and ultraviolet fluorescent lights were placed above the experimental tank. Bardach and his colleagues used two stimulus solutions: droppings from thawed slices of pork liver, diluted 1:10 in water, and cysteine hydrochloride (many other compounds will elicit responses in fishes; see Sutterlin 1975 for a list). The bottom of this experimental tank was divided into six equal-size (1 m by 1 m) grid lines that were coded and could either be followed visually or photographed individually. In most cases, Bardach and colleagues did their tests during the evening when their fishes were active. To monitor the route an individual fish took in response to the stimulus, sequences were timed with a stopwatch, and the camera was set on a long time-exposure setting so the entire track of the fish's movement was recorded. In addition to these tracks, they also studied the behavioral repertoires of individual fishes and qualitatively described these after each experiment.

1. Obtain individuals of the fish or fishes you have chosen to study. It is often informative to pick a species with strong olfactory and taste-bud sensory mechanisms (such as the catfish) and compare it with a species that has only one of the above chemosensory mechanisms well developed. You should consult the literature to help you make your decision (Kleerekoper 1969, Sutterlin 1975). Tiny fish like guppies that only require a modest tank might be more suitable to some laboratory conditions.

2. Set up your holding aquaria so the fishes are kept under optimum conditions, with adequate shelter, flowing or filtered and aerated water, and food.

3. Design and construct your experimental aquarium, perhaps following the design in Bardach et al. (1967), with six 1 m-by-1 m-square grids, each of which is numbered. The incoming water should flow from one end of the tank, and the outgoing water out the other. The flow rate may need to be varied so a control valve is necessary.

4. If you have the facilities, install a camera system so that remote sensing can be used during the experiment. If not, position your aquarium so that several people can observe the behavior of the fish during the experiment and note the fish's behavior and position.

5. Determine the volume of your experimental aquarium so you can calculate the dose of stimuli administered and the influence that the flow rate has on this dose. Consult Bardach et al. (1967) and Sutterlin (1975) for approximate levels of each chemostimulant to administer.

6. Choose one or several stimuli to test with your fish. For example, in the catfish, which finds its food using its olfactory and taste-bud system, chemicals related to the presence of food, such as liver extract or cysteine hydrochloride, might be appropriate (Bardach et al. 1967).

7. Using the stimulus or stimuli you have chosen from your reading for your experiments, evaluate the responses that result from different doses. At first simply administer the chemical near the chemosensory apparatus of the fish and note its response in still water. Vary the dose to see the level at which it no longer increases the response (at the upper end) or no longer initiates the response (at the lower end). In describing the behavioral response, be sure to note the orientation of the fish, its relative activity level (swimming

movements, pectoral beats, opercular beats, and so on), and whether or not certain organs (the barbels, for example) are more active. Also note whether or not the fish stays within the area where the dose had been administered or moves away either early on during the experiment or after receiving sufficient stimulus.

8. Once you have characterized the general response to a particular stimulus, devise an experiment to test whether the response differs between uninitiated fish and those that may be either conditioned or fatigued by continuous stimulus from the substance being studied.

9. Another interesting question is to determine whether or not your fish subjects can detect the stimulus at a distance and then home in on it or avoid it. Administer the stimulus at the incoming water valve with the fish at the other end of the aquarium. Time the sequence and attempt to characterize the response, if any, that the fish makes to each stimulus. Note, for example, the intensity of the initial reaction, where it occurred in terms of distance from the source, and whether or not the fish immediately began to move toward (or away from) the source.

Once you have completed these (and perhaps other) experiments enough times to feel confident that the behavior you observed is a result of the stimulant and is consistent, answer the following questions:

• What organs do you feel your experimental fish is using to sense the substances you have administered? Base your answer on the morphology and behavior of the fish.
• Do you feel this chemosensory mechanism greatly aids the ability this species has to find food or to otherwise survive in its environment? Explain.
• Would changing the direction, concentration, or intensity of the stimulus alter your interpretation of the results?
• Do you think that the chemosensory mechanisms you have studied are as important as any other sensory mechanisms your fish might use to detect this and other stimuli? How would you test this in a laboratory setup?

Exercise 5: Vision

The basic structure of the fish eye is characteristic of all vertebrates (see fig. 2.17, chap. 2), and the eye musculature is relatively constant in size, shape, and position (Winterbottom 1974). Therefore, visual adaptation is limited to changes within the basic vertebrate plan, and extreme adaptations are usually found in the fishes specialized to live in extreme environments, such as dark caves or the deep sea. If no such fishes are available, you may seek out the answers to questions we pose in literature references. However, you can see less bizarre adaptations in commonly available fishes.

First study the general anatomy of the eye of a teleost. You should understand the eye's functional arrangement,

how the eye collects light, and how the various inputs of light intensity, shape, image, and color are detected by the eye as well as how this information is transmitted to the brain for processing. For recent reviews, see Ali (1980) and Bone and Marshall (1982). Consider the following questions:

1. Read the following list of structures:

lens	retina
sclera	rods
pupil	cones
choroid layer	visual pigments
iris	optic nerve
cornea	

• Describe how each works.

2. The choroid layer is highly vascularized and "nourishes" the retina, which requires a great deal of oxygen.

• What is the main function of the retina?
• Why does it require a great deal of oxygen?
• How does the choroid layer provide the retina with so much oxygen?
• Does this system of providing oxygen resemble any other system found in fishes? If so, which one(s)?

3. Fishes may have retinas containing only rods or both rods and cones (Ali 1980). Since these structures have different but complementary functions, many of the adaptations found in fish eyes may depend on the relative number, and perhaps structure, of rods and cones.

• How do rods differ from cones in structure and function? Where are these two kinds of nervous cells located?
• Do they both receive the same kind of innervation?
• Do fishes differing in habitat and behavior have different combinations of rods and cones in their retinas? Explain.
• Rods and cones have pigments that absorb the light of a focused image (Marshall 1966). How do these visual pigments differ among fishes and why?

4. Using the available references as well as your fish specimens and the following guide, tabulate the characteristics of visual adaptations of fishes in the families listed below.
   a. Families of fish:

Carcharhinidae	Opisthoproctidae
Engraulidae	Holocentridae
Myctophidae	Sphyraenidae
Sternoptychidae	Catostomidae

Amblyopsidae   Scombridae
Priacanthidae   Gobiesocidae

b. Table headings
  I. Eye characters
     A. Shape of the eye (round, oval, etc.)
     B. Location (dorsal, lateral, both on one side, etc.)
     C. Orientation (related to above)
     D. Mobility (can the eye itself be moved?)
     E. Size (relative to length of head)
     F. Rods present?
        1. Density
        2. Visual pigment
     G. Cones present?
        1. Density
        2. Visual pigment
        3. Spectral sensitivity
     H. Special adaptations?
        1. Tubular eyes
        2. Aphakic space
        3. Degeneration (i.e., no cornea or lens)
        4. Extra set of eyes
        5. Adipose eyelids (or nictitating membrane)
  II. Habitat characteristics of representative family member
     A. Depth in the water column
     B. Location (i.e., tropics, arctic, etc.)
     C. Amount of light available
     D. Wavelengths of light available
     E. Seasonal variations in light?
     F. Daily variations in light?
     G. Food habits (herbivores, multivores, piscivores, etc.)

5. Using the completed table, characterize the suite of visual adaptations of representative fishes from these five environments:
   a. The deep sea
   b. Coral reefs or near-shore temperate reefs
   c. Caves in freshwater and/or saltwater
   d. The epipelagic zone
   e. Turbid lakes, streams, and rivers

6. In a similar manner, consider the adaptations of fishes that:
   a. Undergo diel vertical migrations
   b. Are crepuscular or nocturnal feeders
   c. Use barbels, taste buds, and free nerve endings to find food
   d. Live in the sediment during the day
   e. Feed on bioluminescent prey in the deep sea

• Do you now agree with our original contention that extreme visual adaptations are often found in fishes specialized to live in extreme environments?

Exercise 6: The Acoustico-Lateralis System

The acoustico-lateralis system includes the lateral-line canal and the inner ear, also known as the labyrinth organ. This system responds primarily to mechanical stimuli such as water movement and sound waves. The basic structures of the lateral line and the semicircular canals of elasmobranchs and teleosts were described in chapter 2 (pp. 19, 26–27). Because these two sensory systems are related embryonically, they are covered in the same exercise; but since they are morphologically separated in an adult fish, they are treated separately.

The Lateral-Line System

The lateral-line system detects movements in the water surrounding the fish, often water displaced by activities of other organisms. As with other sensory systems, its structure varies considerably depending on the specific role it plays and the conditions in which it functions. Marshall (1971) and Bone and Marshall (1982) recognize two kinds of lateral-line canal systems in fishes; one in which the neuromasts are free and the other in which they are enclosed by the canals that open to the water surrounding the fish by pores. Lateral lines with free neuromasts often occur in species that are sedentary, live in crevices, or do not swim actively: that is, in those whose activities do not create much disturbance to the sensors. Fishes that are more continuously active, on the other hand, tend to have enclosed systems. These enclosed canals can either be narrow, with the neuromasts and associated cupula oriented along the main axis of the sensory hair tract, or wider, with the neuromasts—which are often larger—oriented at right angles to the canal. Since neuromasts respond only to disturbances along their axis, the latter large and sensitive kinds are buffered from disturbances by water passing along the swimming fish. Also, fast-swimming fishes tend to have either narrow canals that are relatively unaffected by passing water or broad canals with closed or modified openings to minimize such disturbances.

1. Obtain individuals from some of the following families:
   Anguillidae   Exocoetidae
   Gobiidae   Scombridae
   Gasterosteidae   Engraulidae
   Syngnathidae   Macrouridae
   Cyprinidae

   You can also choose others that might have different lateral-line systems.
2. Carefully examine your specimen's lateral-line system.
   a. Note the distribution on the body and head.
   b. Note whether the neuromasts are exposed or enclosed.

c. If exposed, describe the neuromasts and their associated structures.

d. If enclosed, answer the following questions (for some fishes you may need to make histological preparations):

   • What is the width of the pore openings?
   • In which direction are the neuromasts and cupulae oriented?
   • What is the width of the canal?
   • How large are the cupulae?
   • Is there noticeable fluid in the canal?
   • Do the pores or openings into the canal system appear to be modified, either filled with mucus or having a labyrinthine appearance?
   • Comparatively, do you find that the structure of a fish's lateral-line system reflects its habits, such as swimming and schooling (see Exercise 4 under Swimming in this chapter)?

The Labyrinth

Although the lateral-line system detects water movement around the fish, the inner ear detects the relative position of the fish (i.e., its orientation and balance) and receives sound (i.e., for hearing). The inner ear is a labyrinth of two vertical semicircular canals, one horizontal canal, and three pockets, each containing otoliths (see chap. 2 and Lowenstein 1971). The parts of the inner ear differ among fishes with different lifestyles. For example, fishes that turn slowly tend to have wider semicircular canals with a greater internal surface area because they must detect relatively small angular accelerations (see Marshall 1971 for a review).

Although the shapes and sizes of otoliths tend to vary considerably among species, they remain relatively constant within a species. Thus characteristics of these ear bones obviously adapt different species to different lifestyles, even though exactly how they do this remains unclear. It is generally agreed that otoliths respond primarily to linear accelerations, angular accelerations, and vibrations: They provide the sensory input needed for the fish to orient and balance itself in the water column and to detect sound. Indeed, many fishes have a connection between their swimbladder (a gas-filled structure that resonates sound waves) and the **pars inferior** of their inner ear, which includes two cavities (the sacculus and lagena), each containing otoliths (sagitta and lagena). This suggests that the two cavities work together to detect sound generated by predators, prey, associates, or other important sources. Since it is very difficult to experiment with hearing in live fish, we provide a morphological exercise to introduce you to the basic structure of the inner ear and to how differences in structures among various fishes can reflect their differential abilities to hear various sounds.

1. Choose a fish from each group of the following families if possible:

   A. Cyprinidae
      Sciaenidae
      Pomadasyidae
      Batrachoididae

   B. Pleuronectidae
      Bothidae
      Cynoglossidae

   C. Anguillidae
      Congridae

   D. Engraulidae
      Clupeidae
      Myctophidae

   E. Cottidae
      Gobiesocidae
      Gobiidae

2. Try to pick fishes of similar size so that comparisons are more valid. If this is impossible, devise a method to compare the relative dimensions of the inner ear you measure. Fishes should be preserved in either formalin or alcohol so that their tissues are firm.

3. Decide, either from the literature or from your experience with osteology (see sect. 1, chap. 3), where the otic cavity is. You can begin to dissect either from the dorsolateral portion of the skull, as you did for the brain dissection, or from underneath the skull. If you start from underneath, begin by removing the tissue above and around the last gill arches and continue by slicing the tissue away as you proceed dorsally. Proceed slowly and carefully because inner ear tissues are very delicate.

4. Continue until you have exposed all parts of the inner ear: the two vertical semicircular canals, the single horizontal canal, and the three pockets, each with its otolith (see fig. 2.16). Then answer the following questions:

   • Is there a difference in the inside diameter between the vertical and horizontal canals? If so, why? (Hint: Fish usually turn more quickly from side to side than they do up and down. Recall the relation between sensitivity to detect slow motion and internal surfaces of the canals.)
   • Do the slower moving fishes tend to have wider canals? Explain.
   • Do fish with different shapes have noticeably different forms of their inner ear?

5. Since otoliths rapidly decalcify in formalin, it is best to take them from fresh or freshly defrosted representatives of the groups of fishes listed.

6. Cut into the posterior base of the skull (otic bulla) and remove the otoliths from each side of your fish. Cleanse the bones of extra tissue and place them in a finger bowl with water. The largest and most easily examined is the sagitta.

7. View otoliths displayed in a petri dish or finger bowl against a black surface; perhaps you can spray paint the

dry side of the container. Then the structural details of the transparent bones will stand out against a black background.

8. All otoliths have a medial groove (sulcus) that runs longitudinally and an anterior edge comprised of the rostrum ventrally and the antirostrum dorsally. Other components are listed and shown in figure 5.2.

- Can you distinguish which otolith is from the left and which from the right side? How?
- Are the right and left otoliths identical? If not, list the differences.
- Locate the rings (annuli) that are usually formed one per year and can be used to date the fish (see sect. 3). Why are these rings formed: that is, why are some parts more opaque than others? But if this is not the case in your specimen, explain why the bone is of the same consistency throughout.
- Did you observe any obvious relationship between the otoliths of the inner ear and the swimbladder? Did there appear to be any structures connecting the swimbladder and the inner ear that might transmit sound?

9. Using results from several kinds of fishes, consider the following:

- How much does otolith size and shape differ among species?
- Are these differences as great as among families; that is, is otolith structure relatively the same within families?
- Comparing fish from the groups listed above, do you see any reasons for grouping these fishes as we have done? For example, do you find consistent relations between inner ear and swimbladder?

10. Given sufficient funding and equipment, how would you go about studying the relationship between the inner ear and hearing or balance? How would you design experiments to demonstrate that specific portions of the labyrinth perform specific functions?

Exercise 7: Protective Coloration in Fishes

Antipredator behavior has long been known as important in fishes, and it can take various forms (Keenleyside 1979). Behavioral mechanisms such as flight, evasion, schooling, alarm reactions, and aggressive defense are often quite successful in enabling fishes to escape their predators. However, another mechanism used by many fishes is hiding. This can simply mean existing in crevices where no other organisms can see or some ability of the fish to so closely resemble its surroundings as to become virtually invisible to the predator population.

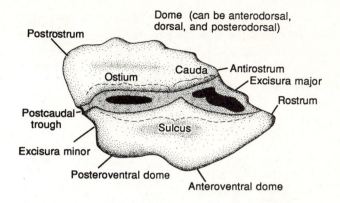

Figure 5.2 Diagram showing the sagitta of a generalized teleost fish with terminology of the various portions following Frizzell and Dante (1965). The inner face of the left saccular otolith is represented here.

In many fishes, the protective coloration mechanism is not alterable. That is, a certain color pattern, such as countershading in small, coastal marine schooling fishes, exists as a result of genetic inheritance and, with the exception of replacement of scales, marks the fish for its life. In other fishes, color patterns can vary considerably, not only among individuals of a species but also within individuals, often over a relatively short time. It is important to distinguish morphological (long-term) color change from physiological (short-term) changes. Indeed, Sumner (1911) studied short-term changes in flatfishes as they adjusted to various backgrounds in aquaria. He followed up with additional studies (Sumner 1934, 1935) in which he not only tested their abilities to change colors but also tested the hypothesis that this color change resulted in greater protection from predation by other fishes and birds.

In this exercise, we will investigate the rate at which color change can occur in fishes. We will also briefly investigate the potential functions that color patterns can have in intraspecific communication.

1. Choose a species of fish for this experiment that readily exhibits different color patterns. One good choice would be members of the freshwater fish family Cichlidae, notably those from the genus *Cichlasoma*. These fishes are capable of rapid color change, and they are readily available in aquarium stores. Other fishes that exhibit color or pattern changes will also work. Make sure that you obtain a sufficient number, perhaps as few as ten of each, and that all are approximately the same size.

2. Set up a holding tank for all the individuals you have chosen. Attempt to keep the tank free of other fish or physical features with color patterns of their own. Also, do not make the density of fish in the tank a factor.

3. Set up two shallow observation tanks, one with the bottom covered in light gravel and the sides covered on

the outside with light plastic sheets. The other tank should have the opposite pattern: dark gravel on the bottom and dark plastic on the sides. These tanks should be relatively shallow so light penetrates enough for you to see the color-pattern changes in the fish.

4. Allow the group of fish to acclimate in your large aquarium for several hours or even days before the experiment. Observe the individuals' color patterns.

   • Do they have bars (vertical) or stripes (horizontal)?
   • Are they spotted?
   • What is their background color?
   • Are all the fish the same color or is there variation among individuals? Make a sketch of the resting color patterns to be used as the "baseline pattern."

5. Now remove five of these fish. Notice whether they change color when they are netted. In most cichlids, this occurs and is considered to be a fear color pattern.

6. Place these fish in the light observation tank. Observe them for ten minutes and record their color patterns at regular intervals.

   • Do they match the background more closely than the remaining fish in the holding tank?

7. Place five more fish from the holding tank into the light tank, one at a time. Record the length of time required for each to change to the color of the color pattern observed in the other fish already in the light tank.

8. Using the same procedure, move the fish from the light tank to the dark tank and note the changes.

   • How long does it take for these fish to assume a dark coloration?
   • Do they eventually match this dark color as well as they had matched the light?

9. Move fish back from the dark to the light tank and record the time it takes them to match the light background.

   • Using times of dark-light and light-dark changes for individual fish, can you determine whether they are able to change more rapidly from one color pattern to the other? Are all individuals equal in their ability to change color?

10. If you would like to investigate the ability of this fish to change details of its pattern further, you can construct a tank with variable patterns. The simplest approach would be to make the tank half dark and half light on the bottom, with the sides matching. A more detailed possibility would be to arrange a checkerboard pattern.

   • Do the fish, when placed in such a tank, tend to prefer one or the other background relative to the color

they were originally adapted to? Transplant fish that are dark-adapted to the light side and vice versa to see how long they will remain in the opposite color portion of the tank as opposed to changing colors.

11. Try adding a shelter or a small amount of food in one section.

   • Do the fish in the other section react?

If they stay where they are, the protective function of color pattern must be stronger than the motivation for food or additional spatial shelter.

12. You have already noted whether or not a fear color pattern showed up. If so, observe now whether color pattern or intensity changes when the fish are doing different things.

   • For example, when one fish is aggressive toward another, which fish tends to change its color?
   • When a fish is feeding, is there any special color pattern exhibited?

As a result of your combined experiments and observations, answer the following questions:

   • What do you think are all the functions of these color patterns?
   • How would you actually test the hypothesis that these functions are operating in the natural world?
   • What would be the major motivations for a fish to become either cryptic or conspicuous at different times in its life?

Slides

Should you wish to follow this exercise with some examples from a marine habitat, you can obtain a series of 20 slides with a written guide explaining them. This series is entitled, "Behavioral Significance of Coloration Among Reef Fishes" and is available from Science Software Systems, Inc., 11899 West Pico Blvd., West Los Angeles, CA 90064, (213) 477-8541 or -8542. This set of slides and guide describes color differences between adults and juveniles, protective coloration, intraspecific communication, conspicuous and warning coloration, and courtship behavior among reef fishes.

A film, entitled *Camouflage in Nature Through Form and Color Matching*, is available from the Pennsylvania State University Audio-Visual Services (number 11174), Special Services Building, University Park, PA 16802.

RESPIRATION AND FEEDING

Since these two quite different functions rely on organ systems lying close together with intricately related muscle action and skeletal movement, we consider them together in the following exercises. A fish may open its mouth to bring in water for respiration or to pull in food particles to be filtered by its gill rakers or to enclose, engulf, or suck in a food item. In either case, both respiratory and feeding structures are involved. Recall from chapters 3 and 4 that the jaws, suspensorium, operculum, and ventral head structures are very closely interconnected; often movement of one structure causes movement of several others. Thus we can reasonably assume that any adaptation to improve the ability of a fish to procure, retain, or process food will also influence structures responsible for passing water over the gills to obtain oxygen for respiration.

The following exercises will introduce you to the dual functioning of the fish respiratory and feeding apparatus. Since the timing of the actions involving the musculoskeletal systems is critical to a complete understanding, you may want to refer to the classic description by Ballintijn and Hughes (1965) of the behavior, cinematography, and electromyography of respiration and feeding in the trout to help you answer some of the following questions.

Exercise 1: Behavioral Observations of Respiration and Feeding

Select live fish that typify different ways of life, perhaps collected during field trips or purchased from fish stores. If facilities are available, you may also observe fish directly, either by snorkeling or by scuba diving. In this exercise, observe fish breathing and feeding. Notice particularly how the two activities interact, how they relate to other behaviors, and how their combined motions reflect the kind of prey eaten and the fish's habitat.

1. Attempt to choose a variety of specimens of fishes that
   a. Constantly swim about in the water column
   b. Remain relatively motionless in the water column
   c. Constantly swim over the bottom
   d. Remain relatively motionless on the bottom
   e. Reside primarily on or in the bottom (substrate)

   and that feed primarily by

   a. Filtering particles or plankton
   b. Grasping or engulfing food out of the water column
   c. Picking prey from the substrate or crevices
   d. Sucking prey into the mouth, whether from the water column or the substrate
2. At first, observe the fish's respiratory motions.

   • Can you detect synchrony in opening and closing of mouth and operculum? Does the operculum open consistently after the mouth closes, or vice versa?

• What muscles are involved in opening and closing the mouth?
• What muscles interact to open and close the operculum?
• What muscles are involved in expanding and compressing the buccal cavity?
• Do many of these muscles have more than one action?
• Decide whether the following muscles are involved in expiration or inspiration, and describe their action:

adductor mandibulae	adductor operculi
adductor arcus palatini	levator operculi
levator arcus palatini	protractor hyoidei
sternohyoideus	hyohoidei
dilatator operculi	

(Hint: Consult Ballintijn and Hughes 1965 and Shelton 1970.)

• Can you detect any difference in mouth/operculum motions—their timing or sequences—between fishes that swim constantly and others that are usually stationary?
• Is rate of opercular beat related to swimming speed?
• Does the size of the mouth opening during respiration vary with swimming speed?
• Judging from your observations and references, do fishes that swim constantly use more or less energy for respiration than sedentary fish do? Why?
• How do bottom-dwelling fishes keep sand and sediment from entering the opercular cavity and clogging the gills? Have you seen this process?

3. Now observe feeding in different fishes. This is easy for fishes that eat readily in captivity but difficult for finicky species with specialized feeding habits. You may have to experiment with different kinds of food. When you have your fish eating, consider the following questions:

• How does the fish approach its prey? Is it a sit-and-wait predator, or does it actively seek its food?
• Once the fish detects its prey, how does it pursue and handle the food item?
• How does the fish manipulate the prey with its mouth, buccal or opercular cavity and other food-gathering structures?
• Is the mouth protrusible in the sense that the fish can move its mouth closer to prey without moving its body?
• Does it grasp the prey between its jaws or engulf the prey in its oral cavity?
• Does your fish appear to suck in its prey? If so, how does it do this?
• Does it modify its respiratory movements while feeding. If so, how?

4. Comparing several different fishes, consider the preceding questions in light of how the fishes obtain food.

   • How many fish protruded their jaws? What proportion were graspers? How many were suction feeders?
   • Do protruders, graspers, and suction feeders differ in the distance from which they captured prey? Was there a maximum or minimum distance between prey and predator before the predator could successfully strike?
   • Is there any evidence that the fish's feeding behavior was correlated with its swimming or respiratory activities?
   • Did feeding tend to disrupt respiratory movements? How?

5. Now recall sensory mechanisms.

   • Which senses does the fish use most effectively to detect its prey?
   • Do some fish reject a food item after having taken it? If so, what sense organs do you think it might be using to determine if the food particle is not a proper one?
   • Is there any other way a fish might reject a food item once it is inside its mouth?
   • A question for you to ponder: How does a remora (shark sucker) breathe and eat? (Hint: Does the shark sucker ever leave its host? Does its morphology suggest an answer?)

Exercise 2: Functional Morphology of the Gills

Now that you know how the pumping mechanism brings water into the fish's buccal and opercular cavities and forces it out the fish's opercular opening past the gills, you need to know how the oxygen dissolved in that water is taken up by the gills. Chapter 2 describes the general morphology of the gill arches, filaments, lamellae, and capillaries (see fig. 2.13, p. 24). Also, recall that water flows past the gill lamellae in a direction opposite to blood flow in the capillaries. Obviously, respiratory structures adapt so fish can extract enough oxygen to breathe in their habitats, whether stagnant or fresh. The following exercise reveals such adaptations by examining the flow of water across the gills together with gill microstructure and surface area. The fish's muscular respiratory pump ensures a nearly unidirectional water flow across the gill lamellae to deliver a constant supply of oxygenated water to the capillary membranes (see Shelton 1970 and Hughes 1980).

1. Using a preserved fish, pull the operculum back to reveal the orientation of filaments on the gill arch. Then tease apart the filaments on the first gill arch, noting their position. Imagine the direction in which water would pass by.

2. Remove the first gill arch and examine the fine structure of the lamellae on each of the demibranchs. Envision again the direction water should flow.
3. While examining gill filaments, closely observe the spacing that occurs between the holobranchs along the gill arch and try to see the lamellae on an individual demibranch.

Now that you have studied the respiratory structures in detail on a preserved fish, obtain a live specimen and anaesthetize it, following the instructions in chapter 10.

1. When the fish is anaesthetized, examine the configuration of its gills to imagine how water flow past the gills is counter to the flow of blood in the gill capillaries.
2. Putting the fish back into the water, try to trace water movement by following particles of india ink or other insoluble crystals in water forced through the mouth of your anaesthetized fish.
3. Now observe the flow as the tagged water proceeds through the gill cavity and over the filaments themselves.
4. Using a technique described by Booth (1978), inject your fish with blood that has been stained with a fluorescent dye. This kind of approach can be used to determine how many of the gill lamellae receive blood and the general progression of blood from one end of the gills to the other.
5. Suggest ways to do the following:
   a. Determine the amount of water passing by the gills per unit of time.
   b. Find the difference in partial pressures of dissolved oxygen in water entering the mouth and the amount exiting past the gills.

   • If you succeed, how could you next estimate the extraction efficiency of the gill lamellae?
   • How could you demonstrate that the blood entering the capillaries in the lamellae contains less oxygen than that leaving them?
   • Does all of the oxygen exchange between water and fish occur through the gills? Where else might such an exchange occur?

Gill surface area varies with the respiratory needs of fish. Smaller fish tend to have a larger gill surface area per gram of body weight than larger fish have; more active fish have a relatively larger gill area than sluggish species have (reviewed by Randall 1970 and discussed for sharks by Benz 1984). Also, fishes living in stagnant waters may have a larger gill surface area than those living in well-oxygenated waters.

1. Considering the procedures in Gray (1954), Hughes (1966, 1980), and Muir (1969), devise your own

method of estimating the effective respiratory surface area of a fish's gills. Effective area is restricted to the lamellar surface area because it is the main site of gas exchange. Since you cannot possibly count all the tiny structures like filaments and lamellae, you must deal with averages and multiples. For example, you may want to measure total lengths of gill arches, count filaments per unit length of arch, find the average length of filaments, and count lamellae per unit length of filament.

a. Pick specimens from the above categories: small and large fishes, fishes that are relatively active and those that are slower swimmers, and, if possible, fishes that live in oxygen-poor conditions.

b. Use your method to estimate surface area on the gills in one of these fishes and compare your result with general values in Randall (1970).

c. Also, note the relative length of individual lamellae, the spacing between them, and their thickness. How might such characteristics become adapted to increase the fish's resistance to desiccation? To test this, find a fish that spends part of the time out of water, such as an intertidal clingfish, and measure the length and spacing of its filaments and the distance between lamellae. Would you expect air-breathing fishes to have similar adaptations?

• What keeps the filaments and their lamellae apart?
• Does surface area of all lamellae equal the total surface area available for respiratory gas exchange? Why or why not?

Exercise 3: Morphological Adaptations for Feeding

Remarkable indeed is the diversity of morphological adaptations for great efficiency at seeking, capturing, retaining, and processing food that allows fishes to inhabit so many different kinds of aquatic environments (Kapoor et al. 1975). Feeding morphology varies considerably among fishes, even within families and lower taxa. You can deduce much about a fish's feeding habits from its morphology. In this exercise, you will examine the feeding apparatus from the mouth—which varies in size, shape, protrusibility, and toothiness—past the gill rakers, which often strain out food particles, through the alimentary canal, which increases surface area for digesting food.

Fishes may be classified by trophic level. Herbivorous fish eat mostly plants; detritivores consume partly decomposed organic materials; multivores ("omnivores") eat a variety of plant and animal prey; and piscivores eat mostly other fish. Some multivores feed mostly on plankton, and their special adaptations for doing so distinguish them as planktivores.

1. Select specimens representing the feeding types just discussed.
2. Design a data sheet for the following observations (remember to compare fish of different sizes, and standardize measurements as proportions of body or head lengths; see chap. 6):
   a. Mouth

gape (length of jaw)	protrusibility
ratio of gape to head length	lip width
cleft (width of mouth)	special adaptations
ratio of gape to cleft	(barbels, taste buds, photophores, and so on)

   b. Teeth (presence, size, kind, and number)

maxilla	palatine
premaxilla	pharyngobranchials
dentary	basibranchials
tongue	gill arches
vomer	gill rakers

   c. Gill rakers (first, second, and third arches)
   number
   mean gill raker length
   ratio of mean gill raker length to head length
   mean gill raker width
   ratio of mean gill raker width to mean gill raker length
   mean distance between rakers
   ornamentation (teeth, spines, and so on)
   d. Stomach
   number (cardiac, pyloric)
   shape
   ratio of length to standard length
   ratio of length to alimentary canal length
   inner structure
   e. Caeca
   number
   mean length
   mean width
   f. Intestine
   shape
   total length (stretched)
   ratio of total length to standard length

3. After slitting the belly from anus to head, expose the coelom and gently pull its contents aside. Locate the anterior portion of the gut (near the esophagus) and cut; then trace the gut back to the anus, pulling it from the body cavity.
4. Remove the liver, pancreas, spleen, gall bladder, and all other extraneous organs. Record observations on your data sheet, starting from the mouth, the buccal cavity, and continuing along the excised gut.

5. After tabulating all results for the array of feeding types, consider and answer the following:

- Do the types differ substantially in mouth structure, toothiness, and the shape, presence, and size of the various organs associated with the gut? Explain.
- Did you see much variation between individuals of this particular species?
- Do different feeding types have characteristic morphologies? For example, do herbivorous fish have fewer teeth, smaller and fewer gill rakers, and an elongated alimentary canal with many caeca? How are these characteristics interrelated?
- Now, can you predict the usual diet of a fish from its feeding morphology? How would you test out your prediction?

Exercise 4: Feeding Rates and Selection of Food

As you learned in exercise 1 of this section, some fishes are often picky about the kinds of food they consume and the rate at which they consume prey, while others are generalized about their prey choice and feeding rates. The numerous factors involved in determining food selection and feeding rate of fish predators have intrigued researchers for some time (Keenleyside 1979, Morse 1980). The factors involved include the size, mobility, and ease of prey capture relative to the size and mobility of the fish predator, the nutritional value and palatability of the prey, and the relative abundance of prey types. Also involved are physical factors such as spatial heterogeneity, prey refuge space, and temperature, which can regulate the metabolism and hence nutritional needs of the fish predator. Diel patterns of feeding are often observed in fish predators and appear related to the ability the fish predator has to visually search for and find prey, the risks associated with feeding through susceptibility to competition and predation, and the role of hunger. Learning also apparently plays a role in prey selectivity, and social factors can influence the amount of feeding that occurs at any given place or time.

In this exercise, we attempt to control as many of these factors as possible to investigate which play significant roles in controlling feeding rates and food selection. We will control environmental factors such as spatial heterogeneity and temperature, the size of the predator and prey, the risks to competition and predation, and the diel patterns that normally occur in the species chosen. We will suggest exercises to evaluate the role that habitat, size, and mobility of prey play in prey selection, the effect that learning has on prey selection, the role that hunger plays in feeding rate, and the social aspects involved with feeding-rate studies.

1. A good candidate for this exercise would be the three-spined stickleback, *Gasterosteus aculeatus*, since it eats a wide variety of food, does well in laboratory conditions, is readily available, and has been studied quite intensively (Wootton 1976, 1985). If it is not available, many other fishes from aquarium stores will do. The number of fish you obtain will be directed by the number of experiments you intend to do, the aquarium facilities available to you, and the sample size necessary to satisfactorily complete each experiment.

2. To control some of the variables listed above, you should choose individual fish that are all of the same size and, if possible, the same sex and reproductive condition. For doing studies on growth rates relative to feeding, young individuals are the most likely to produce significant results. However, for the experiments we are suggesting, the relative size of individuals you choose will mostly be dictated by the facilities you have available.

3. Set up holding tanks with identical conditions. Use the same kind and amount of gravel, keep the aquaria at approximately 20°C (at least for sticklebacks), and use the same setup of filters and bubblers. An ideal shape for the experimental aquarium is rectangular since the habitat or shelter can be at one end of the tank and food can be administered at different distances from that habitat. The holding tank can be any shape, but it should be large enough to minimize aggressive interactions among the individuals. Lighting should closely approximate the native waters of the fish.

Following are four exercises intended to familiarize you with the kinds of studies that can be done on fish feeding rates and selection of food. Each is a separate experiment and will work using freshwater sticklebacks. Conditions could be modified for other species, either from freshwater or saltwater.

Diel Patterns of Feeding

1. It is widely thought that sticklebacks, as with many fishes (see Olla et al. 1972), feed primarily during the day, exhibiting a peak in feeding activities during dawn hours, with the rate diminishing as the daylight period continues (Wootton 1976, 1985). Using a preferred prey type for the stickleback, tubifex worms, observe the feeding activities for a 24-hour cycle in the holding tank. First, offer a known amount of worms—perhaps in a petri dish or plastic cup filled with a thin layer of sediment to prevent dispersal of the prey—to the fish in the tank.

2. Then divide up the 24-hour day into one-hour intervals and assign different people to several of these intervals. During the daylight hours, observations should be made from a blind or behind one-way viewing glass. At night,

make observations under red light so the fish cannot see you, but you can detect their activities. If such lighting is not possible, the next best approach would be to slowly light up the room enough to watch the fish for a short period of time, perhaps every hour. Observations should include (1) the number of fish exhibiting feeding behavior, (2) the number of bites made at the feeding site per fish per time, (3) the number of successful bites made there, and (4) if possible, some measure of individual variation in all three of the above. If you have trouble observing the number of worms consumed, another approach is to count the number of worms remaining after each time period.

3. Once these data are gathered, plot the percent of fish feeding and the mean and standard deviations (see p. 109) of the number of bites and number of successful bites made per hour against time. Examine this curve to see if there is a peak in feeding activity at any time during the 24-hour periods observed.

The Influence of Hunger on Feeding Rate

1. Another factor undoubtedly related to the feeding periodicity you may have observed in the experiment above is the role that hunger plays (Wootton 1976). In this experiment, you will take some of your fish and deprive them of food for different amounts of time. We suggest you try 24, 48, and 72 hours of deprivation for each group of fish.

2. Then starting at dawn on the day following the deprivation period, offer each individual in each group a surplus amount of food (again, tubifex worms in a cup work well). Then for the daylight hours remaining, count the number of tubifex worms each individual consumes per hour for that period.

3. Should partial consumption occur, you can count them as partial worms consumed or can estimate the weight that was ingested by the sticklebacks. You should measure 20 to 30 of the prey worms prior to offering them to fish for feeding, weigh each of them, and plot length versus weight of the prey worms. Then you can calculate a regression to convert numbers eaten into wet weight of worms consumed per hour or per day by fish in the three treatment groups (three levels of deprivation times).

4. Plot the number and wet weight of worms consumed per hour (and the standard deviation of these values) against time for each of the three deprivation treatments. You should observe curves that peak fairly early, then begin to diminish as the fish begin to become satiated from their early meals (Wootton 1976). You should also see a significantly higher peak, or larger early meals, in fish that were deprived the longest.

• If this is true, how does this relate to your diel feeding periodicity results? Be sure to compare your results with those presented by Wootton (1976).

Prey Selection: Choice and the Role of Learning

1. It is known that sticklebacks will consume a wide variety of food, including the benthic tubifex worms we have been using, and other forms, including plankton. Such planktonic prey, such as the brine shrimp, *Artemia salina*, are somewhat smaller, more active, and associated with the water column. We can assume, therefore, that it would cost more energy for the stickleback to feed on brine shrimp than on tubifex worms, both in terms of energy expended to capture prey after searching for it and the nutritional value gained per bite. We might also expect that the kind of food these fish are accustomed to feeding on will influence their choice of prey. That is, fish that have had practice or have learned to feed readily on one type of prey might choose them over another type of prey, especially if the other prey type is more active and less nutritious.

2. Set up two holding tanks with equal numbers of the same-sized fish in each. In one tank, feed the sticklebacks only tubifex for approximately one month, and in the other, feed them only brine shrimp.

3. Remove individuals from each tank and place them in experimental feeding tanks that allow you to observe their feeding activities. If possible, make these tanks rectangular with a shelter located at one end. At an appropriate distance from this shelter, where the fish will presumably situate itself, provide food at the same rate used for feeding the sticklebacks in the holding tanks. You can take several approaches here. First, you need to establish the feeding rates that individual fish will exhibit on the prey that they have been consuming for the past month. That is, you need to estimate the feeding rates of tubifex-fed fish on tubifex worms and brine shrimp-fed fish on brine shrimp. Second, you need to estimate feeding rates on prey opposite to that normally fed to sticklebacks during the acclimation period. That is, estimate the feeding rates of tubifex-fed fish on brine shrimp and brine shrimp-fed fish on tubifex worms. For both sets of treatments, you should estimate the mean and standard deviation of prey items consumed per hour (either as weight or as number) and the percent success rate in feeding attempts.

4. Another approach is to remove an equal number of individuals from the training tanks and place them in the experimental aquaria to offer them equal portions of both species of prey. That is, if you were feeding them 1 gram of tubifex worms or brine shrimp each, offer them 0.5 gram of each. Then for several hours, observe these

individuals and tally the number of each prey they successfully consume per hour.

5. Plot the number of prey of each type consumed per hour by fish in all of the treatments and compare the results.

• Do you see any differences between feeding rates or prey choices in tubifex-trained fish or brine shrimp-trained fish on (1) their trained food type, (2) their untrained food type, or (3) the mixed diet? Explain these observations. These observations can be statistically evaluated using analysis of variance or can simply be evaluated qualitatively.
• Another question is whether the number of prey eaten or the prey choice changes from the start toward the end of the observation periods? That is, did all fish eventually feed more on or choose tubifex prey over brine shrimp or did they stick with the prey they were trained to consume during the acclimation period?
• Which prey do you think, overall, is the more preferred one? Why?

Social Effects on Feeding Behavior

In our experiments to this stage, we have kept groups of fish in holding or training tanks, but we have done all feeding experiments with individuals in separate tanks. Some researchers (Wootton 1976) indicate, however, that the density of fish predators may influence the feeding behavior and intensity of feeding.

1. To evaluate the role that social factors might play in feeding, take fish that have been fed tubifex worms for several weeks in the group holding tank and place them in experimental tanks at different densities. We suggest densities of one, three, and five fish per tank to ease the problems of observing individuals, but you may want to make the differences even more drastic.
2. Feed these fish a surplus amount of food and observe their feeding activities for at least an hour. Qualitatively describe the feeding activities of individuals or groups of individuals in the three density treatments.

• Do they all feed? Do they feed consecutively or at the same time?
• Does the feeding activity of one (or a group of several) appear to influence the feeding activities of the others?
• Does the feeding rate (number of bites or successful bites and worms taken per minute or 15-minute interval) differ among the three treatments? Compare your results with those presented by Wootton (1976).

Films Available on Feeding Behavior of Fishes

Two films are available that might interest you regarding feeding behavior in fishes. One is entitled *Behavior and Ecology of Coral Reef Fishes*, a 28-minute color film produced in 1974 that shows feeding behavioral studies by Dr. E. S. Reese of the University of Hawaii. This film (number 31967) discusses social behavior and ecology of 15 species of butterflyfishes (family Chaetodontidae). The other film, Labroides dimidiatus: *Cleaning of a Different Fish*, describes the ecological aspects of one fish feeding upon the ectoparasites of other fishes and the social interactions involved in such a symbiotic activity. Both films can be obtained from the Pennsylvania State University Audio-Visual Services, University Park, PA 16802, and the second film can also be obtained through the University of California Extension Media Center, Berkeley, CA 96720.

SWIMMING

Fishes use a variety of ways to propel their bodies through water. The primary method is to bend their bodies from side to side, using their lateral musculature as explained in chapter 4 (pp. 44–46). Other methods include moving the dorsal and/or anal fins and sculling the pectorals. Three exercises investigate locomotion in fishes: (1) watching fish swim, (2) explaining how contraction of myotome muscle fibers bends the fish body laterally, and (3) explaining the functional significance of differences in distribution and the relative amounts of red and white muscle in different fishes.

Exercise 1: Observations of Swimming Behavior

From watching fish swim in an aquarium, respond to the following questions:

• What is the main source of thrust used by these fishes, especially during sustained fast movements and bursts? Does each fish propel itself entirely by moving its tail from side to side, by sculling the pectoral fins, by undulating median fins, or by combining these motions?
• Does the way a fish propels itself change from rapid accelerations to steady swimming? Are different "propellers" involved?
• How does the fish steady its position at a particular level in the water column?
• Does the fish have a swimbladder? Contrast the relative importance of regulated buoyancy versus body and fin movements for positioning in the water column.
• Does the fish change its swimming modes during "special" situations, such as when maneuvering to obtain food or in making rapid evasive movements to escape predators?
• How do the swimming modes of the various kinds of fishes relate to body shape, to habitat, and to special objectives the fish has to accomplish?

Exercise 2: The Relation of Myotome Contraction to Body Motion

It is difficult to conceive how the contracting muscle fibers in the epaxial and hypaxial muscle masses can move the fish's body from side to side, especially since the myotomes angle backward and forward toward the backbone. Therefore, you should demonstrate (1) how the zigzag pattern of myotomes relates to the entire muscle mass, (2) exactly which direction the muscle fibers pull within each myotome, and (3) how this pull might act to bend the fish's body.

1. Cut an index card in the shape shown in figure 5.3a, marking the top edge blue and the bottom edge red and tracing the dotted lines and solid arrows onto both sides as shown.
2. Fold on the dotted lines so that when viewed from the blue edge, it resembles the drawing in figure 5.3b. Make sure both the blue and red edges are relatively parallel (i.e., lie flat on a table).
3. Now imagine that the blue edge is a myotome at the skin surface and the red edge is the other end of the myotome at the midline near the vertebral column. Then you can compare this with figure 4.4. Note where the flexures are (recall that anterior is to the left).

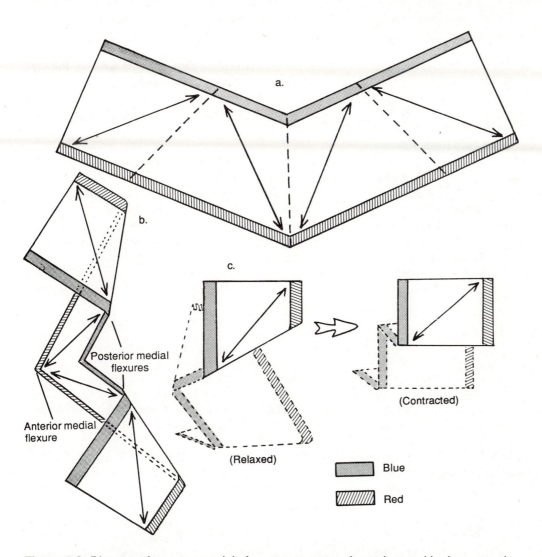

Figure 5.3 Diagram of a cutout model of myotome contraction to be used in demonstrating that contractions of individual muscle fibers in consort can cause a fish's body to move laterally: (a) the shape of the cutout prior to folding; (b) how the cutout appears when it is folded properly along the dotted lines; (c) how a myotome, viewed from the dorsal aspect, changes shape when the muscle fibers contract, causing a lateral bending of the fish body. The blue edge simulates the lateral (skin) edge of the myotome. The red edge represents the midline, where the fibers meet the vertebral column and neural or hemal spines.

4. Now pick up the model myotome, with the blue edge facing left and the top epaxial muscle facing you, and observe each portion. The top portion resembles a rhomboid, as shown in figure 5.3c, and the next one, with a slightly different overall shape, also looks rhomboidal.

5. With arrows indicating the direction of contraction within the myotome and the two sites of attachment of individual muscle fibers, imagine how the muscle changes shape (consult Alexander 1969 and Winterbottom 1974 for a more complete description of the origin and insertion of individual myotome muscle fibers).

6. When you pull the fibers as shown, the myotome should become more rectangular (fig. 5.3c). Why? (Hint: Remember that muscles, upon contraction, retain the same mass or volume and therefore will remain approximately the same size.)

7. Recall that the red line is the flexible vertebral column. Will it bend as the myotomes contract on one side and relax on the other side? Now explain how the myotomes contracting in sequence bend the backbone and cause the fish body to move back and forth. Is your explanation compatible with figure 4.4b? (Hint: Attempt to visualize which axis of the myotome mass moves when the muscle contracts. That is, does the red or blue line axis move more, relatively, when the myotome becomes more rectangular upon contraction of the muscle fibers? This answer explains how the midline moves from side to side.)

8. Admittedly, a piece of relatively inelastic paper does not act like a muscle mass. Suggest a material that might prove more suitable for a realistic model.

Exercise 3: Survey of Red and White Muscles

Fishes have two basic kinds of muscle: (1) white, with relatively thick fibers, no fat or myoglobin, and a primarily anaerobic metabolism; (2) red with fibers of thin diameter, fat and myoglobin, and aerobic metabolism. In most fishes, white muscles predominate, but in some—especially those that swim most of the time and have an adequate oxygen supply—red muscles make up a good portion of the body muscle mass. Boddeke et al. (1959) distinguished those fishes with mostly white muscle ("sprinters") from those with more red muscles ("stayers"). In this sense, the word *sprinters* refers to fishes that swim in short, rapid bursts, while *stayers* refers to those that sustain a slower cruising speed for long periods (continuous swimming). They classified fishes into three different groups based on the distribution of red and white muscle in them: (1) fishes with mostly white muscle fibers and very little red muscle, except in a lateral strip along the body; (2) fishes with a prominent and well-developed lateral strip of red muscles; and (3) those with a very well-developed lateral strip and a mosaic of red muscles within the rest of the body musculature. Since then, many authors have studied red and white muscles in fishes (see Moss and Hudson 1977, Bone et al. 1978, Kryvi and Totland 1978, Greer-Walker et al. 1980, and Totland et al. 1981) and have discovered that some fishes can actually retain the body heat generated by metabolism during swimming. This involves a countercurrent mechanism (rete mirabile) in the lateral musculature that keeps the heat from returning to the gills where it would quickly dissipate into the cooler water flowing by (see reviews by Carey and Teal 1966, Carey et al. 1971, Carey 1973, and Graham 1975).

Examine the distribution of red and white muscle in fishes with different modes of swimming. Because the main forward thrust is provided by the fish's tail, median fins, and pectoral fins, you should carefully examine muscles operating these structures. The proportion of red and white muscles in these structures should reflect whether they are involved in burst or continuous swimming. Also, closely investigate the fibers involved in moving these structures since their characteristics are closely related to their function and their color.

1. Find a relationship between body form and distribution of red muscle in a fresh fish.
   a. Measure head length, standard length, and total weight so that other measurements can be standardized to the relative size of your specimen.
   b. Also measure the caudal fin length and its height and span so that you can calculate the aspect ratio.

      • Since this ratio indicates the surface area in the caudal fin available for thrust, what is the best way to measure it?

   c. Describe the mode of locomotion commonly used by the fish you are studying.
   d. Characterize the shape of your specimen.

      • Is it gibbose like a perch or fusiform and streamlined like a tuna, and so on?

   e. Peel the skin from the entire body of the fish, noting where the muscle tissue appears more reddish than white. Be careful not to pull underlying muscles away from the body. Specifically note whether red muscles, even small ones, are at the base of the dorsal, anal, pectoral, or caudal fins.
   f. Draw your fish from the side view, carefully mapping the distribution of superficial red and white muscle.
   g. To observe the distribution of deeper muscles, cut cross sections of the entire fish at two or three locations along the body. Map the distributions of the two types of muscle in this cross section.

h. To measure relative mass (weight or volume) of red versus white muscle in your fish, cut out and separate all red from white muscle. Accumulate the two types in separate piles. Blot the muscles on paper towels for the same length of time and weigh them as accurately as possible. Save the best pieces of muscle tissue from each pile for later histological examination.

i. Design a data sheet to summarize the following information:

family, genus, species	types of muscles
body shape	red
weight of fish	white
length of fish	mosaic
habitat	rete mirabile
food sources	weight: all muscles
locomotory mode	weight: red muscles
aspect ratio	weight: white muscles
location of muscle types	(express the three weights above as percent of body weight)

• From your tabulated information, describe how its musculature relates to the fish's life history and mode of locomotion. For example, does a fish with a caudal fin of high aspect ratio also tend to have a fusiform body, a narrow caudal peduncle, and a relatively high proportion of red muscle?

2. Examine the fine structure of these two types of muscle fiber. Slice across pieces of each as finely as possible, using a sharp razor or scalpel (consult Greer-Walker and Pull 1975 for suggestions).

a. Using an ocular micrometer, measure the diameter of several muscle fibers in each kind of muscle.

• Are white fibers larger in diameter than red ones? Could you distinguish them on this basis alone if you did not know they were red or white to begin with?
• Can you distinguish the two kinds of fibers based on the amount of red coloration in them?
• Are some fibers intermediate in diameter or coloration? How do you interpret this?
• What is the red pigment? Does it relate to tissue functioning?

b. Examine histological sections if available.

• Do you find differences between red and white muscle cells in terms of number and size of organelles, amount of fat investment around them, and density of capillaries supplying blood to them?

3. Compare various species. Knowing that white muscle functions anaerobically and red muscle aerobically, relate their relative amounts in each specimen to the habitat and environmental conditions of the fishes.

• Do most of the fishes tend to have a predominance of white muscle? Explain.
• Give evidence that red muscle is aerobic and white muscle is mostly anaerobic.
• Design an experiment to test this hypothesis.

Exercise 4: Behavioral and Sensory Mechanisms in Rheotaxis and Schooling

We have known for some time that many fishes swim against currents (exhibiting rheotaxis) and that they must use sensory mechanisms such as touch or lateral-line mechanoreceptors to orient in this fashion. Some fishes exhibit rheotaxis while schooling, and fish biologists have hypothesized that these fishes use vision in addition to the mechanoreceptors already mentioned (McFarland and Moss 1967, Pitcher et al. 1976). Experiments done to elucidate those sensory mechanisms important in both rheotaxis and schooling have been quite complex and have used sophisticated aquaria, photographic systems, and electronic setups (Shaw and Tucker 1965). It would be beyond the scope of this manual to suggest that others repeat these detailed experiments. However, the following simple exercises can give you some ideas about rheotaxis and schooling.

1. Choose fish species that are known to exhibit rheotaxis and to school. Good choices from the field include juvenile trout or silversides. A number of different groups of freshwater fishes that exhibit these behaviors are available at aquarium stores. A general guideline would be to use any small fish with a swimbladder that lives in midwater.

2. The simple setup for this exercise includes a magnetic stirring device, commonly used in chemistry labs to mix solutions. This device has a magnetic motor base with a Teflon stirrer that spins inside a container placed above the motor base and can be adjusted to spin at different velocities inside the beaker or other glass container. Choose a beaker size that will allow individuals of the fish species you have chosen to swim freely, both individually and with several other individuals included. Use water from the holding tanks and keep all other parameters as constant as possible.

3. Make sure the area around the stirring mechanism and beaker has no noticeable dimensions on which the fish could focus and orient. Enclose the beaker setup in a plain, white-sided box with no markings on the inside

and place a light directly above the beaker so no shadows show up.

4. Place individual fish into the water-filled beaker and initiate the magnetic stirrer, starting with low velocities and working slowly up toward higher velocities. Note the response the fish makes to the direction and velocity of the current.

    • At what velocity does the single fish begin to swim against the current (exhibit rheotaxis)?
    • What is the minimum current necessary to initiate this response?
    • How long will the fish continue to orient toward the current? Does it appear to orient for a short time and then simply hover without noticeably reacting to the current?

5. Add a strip of black tape vertically to the outside of the beaker so the fish now has some discrete marker to orient on. Then repeat the experiment outlined in the previous section, using the same fish. (See Shaw and Tucker 1965 for a modification of this exercise.)

    • Does the fish orient to the current more readily? Does it seem to respond to the current at a lower velocity or stay oriented to the current more consistently?
    • How do you account for the differences (or lack of differences) between the fish's responses to the current with and without a marker on the beaker?
    • Is there any indication from your results which sensory mechanisms the fish uses in rheotaxis? Explain.

6. Now repeat these experiments with groups of fish rather than individuals. First place two fish together in the beaker and start the stirrer.

    • Do these fish react to the current in the same fashion as the individual fish did?
    • Does the pair of fish react differently when in the experimental setup with the black strip?
    • Do the fish orient toward each other as well as to the black strip and the current? How would you experimentally demonstrate this?

7. Devise a way to estimate distance between individuals in a schooling and rheotaxis experiment. Remember that the water itself distorts the estimate of linear distance proportional to the amount of water through which the estimate is being made.

    • Relatively speaking, what is the average individual distance between the two individuals?

8. Repeat these experiments with more individuals. In-

stead of two per beaker, try the observations and treatment with four and six individuals.

    • Are there any differences in the intensity with which these individuals respond to the currents?
    • How many individual fish are needed to form a school?
    • Are there narrower individual distances with the denser groups?
    • Do they form schools and orient to the current any more intently than in the lower density experiments?

9. Consider the implications of these experiments:

    • Is there much evidence that vision is important relative to the mechanoreceptors in rheotaxis?
    • Do fish species differ in the relative roles of vision and mechanoreception in rheotaxis and schooling? What would you have to do to evaluate this?
    • Are mechanoreceptors sufficient to initiate rheotaxis or schooling?
    • How would you experimentally test such a hypothesis?
    • Does schooling appear to help the fish orient toward currents?
    • Why do so many species exhibit rheotaxis?
    • What important functions do you think schooling behavior may serve?

Other experiments on schooling behavior suggested by Keenleyside (1975) involve bottles inside aquaria to see if an independent fish would begin to school with fish of the same species in one bottle to one side or with fish of a different species in another bottle on the other side. Keenleyside suggested eight species of aquarium fishes to use in this experiment and designed two experiments that we will briefly review here, should you wish to investigate schooling behavior in fishes further.

In his first experiment, Keenleyside (1975) tested the tendency of a single fish to school with conspecifics. He placed two jars of fish with equal numbers of two different species in the aquarium, one to the far left and the other to the far right. Then he introduced a test fish and noticed the time the test fish spent in each of three areas: near the right jar, near the left jar, or in the middle. He also suggested counting the number of times the test fish moved from one area to another. Then he removed the test fish and repeated the experiments with additional test fish and with reverse positions of schooling fish in jars. These experiments can be repeated using all combinations of available species, and they can also be used to measure the conspecific tendencies of fish to school, either with their own or with different species. At the same time, you can make behavioral observations to ascertain whether the test fish is even responding by schooling with the fish in jars.

In Keenleyside's (1975) second test, he evaluated the effect the density of the fish in a group had on the behavior of the isolated ("test") individual. In this case, jars of the same fish species were placed to the right, but they contained different numbers of fish. For example, the jar on the left might contain two or three fish, whereas the jar on the right had eight to ten. Then the conspecific test fish was placed into the aquarium and the researcher noted whether it orients to one or the other jar. This is repeated several times reversing the jars and using different test fish. The experiment can also be used to compare schooling tendencies in different species of fishes. The variables measured include the time that the test fish spends in each of three areas (left, right, middle) and the number of times the test fish moves from one area to the other.

Keenleyside suggested that the chi-square test would be appropriate to compare the observed distribution of test fish in the aquarium with a theoretical distribution such as the uniform distribution (equal time in each area). He then suggested the following questions:

• Do fish tend to school more conspecifically than with other species?
• Do fish prefer to school in large or small groups?
• Were there any artificial behaviors associated with the experimental setup? That is, did the fish appear to act "normally" in the test situation?
• What were the reactions of the enclosed fish (in the jars) to the test individual?

SWIMBLADDER STRUCTURE AND FUNCTION

The swimbladder allows fish to float effortlessly in the water column. Thus, the energy they save can be used for finding food, avoiding predators, and other survival activities. The two basic kinds of swimbladders—physostomous and physoclistous—differ considerably in structure (chap. 2), which relates to the habits of the fishes (Marshall 1960). Furthermore, physoclistous swimbladders may have their rete mirabile and gas gland (secretory organs) in a separate chamber from the oval (resorptive) organ, a condition called **paraphysoclistic**, or they may have these organs together in the same chamber, called **euphysoclistic**. These two physoclistous forms also differ in the relationship between rete mirabile and gas gland (see Steen 1970 for a thorough review).

You will first study the location and structure of the swimbladders in different fishes. Then you will determine the composition of the gases in the swimbladder and relate any differences to the fish's environment and its inflating mechanisms. Finally, consider other uses of the swimbladder. For example, to amplify sound, some fishes have a connection between the front of the swimbladder and the inner ear.

Exercise 1: Functional Morphology of Swimbladders

Compare the structure of physostomous and physoclistous swimbladders. Obtain a representative of a family whose members have physostomous swimbladders (engraulids, clupeids, or cyprinids) and one from another that has physoclistous members (sciaenids, batrachoidids, or many advanced teleosts). If possible, obtain live specimens. Then inject about 5 cc of a solution of methylene blue and seawater, using a small syringe, into the gill cavity. Wait at least 5 minutes or until the gills turn blue. Usually by this time the rete mirabile will also be stained blue.

1. First dissect the physostomous fish, noting where the swimbladder is in relation to the other internal organs.
   a. Remove the other organs, carefully leaving intact the swimbladder and its blood vessels and tubular connection with the alimentary canal (ductus pneumaticus).
   b. Draw the swimbladder including the pneumatic duct and blood supply. Locate the rete mirabile and gas gland using figure 2.10, page 23. If you injected your fish with methylene blue, they should stand out on the surface of the bladder.

   • Does the swimbladder have any constrictions that may separate it into front and back parts. If so, what is their probable function?
   • Does the swimbladder open posteriorly to the outside? If so, what is the function of this opening?
   • Anteriorly, do you find any evidence of a connection between the swimbladder and inner ear? If so, what does it consist of? If you are dissecting a cyprinid, this connection is collectively called **Weberian ossicles**. In many other fishes, it is called an **otophysic connection**. What differences are there between these two structures and how they function?
   • Considering the size of the pneumatic duct, do you think that this fish fills its swimbladder by gulping air at the surface?

2. Now examine the physoclistous fish, following the same procedures for dissection and drawings.

   • Is this fish a euphysoclist or a paraphysoclist?
   a. Locate the blood vessels serving the superficial structures on the bladder.

   • Which arteries fill the rete mirable ("rete"), and which veins drain it? Again, methylene blue dye injections will help you see details of this system.

   b. Devise a method to estimate the rete size. Since this structure inflates the bladder, its size should increase with the usual depth at which the fish lives because the pressure inside the swimbladder must equal the ambient hydrostatic pressure.

• Does the gas gland appear to be relatively large or small? How do gas gland and rete interrelate?

c. Locate the oval where gas is resorbed into the bloodstream.
d. Examine a histological cross section of the rete, which contains the hairpin countercurrent mechanism to multiply gas pressure. Describe the spatial relation between arterioles and venioles.

• Do you find that each arteriole is surrounded by four to six venioles?
• How would this configuration of vessels in the rete maximize the surface area over which this countercurrent exchange mechanism operates?
• Are any special muscles associated with the swimbladder? In some fishes, like scorpaenids of the genus *Sebastes*, such muscles allow the fish to constrict the bladder. For what purpose? In others, such as croakers or drums (Sciaenidae) and toadfishes or midshipman (Batrachoididae), these muscles vibrate the bladder. Why?
• Is fat invested about the bladder of any fish you have examined? In deep-sea fishes (e.g., myctophids) that rise hundreds of meters toward the ocean surface at night, swimbladders are less pneumatic and more fat invested. Why does a heavier buoyant tissue (fat) replace a lighter element (air)?

e. Design an experiment to test if the swimbladder is large enough to make the fish neutrally buoyant.

• How would you determine the proportion of body volume occupied by the swimbladder?

Exercise 2: Swimbladder Gas Analysis

You can tell a lot about a fish's lifestyle from its gas content. The composition of gases filling a swimbladder reflects the relative availability of gases in the environment, the ambient hydrostatic pressure, the filling mechanism, and the fish's vertical movements. Therefore, the following gives you a method, modified from Scholander et al. (1955) and Hoar and Hickman (1975), to determine volumetric proportions of swimbladder gases and a technique that causes a fish to change the amount and kinds of gas in its swimbladder so you can determine which gases the fish secretes first to readjust buoyancy.

Swimbladder Gas Content

1. You will need a microgasometric analyzer, which is essentially a calibrated pipette tube housed in a plastic container of water to keep the gas sample temperature inside the tube relatively constant. At one end of the tube, a cup receives a small bubble to be analyzed together with reagents to remove components of the gas mixture in the bubble, one by one. A thermometer in the water bath monitors temperature, and a metric rule along the glass tube measures the change in gas volume as components are removed by dissolving in the reagents (fig. 5.4).
2. Assemble the following reagents:
   a. Acid citrate: Dissolve as much as you can of 170 g sodium citrate and 6 g citric acid in 200 cc water to make a supersaturated solution.
   b. Alkaline citrate: Similarly dissolve 70 g sodium citrate and 5 g KOH in 120 cc water.
   c. Oxygen absorber: Cover a few hundred ml of 20% $NaOH$ in a rubber-stoppered bottle with a layer of paraffin oil 2 cm thick. Then add crystals of acid pyrogallol, which drop through the paraffin air seal into the base. Dissolve by stirring the crystals with a glass rod through the seal. The basic coloration of pyrogallol turns purple as it absorbs oxygen on exposure to the air.
   d. Acid-rinsing solution: To a solution of 1 cc concentrated sulfuric acid in 500 cc water, add 10 mg potassium permanganate.
3. Withdraw a sample of gas from live fish specimens having a physoclistous swimbladder and being hardy enough to survive several syringe punctures: for example, species in the families Batrachoididae, Embiotocidae, Gobiidae, Sciaenidae, and Scorpaenidae.
4. To check your technique, analyze a sample of air, which you know contains approximately 80 percent nitrogen and 20 percent oxygen, using the same technique as for gas from inside the swimbladder, as described below.
5. To extract a gas sample from your fish, you must know approximately where its swimbladder is located. It is usually at the top of the body cavity just behind the level of the pectoral fin. But if you are unsure, check its location in a dissected fish.
6. Fit a fine needle (e.g., number 26) to a 5-ml glass hypodermic syringe. To charge the syringe, remove the needle and draw in the acid citrate solution to half full. Replace the needle, hold syringe needle up, and push out any air bubbles. Then cap the needle with a rubber stopper until you are ready to sample.
7. Holding the fish underwater in a net, draw out a 0.5 ml sample of gas. You should pierce the fish by inserting the needle on a forward slant between overlapping scales. Gently pulling the plunger, withdraw the gas slowly. The bubble rises in the acid citrate, where it is

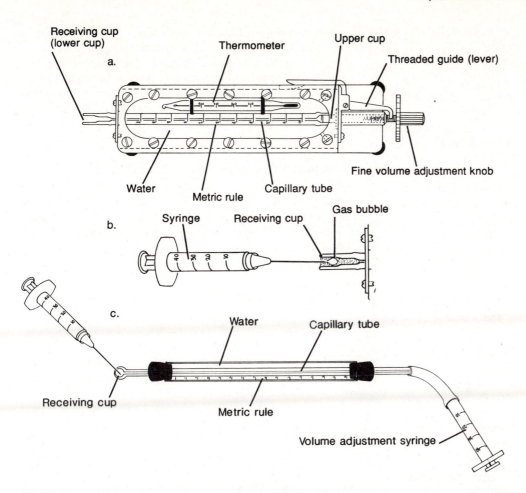

Figure 5.4 Diagrams of microgasometric analyzers: (a) the Hebel gas analyzer with capillary tube, thermometer, metric rule (often on the capillary tube), fine-volume adjustment knob, and receiving cup; (b) syringe used to collect gas sample from the bladder and to introduce a bubble into the cup on the gas analyzer (these can be purchased from Rudolph Holker, 80 Swarthmore Avenue, Rutledge, PA 19070, 215-543-7021); (c) a microgasometric analyzer constructed from capillary tubing, glass tubes, holed rubber corks, and syringes.

preserved because (1) the solution is supersaturated and no oxygen or nitrogen can dissolve and (2) the solution is acid so carbon dioxide remains gaseous.

a. With needle pointed down, push out any contaminants trapped in the front of the syringe and cap with a rubber stopper.

b. The sample is now ready for analysis and can be stored in the syringe indefinitely. However, over longer periods, salts precipitate out of the supersaturated acid solution and tend to freeze the syringe. Therefore, you may have to free the mechanism by gently heating it in warm to hot water.

c. Prepare reagent sources by filling larger syringes holding wide-bore needles with acid citrate, alkaline citrate, and alkaline paragallol solution (withdrawn from under the paraffin). Cap needles with rubber stoppers.

d. Charge the analyzer with acid citrate. First lubricate the analyzer by introducing the reagent from the source syringe into the lower cup of analyzer and pull the fluid up and down the capillary by disengaging the piston from the threaded lever. Then with cup upward, refill and draw reagent down to piston. Push column back up to ensure that capillary and upper cup contain a continuous column of reagent.

e. Set charged analyzer on table with piston end propped slightly higher than cup. Now carefully introduce about 3 mm of gas into the cup from the sample syringe, whose needle is again cleared of any contaminating air (see fig. 5.4).

8. Now that you have charged the analyzer with the gas from your fish's swimbladder, you will need to do the following:

a. Draw the bubble of swimbladder gas into the capillary tube by turning the knob at the end of the analyzer gently and smoothly.

b. Once the complete bubble is within the capillary tube, measure its length, which is V_1.

c. Now draw the bubble back into the upper cup and replace the acid citrate with alkaline citrate solution in the lower cup. Then again draw the bubble into the capillary tube and measure its length, V_2.

d. Leaving the bubble intact within the capillary tube, introduce 1 cupful of pyrogallol with the cup up and allow it to permeate through the solution, past the bubble. Pyrogallol, in excess, effectively prevents the formation of monoxide and removes all oxygen from the bubble. Now measure the remaining bubble, which is mostly nitrogen, and list it as V_3.

e. After analysis, rinse the analyzer several times in tap water, disconnecting the screw feed and removing the plunger. If the water supply is limited, you may find it necessary to rinse with permanganate solution until this retains its color.

9. You can now calculate the relative volumes of the gas components in your sample since the alkaline citrate has removed the carbon dioxide, the pyrogallol has absorbed the oxygen, and the remaining gases are mostly nitrogen. The original gas sample has volume V_1, that with the carbon dioxide removed V_2, and with oxygen removed V_3. The equations for these calculations are as follows:

a. Percent carbon dioxide:

$$\% \, CO_2 = \frac{V_1 - V_2}{V_1} \times 100$$

b. Percent oxygen:

$$\% \, O_2 = \frac{V_2 - V_3}{V_1} \times 100$$

c. Percent nitrogen (and other minor gases):

$$\% \, N_2 = \frac{V_3}{V_1} \times 100 \ (\text{or } 100 - (\%CO_2 + O_2))$$

10. Fish from greater depths contain relatively more oxygen than fish from the surface, which contain gases in about the same proportions as in air.

• Why?
• Does the gas composition in the swimbladder of your fish follow this trend? That is, was your specimen a shallow- or deep-dwelling fish?
• Does the gas composition in your fish's swimbladder appear to be similar to that of its surrounding water?
• Perhaps habitat and depth of water are not the only factors involved. How does the gas composition in your

fish compare with published values for other species (see Steen 1970)? Are there other factors to consider?
• Are all the gases found in the swimbladder biologically secreted by the rete-gas gland complex, or are some inert gases simply concentrated there? How would the concentrating mechanisms differ for these two kinds of gases?

Secretion of Gases into the Swimbladder

At least two ways exist to force your fish to secrete new gases into its swimbladder. One is to increase the ambient pressure for a time, forcing the fish to adjust its bladder volume and buoyancy. The other is to remove the gases from the swimbladder, causing the fish to refill its swimbladder.

1. Devise a method to force your fish to secrete gases into or resorb gases from its swimbladder.
   a. Here are several suggestions: First, you can increase the volume, and hence pressure, of water over the fish by placing it in a very tall aquarium or by having a long tube filled with the aquarium water suspended over the fish and its aquarium. Second, you can place your specimen in a bucket with a meshed screen on it to prevent escape and hang this bucket, with weights if necessary, off a pier to 20 or 30 feet. Third, you can place your fish in a small bowl inside a vacuum pump and run the pump for a sufficient amount of time to reduce the pressure. Fourth, you can remove most of the gases in the swimbladder with a syringe inserted through the lateral musculature just as you would in extracting a sample for analysis.
   b. After performing one or more of the above experiments, allow your experimental fish at least 6 to 12 hours to make the swimbladder adjustments by secreting or harboring new gases. Be sure to keep some fish at ambient pressures or in normal conditions to act as controls.
   c. Retrieve both the experimental and control fish and use the previously described gas analysis techniques to measure the gas composition in their swimbladders.

2. Use the results from your experimental and control fish to consider the following:

• Do the fish kept under pressure behave differently from those kept in ambient conditions? Do the fish with their gases removed behave differently, and does this behavior continue throughout the time they are observed? What symptoms of these experimental fish can be attributed to their swimbladder gas adjustments?
• Does the gas composition in fish placed under higher pressure differ from that of the controls? How? Is there much variation among individuals within either the

experimental or control groups? Which gases were secreted in the experimental fish?
• Does the gas composition in those fish that had their gases removed appear to differ from the controls? If so, which gases are actively secreted to fill an empty swimbladder? Does this answer differ from that given for fish adjusting their swimbladders to increased pressure?
• Do you think your answers to the above questions would differ if your experiments were shorter or longer? Why?

REPRODUCTION

To appreciate the vast diversity of fish reproductive modes, it is best to start out with a basic understanding of how most fishes reproduce (see the reviews by Breder and Rosen 1966, Dodd 1983, and Thresher 1984 and the classification scheme of Balon 1975). Fish reproduction centers around three main processes: egg fertilization, larval and embryonic development, and postzygotic care. Fertilization can be internal or external and can be accomplished by different individual parents, multiple matings, or single hermaphroditic individuals. Development of young can occur within the parent, either in eggs (**ovoviviparity** or **aplacental viviparity**) or in maternal folds of tissue that provide nutrition (**viviparity** or **placental viviparity**) or outside the parent (**oviparity**) in egg clusters variously attached and protected or free within the water column. Parental care ranges from nonexistent, as with free-living larvae, to quite complex parental-offspring interactions. Since reproductive tract morphology closely reflects reproductive habits in fishes, we concentrate on morphology as it pertains to fertilization and development of the young.

Exercise 1: Comparison of Reproductive Morphology of Oviparous and Viviparous Fishes

1. Gather male and female fish that exhibit each of the three reproductive strategies, perhaps using representatives from the following suggested families:
    a. Oviparous   Cyprinidae
        Engraulidae   Labridae
        Clupeidae   Serranidae
        Atherinidae   Centrarchidae
    b. Ovoviviparous   Cottidae
        Elasmobranchs (some) Hexagrammidae
        Scorpaenidae
    c. Viviparous   Poeciliidae
        Elasmobranchs (some) Embiotocidae

2. Search the external surface of your fish for sexual characters.

    • Can you distinguish males from females? How?
    • Some characters, such as intromittent organs, are quite obvious and will always be present in mature characters. Others, such as reproductive color patterns, may only be present at certain times of the year and in certain individuals. Do your fish have both kinds of sexually dimorphic features?
    • Do the sexes of your fish differ in size or shape? If so, what advantage does this difference have?
    • Of the sexually dimorphic characters you have found, what functions do they play in the reproductive life (and success) of the fish involved?

3. In the same manner as with the alimentary canal, remove the reproductive tract of both sexes of your fish.
    a. Draw the reproductive tracts of both species, accurately labeling individual organs and structures.

    • How do testes differ from ovaries? Are these gonadal differences more pronounced with age or time of year? Why?

    b. Compare the sizes, in weight, volume, length, and/or width, of male and female gonads.

    • What portion of the total body weight is gonad in each sex? Does this differ much with age or time of year?
    • Can you determine the state of reproductive maturity in each of these? (Consult sect. 3 for further details.)
    • Does your answer to the preceding questions differ for representatives of the other two kinds of reproductive modes? How?

4. From the literature, summarize how fishes from the three different reproductive modes differ in the way they ensure survival of their young. Describe some of the specialized structures found on these fishes to help their young survive.

5. Describe any morphological specializations that occur in the egg and larval phases of fishes to help these young stages survive. (Hint: See Moser 1982 for examples.)

    • In eggs from oviparous fishes, how would you determine whether they are pelagic or demersal?
    • Discuss the different dispersal mechanisms used by fishes in the three reproductive modes.
    • How are the eggs and larvae of fishes from each mode nourished? How soon do pelagic or demersal fish larvae begin to feed? What specialized structures do viviparous females have to nurture their young?

6. Determine from the literature if all fish have seasonal reproductive cycles.

   • Is the extent of reproductive seasonality related to geographic location? If so, how?
   • Is it phylogenetically linked? Explain.
   • Is food supply or availability implicated in seasonal reproductive periodicity? If so, how?
   • Are any other factors influential in directing or controlling reproductive cycling? Describe and explain how they might operate.
   • Are oviparous, ovoviviparous, and viviparous fishes differentially prone to having seasonal reproductive cycles? If so, why?

7. Many examples of hermaphroditism exist in fishes. They occur in such diverse environments as the deep sea, where it is extremely difficult to find mates due to their rarity and to the harsh, dark conditions, as well as the tropics, where competition for space and perhaps food is a strong factor, and mate selection may be very important. Hermaphrodites can be both male and female concomitantly and synchronously. If synchronous, males can develop into females (**protandrous hermaphrodites**) or females can develop into males (**protogynous hermaphrodites**).

   a. Describe an example of each type of hermaphroditism.
   b. Describe the development of hermaphrodites by answering the following:

      • What happens to the structure of their gonads?
      • What controls their ultimate sex? Their early sex?
      • How do they reproduce?
      • What behavioral constraints are there? (Hint: Do they set up individual pair bonds, multiple sexual encounters, self-fertilize, and so on?)
      • Is there any evidence that hermaphroditism is seasonal?
      • Is hermaphroditism reversible? If so, how?

   c. For each of your examples, describe their environment and their living conditions.

      • Does their geographical distribution appear to be related to their hermaphroditism? If so, how?
      • Does hermaphroditism aid in the survival of their offspring? If so, how?
      • In so many words, what is the advantage of being a hermaphrodite?

8. Consider the various reproductive modes discussed.

   • Do they commonly occur repeatedly in certain groups of fishes, or have they evolved independently in several different groups? Is there any phylogenetic significance to the development of reproductive strategies in fishes?

Exercise 2: Reproductive Cycling and Behavior

For many decades the reproductive habits of fishes have attracted the interest of scientists worldwide. Indeed, some of the classic studies early ethologists made centered on the reproductive behavior of the ubiquitous freshwater and brackish water fish, the stickleback (Tinbergen 1952, 1955). If you consider that well over 25,000 species of fishes inhabit the world, a diverse array of reproductive habits has evolved over time to ensure that these fishes survive from generation to generation. Several recent, comprehensive reviews describe these reproductive habits (Breder and Rosen 1966, Wootton 1976 and 1985, Keenleyside 1979, Morse 1980, Pullin and Lowe-McConnell 1982, and Potts and Wootton 1984).

It would be beyond the scope of this manual to describe all kinds of reproductive behaviors exhibited by marine, brackish, and freshwater fishes, and it would be difficult to describe, in detail, how one would go about studying these behaviors (for more on this, see sect. 3). Experience from teaching about the behavior of fishes has also shown that it is not easy to observe behavior predictably in the laboratory or classroom because the unnatural environment might not allow the fish to follow its normal routine. For example, seasonal variations in temperature and day length induce physiological changes that prepare fish for reproduction. Therefore, it is very difficult to get individuals of a species in the proper reproductive condition to demonstrate nest-building activities. Thus we provide alternate suggestions for learning about the reproductive habits of fishes, using references to specific articles from the literature, several already published laboratory exercises on the subject, and numerous films and slide collections available from commercial sources.

Although the literature on the diverse array of reproductive habits in fishes is abundant, most of it focuses on the sequences and behaviors seen in only a few families. The reproductive biology of salmonid fishes, especially trout and salmon, is quite well known, primarily due to the interest in producing fry in hatcheries around the world both for consumption and for planting (see Tautz and Groot, 1975, for an example). Another family that is well known, primarily because of its aquaculture potential, is the Cichlidae (Pullin and Lowe-McConnell 1982). This diverse family of freshwater fishes has species that spawn on substrates and either guard nests or brood their young in their mouths. Two other families are well studied because of their abundance and territorial defense mechanisms. The Centrarchidae, or sunfishes, have been studied intensively in the lakes of the United States (Keenleyside 1979), and the Pomacentridae, common coral reef fishes called damselfishes, have generated much interest because of their interesting territorial defense behavior (Keenleyside 1979, Morse 1980). Several families of live-bearing fishes, exemplified by the popular poeciliidae fishes (swordtails and guppies), which are common aquarium fishes, have been studied intensively (Breder and Rosen 1966, Keenleyside 1979, Morse 1980, Potts and Wootton 1984). Few families come close to being studied as much as that of sticklebacks (Gasterosteidae), especially *Gasterosteus aculeatus,* the three-spined stickleback (Wootton 1976, 1985).

We divide this exercise into three sections, one on reproductive cycles in general; the second on spawning behavior, such as site selection, territoriality, courtship, and mating activities; and the third on parental care. In each of these sections, we briefly describe the habits known for some fishes, suggest some laboratory studies that could be undertaken, and provide a list of films showing the cycles and behavior that have been described in the literature.

Reproductive Cycles

It is very difficult in a reasonable amount of time to completely observe the entire reproductive cycle of most fishes. Some cycles, however, are relatively brief and predictable. Even so, it would be difficult to observe all component phenomena such as nest building, egg production, mating behavior, fertilization, development, and hatching. Therefore, we have chosen to provide a list of available films that show the reproductive cycles of selected species.

1. *Reproductive Behavior of Brook Trout* (Salvelinus fontinalis): This 24-minute 1971 color film is listed in the American Association for the Advancement of Science (A.A.A.S.) Science Film Catalog and is available (number 22712) from the Pennsylvania State University Audio-Visual Services, Special Services Building, University Park, PA 16802. It demonstrates all behavioral activity leading up to, including, and following the reproductive activities of brook trout in their natural environment.
2. *The Salmon Story*: This is an 11-minute film that covers the life cycle of the salmon. It is also listed in the A.A.A.S. Science Film Catalog and is by Dr. Richard Van Cleve, College of Fisheries, University of Washington, Seattle, Washington.
3. *Life of the Sockeye Salmon*: This 25-minute film, available from Journal Films, 930 Pitner Avenue, Evanston, IL 60202, is listed in the A.A.A.S. Reference Sourcebook (see Newman and McRae 1980). It covers the entire life history of the sockeye salmon, from egg hatching to the return journey upstream to find a spawning site and complete the reproductive cycle.
4. *Behavior of the Shield Darter*: This 9-minute film, available from the Pennsylvania State University Audio-Visual Services (number 11461) is a black-and-white silent film showing fighting among shield darter males, female solicitation, mating, and other behavioral characteristics such as fear responses and sleeping.
5. "The Grunion Story": This is an annotated 25-slide demonstration (number 200-0005) available from Science Software Systems, Inc., 11899 W. Pico Blvd., West Los Angeles, CA 90064. It is a series of color photos depicting the grunion's life cycle, its spawning sequence, and the influence of the tidal regime on this sequence.
6. *Siamese Fighting Fish* (Betta splendens): This 10-minute film is listed in the A.A.A.S. Science Film Catalog and covers the male fighting fish, which plays a major role in courtship and parental care. It covers the fish's bizarre but predictable behavior.

Spawning Behavior

A vast literature also covers the many kinds of behavioral traits that accompany spawning (Breder and Rosen 1966, Keenleyside 1979, Morse 1980, and Potts and Wootton 1984). As before, we suggest exercises on site selection, territoriality, courtship, and mating for well-known species whose behavior is predictable enough to be demonstrated satisfactorily either in the laboratory or by educational films.

Again, the diversity of spawning activities reflects the diversity of fishes. Therefore, we again concentrate on the well-studied stickleback, *Gasterosteus aculeatus* (Tinbergen 1952, 1955, Wootton 1976, Keenleyside 1979, and Potts and Wootton 1984). Males of this species show a predictable ritualized spawning sequence. Other families such as the Salmonidae, Centrarchidae, Cichlidae, Belontiidae (bubblenest builders), and Pomacentridae are represented in some of the films listed at the end of this section on spawning.

The major acts of spawning fall into four categories for species with external fertilization. The first activity is **site selection**. The site the fish selects to make its nest determines the kind of mate it attracts, the structure of its nest, the number of eggs spawned, and the survival of those eggs and hatchlings. The stickleback's site selection is well described by Keenleyside (1979), Wootton (1976, 1985), and Potts and Wootton (1984) and is portrayed in a slide collection available from commercial supply houses.

The second major activity is defense, usually by the male, of the **territory**. Once the fish chooses and prepares a site, it must be defended from all interlopers so only the mate is allowed to enter. Examples of the defense response are well described for sticklebacks in Tinbergen (1952, 1955), Wootton (1979, 1985), Keenleyside (1979), and Potts and Wootton (1984).

Jennings and Olson (1975) present a laboratory exercise to study site defense by the Siamese fighting fish, *Betta splendens*. They describe how to determine the stimuli sufficient (as "social releasers") to elicit agonistic displays of males and suggest experiments prompting males to react to their reflections in a mirror. Males reacting promptly and fully are selected as the more aggressive fish, thus most suitable for laboratory studies. Jennings and Olson suggest

(1) depicting what the male *Betta* does in response to its image; (2) then using the picture of this fish in its threat posture to test other aggressive fish. Presumably, the picture will include those cues (releasers) eliciting the response. These responses include erect fins when the fish is broadside to the picture and spreading the gill covers when the fish is facing the picture. One may then selectively remove features from the picture to see which characters are necessary to initiate a response. Certain combinations of color, size, and shape produce a stronger response than such characters do when presented individually.

• Why does the male *Betta* greet an intruder with agonistic displays rather than immediately engaging it in some sort of physical combat?

Tinbergen (1952, 1955) and others have described similar releasers in sticklebacks. Two features of the male display are essential to elicit a response from an intruder: red coloration and posture. Tinbergen showed this using model fish of various shapes and colors to see which combination elicited the response. He varied posture by placing the males in vials and controlling their vertical or horizontal angles of approach. Keenleyside (1979) and Morse (1980) also offer suggestions on how to study aggressive responses in male sticklebacks and other defenders of breeding sites.

The third category of spawning behavior involves **courtship**, which determines the male and female individuals that actually mate. Courtship is an important step in the discriminatory process and so must be quite complex to ensure that mating occurs between healthy individuals of different sex from the same breeding population. Position, color, and several other features apparently play important roles (Wootton 1976, Keenleyside 1979).

The fourth category involves actual **mating** or **spawning**: the processes controlling fertilization in fishes. For oviparous fishes, such as the stickleback and brook trout (see Tautz and Groot 1975), spawning involves a fairly detailed series of events, determining which male will fertilize which female's clutch of eggs after courtship. For viviparous fishes—for example, the Poeciliidae (swordtails or guppies)—several behavioral interactions lead up to the actual impregnation of the female (see Keenleyside 1979, Morse 1980, and Potts and Wootton 1984, for examples).

The Three-Spined Stickleback. The following is a brief description of the reproductive behavior of the three-spined stickleback, *Gasterosteus aculeatus* (after Tinbergen 1952, 1955, Wootton 1976 and 1985, and Keenleyside 1979). If you can obtain specimens in breeding condition, you may see these behavior changes as the fish progress through their normal reproductive cycles.

When nonreproductive, both males and females are similar in color: dull gray to green with faint darker vertical bars. When becoming reproductive, under the proper conditions the males develop a red belly or throat and a whitish back, and the females become silvery and, when full of eggs, exhibit a distended belly.

The male's behavior is both interesting and predictable as he takes the lead role in reproductive interactions. He builds a nest in sand, using bits of surrounding vegetation as construction materials and to keep the nest together. Once the nest is built, he defends it from all intruders. When a female enters the territory, the male initiates courtship with a zigzag dance and eventually leads the female to the nest. He then lies on his side, pointing his snout at the nest entrance. Once the female enters the nest, which does not always happen at the end of courtship, the male begins his mating behavior. First, he prods the female or quivers alongside her. Then the female releases her eggs inside the nest, and the male enters immediately to deposit his milt or sperm. From this point on, the male chases away all intruders, even his mate, to protect the eggs from being eaten. He also fans the eggs to keep them well oxygenated. Once the young hatch, the male tends the young, fans them, and often returns wandering fry back to the nest by putting them inside his mouth.

Several experiments may reveal all or part of this sequence of site selection, defense, courtship, and spawning. It is difficult to get the fish to cooperate in the entire series of activities in the artificial laboratory environment, but with patient attention to individuals in the right breeding condition, you can usually see several of these activities.

One experiment is to induce reproductive males to establish territories by providing them with shelter and observing their reactions to other males. For example, place two fish in an aquarium with three shelters (rocks with plastic plants attached). Then, after the two set up residence in the shelters, introduce a third male. Observe the reaction of the first two to the intruder. Usually this intruder is relegated the least favorable (smallest or poorest condition) site, and it may even have difficulty defending this.

Another classic experiment is to put two territorial and aggressive males into clear glass test tubes so they can be moved and oriented within the tank. If one introduces both fish (fish *a* and fish *b*) into fish *a*'s territory, fish *a* will be the more aggressive and displace fish *b*. The opposite will be true in fish *b*'s territory.

You can see all four of these behavioral categories (site selection, territoriality, courtship, and mating) in the following films and slides.

1. *In Search of a Mate*: This 24-minute color film made in 1972 is available from the Pennsylvania State University Audio-Visual Services, University Park, PA 16802. It is number 32196 and shows how males and females of various kinds of organisms find each other. It describes signals, postures, colors, and sounds animals use in their mating quest. The material is taken mainly from the work of Niko Tinbergen.

2. *Reproductive Behavior of the Guppy*: This relatively old black-and-white film is also available from the Pennsylvania State University Audio-Visual Services and deals mostly with male displays in attracting a female mate for internal fertilization in this live-bearing (viviparous) fish.

3. Betta splendens (*Siamese Fighting Fish*): This 21-minute color film (number 21728) is also available from Pennsylvania State University Audio-Visual Services and deals with the reproductive cycle of *Betta splendens*, showing the sequence from mating ritual to courtship, nest building, egg laying, and the protection of eggs and fry by the male.

4. Haplochromis burtoni: *Ritualized Fighting* (number E722) and Haplochromis burtoni: *Courtship and Spawning* (number E470): These two films, available from the Pennsylvania State University Audio-Visual Service, depict the reproductive behavior of the genus *Haplochromis*, a cichlid exhibiting typical reproductive behavior.

5. "Stickleback": This is a series of 20 color slides (175 W 0563) with a guide, available from Ward's Natural Science Establishment, Inc., either through their East Coast facility at 5100 West Henrietta Road, P. O. Box 92912, Rochester, NY 14692-9012 or from their West Coast facility, 11850 East Florence Avenue, Santa Fe Springs (Los Angeles), CA 90670-4490. It illustrates the mating behavior of the stickleback and the important role played by the male in building a nest and caring for the young.

Parental Care

The amount and kind of care that parents provide their young vary a great deal among fishes (Breder and Rosen 1966, Keenleyside 1979, Morse 1980, and Potts and Wootton 1984). Fishes providing the most care tend to have relatively low fecundities; the parents make up for the smaller number of offspring by ensuring better survival than if the young were allowed to fend for themselves. Thus, though parental care is relatively rare among fishes, it is an essential focus for study in order to learn about its survival value.

Members of the family Cichlidae provide excellent demonstrations of parental care because they include substrate spawners and nest guarders (*Tilapia zillii* is one example) and mouth brooders (*Tilapia mossambica*). In designing a laboratory session using several species of cichlids to demonstrate parental behavior, Reynierse (1975) noted three components: (1) care of the spawn or eggs, (2) care of the wrigglers or young fry, and (3) care of the free-swimming older fry. He also described how to observe and quantify various aspects of parental behavior in cichlid fish during each of these three stages.

First you set up aquaria with pairs from two or three of the species recommended. Allow the fish to complete the part of their reproductive cycle leading up to fertilization of offspring. Then observe during 5–10 minute intervals:

1. The frequency of head-stand nibbling as parents clean out decayed eggs or other debris from the egg mass
2. The frequency and amount of time spent by parents fanning eggs with their pectoral fins
3. The frequency of parents picking up wrigglers and returning them to the "nursery" pit
4. The frequency that parents retrieve free-swimming fry that stray
5. The frequency of such agonistic behaviors as bites or chases directed either at the mate or a neighboring pair

Reynierse suggested several questions for observers to ask relative to their results:

- Did both sexes show parental care equally?
- Were behavioral traits in the parents consistent over time or did they change?
- What are the adaptive advantages of cichlids' activities during each of the three stages of parental care?

Reynierse also suggested some additional studies that could be done on cichlid fishes. One could measure the amount of parental motivation by using responses (usually in the form of bites at the image) to its own mirror image at one end of the experimental aquarium. Fin erection and gill-cover erection are other behaviors that indicate agonism toward an image and could be recorded and measured. These experiments should be repeated several times during the three stages of parental care, and one should plot the frequency of biting as a function of time during each of the three parental care stages.

- Can you think of any major problem with this research approach?
- Would these fishes respond to the image seen of themselves in the mirror in the same way they would to a real intruder? Why or why not?
- How would you test your answer to the previous question?

In addition to the several films already suggested on fish reproductive behavior, two films illustrate parental care behavior.

1. Tilapia zillii: *Care of the Fry*: This film, number E 1136 in the Pennsylvania State University Audio-Visual Services Catalog, demonstrates how parents in this substrate brooding species care for their young.

2. *Reproductive Behavior in African Mouth-Breeding Fishes*: Tilapia mossambica *Courtship and Spawning*: Another film from the Pennsylvania State University Audio-Visual Services (number E771) details reproductive behavior, including the mouth-breeding approach to parental care.

82   Section One/Morphology of Fishes: Form and Function

References and Suggested Readings for Section One

Alexander, R. M. 1969. The orientation of muscle fibres in the myomeres of fishes. *J. mar. biol. Ass. U.K.* 49:263–90.

Ali, M. A., ed. 1980. *Environmental physiology of fishes.* 723 pp. New York: Plenum Press.

Allen, D. M.; Loew, E. R.; and McFarland, W. N. 1982. Seasonal changes in the amount of visual pigment in the retinae of fishes. *Can. J. Zool.* 60:281–87.

American Association for the Advancement of Science. 1975. *Science film catalog.* New York: R. R. Bowker.

Appelbaum, S., and Schemmel, C. 1983. Dermal sense organs and their significance in the feeding behavior of the common sole *Solea vulgaris. Mar. Ecol. Prog. Ser.* 13(1):29–36.

Ashley, L. M. 1976. *Laboratory anatomy of the shark.* 75 pp. Dubuque, Iowa: W. C. Brown.

Ballintijn, C. M., and Hughes, G. 1965. The muscular basis of the respiratory pumps in the trout. *J. exp. Biol.* 43:349–62.

Balon, E. K. 1975. Reproductive guilds of fishes: A proposal and definition. *J. Fish. Res. Bd. Can.* 32(6):821–64.

Bardach, J. E.; Todd, J. H.; and Crickmer, R. 1967. Orientation by taste in fish of the genus *Ictalurus. Science* 155:1276–78.

Batts, B. S. 1964. Lepidology of the adult pleuronectiform fishes of Puget Sound, Washington. *Copeia* 1964(4):666–73.

Bauchot, R.; Platel, R.; and Ridet, J. M. 1976. Brain-body weight relationships in Selanchii. *Copeia* 1976(2):305–10.

Bauchot, R.; Bauchot, M. L.; Platel, R.; and Ridet, J. M. 1977. Brains of Hawaiian tropical fishes: Brain size and evolution. *Copeia* 1977(1):42–46.

Beamish, R. J., and McFarlane, G. A. 1983. Validation of age determination estimates: The forgotten requirement. *Trans. Am. Fish. Soc.* 112:735–43.

Benz, G. W. 1984. On the conservative nature of the gill filaments of sharks. *Env. Biol. Fishes* 10(1/2):111–16.

Bernstein, J. J. 1970. Anatomy and physiology of the central nervous system. In *Fish physiology,* vol. 4, ed. W. S. Hoar and D. J. Randall, pp. 2–90. New York: Academic Press.

Boddeke, R.; Elijper, G. J.; and Van Der Stelt, A. 1959. Histological characteristics of the body-musculature of fishes in connection with their mode of life. *Proc. Koninkl. Ned. Akad. Wetenschap.* 620:576–88.

Bond, C. E. 1979. *The biology of fishes.* 514 pp. Philadelphia: W. B. Saunders.

Bone, Q. 1971. On the scabbard fish, *Aphanopus carbo. J. mar. biol. Ass. U.K.* 51:219–25.

Bone, Q.; Kiceniuk, J.; and Jones, D. R. 1978. On the role of the different fibre types in fish myotomes at intermediate swimming speeds. *Fish. Bull.,* U.S. 76(3):691–99.

Bone, Q., and Marshall, N. B. 1982. *Biology of fishes.* 253 pp. New York: Chapman and Hall.

Booth, J. H. 1978. The distribution of blood flow in the gills of fish: Application of a new technique to rainbow trout *(Salmo gairdneri). J. exp. Biol.* 73:119–29.

Breder, C. M., and Rosen, D. E. 1966. Modes of reproduction in fishes. 941 pp. Garden City, N.Y.: Natural History Press.

Brett, J. R., and Groot, C. 1963. Some aspects of olfactory and visual responses in Pacific salmon. *J. Fish. Res. Bd. Can.* 20(2):287–303.

Brogal, A., and Fange, R., eds. 1963. *The biology of myxine.* 588 pp. Oslo, Norway: Universitetsforlaget.

Brubaker, J. M., and Angus, R. A. 1984. A procedure for staining fish with alizarin without causing exfoliation of scales. *Copeia* 1984(4):989–90.

Burne, R. H. 1909. The anatomy of the olfactory organ of teleostean fishes. *Proc. Zool. Soc. Lon.* 610–63.

Carey, F. G. 1973. Fishes with warm bodies. *Sci. Am.* 228(2):36–44.

Carey, F. G., and Teal, J. M. 1966. Heat conservation in tuna fish muscle. *Proc. Nat. Acad. Sci.* 565(5):1464–69.

Carey, F. G.; Teal, J. M.; Kanwisher, J. W.; and Lawson, K. D. 1971. Warm-bodied fish. *Am. Zool.* 11:137–45.

Chiasson, R. B. 1974. *Laboratory anatomy of the perch.* 125 pp. Dubuque, Iowa: W. C. Brown.

Delamater, E. D., and Courtenay, W. R., Jr. 1974. Fish scales as seen by scanning electron microscopy. *Fla. Scient.* 37(3):141–49.

Dingerkus, G. 1981. The use of various alcohols for alcian blue in-toto staining of cartilage. *Stain Technology* 56:128–29.

Dingerkus, G., and Ohler, L. D. 1977. Enzymes clearing of alcian blue stained whole small vertebrates for demonstration of cartilage. *Stain Technology* 52(4):229–32.

Dodd, J. M. 1983. Reproduction in cartilaginous fishes (Chondrichthyes). In *Fish physiology,* vol. 9, part A, ed. W. S. Hoar and D. J. Randall, pp. 31–95. New York: Academic Press.

Flock, A. 1971. The lateral line organ mechanoreceptors. In *Fish physiology,* vol. 5, ed. W. S. Hoar and D. J. Randall, pp. 241–64. New York: Academic Press.

Fraser, T. H., and Freihofer, W. C. 1971. Trypsin modification for Sihler technique of staining nerves for systematic studies of fishes. *Copeia* 1971(3):574–76.

Freihofer, W. C. 1966. The Sihler technique of staining nerves for systematic study, especially of fishes. *Copeia* 1966(3):470–74.

Freihofer, W. C.; Compagno, L.J.V.; and Rogers, W. 1977. Additional notes on the use of the Sihler technique of staining nerves of small, whole specimens of fishes and other vertebrates. *Copeia* 1977(3):587–88.

Frizzell, D. L., and Dante, J. H. 1965. Otoliths of some early Cenozoic fishes of the gulf coasts. *J. Paleo.* 39(4):687–718.

Gans, C., and Parsons, T. S. 1981. *A photographic atlas of shark anatomy: The gross morphology of Squalus acanthias.* 106 pp. Chicago: University of Chicago Press.

Gilbert, S. G. 1973. *Pictorial anatomy of the dogfish.* 59 pp. Seattle: University of Washington Press.

Goodrich, E. S. 1930. *Studies on the structure and development of vertebrates.* 837 pp. London: Macmillan.

Graham, J. B. 1975. Heat exchange in the yellowfin tuna, *Thunnus albacares,* and skipjack tuna, *Katsuwonus pelamis,* and the adaptive significance of elevated body temperatures in scombrid fishes. *Fish. Bull. U.S.* 73(2):219–29.

Gray, I. E. 1954. Comparative study of the gill area of marine fishes. *Biol. Bull., Woods Hole* 107:219–25.

Greer-Walker, M., and Pull, G. A. 1975. A survey of red and white muscle in marine fish. *J. Fish. Biol.* 7:295–300.

Greer-Walker, M.; Horwood, J.; and Emerson, L. 1980. On the

morphology and function of red and white skeletal muscle in the anchovies *Engraulis encrasicolus* L. and *E. mordax* Girard. *J. mar. biol. Ass. U.K.* 60:31–37.

Gregory, W. K. 1933. Fish skulls: A study of the evolution of natural mechanisms. *Trans. Am. Philos. Soc.*, New Ser. 23, art. 2:vii, 75–481.

Hara, T. J. 1971. Chemoreception. In *Fish physiology*, vol. 5, ed. W. S. Hoar and D. J. Randall, pp. 79–210. New York: Academic Press.

Harder, W. 1975. *Anatomy of fishes*. Part I (text), 612 pp.; part II (figures and plates), 132 pp. Stuttgart, Germany: E. Schweizerbartsche Verlagsbuchhandlung (Nagele u. Obermiller).

Hardisty, M. W., and Potter, I. C. 1972. *The biology of lampreys*. Vol. 2. 466 pp. New York: Academic Press.

Harrington, R. W., Jr. 1955. The osteocranium of the American cyprinid fish *Notropis bifrenatus* with an annotated synonymy of teleost skull bones. *Copeia* 1955(4):267–90.

Hildebrand, M. 1968. *Anatomical preparations*. 100 pp. Berkeley: University of California Press.

Hoar, W. S. 1955. Reproduction in teleost fish. *Mem. Soc. Endocrinol.* 4:5–24.

———. 1969. Reproduction. In *Fish physiology*, vol. 3, ed. W. S. Hoar and D. J. Randall, pp. 1–72. New York: Academic Press.

Hoar, W. S., and Hickman, C. P., eds. 1975. Analysis of respiratory and bladder gases. In *A laboratory companion for general and comparative physiology*, 2d ed., pp. 82–89. Englewood Cliffs, N.J.: Prentice-Hall.

Hoar, W. S., and Randall, D. J., eds. 1971. *Fish physiology*, vol. 5. *Sensory systems and electric organs*. 600 pp. New York: Academic Press.

Hollister, G. 1934. Clearing and dyeing fish for bone study. *Zoologica* 12:89–101.

Hughes, G. M. 1966. The dimensions of fish gills in relation to their function. *J. exp. Biol.* 45:177–95.

———. 1980. Morphometry of fish gas exchange organs in relation to their respiratory function. In *Environmental physiology of fishes,* ed. M. A. Ali, pp. 33–56. New York: Plenum Press.

Jennings, J. W., and Olson, D. L. 1975. Releasers for agonistic display in male Siamese fighting fish. In *Animal behavior in lab and field*, ed. E. O. Price and A. W. Stokes, pp. 98–100. New York: W. H. Freeman.

Kapoor, B. G.; Smit, H.; and Verighina, I. A. 1975. The alimentary canal and digestion in teleosts. *Adv. Mar. Biol.* 13:109–239.

Keenleyside, M.H.A. 1975. Schooling behavior in fish. In *Animal behavior in lab and field*, ed. E. O. Price and A. W. Stokes, pp. 35–38. New York: W. H. Freeman.

———. 1979. *Diversity and adaptation in fish behavior*. Zoophysiology, vol. 11. 208 pp. New York: Springer-Verlag.

Kleerekoper, H. 1969. *Olfaction in fishes*. 222 pp. Bloomington: Indiana University Press.

Konnerth, A. 1965. Preparation of ligamentory articulated fish skeletons. *Curator* 8(4):325–32.

Kryvi, H., and Totland, G. K. 1978. Fibre types in locomotory muscles of the cartilaginous fish *Chimaera monstrea. J. Fish. Biol.* 12:257–65.

Lacy, E. R.; Reale, E.; Schlusselberg, D. S.; Smith, W. K.; and Woodward, D. J. 1985. A renal countercurrent system in marine elasmobranch fish: A computer-assisted reconstruction. *Science* 227:1351–54.

Lagler, K. F.; Bardach, J. E.; and Miller, R. R. 1962. *Ichthyology*. 542 pp. New York: Wiley.

Lagler, K. F.; Bardach, J. E.; Miller, R. R.; and Passino, D.R.M. 1977. *Ichthyology*. 2d ed. 528 pp. New York: Wiley.

Lauder, G. V., Jr. 1981. Intraspecific functional repertoires in the feeding mechanism of the characoid fishes *Lebiasina, Hoplias,* and *Chalceus. Copeia* 1981(1):154–68.

———. 1982. Structure and function in the tail of the pumpkin-seed sunfish *(Lepomis gibbosus). J. Zool. Lond.* 197:483–95.

———. 1983a. Prey capture hydrodynamics in fishes: Experimental tests of two models. *J. exp. Biol.* 104:1–13.

———. 1983b. Functional and morphological bases of trophic specialization in sunfishes (Teleostei, Centrarchidae). *J. Morph.* 178:1–21.

———. 1983c. Neuromuscular patterns and the origin of trophic specialization in fishes. *Science* 219:1235–37.

Liem, K. F. 1973. Evolutionary strategies and morphological innovations: Cichlid pharyngeal jaws. *Syst. Zool.* 22(4):425–41.

Lowenstam, H. A. 1981. Minerals formed by organisms. *Science* 211:1126–31.

Lowenstein, O. 1971. The labyrinth. In *Fish physiology*, vol. V, edited by W. S. Hoar and D. J. Randall, pp. 207–40. New York: Academic Press.

Lythgoe, J. N. 1980. Vision in fishes: Ecological adaptations. In *Environmental physiology of fishes*, edited by M. A. Ali, pp. 431–46. New York: Plenum Press.

Marshall, N. B. 1960. Swimbladder structure of deep-sea fishes in relation to their systematics and biology. *Discovery Reports* (31):1–121.

———. 1966. *The life of fishes*. 402 pp. New York: World Publishing.

———. 1971. *Explorations in the life of fishes*. 204 pp. Cambridge, Mass.: Harvard University Press.

Mayden, R. L., and Wiley, E. O. 1984. A method of preparing disarticulated skeletons of small fishes. *Copeia* 1984(1):230–32.

McFarland, W. N., and Moss, S. A. 1967. Internal behavior in fish schools. *Science* 156:260–62.

McFarland, W. N.; Ogden, J.; and Lythgoe, J. N. 1979. The influence of light on the twilight migrations of grunts. *Env. Biol. Fishes* 4:9–22.

Mead, G. W., and Bradbury, M. G. 1963. Names of bones. In *Fishes of the western North Atlantic*, mem. (1), pp. 20–23. New Haven, Conn.: Sears Foundation for Marine Research, Yale University.

Miller, D. J., and Lea, R. N. 1972. *Guide to the coastal marine fishes of California*. 235 pp. Bulletin 157. Sacramento, Calif.: Department of Fish and Game.

Morgenroth, P. A., and Morgenroth, A. M. 1969. *Skeletal anatomy of the rockfish*. 13 pp. Eureka, Calif.: Department of Fisheries, Humboldt State College.

Morse, D. H. 1980. *Behavioral mechanisms in ecology*. 383 pp. Cambridge, Mass.: Harvard University Press.

Moser, H. G. 1982. Morphological and functional aspects of marine fish larvae. In *Marine fish larvae*, ed. R. Lasker, pp. 90–131. Seattle: University of Washington Press.

Moss, P.R.L., and Hudson, R.C.L. 1977. The functional roles of different muscle fiber types identified in the myomeres of marine teleosts: A behavioral, anatomical, and histological study. *J. Fish Biol.* 11:417–30.

Motta, P. J. 1984. Mechanics and functions of jaw protrusion in teleost fishes: A review. *Copeia* 1984(1):1–18.

Moyle, P. B., and Cech, J. J. 1982. *Fishes: An introduction to ichthyology.* 592 pp. Englewood Cliffs, N.J.: Prentice-Hall.

Muir, B. S. 1969. Gill dimensions as a function of fish size. *J. Fish. Res. Bd. Can.* 26:165–70.

Mujib, K. A. 1967. The cranial osteology of the Gadidae. *J. Fish. Res. Bd. Can.* 24:1315–75.

Munk, O. 1964a. The eyes of some ceratioid fishes. *Dana Reports* (61):1–15.

———. 1964b. The eyes of three benthic deep sea fishes caught at great depths. *Galathea* 7:137–49.

Nelson, E. M. 1963. A preparation of a standard teleost study skull. *Turtox News* 41(2):72–74.

Newman, M. M., and McRae, M. A., eds. 1980. Films in the sciences, reviews and recommendations. *A.A.A.S. Reference Sourcebook.* Washington, D.C.: American Association for the Advancement of Science.

Norden, E. M. 1963. Comparative osteology of representative salmonid fishes, with particular reference to the grayling *(Thymallus arcticus)* and its phylogeny. *J. Fish. Res. Bd. Can.* 18(5):679–791.

Northcutt, R. G., and Davis, R. E., eds. 1983. Fish Neurobiology. Vol. 1, *Brainstem and sense organs,* 414 p.; vol. 2, *Higher brain areas and functions,* 375 p. Ann Arbor: University of Michigan Press.

Northmore, D.; Volkmann, F. C.; and Yager, D. 1978. Vision in fishes: Color and pattern. In *The behavior of fish and other aquatic animals,* ed. by D. I. Mostofsky, pp. 79–139. New York: Academic Press.

Nursall, J. R. 1956. The lateral musculature and the swimming of fish. *Proc. Zool. Soc. Lon.* 126(1):27–143.

———. 1963. The caudal musculature of *Hoplapagrus guntheri* gill (Perciformes: Lutjanidae). *Can. J. Zool.* 41:865–80.

Oakley, B., and Schafer, R. 1978. *Experimental neurobiology: A laboratory manual.* 384 pp. Ann Arbor: University of Michigan Press.

Olla, B. L.; Samet, C. E.; and Stuoholme, A. L. 1972. Activity and feeding behavior of the summer flounder *(Paralichthys centatus)* under controlled laboratory conditions. *Fish. Bull.,* U.S. 70:1127–36.

Osse, J.W.M. 1969. Functional morphology of the head of the perch *(Perca fluviatilis L.):* An electromyographic study. *Neth. J. Zool.* 19(3):289–92.

Ossian, C. R. 1970. Preparation of disarticulated skeletons using enzyme based laundry "pre-soakers." *Copeia* 1970:199–200.

Pankhurst, N. W., and Lythgoe, J. N. 1983. Changes in vision and olfaction during sexual maturation in the European eel, *Anguilla anguilla* (L.). *J. Fish Biol.* 23:229–40.

Pitcher, T. J.; Partridge, B. L.; and Wardle, C. S. 1976. A blind fish can school. *Science* 194:963–65.

Price, E. O., and Stokes, A. W., eds. 1975. *Animal behavior in lab and field.* New York: W. H. Freeman.

Potts, G. W., and Wootton, R. J., eds. 1984. *Fish reproduction: Strategies and tactics.* 410 pp. New York: Academic Press.

Pullin, R.S.V., and Lowe-McConnell, R. H., eds. 1982. *The biology and culture of Tilapias.* 432 pp. International Center for

Living Aquatic Resources Management Conference (Manila, Philippines) Proceedings, no. 75.

Raikow, R. J. 1978. *A guide to the anatomy of* Chimaera colliei *(Holocephali).* The Morphology Teacher, no. 17. 6 pp. Pittsburgh, Pa.: Department of Biological Sciences, University of Pittsburgh.

Randall, D. J. 1970. Gas exchange in fish. In *Fish physiology,* vol. 4, ed. by W. S. Hoar and D. J. Randall, pp. 253–92. New York: Academic Press.

Regan, C. T. 1910. Notes on the classification of the teleostean fishes. 16 pp. *Proc. Seventh Int. Zool. Congr.*

Reynierse, J. H. 1975. Parental behavior in cichlid fish. In *Animal behavior in lab and field,* ed. by E. O. Price and A. W. Stokes, pp. 78–80. New York: W. H. Freeman.

Russell, E. S. 1982. *Form and function: A contribution to the history of animal morphology.* 383 pp. Chicago: University of Chicago Press.

Scholander, P. F.; Van Dam, L.; Claff, C. L.; and Kanwisher, J. W. 1955. Microgasometric determination of dissolved oxygen and nitrogen. *Biol. Bull.* 109:328–34.

Shaw, E., and Tucker, A. 1965. The optomotor reaction of schooling carangid fishes. *Animal Behav.* 13(2–3):330–36.

Shelton, G. 1970. The regulation of breathing. In *Fish physiology,* vol. 4, ed. by W. S. Hoar and D. J. Randall, pp. 293–360. New York: Academic Press.

Simons, E. V., and Van Horn, J. R. 1970/71. A new procedure for whole-mount alcian blue staining of the cartilaginous skeleton of chicken embryos, adapted to the clearing procedure in potassium hydroxide. *Acta Morphol. Neerl.—Scand.* (Utrecht) 8:281–92.

———. 1971. An in-toto staining procedure for the cartilaginous skeleton of chicken embryos. *Acta Morphol. Neerl.—Scand.* (Utrecht) 9:138–39.

Smeets, W.J.A.; Nieuwenhuys, R.; and Roberts, B. L. 1983. *The central nervous system of cartilaginous fishes: Structure and functional correlations.* 266 pp. New York: Springer-Verlag.

Squire,, J. L., Jr., and Smith, S. E. 1977. *Angler's guide to the United States Pacific coasts.* 139 pp. National Marine Fisheries Service publication. Washington, D.C.: U.S. Government Printing Office.

Stahl, B. J. 1967. Morphology and relationships of the Holocephali with special reference to the venous system. *Bull. Mus. Comp. Zool.* 135(3):141–213.

Starks, E. C. 1930. The primary shoulder girdle of the bony fishes. *Stanford Univ. Publ. Sci.* 6(2):149–239.

Steen, J. B. 1970. The swimbladder as a hydrostatic organ. In *Fish physiology,* vol. 4, ed. by W. S. Hoar and D. J. Randall, pp. 414–44. New York: Academic Press.

Stokely, P. S. 1952. The vertebral axis of two species of centrarchid fishes. *Copeia* 1952(4):255–61.

Sumner, F. B. 1911. The adjustment of flatfishes to various backgrounds: A study of adaptive color change. *J. Exp. Zool.* 10:409–505.

———. 1934. Does "protective coloration" protect?—Results of some experiments with fishes and birds. *Proc. Nat. Acad. Sci., U.S.A.* 20:559–64.

———. 1935. Studies of protective color change. III: Experiments with fishes both as predators and prey. *Proc. Nat. Acad. Sci., U.S.A.* 21:345–53.

Sutterlin, A. M. 1975. Chemical attraction of some marine fish in their natural habitat. *J. Fish. Res. Bd. Can.* 32:729–38.

Tautz, A. F., and Groot, C. 1975. Spawning behavior of chum salmon *(Oncorhynchus keta)* and rainbow trout *(Salmo gairdneri). J. Fish. Res. Bd. Can.* 32:633–42.

Taylor, W. R. 1967a. An enzyme method of clearing and staining small vertebrates. *Proc. U.S. Nat. Mus.* 122(3596):1–17.

___. 1967b. Outline of a method of clearing tissues with pancreatic enzymes and staining bones of small vertebrates. *Turtox News* 45(12):308–9.

Thresher, R. E. 1984. *Reproduction in reef fishes.* 399 pp. Neptune City, N.J.: T.F.H. Publications.

Tinbergen, N. 1952. The curious behavior of sticklebacks. *Sci. Am.* 187(6):22–26.

___. 1955. *The study of instinct.* 338 pp. London: Oxford University Press.

Totland, G. K.; Kryvi, H.; Bone, Q.; and Flood, R. F. 1981.

Vascularization of the lateral muscle of some elasmobranchiomorph fishes. *J. Fish. Biol.* 18:223–34.

Wake, M. H., ed. 1979. *Hyman's comparative vertebrate anatomy.* 3d ed. 788 p. Chicago: University of Chicago Press.

Wessells, N. K., and Center, E. M. 1975. *Vertebrates: A laboratory text.* 216 pp. Los Altos, Calif.: William Kaufmann.

Willemse, J. J. 1959. The way in which flexures of the body are caused by musculature contractions. *Koninkl. Nederl. Akad. Wetensch. Proc.* 62:589–93.

Winterbottom, R. 1974. A descriptive synonymy of the striated muscles of the Teleostei. *Proc. Acad. Nat. Sci. Phil.* 125(12):225–317.

Wischnitzer, P. 1972. *Atlas and dissection guide for comparative anatomy.* 203 pp. New York: W. H. Freeman.

Wootton, R. J. 1976. *The biology of sticklebacks.* 387 pp. London: Academic Press.

___. 1985. *A functional biology of sticklebacks.* 265 pp. Berkeley: University of California Press.

SECTION TWO
TAXONOMIC CHARACTERS IN IDENTIFICATION, VARIATION, AND CLASSIFICATION

In section 1, we examined fishes to learn how to disassemble them and how to infer their inter-relationships in a structural and mechanical sense. Now in this section, we examine fishes to learn how to identify them and how to reason about their relationships from an evolutionary perspective. Both sections deal with morphological characteristics of fish: the first from a functional viewpoint, the second from a taxonomic one. Thus the study of fish characters is fundamental to a large body of ichthyological research.

Taxonomic characters are the building blocks of any systematic analysis.[1] Knowing the characters and how they vary among species and other taxa is what allows us to identify fishes in the first place. Then, the assumptions we make about the inheritance and evolution of characters form the basis for reasoning about how species originate and relate to one another genealogically. In this section, we discover and measure "good" taxonomic characters (chap. 6). From a practical standpoint, it is essential to find easily observable morphological characters for use in identifying species and other taxa. We do this by constructing and using taxonomic keys (chap. 7). Learning how to measure and interpret character variation among individual examples provides a technique for detecting geographic patterns in morphological variation and for inferring genetic events from their presumed phenotypic outcomes. This is the circumstantial evidence needed to distinguish species from genetically distinct populations within species. To assemble this evidence, we sample fish populations, find good characters that vary between samples, and analyze the variation statistically (chap. 8). Finally, we see how characters that distinguish species and groups of species can be used to construct hierarchical classifications that are suggested phylogenies of the species. We achieve this by emphasizing characters that are uniquely shared by pairs of species and groups of species (chap. 9).

These chapters provide only the essential background information for the laboratory exercises around which they are built: measuring characters on fish specimens, identifying fish specimens, measuring morphological variation between samples of fish, and classifying a group of fishes by means of uniquely shared characters. For further general reading, E. O. Wiley (1981) provides an unusually complete treatment of modern systematic theory and practice, including briefs on taxonomic mechanics such as rules of nomenclature. Many recent and comprehensive ichthyological texts (e.g., Lagler et al. 1977, Bond 1979, Moyle and Cech 1982) summarize the higher classification of fishlike vertebrates.

---

1. Following current usage, Wiley (1981) distinguishes the terms *comparative biology, systematics,* and *taxonomy.* Comparative biology is the general study of patterns and causes of diversity of life. A part of comparative biology, systematics deals with the evolutionary relationships among populations, species, and higher taxa of organisms. Taxonomy is the subdivision of systematics concerning the theory and practice of describing, identifying, and classifying taxa. (A *taxon,* plural *taxa,* is a group of organisms having a common evolutionary history: for example, a particular species, genus, or family.)

Chapter 6
Finding and Measuring Characters

GOOD TAXONOMIC CHARACTERS

A **character** is any attribute of any organism that we can detect and describe. To be good, however, a taxonomic character must be easily observable and vary from one taxon to another. Therefore, **good characters** must be genetically, rather than environmentally, determined. For instance, fish that live in impoverished waters may have relatively large heads and thin bodies because they are undernourished. In this situation, one might mistake emaciated fish with big heads for a separate species simply because the fish were starving due to environmental conditions. Nonetheless, differences in head size and body shape are often determined genetically and as such can be used as good characters.

Even genetically determined characters can mislead ichthyologists if, for example, they vary between sexes of the same species. A case in point was confusion about identifying species of sexually dimorphic parrotfishes (Scaridae), which inhabit coral reefs. For many years, some parrotfishes had two species names, one for the larger, more colorful males, another for females. Finally, observation and sexing of the fish corrected the error (e.g., Randall 1963). Ordinarily, color pattern can only be used for identifying parrotfish of the same sex.

- Would counting the number of eggs in the ovary of a female be a good taxonomic character?
- Might the shape of a fish's otolith—the hard, calcified bone in the inner ear—be a good character?
- Fish living in the cooler part of a species' range often have a larger number of fin rays or vertebrae than fish living in the warmer part. How could you judge whether this difference was more likely **ecophenotypic** (under direct environmental control) or genetically based?

KINDS OF CHARACTERS

Quantitative Morphological Characters

Most good characters used in fish taxonomy are morphological—that is, they are attributes of body form and structure—because such attributes are the easiest to observe. Morphological characters may be divided into those that are directly measurable and those that are not. Measurable, or quantitative, characters include those like length of body parts, which can be measured with a millimeter scale (**mensural** or **morphometric** characters) and those like number of fin rays (**meristic** characters), which can be counted. Statistically speaking, morphometric characters are continuous variables. This means that, theoretically, any number of values exists between one measurement of, say, head length and another, depending on degree of accuracy (see p. 106, chap. 8). For example, if measurements were taken to the nearest 1 mm, there would be 9 values between measurements of 50 and 60 mm; but if measurements were taken to the nearest 0.1 mm, there would be 99 values between 50.0 and 60.0. On the other hand, meristic characters are discontinuous or discrete variables. There might be 9 or 10 rays counted in a fin, but there will not be 9.5.

Ratios and Scattergrams

Morphometric characters present a problem of scaling. Obviously, head length as an absolute measurement could not be used to distinguish two species of fish if one species were to be represented by a juvenile individual and the other by a fully grown adult. As a fish grows, so does its head. Therefore, morphometrics are usually expressed as proportions or percents of the fish's **standard length (SL)**, the straight-line distance from tip of the snout to the base of the caudal fin.

Yet this normalization to relative measurement does not correct for size if, for example, young fish have relatively larger heads or eyes than adults, that is, if some body parts grow disproportionately slower (or faster) than overall length. We can detect this **allometric growth** by plotting the percentage values of the character against standard length to get some idea of where the resulting **scattergram** of points deviates from a trend that is generally horizontal or "flat." (A horizontal trend would be expected if relative size of the body part did not vary with fish size.) The pattern of open circles in figure 6.1 is a scattergram of eye diameter expressed as a percent of standard length, plotted against the standard length. Notice that the scatter does not

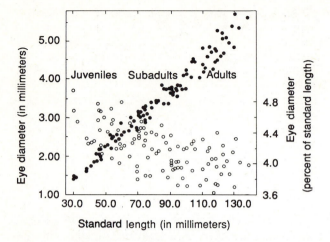

Figure 6.1 Relation of eye size to body size of a small oceanic fish. The tighter scattergram of solid circles is a bivariate plot of absolute values of eye diameter (left vertical axis) versus standard length (horizontal axis); the looser scattergram of open circles is a plot of relative values of eye diameter expressed as percent SL (right vertical axis) versus standard length (horizontal axis). Eye diameter was measured by ocular micrometer to the nearest 0.01 mm; standard length was measured by dividers to 0.1 mm.

describe an entirely flat trend; it first curves downward and then becomes horizontal only for fish longer than about 90.0 mm SL. Thus the scattergram shows that eye size is relatively large in younger individuals of this species. We might even (somewhat arbitrarily) divide the domain of percent values into three ranges to represent different growth stages: juvenile, subadult, and adult. Some published species descriptions, in fact, give such subdivisions for allometric characters (e.g., Ebeling and Weed 1963).

Figure 6.1 also illustrates one problem with using percentages to scale body measurements. Percentages represent ratios of values using two characters, each of which is subject to measurement error. Thus, as we explain in greater detail later, percentages can compound errors in both original measurements. This means they may be more erratic than either measurement individually (Sokal and Rohlf 1981). Note that the scattergram for percent eye diameter (open circles) is much more diffuse than the scattergram for absolute eye diameter plotted against standard length (solid circles).

For this and other reasons, the latter **bivariate** plot of original measurements is said to be the more correct and accurate representation of a morphometric character (Marr 1955). It identifies a mathematical function subject to statistical **regression analysis**, wherein, for instance, eye diameters are predictable for the entire domain of standard lengths. Instead of summarizing relative values for morphometric characters, some authors have tabulated parameters that determine **regression lines** "fitting" the scattergrams

(e.g., Cohen and Russo 1979). While we don't deny the elegance of regression models, we regard ordinary proportions and percents as easy to calculate, display, and interpret. They are still commonly used to help describe and compare fish species and other taxa (in, for example, Emery and Smith-Vaniz 1982).

Qualitative Morphological Characters

Values of qualitative characters are not so easily expressed as numbers are. Such attributes as color or shape are usually described in words such as *red* or *fusiform*. But with technological advances, more and more qualitative characters have the potential to become quantitative. Photographic image analysis by computer can render differences in tints and outline in digital terms. More simply, qualitative characters can be scored subjectively. For example, body shape might be scored from 1 (slender) to 5 (robust) or body color shade from 1 (light) to 5 (dark).

Nonmorphological Characters

Taxonomic characters need not always be morphological, even though morphological characters are often easiest to observe and measure. Characters can also be functional (physiological), behavioral, distributional, cytological, or biochemical (see Wiley 1981 for an excellent summary of different kinds of characters and how they are measured). We do not mean to practice "character discrimination." Every kind of taxonomic character is potentially important and should be used if it proves valuable in identifying fish taxa (and if you have the resources to measure it).

Physiological characters are difficult to measure precisely and have seldom been used for systematic purposes. In a rare exception, Barlow (1961a) was able to distinguish populations of goby fishes by differences in their respiratory rate. To do this, he applied the general knowledge that fishes adapted to living in waters of different average temperature consume oxygen at characteristically different rates when acclimated to the same intermediate temperature.

The entire science of **ethology** (comparative behavior) is based on genetically determined differences in the behavioral patterns of species. Differences in breeding behavior, for example, may mark closely related fish species that are otherwise quite similar (e.g., Keenleyside 1979). Behaviors also make good characters for field identification. With a "good eye" and knowledge of species habits, an experienced field observer may first distinguish morphologically similar species according to where they are and what they are doing.

All good fish-identification books give species distributions. Frequently the best check on an identification is to find out where the specimen was collected. Morphologically similar species often occupy different geographic ranges, with little or no distributional overlap (i.e., they are often **allopatric**). The identification of a specimen from well beyond the species' previously known range is always suspect.

With improving techniques of cytological preparation, chromosomal patterns, or **karyotypes**, are also providing good characters for taxonomic analysis. Not only the numbers but also the shapes and sizes of fish chromosomes can distinguish certain different species or even higher taxa (Gold 1979).

Biochemical characters provide direct measures of genetic "distance" between taxa because, for instance, different genes may encode characteristically different enzymes. Protein (enzyme) separation by electrophoresis is gaining wide popularity as a modern tool for work in fish systematics. It is a highly sensitive way of determining whether samples of similar fish represent genetically distinct populations or a single species (Buth and Mayden 1981). Electrophoretic characters, or **electromorphs**, can also supplement morphological characters in constructing phylogenetic classifications (Buth et al. 1980). In fact, three kinds of characters—biochemical, chromosomal, and morphological—can be mobilized to tackle more difficult systematic questions concerning, for example, the identity of trout populations (Busack et al. 1980).

Character Combinations

If a single character does not efficiently separate individuals of two different populations or species, a group of characters whose values are combined mathematically into a **discriminate function** may do so. Thus, usually by computerized correlative procedures, "virtual" characters are created as combinations of "real" (directly observable) characters. Examples include studies of marine damselfishes (Emery and Smith-Vanez 1982) and freshwater minnows (Matthews et al. 1982). The informational content of an analysis does not necessarily increase in direct proportion to the number of intercorrelated characters, however. Some characters can be redundant; that is, they can be different measurements of the same thing or genetic effect. If a fish species has a relatively long head, for example, this distinction could be expressed not only by overall head length but also by lengths from snout to eye, from eye to preopercle, from preopercle to end of opercle, and measurements of all the landmarks in between. If the head shape of the fish is not particularly unusual, a discriminant function produced by combining these measurements, which are simply the parts, contains little more useful information than the whole.

• Give reasons why metabolic rate as measured by oxygen consumption may not be a good taxonomic character.

• Basically, in identifying a fish, how does the criterion of capture locality differ from that of morphological distinctiveness?

• What kinds of characters are useful in identifying living fish in their natural habitat? Are these necessarily the same as the best characters to distinguish preserved specimens?

• Would gill-raker counts from both sides of a fish provide twice the useful taxonomic information as a single count from the left side?

EXERCISE: MEASURING MORPHOLOGICAL CHARACTERS

For convenience, characters used to describe and identify fishes are usually superficially located and relatively easy to observe. These include counts (meristics) such as the numbers of fin rays or gill rakers, measurements (morphometrics) such as the head length or body depth, and qualitative characters such as shape and color. Table 6.1 lists commonly used characters, many of which are diagrammed in figures 6.2 and 6.3. If many of these prove not to be diagnostic (that is, capable of distinguishing the taxon at hand from all others), seek out others that are. For example, some species of the tiny freshwater darters (Percidae) are best distinguished by characteristic patterns in head canals of their acoustico-lateralis sensory system (Page 1977; and see sect. 1, p. 25).

Using figures 6.2 and 6.3 and the following directions as a guide, measure the characters on a fish listed in table 6.1, recording values in the spaces provided. Double check all your values because your completed individual data sheet can also contribute to group exercises in identifying fish specimens, measuring morphological variation, and constructing a phylogenetic classification. Definitions of commonly used characters follow those of Hubbs and Lagler (1958), the widely accepted authority.

Before measuring characters, place the fish in a dissecting tray with water or a moist paper towel over the bottom to prevent drying. Observe the larger structures under a desk lamp; measure the smaller structures using a magnifying glass or dissecting microscope at low power.

Counts

Among the most obvious and useful meristic characters are the numbers of rays (spines or soft rays) in the different fins. Fin rays are most easily distinguished against light transmitted through the fin's membrane. To make a count, simply pull the first element to be counted (ray or spine) forward, which erects the fin and separates the rays. Against background light, either from a lamp or transmitted upward

Table 6.1. Suggested data sheet for recording morphological characters. (All measurements of morphometric characters should be taken to the nearest 0.1 mm.)

Your name _____

Species _____

Specimen number _____

COUNTS

  1. Dorsal-fin spines _____

  2. Dorsal soft rays _____

  3. Anal spines _____

  4. Anal soft rays _____

  5. Total pectoral rays _____

  6. Scales along lateral line _____

  7. Scales above lateral line _____

  8. Scales below lateral line _____

  9. Scales before dorsal fin _____

10. Scales around caudal peduncle _____

11. Branchiostegal rays _____

12. Pyloric caeca _____

13. Total gill rakers on first arch _____

14. Total vertebrae _____

	PERCENT STANDARD LENGTH
MEASUREMENTS	
Standard length _____	_____
15. Body depth _____	_____
16. Caudal-peduncle depth _____	_____
17. Caudal-peduncle length _____	_____
18. Predorsal length _____	_____
19. Length of dorsal base _____	_____
20. Length of anal base _____	_____
21. Height of dorsal fin _____	_____
22. Height of anal fin _____	_____
23. Length of pectoral fin _____	_____
24. Length of pelvic fin _____	_____
25. Length of longest dorsal spine _____	_____

Table 6.1. *Continued*

26. Head length _____   _____

27. Head width _____   _____

28. Snout length _____   _____

29. Suborbital width _____   _____

30. Orbit to preopercle angle _____   _____

31. Eye diameter _____   _____

32. Upper-jaw length _____   _____

33. Gape width _____   _____

SCORED ATTRIBUTES

34. Position of mouth (1 inferior, 2 terminal, 3 superior) _____

35. Snout profile (1 convex, 2 straight, 3 concave) _____

36. Upper-jaw teeth shape (1 simple pointed, 2 simple blunt, 3 multicuspid) _____

37. Shade of body background color (1 light, 2 dark) _____

38. Pattern of body color (1 plain, 2 complex) _____

through the stage of a dissecting microscope, fin rays contrast markedly with the translucent interradial membrane.

In specification of fin-ray counts, the name of the fin is often abbreviated in the following way: D, dorsal fin; A, anal; C, caudal; P_1, pectoral; P_2, pelvic. **Spines**, which are stiff, sharp, and unsegmented rays, are designated by roman numerals. **Soft rays**, which are flexible rays often branched at the tip and segmented, are designated by arabic numbers. For example, the dorsal-ray count of the fish in figure 6.2 may be written as: D. XIII, 14, which signifies 13 spines in the spinous dorsal fin, followed by 14 soft rays in the soft dorsal.

If the count were for the whole species, a range of values is given. The olive rockfish, *Sebastes serranoides*, a common subtidal resident of California reefs, has a dorsal-ray count of D. XIII, 15-17, meaning that all individuals have 13 dorsal spines, but individuals may have 15, 16, or 17 soft rays. Dorsal, anal, and caudal fins are **median** (unpaired) fins so they require only one count. Pectoral and pelvic fins are paired so count them either on the left side of the fish or, for completeness, on both sides. For example, the complete pelvic-ray counts for this species is P_2, I, 5 - I, 5, for the left and right sides, respectively.

Some fin-ray counts are difficult to interpret. Often a series of tiny **procurrent rays** precede the large, obvious **principal rays** in the caudal fin: then the first principal ray

forming the fin edge at the top or bottom is an **unbranched ray** followed by a series of rays, which are more and more deeply branched toward the middle of the fin. Because the procurrent rays may be attached to the principal rays, it is often easiest to count principal rays by counting branched rays and adding 2. A complete caudal-fin count might be 3 + 17 + 3, indicating 3 upper and lower procurrent rays and 17 (15 branched + 2 unbranched) principal rays. In other fins, the first or uppermost ray of the pectoral fin may be rudimentary and splintlike. The last soft ray of the dorsal and anal fins is usually branched to its base and so appears as two elements, which, however, should be counted as one; consequently, soft-ray counts of median fins may seem to equal the total number of separable elements minus one.

For typical perchlike fishes (Perciformes), which form the largest group of teleosts, pelvic-ray and caudal-ray counts are not always good characters because they seldom vary between taxa. Most such species have P_2, I, 5 and C, 17.

Before counting scales, blot the fish lightly to eliminate confusing highlights and reveal scale margins. Then, to accentuate the margins, lightly rub the scaled flank with your finger from tail to head against the grain. As with paired-fin counts, count scales on the left side only or, for completeness, on both sides.

A common count is of the scales along the lateral line,

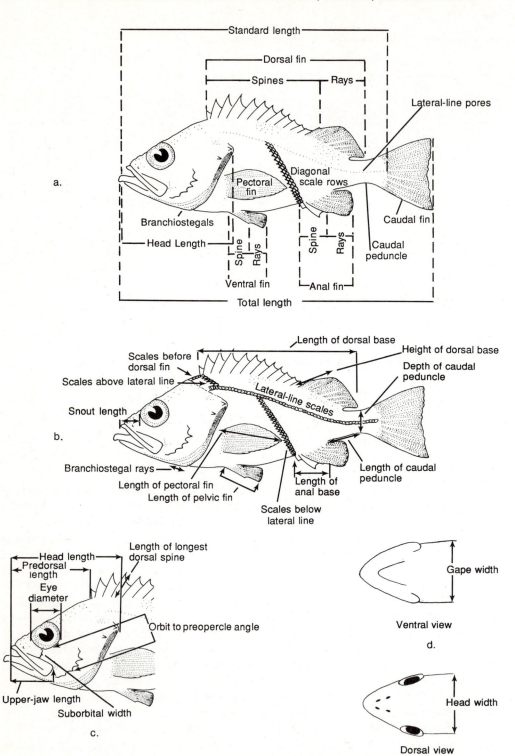

Figure 6.2 Common external meristic and morphometric characters (counts and measurements, respectively): (a) and (b) fish with labeled counts, measurements, and various reference features listed in table 6.1; (c) closeup of head showing measurements; (d) diagrammatic ventral and dorsal views of head showing measurements.

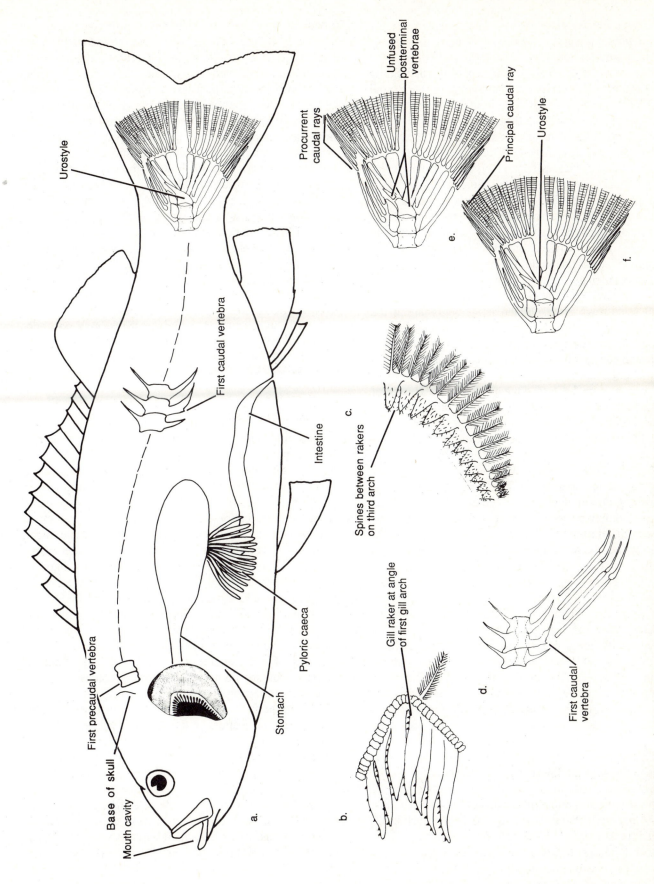

Figure 6.3 Diagram of the location of commonly used internal characters (a); features of the gill arch (b and c); the vertebral column (d); and the caudal skeleton (e and f). These are reference features, some of which are found in Table 6.1.

which is superficially manifest by a line of pores, one per scale, extending along the flanks from head to base of caudal fin. Count all pored scales from the beginning of the lateral line just behind the head at the top of the operculum to the caudal base, which is identified by moving the caudal fin from side to side. The last scale in this series is the one that lies on the crease marking the caudal base when the fin is moved. For species that lack a typical pored lateral line along the flanks, such as herring (*Clupea*), or have the line interrupted, such as wrasses (Labridae), simply count scales in a longitudinal series from head to caudal base.

Also count scales above and below the lateral line, before the dorsal fin, and around the caudal peduncle. Begin with the median scale at the fin's origin and count scales in an oblique row downward and backward to, but not including, the lateral-line scale. Below the lateral line begin with the medial scale before the anal-fin origin and count obliquely upward. For fishes with atypical lateral lines, count all scale rows in an oblique series beginning at the origin of the dorsal fin. Or, you can do a circumference scale count of all scale rows around the body at the same point. The caudal peduncle scale count is a circumference count around the narrowest part of the caudal peduncle.

You can also make less obvious counts or counts of internal structures (fig. 6.3), such as branchiostegal rays, pharyngeal teeth, and pyloric caeca, which are blind sacs marking the junction of the duodenum and the stomach. As with more superficial characters, it is useless to describe all of them here because characters that are good for distinguishing taxa in one group of fishes may not be good for distinguishing taxa in another. For example, branchiostegal rays may distinguish species of subperciform fishes but be almost constant in number for some groups of perch and basslike species. Some species either lack pharyngeal teeth or jaw teeth or they have highly variable numbers. Other fishes, such as surfperches (Embiotocidae), lack pyloric caeca.

Two important internal counts listed in most species descriptions, however, are gill rakers and vertebrae. Gill rakers are usually aligned in two rows on each gill arch, an outer row of longer rakers and an inner row of short stubs. Count all long outer rakers on the left first arch, including the smallest in the series at top and bottom of the arch. Note that the rakers are longest at the angle of the arch; then they progressively shorten toward the top and bottom ends. Counts are often expressed as numbers on upper and lower limbs, separated by a plus sign. Include the long raker straddling the angle with the lower count. Thus a count of 7 + 20 includes 7 in the upper limb, 1 straddling the angle, and 19 in the lower limb of the first gill arch; a count of 7 + 20, 8 + 20 shows that the first arch on the right side of the fish has 1 more raker in its upper limb than that on the left side.

Vertebral counts indicate body **metamerism** or segmentation. There is one vertebra per body segment, which extends outward as a lateral muscle segment (myotome).

Horizontal scale rows and even fin rays in dorsal and anal fins usually reflect metamerism so all these characters are frequently intercorrelated. If, say, vertebrae, myotomes, and scale rows are related one-to-one, the three characters together provide little more taxonomic information than any one because they may all be an expression (**phenotype**) of the same group of genes. Vertebral counts are best made from x-ray photographs (radiographs) of whole fish or from specimens that have been cleared and stained (see sect. 1). Count all elements from the base of the skull backward to and including the urostyle (fig. 6.3). Precaudal are often distinguished by a plus from caudal vertebrae. The first caudal vertebra has a complete hemal arch projecting downward from the centrum; a count of 10 + 16 indicates that 10 precaudal elements without hemal arches precede 16 caudal elements with hemal arches, including the urostyle (or postterminal elements).

- Give evidence that the numbers of vertebrae, myotomes, and scales in a horizontal row may be under common genetic control.
- What information does a gill-raker count of 7 + 20, 7 + 21 convey?

Measurements

All measurements are straight-line projections between two reference points; that is, they are never taken along the curve of the fish's body. Therefore, use needle-point dividers to measure distances, which can be read to nearest 0.1 mm by laying the extended divider on a good-quality millimeter scale calibrated to 0.5 mm. Take care not to move the divider arms before reading the measurement. Alternatively, you can use a dial-reading or vernier caliper calibrated in mm for more direct readings. To improve accuracy, measure each distance three times, and record the average of the two closest values to the nearest 0.1 mm. Special meter sticks with sliding needle points are available for measuring large fish. Measurements for taxonomic analysis must be more accurate and precise than rapid measurements of fish lengths suitable for fisheries studies. Therefore, you should not use measuring boards and other such quick-processing devices in this exercise.

Measure the fish's standard length: the distance from the most anterior projection of the snout or upper lip to the **caudal base** (marked by a crease found by moving the caudal fin laterally against the fish's body). Lightly squeeze one needle point against the lip, moving the other to the crease at the caudal base. Take special care to measure standard length accurately because it is the denominator of all ratios. Recall that other measurements are expressed as a percent or proportion of standard length so that they measure fish shape by eliminating the effect of fish size. Hence, if standard length is measured incorrectly, the relative values of all other measures will be wrong. This is the main reason ichthyologists record standard length instead of total fish length for most taxonomic studies. As a reference point, the caudal-fin base is more reliable than the tip, which is fragile and often broken.

Complete the set of four measurements listed on your data sheet (table 6.1), using the reference points indicated in figure 6.2. Body depth is the greatest vertical dimension, usually from a point near the origin of the first dorsal fin. Caudal peduncle depth is the least depth near the caudal base, while its length is the oblique distance from anal-fin insertion to mid-caudal base. Predorsal length extends from tip of the snout to the origin of the first dorsal fin. Lengths of fin bases are distances between **origin**, at the front of the base of first ray or spine, and **insertion**, where the membrane behind the last ray meets the body. Heights of median fins and lengths of paired fins are measured from the fin's origins to the tips of their nearest lobes or projections. Fin-ray lengths extend from their extreme bony base to their outermost tip when the ray is set as straight as possible.

Head length extends from the tip of snout backward to the farthest point on the fleshy opercular membrane; depth is directly downward from the midpoint of the **occiput** (back part of head); and width is the greatest dimension when gill covers are normally placed. Several common measurements have the margin of the orbit or eye socket as reference point. For all, slightly squeeze your dividers so that the needle points compress the fleshy rim toward the bony margin. Using this method, snout length is from the tip of the snout to the front of the orbit. Postorbital head length is from the back of the orbit to the farthest point on the opercle. Suborbital width is the least distance from the orbit bottom to the suborbital edge, located just above the upper jaw. Cheek width is between the back of the orbit and the margin of the preopercle. Orbit to preopercle angle includes any spine at this point. Interorbital width is the least distance between the tops of the orbits on either side of the head. And orbit length is the greatest diameter between the orbit margins. In contrast with orbit length, eye diameter is the greatest distance across the cornea of the eyeball, found by lightly probing the eye surface to depress the relatively pliant cornea. Eye diameters of small fish are measured more accurately with an ocular micrometer, which can be mounted in an eyepiece of the dissecting scope. Other common measurements in the head region include upper-jaw length, from the tip of the snout backward to the end of the maxillary bone, which is the posterior extent of the jaw; and gape width, the greatest ventral distance across the mouth opening.

Of course, an effectively infinite number of measurements are possible. Various distances from snout to fin origins or insertions are often recorded, and distances between fins are commonly measured. Recall, however, the possibility of proliferating measurements around the same essential character. For example, it is probably a waste of time to measure snout to pectoral origin, pectoral origin to anal-fin origin, then snout to anal origin because the last measurement is the sum of the first two and is thus redundant. If the relative position of the pectoral fin is a good character, then both component distances should be measured. On the other hand, distance from snout to anal origin may be a better measure of general body shape.

Additional Morphological Characters

Characters that cannot be counted or measured (are neither meristic nor morphometric) can either be described in words or scored for numerical analysis. For example, the position of the fish's mouth relative to the fish's horizontal body axis may be described as **inferior** (directed slightly downward), **terminal** (projecting straight ahead), or **superior** (directed slightly upward). Or its position may be simply scored 1 for inferior, 2 for terminal, and 3 for superior. Even colors can be scored: for example, 1 for relatively light and 2 for relatively dark. Colors of specimens preserved for a long time tend to fade so color patterns may be more reliable than shades or tints. For instance, the presence or absence of dark spots or blotches are recognizable even on badly faded specimens.

• The condition factor of a fish has been defined as the fish's weight (gms) divided by its length (mm) cubed. What problems arise in using condition factor as a taxonomic character?
• Why is relative eye diameter (eye diameter expressed as percent of standard length) usually greater in juveniles than in adult fish?
• What problems may occur in describing and encoding (scoring) color characters? Once the states of a color character are scored, is the character objectively determined (as with counts and measurements)?

Chapter 7
Key Characters and Identification of Taxa

To identify unknown specimens logically and efficiently, information about characters and how they vary among species and other fish taxa must be assembled in an orderly fashion. A taxonomic "key" to fish identification is a hierarchical analysis of good characters that are usually morphological (see chap. 6). Thus the particular characters good for identifying members of a given fish group are **key characters** for that group. We use key characters to determine the correct taxon for an unknown fish specimen.

This process of identification requires keying and checking. If you do not know the classification of the specimen, you should first key out the fish to a family in a **preliminary key** like the family key in Moyle (1976) for inland fishes or the one in Miller and Lea (1972) for coastal fishes of California. Others are listed toward the end of this chapter (pp. 103–104). Preliminary keys often include outline drawings of characters and representative species as models. Once you have determined its family, you can tentatively identify the specimen to species by using another key to the family's genera and species. Finally, check the tentative identification by seeing if the capture locality is within the known range of the species and by comparing the specimen you have with published illustrations, descriptions, and authentically identified reference specimens.

Before we get too "keyed up," however, we need to make sure we understand the significance of the name given to the specimen's taxon during the identification process. To this end, we begin with a review and practice of **taxonomic nomenclature** as applied to fishes.

TAXONOMIC NOMENCLATURE

The **species** forms the basic taxonomic category of a **gonochoristic** (sexually reproducing) organism like a fish. A species is a group or groups of individuals that do not ordinarily interbreed with other such groups. This genetic distinctness implies a morphological distinctness; a species can be identified and distinguished from all other species by a unique set of characteristics. In practice, we first recognize a discontinuous pattern of variation between groups of

fish,[1] then we seek genetic or other factors that may explain the pattern.

A few fishes, such as the small, live-bearing Amazon molly (*Poecilia formosa*), reproduce asexually in that sperm and egg do not unite to form a zygote. Thus all Amazon mollies are females, and their eggs are stimulated to develop by simple contact with sperm of closely related sexually reproducing species.

- Is the Amazon molly a species in the true sense?

Unlike species, all other taxonomic categories, either lower or higher in rank, are subjectively delimited by degree of difference from other such groups. For example, **subspecies** are genetically determined geographic variants or races within a species, while **genera, families, orders,** and so on, are groups of similar and presumably related species. Human beings—usually the variety called *scientist*—decide the limits, say, of a genus or family, not the fish themselves. And since these limits are ultimately subjective, they may be reinterpreted and changed. For example, we may find a group of species once considered a single genus split into several genera, or several genera lumped into a single genus.

- If there were no human beings to classify them, would fish genera, families, orders, and so on, exist? Would fish species exist?

Nomenclatural Rules

The naming of taxa (**scientific nomenclature**) often follows various rules. The most rigid of these rules govern the naming of a species. The scientific name of a species consists of two parts, a genus name, in which the first letter is

---

1. Recall that we use the plural *fishes* to emphasize more than one species, while the plural *fish* simply means more than one individual, no matter what species. For example, one would do a taxonomic analysis of the fishes of California but would ask how many fish were caught on a party boat.

always capitalized, and a species name, in which the first letter is never capitalized. Both names are italicized. For example, *Perca flavescens* is the common yellow perch that inhabits lakes and streams in the midwestern United States. Sometimes you will see the name written as *Perca flavescens* (Mitchill 1814). This tells us that the species was first described by an ichthyologist named Mitchill in a publication issued in the year 1814. The parentheses indicate that Mitchill had named the species in a genus other than *Perca*; thus, the name we now use for the species is a new combination compared to what appeared in the original description published in 1814. Although other names have mistakenly been proposed for the same species, we use *flavescens* because it was the first published; thus it has priority. If there is confusion as to whether two published names and descriptions refer to the same species or not, ichthyologists often visit museums to examine the **type specimens**, which are typical fish representing the **nominal species** or species named in the original descriptions. If the type specimens of both nominal species are judged to be of the same species, the earliest published name is declared the correct name of the single valid species, and the later-published nominal species is called a **junior synonym**.

• In 1818, Rafinesque described common yellow perch from Lake Erie and named them *Perca notata*. Is this the correct (valid) name of the species?

Fish species are classified into progressively larger taxa containing species that share unique sets of characteristics. *Perca flavescens* is a taxon in the taxonomic category of species. This species, in turn, is a member of a larger taxon, *Perca*, which is the category of genus and contains other species that resemble *Perca flavescens*, such as *Perca fluviatilis*, the European perch. Thus, classification is hierarchical, with genera classified into families (Percidae), families into orders (Perciformes), orders into classes (Osteichthyes), and classes into phyla (Chordata). Note that all family names have the suffix *-idae*, and fish orders have the suffix *-iformes*. Also the prefixes *sub* and *super* are used to insert taxonomic categories at intermediate levels. For example, our yellow perch is classified in the suborder Percoidei and in the superorder Teleostei. Unfortunately, ichthyologists often differ about the definitions of higher classifications of fishes.

Classification thus involves the study of relationships among fish species and groups of related species. As such, it has a long history. Carolus Linnaeus's *Systema Naturae*, published in 1758, marked the official beginning of the organized and scientific naming of species and higher categories. No name published before 1758 is recognized and so cannot have priority. But Linnaeus believed that species were created once and fixed in time. He did not consider variability within species, and a type specimen represented the assumed uniformity of characteristics. Hence,

classification was simply a process of grouping similar species together by arbitrarily weighted characters without considering their evolutionary relationships. With the publication of his remarkable *Origin of Species* in 1859, Charles Darwin introduced the dimension of time into biological thought and systematics. This sped replacement of Linnaeus's typological concept with the present dynamic concept of evolving species made up of populations of interbreeding individuals, which vary among themselves in **genotypic** (genes) and **phenotypic** (physical expression of genes) characteristics. For the modern systematist, this meant replacing the concept of typology or uniformity and the reliance on type specimens with the concept of variability and the importance of statistical samples.

Multiplicity of Scientific Names

Several objective reasons explain why a species might have been called by different names. Remember that the valid name of a species or genus is the first one published along with a description, diagnosis, illustration, type locality (where collected), and deposition of at least one type specimen. (Older names still have priority if they are backed up by little more than a brief description and type specimen.) But the original name may have been overlooked, especially if published in an obscure journal missed by most bibliographic aids. If the biological species is discovered anew and redescribed, the later name is then mistakenly used unless the earlier name is uncovered by a thorough reviser. If this happens, the later name becomes a **junior objective synonym** to be replaced by the **senior objective synonym** (valid name) which has priority. Or, by mistake, two or more identical names may be proposed for different genera or for different species in the same genus. Among these (objective) homonyms, the first published or **senior homonym** is the valid name of the taxon to which it is then applied; thus all **junior homonyms** used for other taxa described later must be replaced with different names. A genus name is unique. Hence if an ichthyologist gives a new genus of fishes a name that has already been used for another genus of animals in any phylum, this name becomes a junior homonym and must be changed.

Scientific names are also changed for subjective reasons. Concepts of what makes up a species or genus change as the animal group in question becomes better known. Fish once believed to be in a single genus or species may later turn out to comprise more than one. When this happens, all the species in the original heterogeneous group except the one that best fits the original description and matches the type specimen must be renamed. Taxonomists also develop new ideas as to the relationships among species. Thus these authorities may shift species from one genus to another, creating new combinations of genus and species names. In this case, the latest or **senior subjective synonym** is valid, and earlier combinations lose status as junior synonyms. Despite the obvious potential for taxonomic machinations, we like to believe that name changes are due less to egocentricity and obfuscation and more to scientific progress and growing knowledge about the fish we study.

• Distinguish between objective and subjective reasons for changing scientific names. Give some good reasons for subjective changes.

• One on-again off-again rule of animal nomenclature states that a senior objective synonym that has not appeared in the literature for 50 years may be discarded in favor of a well-known junior synonym. Does this tend to stabilize or destabilize nomenclature? Do you prefer the current case-by-case legislation by the International Zoological Commission to protect "time-honored" names from preemption by obscure senior synonyms?

• Why must a genus name be unique to one animal group?

Synonymies

A **synonymy** is an annotated list of published scientific names (synonyms) that taxonomists have given a single valid genus or species. It serves as a brief nomenclatural history of the taxon. Though scientific names are meant to stabilize nomenclature, they nevertheless change, much to the consternation of nontaxonomists who simply want to know what to call a fish. Therefore, each account of a previously described genus or species in a taxonomic revision includes a synonymy that determines the status of each name. This assures that the names will not be misapplied in the future.

Anyone working with a fish species—whether studying its population, ecology, feeding, age and growth, or physiology—needs to know what to call it and therefore needs to be able to track its synonymy. For many, these are already published, but for others, the work remains to be done. To help you through this often tedious and confusing process, we have compiled made-up generic and specific synonymies to illustrate how it is done. The synonymy for the genus *Bassus* follows:

Bassus Jones

Crassus Smith, 1864: 102 (type species *Perchus macrocephalus* Guttstrain, by original designation).

Bassus Jones, 1899: 76 (substitute name for *Crassus* Brown, 1851, which is preoccupied by a genus of insects).

Here we find that a new genus requires a **type species**, just as a new species has its type specimens. Type species are designated either explicitly or implicitly. If, as above, more than one species are originally placed in the genus, the "most typical" of the lot is selected as type by **original designation**. But if only one species is placed in it, then the

species is automatically the implied type by **monotypy**, no matter how many other species may be added by later revisers.

The generic synonymy also tells us that *Bassus* is the valid genus name because the first name *Crassus* had already been used for (i.e., was *preoccupied* by) another genus of animals. The page number of the account follows its date of publication, leaving the full citation for a reference or literature-cited section.

An example of a species synonymy in this genus, written by the latest reviser, follows:

Bassus macrocephalus (Guttstrain)

Perchus macrocephalus Guttstrain, 1862: 86-87 (original description; illustration; type locality: Lake Torpid, Mississippi).

Crassus macrocephalus. Smith, 1864: 102 (type species of new genus; comparisons with congeners and with *Perchus* species).

Bassus macrocephalus. Jones, 1899: 76-77 (new genus name for preoccupied *Crassus*).

Massus macrocephalus. McGonigle, 1910: 364 (new combination; comparisons with *Massus* species).

Bassus guttstraini. White, 1952: 10-13 (original description; illustration; type locality: Red River, Florida).

This tells us that someone named Guttstrain originally described the species *macrocephalus* from specimens (types) collected out of a lake in Mississippi. Then along came Smith, who thought that the species was different enough from other fishes in the genus *Perchus* that it and its look-alikes warranted their own genus, *Crassus*. But later, Jones realized that *Crassus* was preoccupied. So he substituted the unique name *Bassus* for this genus of fishes distinct from *Perchus*. McGonigle, on the other hand, decided that *macrocephalus* resembled species in a third genus *Massus* and transferred the species accordingly. The latest reviser who composed this synonymy disagreed with McGonigle. He concluded that the valid binomen is *Bassus macrocephalus*; that is, that *macrocephalus* is indeed a bona fide member of the genus *Bassus* of Jones. To further complicate matters, White described the new species *Bassus guttstraini* from a collection made in a Florida river. She named the new species honoring the memory of Guttstrain who pioneered the study of *Bassus*-like fishes. However, our latest reviser could find no differences between type specimens of *macrocephalus* and *guttstraini* and so concluded that the nominal species *guttstraini* was merely a junior synonym of the valid species *macrocephalus*. Nonetheless, the name of the author of this species, Guttstrain, is in parentheses because he originally described the species under another genus.

• Given the natural variability among individuals of a single species, is the designation of one specimen to be a **holotype** of the species worthwhile? Why not simply declare all or more of the specimens at hand for the species' original description to be **paratypes** and be done with it?

• In describing a wide-ranging species, why is it still a good idea to specify a type locality?

Exercise: Compilation of Synonymy

Compile a complete species synonymy for your favorite local fish. Look up as much of the taxonomic literature dealing with your species and its close relatives as possible. Start with recent faunal works covering fishes of your geographic area, where you should find references to the original description and, perhaps, a recent revision of the group to which your species belongs. If you are lucky enough to find your species treated in an up-to-date and thorough revision, many of the essential inquiries have already been made. The species account should include a synonymy, which reduces your problem to interpreting the synonymy and updating the nomenclatural history with more recent references.

Consult general bibliographies if need be. For example, the *Zoological Record*, published annually by the Zoological Society of London (1864-date), references species names in its Subject Index of Part Pisces. To see if the genus name was preoccupied before 1935, check in S. A. Neave's (1939-1940) *Nomenclator Zoologicus*, which lists all names of genera described earlier. Prepared annually by the American Museum of Natural History, the *Dean Bibliography of Fishes* (Atz 1971, 1973) indexes many recent references. Try to find a reference to "synonymy" under the family and species of your fish. This compendium updates the original *Bibliography of Fishes* by Bashford Dean (1916-1923). The American Fisheries Society's *List of Common and Scientific Names of Fishes from the United States and Canada* (Robins et al. 1980) gives names that are currently recognized as valid, along with nomenclatural footnotes.

Write your own synonymy formally as an annotated list of names as in the earlier made-up example; then translate it in a paragraph or two. Some of the following questions may confront you:

1. Who first named and described the species?
2. What are the diagnostic characters of the species?
3. Who later renamed the species and why?
4. Where are the type specimens deposited?
5. On how many specimens was the original description based, and do they seem to represent the species well?
6. Is there a good, detailed illustration of a type specimen?
7. Is the species common now, and are specimens readily available for comparison?
8. Where were the original specimens collected?
9. What is the present range of the species?
10. Is the nominal species a valid one and why?
11. Is there any reason to believe that the species actually consists of more than one?

TAXONOMIC KEYS

A taxonomic key is an **algorithm**: a set of rules or steps to be followed in sequence for solving a problem. The problem here is to identify a fish specimen. Steps to follow are sequenced observations of key characters on the specimen; the result of each observation specifies which alternative paths lead to the next observation. The goal is to identify the specimen by following the correct path to its end point. Using a taxonomic key is something like playing the old parlor game of 20 questions to identify some unknown object that the person being questioned has in mind. With each yes or no answer, questioners eliminate increasingly large sets until, by this process of elimination, only the object itself remains. In using a fish key, however, the "object" is an unknown fish specimen and the "questions" are contrasting statements about conditions (states) of key characters.

For the particular specimen, each statement must be found either true or false, which definitely excludes a subset of taxa to which the specimen does not belong. The statement must be unambiguous. Take, for example, "Anal soft rays many." This is an unsatisfactory statement because it defies definite judgment. Many, relative to what? one would ask. On the other hand, look at, "Anal soft rays more than 20." This is unambiguous because it can be verified or denied with certainty by counting fin rays accurately. If a step specifies a single character to be observed, the character must, with a true or false decision as to its state, eliminate all (or just about all) individuals in the set of excluded taxa. This leaves all individuals of the specimen's taxon together with others of the included set. If, for example, females of a species had twice as many anal rays as males, "Anal soft rays more than 20" becomes ambiguous unless the statement is qualified as to whether it refers to males or females. Keys may specify observations on more than one character per alternative. For example, "Anal soft rays more than 20; eye diameter less than 25 percent head length." This provides further information as fail-safe. The order of characters implies that the count of soft anal rays is perhaps the better (more reliable) of the two characters, but if anal rays are damaged or missing, a decision based on eye diameter will probably not lead you astray.

Kinds

For unequivocal pathfinding, a taxonomic key should be **dichotomous**. This means that it should have no more than two alternative statements about contrasting states of a key character per step or observation. Then if one alternative is false, the next step is specified automatically, and the direction of the path is clear. Dichotomous keys usually fall into two categories: indented and bracketed. An indented key places the set of all included taxa under one alternative and all excluded taxa under the other. For example:

A. Anal soft rays more than 20
    B. Total gill rakers on first arch fewer than 15; head length more than 30 percent SL
        Bassus macrocephalus
    BB. Total gill rakers on first arch more than 20; head length less than 25 percent SL
        Bassus microcephalus
AA. Anal soft rays fewer than 18
    B. Side of body with large black spots, no stripes
        Perchus nigromaculosus
    BB. Side of body with thin black stripes, no spots
        Perchus nigrofasciatus

Indented keys have the advantage that similar taxa are set off together. But long keys are hard to follow because they have initial contrasts located far apart, and they also waste page space since they have progressively longer indentations.

Bracketed keys are more commonly used for identifying fish. Long keys are relatively easy to use and save space; alternatives are placed together as couplets, and statements are not indented. For example:

1a. Anal soft rays more than 20 2
1b. Anal soft rays fewer than 18 3
2a(1a). Total gill rakers on first arch fewer than 15; head length more than 30 percent SL
2b. Total gill rakers on first arch more than 20; head length less than 25 percent SL
        Bassus microcephalus
3a(1b). Side of body with large black spots, no stripes
        Perchus nigromaculosus
3b. Side of body with thin black stripes, no spots
        Perchus nigrofasciatus

Notice that you can backtrack if you take the wrong path. Alternative "A" of all couplets except the first refers back (in parentheses) to the preceding step. Unfortunately, many bracketed keys lack this provision.

Most fish keys are made primarily for identifying specimens along the easiest and quickest path possible. Nonetheless, they may reflect phylogenetic classification by having closely related species near each other wherever the utilitarian purpose is not compromised. For example, species in the same genus (**congeners**) are usually together because they are readily distinguishable as a group from noncongeners. Such keys that are based on easily observed external characters showing clear-cut differences and that do not necessarily reflect phylogenetic order are called

artificial. Many characters—for example, internal skeletal characters—used to measure phylogenetic relationship are not easily observed and so are not good key characters. It follows that **phylogenetic keys**, which group taxa strictly by their presumed phylogenetic relationship, become difficult to use as internal characters obstruct the path. Phylogenetic keys are usually indented.

• What is the difference, if any, between *good character* and *key character*? Would a key character used in distinguishing families necessarily be a key character for identifying taxa within a family?

Exercise: Construction of a Key

The best way to learn how keys are made and used is to do one yourself. This requires making time-consuming observations on several specimens of each taxon to be represented, then sifting through the observations to find the useful, clearly diagnostic characters. To save time, you can use all the information gathered by a group or else by yourself on numerous specimens or gleaned from species descriptions in a detailed taxonomic work already published.

Once you have a data base, systematize it so that all but key characters can be culled and the hierarchies of inclusive sets of taxa are revealed. A good beginning is to tabulate characters by species. On a large ruled sheet of paper, prepare a matrix of observations with species as rows and characters as columns. Then begin to fill in the cells of the matrix with ranges of values for the observations. Add all the data available and continue by adjusting ranges and so on until the matrix is complete (see Table 7.1).

Eliminate characters that are not key characters. Looking down the columns in Table 7.1, we quickly eliminate the anal-spines character because its value is constant. Similarly, scales along lateral line and eye diameter have overlapping ranges and provide no clear-cut distinctions. Alternative statements based on position of mouth, upper-jaw teeth shape, and shape of body color would be ambiguous. For example, we must agonize over what the difference is between a "terminal" and "slightly superior" position of mouth or between "simple pointed" and "slightly blunt" shapes of upper-jaw teeth. This leaves four key characters useful to arrange the taxa into exclusive sets.

Paths to identification are shortened by finding any key characters that initially segregate the taxa into two mutually exclusive sets of equal or near equal sizes. This saves steps along the path because about half the taxa and steps would be eliminated at the outset. Find such characters by examining the columns of your matrix, one by one, and marking equal or overlapping states. Use a different mark for each different state (checks, crosses, and so on). Then, if a character has all values marked in one way or another and near-

Table 7.1 Characters tabulated by species.

	Anal Spines	Soft Rays	Scales Along Lateral Line	Total Gill Rakers on first Arch	Head Length (Percent SL)	Eye Diameter (Percent) SL)	Position of Mouth	Upper-Jaw Teeth Shape	Shape of Body Back-ground Cover	Pattern of Body Color
1. *Bassis macrocephalus*	III	21–25	58–63	12–14	32–36	7–10	Terminal	Simple pointed	Light	Mottled darkish
2. *B. microcephalus*	III	23–27	57–62	21–23	21–24	8–10	Terminal	Slightly blunt	Light silvery	Mottled black
3. *Perchus nigromaculatus*	III	15–18	55–60	20–22	31–34	6–9	Slightly superior	Some pointed, some blunt	Light	Distinct black spots
4. *P. nigrofasciatus*	III	14–16	54–59	21–23	27–31	7–10	Terminal	Simple pointed stripes	Light	Distinct thin black

equal numbers of, say, check marks and cross marks, it is a good candidate for the first couplet.

In the example given, only anal soft rays, total gill rakers on first arch, head length, and pattern of body color remain as useful key characters. Anal soft rays (first column) has check marks for species 1 and 2, which have relatively high counts, and cross marks for species 3 and 4, which have low counts. Clearly, this character segregates the species into two equal groups as it does in the first couplet of the above keys. Total gill rakers on first arch distinguishes only species 1 and 2 in couplet two of the bracketed key. At first glance, head length also seems to segregate species into two equal groups: species 1 and 3 with relatively large heads, and 2 and 4 with small heads. However, the difference between 3 and 4 is not clear-cut. Furthermore, setting these groups off violates the rule of following phylogenetic order wherever possible; difference in head length does not distinguish the two pairs of congeners. Head length, therefore, is used to distinguish species 1 and 2 in couplet two. Although pattern of body color may distinguish species 1 and 2 from the others, the profusion of terms—mottling, spotting, darkish, and black—adds little useful information to couplet one. Spots versus stripes in black, which is the most durable color in preserved specimens, is better used as an easy-to-see difference between congeners 3 and 4.

Another strategy of making keys puts couplets identifying bizarre, quickly distinguishable species at the beginning, leaving the most similar species for more tortuous pondering at the last. If species 1 in the example had no pelvic fins, it could be identified at a glance in a first couplet:

1a. Pelvic fins absent . . . . *Bassus macrocephalus*
1b. Pelvic fins present 2

In effect, this eliminates one species from the ponderables and so speeds the way down the first part of the path and minimizes early mistakes that could lead us to a completely wrong trail.

In effect, this eliminates one species from the ponderables, and so speeds the way down the first part of the path and minimizes early mistakes that could lead us to a completely wrong trail.

Now you can write a bracketed artificial key to the species in your list. Once you know the key characters and the species they distinguish, the actual construction is easy. If several species are involved, however, it may help to somehow arrange groups by their key characters, as shown in figure 7.1.

Write statements for each couplet in telegraphic style, eliminating articles and verbs whenever possible. A couplet's contrasting statements should always be parallel: that is, all words and their order should be the same except for the one or two words that give distinction: fewer versus more, more versus less, large spots versus thin stripes, and so on. When finished, compare your key with either a published one or one prepared by another group, and use it to key out the available specimens of the included species.

• Which key works the best and why? Be objective in your appraisal.

Checking Identification

A taxonomic key is merely a shortcut that does away with the necessity of reading page after page of description or groping through jar after jar of smelly preserved fish in reference collections. All identifications from keys, therefore, should be double checked in one way or another.

One way to do this is to compare the collection locality and characteristics of the specimen with distributions, descriptions, and pictures in published monographs and faunal works. If the geographic distribution (range) of the presumed species excludes the locality where the specimen was collected, then the identification is probably wrong and

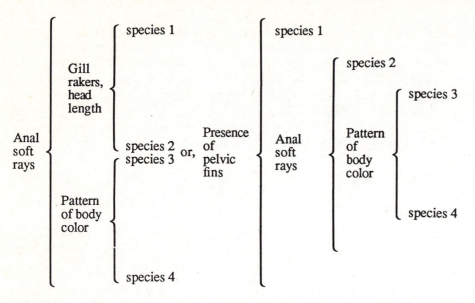

Figure 7.1 Key arranged according to key characters. Brackets indicate where key characters separate species or species groups.

an agonizing reappraisal of the keying out is required. In checking descriptions, you may have difficulty interpreting highly technical monographs (revisions of families or genera). Instead, many faunal works provide briefer, more easily interpretable descriptions accompanied by ranges and pictures, often in color. A disadvantage of faunal works is that their coverage is usually limited to a particular region. Since literally hundreds of such works deal with just about all marine and freshwater regions of the world, a comprehensive listing is beyond the scope of this manual. Your public and academic libraries should contain faunal references for your area. A few examples of comprehensive faunal works include Hubbs and Lagler (1958), Sterba (1962), Liem and Scott (1966), Böhlke and Chaplin (1968), Hart (1971), Hildebrand and Schroeder (1972), Miller and Lea (1972), Moyle (1976), Thomson et al. (1979), and Eschmeyer et al. (1983).

Technical monographs, revisions, and papers describing new species are even more numerous. If you must check your specimen with its presumed original description, you can find the reference in a revision of the family. One heroic attempt at publishing differently authored technical revisions of families and higher taxa of an entire fauna is *Fishes of the Western North Atlantic*, published by the Sears Foundation for Marine Research, New Haven, Connecticut, beginning in 1948. To date, this literary crusade has grown to eight volumes, with several thousand pages of descriptions, statistics, distributional maps, keys, and technical discussions.

Another check is to compare the characteristics of your specimen with identified fish in a **reference collection** (see sect. 3). A reference collection's main purpose is to facilitate determinations. Most species in a good reference collection are represented by a series of individuals of different sizes. Therefore, you can compare your specimen with known fish of about the same growth stage. If it does not match any in the series, try a similar species.

• Almost no key is perfect; most keys are corrected and amended with each new revision of the taxon. Why is this so?

• Some publications give a variety of keys to the same group of related species: a key to larvae and perhaps two others for adults—one for freshly caught fish, the other for preserved specimens. Why these different keys? Can you think of any other keys to these species that could be added? How could two of these keys, say, be combined into one? Is it possible for a species (or family) to come out at more than one end point of a key?

Exercise: Identifying a Collection of Local Fishes

With your newly acquired expertise, help identify species in a collection, perhaps made during a group field trip. First sort the collection to what you think are species—all the different kinds of fish you can recognize. Segregate individuals by kind into trays containing some water to keep the fish moist. Reexamine each specimen to make sure that segregated lots do not contain more than one species.

Key out a representative specimen to its family in a preliminary key, then "run it down" to species in a key to local fishes. Recall that a taxonomic key is already a shortcut to identification. Do not skip couplets or, in this first try, start at the end and work backward. Read both statements of the couplet carefully before you decide on the path; assuming that your specimen is not a novelty, you should find it fits one or the other mutually exclusive alternatives. Be sure you understand each key character and what its contrasting states are. Nothing is more frustrating than blundering down the wrong path by rationalizing poor decisions. "Well, let's say that it does anyway," are the famous last words of incorrect keying. If possible, examine more than one specimen before making a decision, because individual fish may be damaged or abnormal. Also, fish of the same species vary within character states, and extremes may exceed the limits to values stated in an alternative. No key is perfect. Keys evolve to more complete accuracy as mistakes and inconsistencies are uncovered through more and more use. Expect some difficulties, and never give up in frustration.

Check your result. Compare the fish you have keyed out with descriptions and pictures of its presumed species and with an identified series of reference specimens. Remember to establish that its capture locality is within the known range of the species. Finally, check with an authority. If you erred, you need not start at the key's beginning. Carefully checking alternatives, work character by character from the false species name backward to the point where you took the wrong turn and correct your path.

When you are sure of the identification, write the species name, collection number, locality, date, and your name and today's date in pencil on a suitable label. Bottle the identified series of fish in preservative together with the correct label.

• Say that you reach a particular couplet in a bracketed key and find to your dismay that your specimen fits neither alternative. List several possible reasons for this and their remedies.

• You find that your fish has one more lateral-line scale than the maximum "permitted" in a key. Otherwise, it is a perfect match with the species arrived at and closely resembles pictures and voucher specimens. Do you immediately conclude that you have found a species new to science? If not, give an alternative explanation for the high scale count, assuming that it is correct.

Chapter 8
Character Trends and Morphological Variation

So far we have only used characters in a determinate sense; that is, key characters were simply involved in yes-or-no and does-or-does-not decisions. Except by implication, we did not treat characters as vectors showing trends of values within as well as between species. In this chapter we analyze morphological characters as variables whose values may differ from fish to fish as well as from one group of fish to another. We must describe samples of values in terms not only of a measure of central tendency or "norm" but also of a measure of variation of values (due to individual differences and other "sources of error") about this norm. This information provides the insight needed to judge from arrays of character values whether or not actual samples represent different fish populations. Furthermore, it is obviously best to make such judgments with a known degree of confidence. To accomplish this, an analysis of morphological variation requires a basic knowledge of descriptive and inferential statistics. Do not be alarmed, however; the example we describe is limited to a relatively simple, straightforward graphical representation of variation.

You might ask, Why bother? Counting and measuring enough good characters to provide a sufficient statistical sample from each of several localities can, indeed, be quite a job. We bother because an analysis of character variability is fundamental to systematic study. The process of speciation and its genetic basis imply that not only do fish vary in their genetic makeup between species but they also vary within the same species. Samples showing values of good characters express this variation. Thus we recognize species and distinct populations within species by analyzing geographic trends in morphological variation from, say, one drainage system, lake, coastal area, ocean basin, or climatic zone to another. Different "shapes" of trends suggest different kinds of genetically determined groups. For instance, geographically distinct (allopatric) **subspecies** intergrade in characters at the margins of their ranges and make up one **polytypic species**; allopatric **semispecies** cannot intergrade, are each good species in their own right, and comprise a **superspecies**; and geographically overlapping or coinciding **sympatric species** do not intergrade and make up a **species group**.

In this chapter you learn to use simple statistical procedures to infer morphological properties of fish populations from samples of character values. Each value is a measurement from an individual fish. You can then interpret differences in these properties in terms of genetic discontinuities. The statistical methods are largely from Sokal and Rohlf (1981).

VARIABLES

Morphological characters such as counts and measurements are variables. A variable is a set of values that describes a given attribute. Each value is an individual measurement expressed as a single number. For instance, 34.3, 32.6, and 35.1 might be three values of the variable "head length." Thus variables are properties through which individual fish in a sample are observed to differ in some quantifiable way.

Accuracy and Precision

To consider these components of measurement reliability, first recall that body measurements are continuous variables even though any single value seems discrete because it is approximate. Here is an example: Suppose you were sufficiently sure-handed to measure the head length of your fish to the nearest 0.1 mm, and you obtained a value of 34.3. This value may look like a measurement of a discrete variable because it is recorded to one decimal place, but this apparent "discreteness" only reflects the limit of accuracy (closeness to a true value) of your measuring method. You have reason to believe that your measurement was accurate to one decimal place but not to two (e.g., 34.32) or to three (34.321). Thus the single decimal (.3) implies the degree of precision (ability to repeatedly obtain the same value) to which the measurement was made. Or, in another sense, it implies that on a scale of measurements there are upper and lower limits between which the true value presumably lies. These implied limits are 34.25 and 34.35, extending one more decimal place than the recorded value. You simply assume that any measurement error is confined to the interval between these limits. Your measurement was simply the most accurate you could make, with any degree of precision, of a truly continuous variable.

Discrete variables such as fin-ray counts, of course, have no implied limits. You can achieve complete accuracy and precision in counting fin rays as long as you are careful and do not overlook an element. (Theoretically, statistical procedures differ for treating discrete and continuous variables. But in practice, as you will see later on, these procedures need not differ when applied to taxonomic data.)

• How could you determine if your measurements were precise enough to warrant your recording them to the nearest 0.1 mm?

Sources of Error

Recall the problem with scaling a measurement to correct for the fish's body size (chap. 6): Automatically there is greater latitude for error. This is because you compound measurement error between numerator and denominator of the derived ratio. You have as an example the value of 34.3 mm with implied limits of 34.25 and 34.35 for head length. Say you obtained a value of 102.7 mm with limits of 102.65 and 102.75 for the standard length of your fish. Hence the implied limits of the derived ratio of head length to standard length (34.3/102.7 = 0.334) are 34.25/102.75 (0.333) and 34.35/102.65 (0.335). Although the maximum error would be only 0.15 percent (34.35 - 34.3/34.3 x 100) for the original measurement of head length, it would be 0.30 percent (0.335 - 0.334/0.334 x 100), or twice as great, for the ratio.[1]

Well, an error of only 1/3 of a percent does not sound significant, does it? Actually it is not. It is unrealistically low. As an example of the natural world, the scattergram in figure 6.1 indicates that the observed difference between largest and smallest values of percent eye diameter (measured to 0.01 mm) is more than 20 percent for adult fish of this particular species. Yet calculations like those in the previous paragraph show "maximum error" to be only 0.25 percent, almost two orders of magnitude less. Perhaps the assumed measurement accuracies of 0.01 mm for eye diameter and 0.1 mm for standard length were too optimistic.

More likely, most of the observed "error" in the original measurements as compounded in the derived percents was beyond our control. Specimens differ in their state of preservation so that parts can be distorted. Even more im-

portant are natural morphological differences between individual fish, each of which has a unique genotype and environmental-nutritional history. Thus discrete variables reflect this natural individual variability as well.

This is why **random variables** do in fact vary, and we must treat them statistically. We can estimate a "true" value so long as "errors" from all sources are as likely to be in one direction as the other.

• What are the various sources of error in taking measurements or making counts on fish specimens?
• Which would be the more accurate representation of the head length in a fish species: head length expressed as a proportion of standard length and averaged over a series of young to adult individuals or a plot of head length versus standard length for these same individuals?

INFERENCES FROM SAMPLES

Samples and Populations

A sample is a set of **variates** (values of a variable) collected in some specified way. A **statistical population** (or, simply, population) is made up of the total possible variates. In systematics, the statistical population usually consists of all possible values of a character, one per every individual organism in a particular, genetically distinct **biological population**. To exemplify these and other concepts, we select data from a taxonomic study (by Collette et al. 1978) of Spanish mackerels, which are large (60 cm long), fast-swimming predatory fish species of tropical American coastal waters. One sample from this study is a set of 34 counts of total gill rakers on the fish's left first gill arch, made from 34 sierra mackerel (*Scomberomorus sierra*) collected from along the Pacific coast of Central and South America (table 8.1). Hence, **sample size** (*n*) is 34. The (statistical) population sampled consists of gill-raker counts from all subadult and adult sierra mackerel living in this area, which comprise the presumed biological population, may number in the billions, and of course can never be enumerated, let alone observed. As you see, the size of most statistical populations in taxonomy is effectively infinite so a calculation from a sample (or **statistic**), such as an average, is not fixed and can easily be known, but a calculation from a population (or **parameter**) is fixed and usually cannot be known (i.e., is theoretical).

• Say you have 64 goldfish in an aquarium. If you removed all 64 fish, counted gill rakers, and calculated an average, would the average be a statistic or a parameter?
• A jar contains 100 fish of the same species. You tag each one with a number from 1 to 100, then select only the even numbers for counts of lateral-line scales. Would the counts so obtained constitute a random sample?

---

1.   Also, ratios present some statistical problems, which we will discuss later. Yet body proportions derived from ratios are themselves continuous variables and are the best single measures to correct for size (i.e., they measure "shape"). Alternatively, as suggested in chapter 6, a **bivariate analysis** (analysis of the relation between the two original variables) can be made for each morphometric character.

Table 8.1 Frequency tabulation of gill-raker counts making up three samples from presumably different biological populations in two species of Spanish mackerel (*Scomberomorus*).

Species and Geographic Population	11	12	13	14	15	16	17	18	Sample Size
Scomberomorus sierra (E. Pacific)									
Mexico			4	10	10	8	1		33
Central and South America			1	5	14	12	2		34
S. maculatus (W. Atlantic)	2	7	16	6	2	1			34

Adapted from Collette et al. (1978)

Ideally, samples should be **random**: Each variate should have an equal chance of being observed so that no bias toward selecting certain values in preference to others can occur. In the Spanish mackerel study, total sample randomization would require that each fish in the area have an equal chance of being selected for the gill-raker count. Obviously, this is impossible. As in most taxonomic studies, fish—which occur nonrandomly to begin with—were collected in different ways as opportunities arose. Hence, we simply assume that the sample is representative and not misleadingly biased: There is no good reason to believe that fish were selected for their gill-raker number, and there was about equal chance of finding large values as well as small values among the fish at hand. This assumption seems reasonable, as we show later.

Frequency Distribution and Probability

Of course, the sample as a whole contains no more information than is in the *n* variate values. Yet statistics allow us to realize these data in a way that takes us beyond the scope of the sample to make educated guesses about values of population parameters. Statistics also provide a measure of just how good these guesses may be.

To do this, statisticians have developed ways to deal with the variability of values in a sample. If the observations are random so that an equal chance of finding both high values and low values exists, then the sizes of values should fluctuate above and below a "true value," which can be defined and estimated. A fluctuation of specified amount occurs with a particular chance or **probability**. In table 8.1, for example, counts of as few as 13 or as many as 17 gill rakers in sierra mackerels appear less probable than a count of 14. This can be seen by plotting the frequencies of each count in table 8.1 as a **histogram** (fig. 8.1). The heights of the bars represent the frequencies (numbers of times observed) of the different variate values. Imagine now that the histogram represents the frequency distribution of a continuous, rather than discrete, variable. We convert the histogram to a smooth curve by connecting the tops of the

bars as shown in figure 8.1. The percentage of the area curve between any two vertical lines gives the relative frequency of the range of values between the lines. With the total area under the curve set at 100 percent, the **relative frequency** is the best and least biased guess you can make from the sample as to the probability (chance) that a count taken at random would be within the range of values. Statistically speaking, the relative frequency of an "event" (e.g., count) is used to estimate the event's probability. The distribution indicates, for instance, that the best guess you can make is that there is about a 91 percent chance (31/34 x 100) of a sierra mackerel chosen at random having 14, 15, or 16 gill rakers on its first arch.

Ideally, the smoothed curve is bell shaped and approaches a "normal" frequency distribution. The **normal distribution** is basic to a considerable body of statistics because its areas are theoretically known and tabulated. Therefore we can determine the probability of selecting particular values of a random variable. It has been shown that any variable whose different values are responses to the actions of many factors is likely to be a random variable with a normal distribution. Even though normal distributions describe continuous variables, a discrete variable like a gill-raker count can, in a sense, be treated as though normally distributed because its expression is under complex control. There is good reason to believe that underlying factors—such as the actions of gene complexes and developmental processes that cause individual variation in counts—are really continuous even though they are ultimately expressed in discrete "morphological packages."

Descriptive Sample Statistics

Since sample distributions of random variables have similar shapes, we can describe them with just a couple of calculations from the samples (statistics). The **mean** (average) locates the center of the distribution. The **variance** measures the dispersion of values about the mean. Just as the frequencies of sample values provided the best way to guess what the frequencies of values in the sampled population might be, the mean and variance of these sample values are the best estimates we can make of what the unknowable

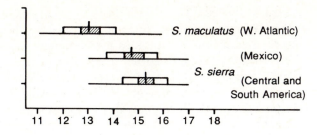

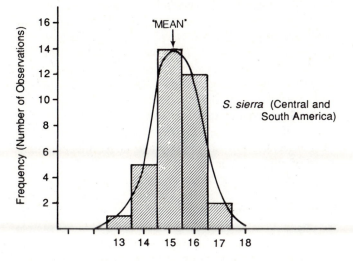

Figure 8.1 Graphical analysis of samples of gill-raker counts from Spanish mackerel. Upper graph is of Dice-diagrams showing sample range (horizontal line), mean (vertical line), one standard deviation on either side of mean (open bar), and t standard errors on either side of mean (hatched bar). Thus, nonoverlapping hatched bars indicate that there is only a 5 percent chance or less of the two means being from samples of the same population (see text). Lower graph is a frequency histogram (hatched vertical bars) of gill-raker counts describing a sample from one population. Areas under the smooth curve estimate the probabilities of counting the included numbers of rakers (see text).

mean and variance (parameters) of the population might be.

The mean is the sum of all sample values divided by the set sample size. The mean is written in mathematical short-hand as

$$\bar{x} = \frac{1}{n} \sum_{i=1}^{n} x_i$$

The symbol $\bar{x}$ stands for mean, and n represents sample size. The large Σ, which is capital sigma in Greek, is a summation sign, meaning add up a series of numbers. The subscripted symbol x_i stands for the ith number (value of variate) to be added; thus the complete summation,

$$\sum_{i=1}^{n} x_i$$

means the sum of the first ($i = 1$) through n values of the variable x. The prefix $1/n$ means that this sum should be divided by the sample size to obtain the mean. The mean gill-raker count (table 8.1, row 2)

$$\left(\frac{1}{34} \sum_{i=1}^{n=34} x_i \right)$$

is $[(1 \times 13) + (5 \times 14) + (14 \times 15) + (12 \times 16) + (2 \times 17)]/34 = 519/34 = 15.26$.

The variance is something like an average of squared deviations about the mean and is represented as:

$$s^2 = \frac{1}{n-1} \sum_{i=1}^{n} (x_i - \bar{x})^2$$

The symbol s^2 stands for variance, and the other symbols are the same as those used in representing the mean. Since variances calculated from small samples (size less than 100) tend to underestimate population variance, the sum is divided by $n - 1$ instead of the sample size n in order to obtain the best unbiased estimate of the population statistic. The value of $n - 1$ is called *degrees of freedom* and equals the sample size minus the number of previous constraints imposed on a statistic. The previous constraint on the variance was the calculation of the mean, which fixes the location. To undo the effects of squaring deviations from the mean, dispersion is often expressed as the square root of the variance, which is called the **standard deviation** (s). If you use a hand calculator, an algebraic rearrangement of the variance formula saves computational time:

$$s^2 = \frac{1}{n-1} \left[\sum_{i=1}^{n} x_i^2 - \frac{\left(\sum_{i=1}^{n} x_i \right)^2}{n} \right]$$

Here the first term in the bracketed expression means the sum of each variate value squared; in the gill-raker example, this would be $(1 \times 13^2) + (5 \times 14^2) + (14 \times 15^2) + (12 \times 16^2) + (2 \times 17^2) = 7949$. The second term is the square of the sum of values, divided by sample size: $(519)^2/34 = 7922.382$. Thus, variance is $(7949 - 7922.382)/(34 - 1) = 0.807$, and standard deviation is $\sqrt{0.807} = 0.898$.

• Suppose you tried to calculate the variance of gill-raker counts from a random sample of sierra mackerel but forgot to square each deviation from the mean. What would you expect the resulting value to be?

Since the shape of the frequency distribution is presumed to be normal, the percentage of variate values that should fall within certain numbers of standard deviations about the mean has been calculated. For instance, 68 percent of the values should lie within one s on either side of the mean, while 95 percent should lie within $1.96s$'s. Thus in our sample of 34 gill-raker counts with a mean of 15.26 and an s of 0.898, 68 percent should lie within 14.36 (15.26 - .898) and 16.16 (15.26 + .898), and 95 percent should lie between 13.5 [15.26 - (1.96 x 0.898)] and 17.0 [15.26 + (1.96 x 0.898)]. But this is difficult to judge because the counts are discrete. About all we can say is that between 68 and 95 percent of the counts should have values of 14, 15, or 16.

We can use these descriptive statistics—mean and standard deviation—to summarize the properties of a sample. Yet this tells us little about the reliability of these as estimates of population parameters. With what amount of confidence can we use the sample mean to estimate the unknown population mean?

Confidence Interval of the Mean

We judge the reliability of the sample mean by calculating its **confidence limits**, which allow us to be 95 percent certain that a specified range of values will contain the population mean. (This "95 percent certainty" is an arbitrary level of probability but is accepted by most ichthyologists and other biologists.)

To find confidence limits, we first calculate the **standard error** of the sample mean. Much as the variate values themselves, the sample means are also distributed randomly with a deviation called the standard error. It can be shown algebraically, furthermore, that the sample estimate of standard error (se) is simply $s/\sqrt{n}$, where s is the sample standard deviation and n is sample size. Thus the standard error indicates the most probable or frequent values of sample means, just as the standard deviation indicates the most probable or frequent of the individual variate values. Note that as n decreases, standard error increases; smaller samples have larger standard errors.

Probability areas (relative frequencies) under each curve, one for each sample size (actually degrees of freedom, n - 1), have been tabulated as in table 12 of Rohlf and Sokal (1981). These curves are called student's t-distributions, and curves based on smaller samples are flatter than those for larger samples because standard errors for smaller samples are larger than those for larger samples from the same population. Consequently, the central interval defining 95 percent of the area under the curves for smaller samples will be relatively larger. The t table shows that for degrees of freedom equaling, say, 10 (sample size 11), 95 percent of the curve area falls within an interval of 2.228 standard errors on either side of the mean. But for degrees of freedom equaling 30 (sample size 31), 95 percent falls within only 2.042 se's of the mean. The numbers 2.228 and 2.042

are called t values. To calculate the 95 percent confidence interval of a sample mean, first find the row of t values for the degrees of freedom specified by the sample size, then the particular t value listed under the column headed by 0.05. The number 0.05 (1.0 - 0.95) is the proportion of area in the "tails" of the particular t distribution laying outside the central 95 percent. Multiply this t value by the sample standard error. The interval extends from a lower limit (L_1), obtained by subtracting the result from the sample mean, to an upper limit (L_2), obtained by adding the result to the sample mean. In our gill-raker example, standard error ($s/\sqrt{n}$) is $0.898/\sqrt{34} = 0.139$. The value of t95 percent is 2.036 for 33 (34 − 1) degrees of freedom. Thus the 95 percent limits are L_1 = 15.26 (x) - (2.036 x 0.139) = 14.997; and L_2 = 15.26 + (2.036 x 0.139) = 15.543. From this, we can be 95 percent certain that this interval (14.997 – 15.543) covers the true mean. Or, stated another way, 19 of 20 such intervals will on the average cover the population mean of gill-raker counts.

To reflect a bit, it makes common sense that we should have less confidence in the ability of a mean calculated from a small sample to accurately estimate a population parameter than in that of a mean from a large sample. Indeed, we have seen that the t component of a 95 percent confidence interval decreases by more than 8 percent when sample size is increased from 11 to 31. However, a further increase in sample size to about 120 gains a further decrease of only 3 percent. Except for the sustained decrease in magnitude of standard error, therefore, little is gained by collecting more than about 30 individuals per sample, especially if sampling effort and expense are relatively great.

In reports of sample statistics from a taxonomic study, the range, mean, standard deviation, and 95 percent confidence interval are often presented as a bar graph with a straight-line base spanning the range (smallest to largest variate value), a spike marking the mean, and bars delimiting standard deviation and 95 percent confidence interval. This allows a quick visual comparison of several samples, each from a possibly different biological population or species.

We can now interpret such so-called **Dice-diagrams** calculated from the Collette et al. Spanish mackerel data in table 8.1. In figure 8.1, three Dice-diagrams compare three samples, two of sierra mackerel (*Scomberomorus sierra*) from different areas of the eastern tropical Pacific and one of a closely related species (*S. maculatus*) from the western Atlantic Ocean. Of the two samples of sierra mackerel, we say that there is a better than 5 percent chance that both confidence intervals cover the same true population mean because the intervals overlap each other (i.e., the two intervals are most likely among the 95 percent that, on average, covers a single true mean). So, to be conservative, we conclude that the sample means are simply different estimates of the same population parameter and that the samples are from the same statistical population of gill-raker counts.[2] And with only this information, no good reason exists to believe that the fish are from different biological populations. For the sample of *S. maculatus*, on the other hand, there is less than 5 percent chance that the confidence interval covers the same population parameter covered by the intervals for sierra mackerel samples because the interval for *S. maculatus* does not overlap those for *S. sierra*. So here we conclude that the sample is from a different population. From barely overlapping standard deviations, we may also infer that most individuals of *S. maculatus* are distinguishable from most individuals of *S. sierra* by their gill-raker counts.

We emphasize that such inferences are inexact. They are not based on an accurate value of the probability (**P value**) that a **null hypothesis** of no difference between population means is correct. This requires a *t* test between two samples (footnote 2) or an **analysis of variance** among more than two. Only when such a test gives an exact probability of no difference can we infer that sample means do or do not differ **significantly**. Therefore, we have shied away from speaking of means as being "significantly different" or "not significantly different" from one another.

Statistics of Body Proportions

We have already mentioned some difficulties in analyzing morphometric variables expressed as proportions of fish standard length. Yet as with the original measurements, proportions and percentages are continuous variables so the way we analyze them statistically depends on whether they are distributed normally. Two opposing tendencies may cause body proportions to be normally distributed. If both numerator and denominator of a ratio are random variables but vary independently of one another, the ratio's frequency distribution tend to be flatter or more "squarish" than normal with many values occurring between mean and extremes. But when numerator varies with denominator, values tend to pile up in the middle classes so that the distribution is more peaked than normal. Thus body proportions tend to be normally distributed because the two effects may cancel each other out. Both numerator and denominator are random variables, and the numerator (particular measurement) invariably increases with the denominator (standard length).

The sample range of a proportion may be divided into **class intervals** and the distribution of proportions plotted as a **frequency histogram**, as though the variable were discrete (fig. 8.2). Then if the smoothed distribution appears bell shaped and normal, its mean, standard deviation, and confidence interval can be calculated as above. Even if not, however, the proportion can be transformed into angles and be analyzed statistically. An **angular transformation** compresses the middle of a squarish or flattened curve so that it is more nearly bell shaped. This transformation is called **arcsine**, which stands for the angle whose sine is the value of a body-proportion variate. As a general rule, if body proportions vary within the interval 30-70 percent, they need not be transformed to angles (see Sokal and Rohlf 1981).

Robert Gibb's (1961) taxonomic analysis of two closely related species of common freshwater shiner minnow provides data to exemplify Dice-diagrams comparing a measurement (body depth) expressed as a percent standard length (fig. 8.2). Body depth of these shiners is less than 30 percent standard length so we shall transform values to angles from Rohlf and Sokal's (1981) table 5. An observed value of 22 percent corresponds to an angle 27.97°, 24 percent to 29.33°, 25 percent to 30.00°, and so on. Histograms in figure 8.2 show sample distributions of percentages on the left and of angles (whose values are larger than the percentages) on the right. Note that the sample of bluntface shiner (*Notropis camurus*) from the Arkansas River already has a bell-shaped distribution of percent body depth so the transformation does little. However, the sample from the lower Mississippi River appears irregular and flattened, and transformation compresses the middle to a bell shape.

Inferences from the Dice-diagrams follow the same logic as those for Spanish mackerel gill-raker counts. For the bluntfaced shiner, we conclude that the two body-depth samples are from the same statistical population. Thus this single character provides no evidence that the two samples are from taxonomically different biological populations. For the whitetail shiner, *Notropis galacturus*, however, chances of both confidence intervals covering the same statistical-population mean are less than 1/20 so the two samples probably represent two different biological populations, assuming that body depth is a genetically based character.

---

2.   Comparison of 95 percent confidence intervals is not a true test of the difference between two means, which is usually performed as a *t* test. Means may differ significantly (at the 5 percent probability level) by *t* test even though their 95 percent confidence intervals overlap. Less frequently, means with non- or barely overlapping intervals do not differ significantly. Yet you can apply rules of thumb to the interpretation of confidence intervals with some assurance (Simpson et al. 1960): (1) if the confidence interval of one sample covers the observed mean of a second sample, the two means do not differ significantly by *t* test (i.e., we conclude that they are merely different estimates of the true mean of a single population); (2) if intervals from two samples overlap, but if the interval from one does not cover the mean of the second sample, the means may or may not differ significantly; but (3) if the two intervals do not overlap, the means differ significantly, especially if the intervals are about the same length (or if the shorter of the two is arbitrarily lengthened to equal the longer).

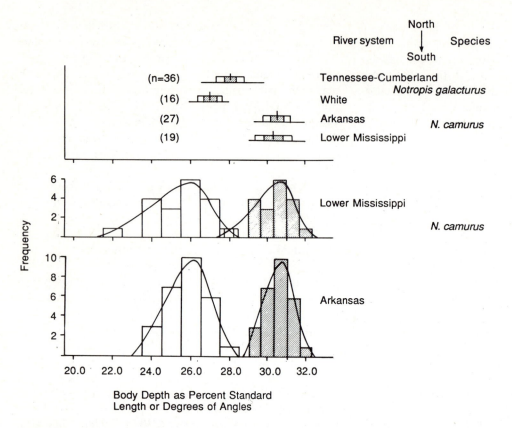

Figure 8.2 Graphical analysis of samples of arcsine-transformed body-depth proportions from shiner minnows of the midwestern United States. Upper graph is of Dice-diagrams showing sample statistics (see fig. 8.1) with sample size in parentheses. Lower graphs are frequency histograms describing samples from two populations of one species; open bars are frequencies of class intervals of body depth expressed as percent standard length; hatched bars are for these values transformed to angles by arcsine to make the smooth curves describing probability densities more "normal" in shape (see text). Note that the upper curve is skewed to the left so the arcsine transformation helps quite a bit. (Adapted from Gibbs 1961, table 4)

INTERPRETATION OF MORPHOLOGICAL VARIATION

The study of fish species and biological populations within species concerns geographic variation and its meaning. Distinguishing valid species from geographical populations of the same species usually begins by studying variability of good characters among samples, perhaps using Dice-diagrams.

Character variability often describes **clines**, which are directed changes in sample means of characters over a geographical range (fig. 8.3). An **even cline** describes gradual change without abrupt discontinuities between ranges of gradual change. Genetically based clines in character means reflect an evolutionary response, by means of natural selection, to geographically varying environmental factors such as temperature. This is shown by frequent correlation between clines in morphological characters (**morphoclines**) and clines in **allelic frequencies**, as indicated by electrophoretically determined enzyme variants (e.g., Buth and Mayden 1981). Thus significant dif-

ferences between means of geographic samples suggest that the samples are from different, taxonomically recognizable biological populations.

But what suggests that a step in a cline actually distinguishes different species? This requires a bit of deductive reasoning. Given that members of one species usually do not or cannot mate successfully with members of the other, there is little genetic exchange between the two. It follows that few, if any, **hybrids** occur between the two species. That is, there are few, if any, individuals with intermediate genotypes. Now if we make a big jump and assume that such **genetic nonintergradation** implies phenotypic or, more explicitly, **morphological nonintergradation**, we assume that two species differ in some characters whose sample ranges of variation do not or almost do not overlap. In particular, then, we predict that the two species of shiner minnows referred to in figure 8.2 are distinguishable by some such characters. Indeed, as diagrammed in figure 8.2, probably just about all individuals of *Notropis camurus* in the Arkansas River system have relatively deeper bodies than White River individuals, even though the river systems

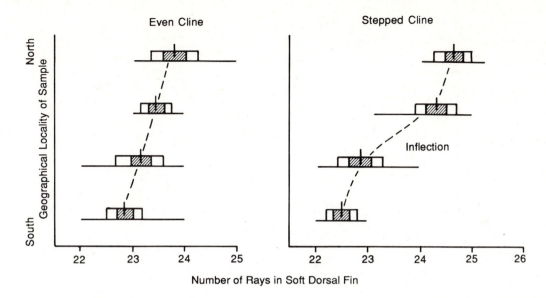

Figure 8.3 Even and stepped clines of geographic variation in numbers of anal-fin rays, as shown in Dice-diagram analyses of hypothetical samples. Figures 8.1 and 8.2 and the text explain Dice-diagrams. The text discusses the taxonomic significance of clines and inflections in clines.

are adjacent and include only areas where the ranges of the two species overlap. Furthermore, the original analysis showed that the two species are completely distinguishable by differences in scale counts so our prediction is corroborated.

Data selected and simplified from George W. Barlow's (1961b, 1963) extensive study of the genus of mudsucker fishes *Gillichthys* exemplifies clines and species characters (fig. 8.4). The longjaw mudsucker, *Gillichthys mirabilis*, inhabits coastal sloughs and estuaries along the North American Pacific coast from central California to southern Baja California, Mexico, and along most of the Gulf of California. Its only **congener** (member of the same genus), *G. seta*, however, inhabits just the rocky intertidal areas of the northern Gulf of California. Samples of anal-ray counts from *G. mirabilis* describe a more or less even north-south cline of variation along the Pacific coast, from slightly higher counts in California to slightly lower counts in southern Baja California. Gulf samples reveal a similar, though nonsignificant, trend. Based on this one character, it is difficult to say whether the clines reflect genetic differences among populations or **ecophenotypic** differences, wherein the number of anal-fin rays is directly influenced by the environment—perhaps water temperature—during a critical period in the fish's larval development. In the original analysis, however, **concordant variation** in other characters suggests that the morphocline has a genetic basis, and so *G. mirabilis* may be a **polytypic species**. The anal-ray count is also a good species character: Predictably, therefore, there is little if any overlap in this character between *G. seta*, which has relatively few anal rays, and *G. mirabilis*. Other characters in Barlow's original analysis

substantiate the morphological distinctness of the two. *G. seta* also occupies a different habitat and shows certain different physiological adaptations (Barlow 1963). Hence, all evidence indicates that *mirabilis* and *seta* make up a **species group** of the two species that are sympatric in the north Gulf of California.

EXERCISE: VARIATIONAL STUDY

This exercise incorporates much of the technique and theory described in this chapter and in chapter 6: finding and measuring morphological characters, then treating them as continuous variables for statistical analysis and inference, and finally interpreting the results in terms of other characters, genetic isolation, and speciation theory.

If adequate samples are available, this can be a cooperative group exercise. Assign groups of people to measuring characters on different subsets of fish from the samples. If fish samples are unavailable, however, original counts and measurements from a previous study are given in table 8.2. This eliminates the necessity for preliminary handling of fish as well as observing the variates; each person can complete a statistical analysis of the data and biological interpretation of the outcome. Without fish, therefore, go directly to the section titled Analyze Statistically on page 117.

Study Material

Collect or otherwise acquire at least three or four samples of 20 to 30 fish each from populations in different geo-

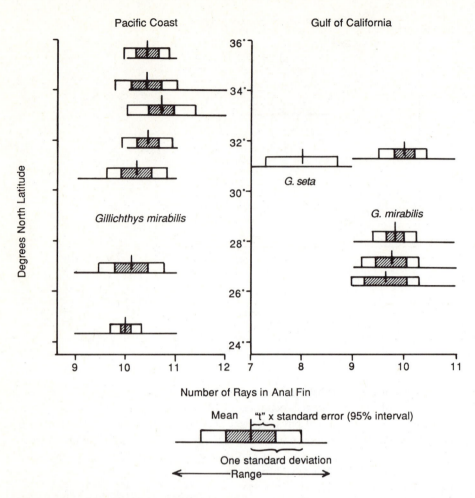

Figure 8.4 Geographic variation in numbers of anal-fin rays in mudsucker fishes of the genus *Gillichthys*. (Data for *G. mirabilis* selected and adapted from Barlow 1963, fig. 7; those for *G. seta*, from Barlow 1961b)

graphical localities. Samples may be of marine fish from different oceanic or coastal areas, of freshwater fish from different river or lake systems, or of intertidal or estuarine fish from different coastal areas. Some samples may be from the same general area: for example, from the headwaters and mouth of the same river or stream, from either side of a point of land, or from an island and its adjacent mainland. One or more samples may be of a different species that resembles the first. Fish should be preserved in alcohol for easy handling (see sect. 3).

Because the exercise involves considerable observation and recording of data, work should be shared among study groups of three or four people each. Follow these procedures to prepare the samples for cooperative observations:

1. Distribute the intact samples among the study groups.
2. Tag each fish with a letter or number identifying its particular sample. Mark tags with soft lead pencil or indelible ink that does not run in alcohol and secure firmly with string or thread to the fish's caudal pe-

duncle. Alternatively, mark narrow slivers of paper and push them through the gill cavity so that the unmarked end protrudes out the fish's mouth and the marked, wider end is displayed behind the gill slit. Tags should be of high-quality rag paper or cardboard that does not deteriorate in preservative.

Find Good Characters

Many different characters should be measured on a few specimens from each sample to find potentially good characters—those likely to vary among the samples. Recall that characters which do not vary among the taxa and populations under study are not good, in the sense of distinguishing one taxon or population from another. Therefore, it is a waste of time to measure any characters that lack promise of being good distinguishers.

1. Choose two larger specimens in good condition from each sample and distribute them among the teams so

Table 8.2. Data for laboratory exercise in assessing morphological variation: Selected body measurements and gill-raker counts for geographically separated samples of individuals of deep-sea fish of the genus *Scopelogadus* in the beryciform family Melamphaidae (see Ebeling and Weed 1963). Such individuals are small, black, soft-bodied fish that live in the cold, dark mid-depths of the open ocean in roughly the same depth interval hundreds or even thousands of meters below the surface. Individuals in all samples resemble one another, superficially at least. All measurements are to the nearest 0.1 mm. Standard lengths (SL) and sex (if known) of specimens precede columns for body depth (BD), head length (HL), suborbital width (SW), and total gill rakers on first arch (GR).

Sample 1: Atlantic Ocean, between 40°N and 20°S Latitudes

SL	(Sex)	BD	HL	SW	GR
82.0	(f)	21.0	31.7	4.9	24
84.0	(f)	20.8	32.0	5.3	24
62.9	(f)	17.2	23.5	3.4	23
75.0	(f)	21.7	29.4	4.4	24
71.5	(f)	18.8	25.1	3.4	24
75.0	(f)	19.4	29.5	3.6	23
49.0	(m)	11.8	19.1	2.5	24
40.8	(f)	10.4	14.5	2.1	23
53.6	(m)	13.5	20.5	2.7	24
67.5	(f)	16.5	25.6	4.3	24
72.6	(f)	17.5	27.9	3.9	24
68.3	(f)	17.9	27.1	3.9	24
48.4		12.8	19.0	3.1	24
82.5	(f)	21.0	31.8	4.9	24
56.9	(f)	15.4	20.9	2.5	24
59.5	(f)	15.0	21.7	2.8	22
56.1	(f)	14.0	21.2	3.0	23
55.9		12.3	20.0	2.8	26
63.0	(m)	15.5	24.2	3.7	24
71.0	(m)	18.8	27.7	4.8	24
61.2	(f)	15.7	21.8	3.0	24
56.3	(m)	14.9	21.8	3.3	23
61.5	(m)	16.1	22.8	3.3	24
55.8	(f)	13.1	21.4	2.8	25
51.1	(m)	13.4	18.5	2.7	25
52.4		13.1	19.1	2.5	24
57.6	(m)	14.9	21.6	3.0	22
57.0	(f)	14.7	21.6	3.0	25
30.3		8.7	12.3	2.5	22
28.4		9.0	13.0	2.9	23
23.2		7.0	8.9	2.2	22
21.6		5.8	7.5	1.6	22

Sample 2: Indian Ocean and Western Tropical Pacific Ocean (Indo-Pacific Region)

SL	(Sex)	BD	HL	SW	GR
70.5	(f)	18.8	27.1	3.8	23
66.4	(m)	17.9	25.6	3.7	23
80.4	(f)	20.0	30.7	4.6	23
68.0	(m)	17.4	24.5	3.5	23
92.0	(f)	24.2	38.4	4.8	23
86.6	(f)	22.5	34.5	4.6	23
91.4	(f)	23.4	34.0	4.3	23
93.7	(f)	24.1	36.1	4.9	23
51.2	(m)	14.0	18.5	3.7	23
50.0	(f)	11.6	17.2	3.4	24
85.3	(f)	24.5	28.0	4.5	24
92.0	(f)	23.0	36.0	5.1	22
59.1	(m)	15.2	23.0	3.1	23
67.2	(f)	18.0	25.9	4.3	23
57.0	(m)	16.0	19.9	3.4	24
61.0	(m)	15.6	22.0	4.2	23
52.2	(f)	14.3	20.5	3.0	24
47.0		11.6	17.2	3.2	24
44.8		23.9	16.6	2.8	21
48.9	(m)	13.0	19.7	3.7	22
46.1	(f)	12.0	17.0	3.1	23
44.0	(m)	10.0	16.2	3.0	23
44.0	(f)	10.1	16.0	2.8	24
33.4		8.6	13.6	2.0	24
29.8		8.0	10.6	1.8	22
37.3		9.8	14.0	2.5	24
38.2		9.8	14.0	2.1	22
29.3		7.5	13.0	1.6	23
25.0		7.3	10.0	1.8	23
21.5		6.5	8.3	1.2	23

Sample 3: Indo-Pacific Region (same as sample 2). All individuals in this sample have only one spine in the dorsal fin; all individuals in all other samples have two spines.

SL	(Sex)	BD	HL	SW	GR
83.5	(f)	29.8	33.1	7.4	26
93.5	(m)	32.0	35.2	6.7	28
82.8	(f)	29.7	31.0	7.0	28
85.4	(f)	24.1	30.1	5.8	29
84.7	(m)	24.2	31.2	5.9	29
87.6	(f)	26.4	31.0	6.3	27
88.5	(m)	22.9	30.5	5.8	28
81.9	(m)	21.9	29.8	5.7	28
95.3	(f)	31.6	37.0	6.7	26
84.0	(m)	27.2	30.8	6.4	26
85.0	(m)	27.9	34.5	6.2	25
69.7	(m)	19.1	25.5	4.6	26

Sample 4: Central Tropical Pacific Ocean between 2 and 20°N Latitudes, and West of 100°W Longitude

SL	(Sex)	BD	HL	SW	GR
41.2	(f)	25.3	38.2	5.6	25
81.2	(f)	23.6	35.0	5.5	26
86.0	(m)	24.0	33.2	6.2	23
102.0	(f)	29.5	37.2	6.5	25
53.0		14.5	20.6	3.8	25
73.1	(f)	20.5	28.0	5.0	26
59.0	(f)	16.7	24.0	4.4	23
54.4	(f)	14.9	21.2	3.5	22
78.2	(m)	23.0	32.0	5.9	23
70.3	(f)	18.5	28.9	4.5	27
57.1	(m)	15.0	22.0	3.4	23
55.2	(f)	15.0	24.2	4.2	22

Table 8.2 *Continued*

SL	(Sex)	BD	HL	SW	GR		SL	(Sex)	BD	HL	SW	GR
91.5	(m)	30.5	35.1	6.6	25		41.0		10.4	19.0	2.7	21
61.2		16.1	22.7	4.5	25		42.4		12.0	18.0	3.1	22
83.3		22.7	32.9	6.2	27		74.2	(f)	23.0	33.6	5.9	22
86.3		22.8	31.0	6.0	27		47.2	(f)	13.6	20.4	3.7	23
80.6		20.7	29.1	5.5	27		40.2	(m)	10.8	17.5	3.0	22
60.3		16.2	22.0	4.2	26		44.8		11.8	21.8	3.9	22
82.2		20.3	28.7	5.7	26		59.5	(f)	16.8	27.0	4.5	22
80.0		21.2	29.7	6.9	28		51.5	(f)	13.5	23.5	3.7	24
85.3		23.6	31.7	7.2	26		54.2	(m)	15.4	25.2	3.9	21
78.3		20.4	28.9	5.3	25		52.5	(f)	13.3	23.8	4.0	23
49.9		12.7	19.7	3.5	27		47.2	(m)	13.0	21.8	3.7	22
86.0		27.8	31.1	7.0	25		63.5	(f)	16.6	28.5	4.8	21
21.7		6.0	9.0	1.4	27		63.0	(f)	17.5	27.5	4.6	22
20.7		5.8	8.9	1.6	26		54.0	(m)	15.0	25.0	3.4	24
19.9		5.7	8.7	1.4	25		33.2		9.5	14.8	2.4	22
19.8		5.6	9.0	1.5	25		29.4		8.9	12.1	2.4	22
19.8		5.5	8.7	1.3	27		28.6		7.5	11.9	2.7	24
							27.7		7.7	11.9	2.0	23
14.7		4.0	7.1	1.1	25		67.5		18.8	28.0	4.5	24

Sample 5: Eastern Tropical Pacific Ocean between 2 and 20°N Latitudes and East of 100°W Longitude	Sample 6: Eastern North Pacific Ocean North of 20°N Latitude and East of 130°W Longitude

SL	(Sex)	BD	HL	SW	GR		SL	(Sex)	BD	HL	SW	GR
95.0	(f)	31.8	43.1	6.7	24		73.5	(f)	22.0	31.0	3.9	25
78.5	(m)	21.1	30.4	5.6	24		80.0	(f)	24.0	35.0	3.9	24
74.1	(m)	20.1	28.2	5.5	23		71.8	(f)	23.4	30.8	3.6	25
60.8	(f)	19.0	25.6	4.6	22		72.0	(f)	20.9	30.1	5.0	25
60.0	(f)	16.8	26.0	4.2	23		71.1	(m)	21.0	29.4	4.6	24
48.2	(f)	14.3	20.0	3.4	24		71.5	(f)	23.0	29.6	4.7	23
48.8	(f)	14.1	20.0	3.3	23		90.7	(f)	25.4	35.9	5.8	26
46.0	(m)	10.8	19.1	3.1	24		86.1		24.0	33.3	5.7	23
43.3	(m)	11.2	16.0	3.1	23		65.2	(m)	19.1	28.1	4.3	24
64.0	(f)	18.4	25.8	4.3	23		57.2		14.4	24.0	3.7	24
55.3	(m)	15.5	22.7	4.0	24		55.2		15.5	22.4	3.1	24
47.1	(f)	12.6	17.1	3.6	24		62.0	(f)	15.8	25.2	3.4	24
60.7	(f)	18.2	23.4	4.6	24		67.8		18.6	27.2	4.7	24
54.3	(f)	15.8	23.0	3.4	22		59.9	(m)	15.5	23.5	3.6	23
62.2	(f)	18.0	25.9	4.3	23		76.5	(f)	22.3	31.1	4.8	26
48.0	(f)	13.2	18.0	3.6	24		74.4	(f)	20.5	32.0	4.4	25
47.2	(m)	12.1	18.8	3.4	23		75.5	(f)	21.3	32.6	4.7	24
42.0	(m)	11.0	16.2	3.1	23		62.3		17.5	26.5	3.5	24
60.5	(f)	18.0	25.2	5.2	24		66.0		17.4	27.0	4.0	26
57.3	(f)	16.4	21.0	4.0	22		58.0		14.7	22.8	4.2	24
53.7	(m)	16.0	22.0	3.7	24		63.0	(f)	17.6	25.0	4.3	23
43.0	(m)	10.1	18.3	3.4	23		69.0	(f)	19.0	28.2	4.5	24
63.5	(f)	19.7	25.2	4.6	23		62.8	(f)	18.2	25.1	4.0	22
66.7	(f)	20.2	27.5	4.8	23		62.1	(m)	17.8	24.9	3.9	24
57.8		17.5	22.9	3.6	22		53.4		14.2	21.5	3.5	24
59.3	(m)	16.5	22.2	3.9	23		84.0	(f)	23.0	34.0	5.6	25
61.0	(f)	19.1	25.8	4.6	22		77.8	(f)	21.9	32.0	4.9	24
35.8		9.8	14.5	2.7	24		51.2	(m)	13.4	22.2	3.3	23
37.2		10.0	14.5	2.3	24		37.2		9.8	15.7	2.2	22
23.6		6.5	11.0	1.8	24		49.0		13.1	21.0	3.4	24
30.2		9.6	12.2	2.4	22		36.9		10.0	14.6	2.4	24
23.3		6.0	9.1	1.8	23		32.8		9.8	12.9	1.9	24
28.0		8.0	12.0	2.2	23							
19.0		6.0	7.8	1.6	23							
20.0		6.3	8.5	1.8	22							
19.4		6.1	8.2	1.8	23							

that no team has both specimens. This eliminates any team bias in measuring the variates.

2. Observe a standard array of 30 to 50 characters on these specimens. Use those listed in table 6.1 and defined in chapter 6, or make up your own list by deleting any that do not initially appear promising and adding others that look different when you compare specimens. To find characters that initially look different, align specimens, one from each sample, in a dissecting tray and subjectively compare by simply looking at them. Pass the tray among the groups so that everyone has a chance to test her or his eye for differences. When the list of characters is decided, distribute the labor of observing and recording values among team members. One member can make a few measurements, while another records; later other members can take their places.

3. After measuring and recording the long list of characters on the few typical specimens, assemble the data, recorded on one sheet per fish, by sample. Then convert any morphometric measurements to proportions or percentages of standard length, and calculate average values for two fish, say, per sample.

4. Compare the arrays of character averages, one array per sample, and note the characters that differ most noticeably between arrays. These are the characters most likely to be good.

5. If possible, sex the specimens to make sure differences are not sexual dimorphisms (see sect. 3, chap. 14). By chance, two females may have been selected from one sample and two males from another.

6. Depending on time available for the project, select two or more of the presumably good characters showing the most marked differences. Ideally, this subset will include counts and morphometric measurements.

7. Record values of these good characters measured from all fish in all samples. Set up data sheets as in table 8.2, and pass out samples and data sheets among teams to minimize bias. For example, one team could measure the first five specimens in sample 1 and then pass the sample and data sheet to another team, which measures the second five, and so forth. Continue until all specimens in all samples are observed and all data sheets, one per sample, are completed.

Analyze Statistically

If you observed actual specimens, use the data sheets you completed. If not, use the original data from a taxonomic analysis of a genus of deep-sea fishes as tabulated in table 8.2. Calculate sample statistics as described on pages 108–111.

1. Express all measurements as a percent or proportion of the standard length.

2. Plot body proportions versus standard length, as in figure 6.1, to see if growth is allometric. If, for example, relatively small fish have disproportionately large heads, and head length is a good character, sample size should be reduced to include only the values to the right of the growth inflection (i.e., the values from the larger specimens).

3. Using table 5 in Rohlf and Sokal (1981), transform the proportions to angles by arcsine if required, that is, if most values are less than 30 percent or more than 70 percent.

4. Calculate sample mean, standard deviation, and standard error of the mean for each variable (character). Look up the value of t (Rohlf and Sokal 1969; table Q) for the sample degrees of freedom ($n - 1$), and determine the 95 percent confidence limits of the mean.

5. Plot Dice-diagrams, representing sample statistics for each character. As in figures 8.1 to 8.4, include sample range, one standard deviation on either side of the mean, and t times the standard error about the mean.

Interpret Results

Interpret your Dice-diagrams, which can be compiled by team members and duplicated for the whole group, in terms of theory presented earlier in this chapter. Write up the variational study in proper scientific format, using recent journals as examples. Consider the following questions:

• Are the samples probably from different statistical populations?
• Is clinical variation indicated?
• Do morphological gaps indicate a stepped cline?
• Are differences great enough to suggest stoppage of gene flow between biological populations? That is, does morphological nonintergradation indicate genetic nonintergradation? Are the samples of more than one species?
• Do other characters corroborate the hypothesis that samples are from more than one biological population or species?
• If there is morphological evidence that samples represent more than one species, can predictions be tested to confirm this hypothesis? Different species may overlap in geographic range (be sympatric) with little hybridization. Sympatric species occupy different habitats or microhabitats.

Chapter 9
Shared Characters and Classification

By now you should be convinced that, taxonomically speaking, we can look at a fish as an assembly of good characters to be used for different purposes. In chapter 7 we used characters in a determinate sense as key characters to identify individuals. Yet as we found in chapter 8, the same characters may be used statistically as variables to identify populations. Now we return once more to using characters in a determinate sense, but here we do so for classification rather than identification.

As best we can, we construct a **phylogenetic classification** based on how characters differ between fish species and groups of species. A phylogenetic classification is an evolutionary hypothesis. It suggests that species or groups of species classified together are more closely related genealogically to each other than they are to any other taxa. Together they form a **monophyletic group**, all ultimately derived from a single (hypothetical) species called a **common ancestor**. Various ways exist to construct classifications interpretable as phylogenetic. Some have a more concrete theoretical framework than others and so have a more definite set of rules to follow. For this exercise, it is easiest to follow definite rules without exceptions. Therefore, we use a method of **phylogenetic systematics** (see Wiley 1981) to assemble a **cladogram** suggesting relationships among taxa in a fish family. It is true that many ichthyologists use more "traditional" methods for phylogenetic classification. Nevertheless, the method of inferring a phylogenetic tree from a cladogram is gaining favor.

CLADOGRAM

A cladogram is a branching diagram (dendrogram) in which species or other taxa are linked by sharing one or more characters in a unique state or condition. "Alternative X" in figure 9.1 exemplifies a cladogram that links four taxa (A-D) into monophyletic groups by means of their sharing three characters (1-3) in unique states. The uniqueness of the character state indicates that it is an evolutionary novelty (i.e., is **apomorphic**). This means that it has evolved (i.e., was derived) from a more ancestral (**plesiomorphic**)

condition found in related species outside the monophyletic group.[1] (In fig. 9.1 and thereafter, the plesiomorphic state is indicated by 0, the apomorphic state by 1.)

Each monophyletic group is defined by the presence of the same uniquely derived character states in all its members (**synapomorphies**) and typically consists of two **sister groups** or species. A fork in the cladogram represents the common ancestor of the two sister groups. In our example (fig. 9.1), B and CD are sister groups of a monophyletic group, defined by a synapomorphy in character 1, with hypothesized common ancestor B'. Within this assemblage, C and D are sister taxa of a more recent monophyletic group, defined by synapomorphies in characters 2 and 3, with common ancestor C'. The common ancestor is the hypothetical species from which the sister groups were derived sometime in the past. At that time, the common ancestor presumably gave rise to the forerunners of the sister species through the process of speciation, and when speciation was completed, the common ancestor necessarily ceased to exist.

Thus the cladogram example implies a phylogenetic classification based on a nested hierarchy of monophyletic groups. At the top of the hierarchy is a group A-D, consisting of subgroups A and B-D; then within group B-D are subgroups B and CD; at the bottom are C and D of CD. The classification might look something like this:

Families	A	B-D		
Genera		B	C-D	
Species			C	D

---

1. As defined by Willi Hennig (1966) a plesiomorphic character condition (state) is ancestral; an apomorphic state is derived. Thus, a **symplesiomorphy** is the presence of plesiomorphic character states (or, simply, characters) in different species or groups. Symplesiomorphies give little useful phylogenetic information because ancestral characters cannot determine monophyletic sister groups. A **synapomorphy**, the sharing of the apomorphic characters between different species, is phylogenetically more meaningful because it always determines sister groups. **Autapomorphic** characters are derived characters peculiar to (diagnostic of) a single species or group; they are unshared.

There is a distinction between a cladogram and a phylogenetic tree (Wiley 1981). Strictly speaking, a cladogram is only a construct wherein synapomorphies define branch points of a particular genealogical dendrogram. A phylogenetic tree has all evolutionary connotations and is a hypothesis of a historical sequence of speciational events. Hence, we may infer a phylogenetic tree from a cladogram.

• What assumptions should be made to deduce that a cladogram is a phylogenetic tree?
• How would you test a hypothesis of phylogenetic classification?
• In phylogenetic classifications of fishes, why are common ancestors always hypothetical? Can a living species ever be morphologically identical to a common ancestor?

CHARACTER TRANSFORMATION SERIES

An evolutionary transformation series, or simply a **transformation series**, is a pair or more of **homologous** character states ordered from ancestral (plesiomorphic) to derived (apomorphic) condition. Characters states are homologous if one is directly derived from the other by evolutionary modification. The plesiomorphic state is the original; the apomorphic state is an evolutionary novelty. (We will assume here that a character "never" reverts from derived to ancestral state.) In figure 9.1, therefore, an 0-1 pair of states for any of the three characters is a transformation series.

Nonhomologous character states cannot make up a transformation series because one is not the precursor of the other. Thus a nonhomology occurs when the same state is derived more than once in different common ancestors or derived independently in different branches from the same common ancestor. Say, for instance, that character 2 in figure 9.1 is body size of a fish and that the ancestral state is "large-bodied" (as defined by average adult standard length) and the derived state is "small-bodied." In alternative Y, there is a nonhomology in character 2 because small-bodiedness evolved independently in species C and D after they branched off from their common ancestor but not in species B. Alternative cladogram Z also requires a nonhomology in character 2 because small-bodiedness was derived independently in branches from two different common ancestors.

OUT-GROUP COMPARISONS

How do we know the direction, from ancestral to derived states, of the transformation series? We lack direct information because a suitable historical record showing the evolution of the group of fishes being classified almost

Taxon	Character		
	1	2	3
A	0	0	0
B	1	0	0
C	1	1	1
D	1	1	1

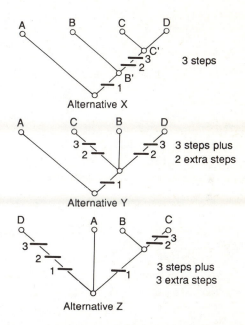

Figure 9.1 Finding the most parsimonious cladogram—the one with fewest steps or transformations from ancestral to derived character states—to classify four taxa (A-D) by three characters (1-3). First a character matrix orders taxa from presumed most ancestral (A) to most derived (D), based on increasingly larger groups of derived character states. Ancestral (plesiomorphic) states are indicated by 0; derived (apomorphic) states are signified by 1. As constructed from the character matrix, alternative cladogram X with the fewest steps (fewest nonhomologous characters) is the most parsimonious of the three (X-Z). See the text for further explanation.

never exists. Consequently we must usually infer the direction obliquely by making out-group comparisons. Typically, an **out-group** is the sister group of the taxon containing the species you want to classify. If the character occurs in two homologous states among species you are classifying, the state that also occurs in most or all members of the out-group is assumed to be the plesiomorphic one. It seems reasonable to suppose that the other state is apomorphic; that is, it arose as an evolutionary novelty in an ancestral species of your group.

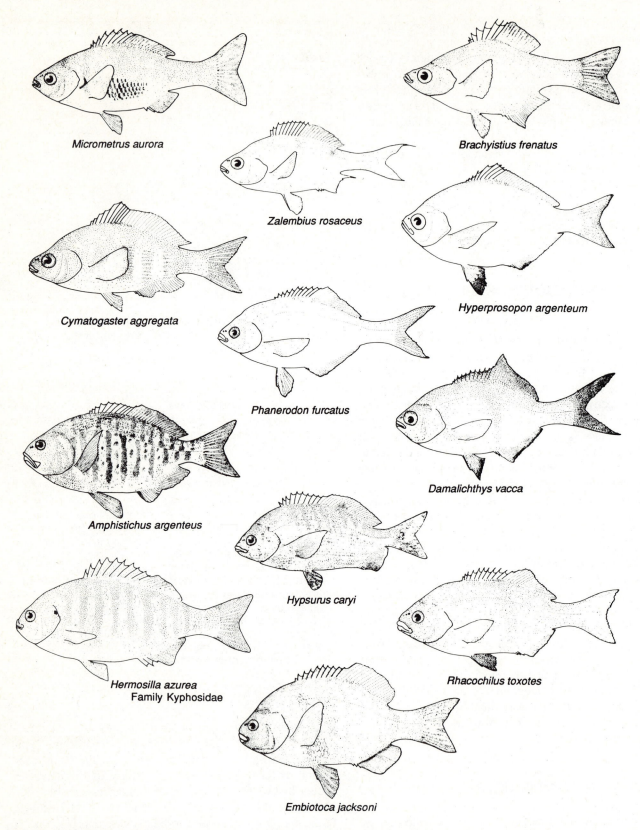

Micrometrus aurora

Brachyistius frenatus

Zalembius rosaceus

Cymatogaster aggregata

Hyperprosopon argenteum

Phanerodon furcatus

Amphistichus argenteus

Damalichthys vacca

Hypsurus caryi

Hermosilla azurea
Family Kyphosidae

Rhacochilus toxotes

Embiotoca jacksoni

Figure 9.2 Genera of surfperches to be classified phylogenetically by cladogram and a representative of the presumed sister family of rudderfishes. (Miller and Lea 1972)

As an example, let us assemble a cladogram for only the monophyletic group B-D of cladogram X in figure 9.1. You want to determine the direction of the transformation series for character 2, body size. Let species B be large-bodied, but let species C and D be small-bodied. This indicates two possibilities: Common ancestor B' was small-bodied so small-bodiedness is the ancestral state; or species B is apomorphic for body size, and C and D are symplesiomorphic for body size. Alternatively, B' was large-bodied and so C and D are synapomorphic for body size. To decide between the alternatives, let out-group A contain several species, all of which are large-bodied. Thus from out-group comparison, we accept the first alternative. Now the direction of character transformation is determined: Large-bodiedness is the plesiomorphic state.

MOST PARSIMONIOUS CLADOGRAM

A widely accepted rule is that the cladogram chosen should be the most parsimonious among possible alternatives: It should be the one assembled from the fewest evolutionary steps (transformations from ancestral to derived character states). This amounts to choosing the cladogram containing the fewest nonhomologies or extra steps. Of course no inherent biological reason indicates that species diversify from a common ancestor in the most parsimonious way. From our standpoint, however, the fewer the steps or transformations we must hypothesize, the fewer the ways we could be wrong.

Felsenstein (1982) reviewed and evaluated different "minimum evolution methods" of finding the most parsimonious cladogram. Of these, we will use a relatively simple and straightforward method invented by Camin and Sokal (1965). Figure 9.1 illustrates the most parsimonious assembly of a cladogram of four species (A-D) using three characters (1-3). In cladograms X-Z, "steps" are indicated by dark cross-lines numbered for each character. In alternative cladogram X, taxa B and CD are sister groups determined by a synapomorphy in character 1, and C and D are sister species by synapomorphies in characters 2 and 3. In alternative Y, however, C, B, and D are sister taxa of equal rank, all arising simultaneously in a trinary speciational event. Since B retains the ancestral states of characters 2 and 3 and since for this example we disallow reversions from derived to ancestral states, we assume that apomorphies were derived independently in lines evolving C and D. Similarly in alternative Z, apomorphies in character 1 evolved both in lines producing D and BC. Also apomorphies in characters 2 and 3 arose independently in two lineages (D and C), each from a different common ancestor. To sum up, we simply count steps. Clearly, alternative X with three steps and no nonhomologies (extra steps) is the most parsimonious. It has fewer constructs than

alternative Y with two added extra steps and fewer than Z with three extras.

- Review the rules for assembling "most parsimonious" cladograms: (1) Only synapomorphies (never symplesiomorphies) may be used to define monophyletic groups of sister taxa; (2) directions of transformation series (ancestral to derived character state) may be inferred from comparisons with out-groups; (3) among alternative cladograms, accept the one with fewest extra steps. Which rules have the most biological meaning?
- What subjective decisions must you make in constructing a phylogenetic tree for a group of fish taxa?
- Even the most parsimonious cladograms may include some extra steps. What factors might contribute to this, that is, the independent evolution of similar derived characters in different lineages?

EXERCISE: CLADOGRAM ASSEMBLY

You can now construct a most parsimonious cladogram to interpret as a hypothetical phylogeny of a monophyletic

Table 9.1 Ancestral and Derived States of Characters Used to Construct a Cladogram of the Genera of Surfperches (Embiotocidae). Direction of the evolutionary transformation series from ancestral (o) to derived (1) was determined by out-group comparison with the family's presumed sister group of rudderfishes (Kyphosidae).

Data are mostly from Tarp (1952).

1. Viviparity
   0. No
   1. Yes

2. Males with flask organ
   0. No
   1. Yes

3. Orbit without bony front wall
   0. Yes
   1. No

4. Caudal peduncle length
   0. Short
   1. Long (>18% SL)

5. Body depth
   0. Deep
   1. Narrow (<44% SL)

6. Body size
   0. Large
   1. Small (generally < 160mm SL)

7. Length of dorsal-fin base
   0. Long
   1. Short (generally < 45% SL)

8. Eye diameter
   0. Moderate
   1. Large (>8.9% SL)

9. Males with anal crescent
   0. No
   1. Yes

10. Cleithrum with process
    0. No
    1. Yes

11. Length of dorsal sheath
    0. Long
    1. Short (<70% dorsal base)

12. Body mostly darkish colored
    0. No
    1. Yes

13. Flanks with large black bars
    0. No
    1. Yes

Table 9.2 Character Matrix Ordering Surfperch Genera. These are data given relative to a representative of the surfperch's sister group of rudderfishes from more ancestral taxa (top) to more derived taxa (bottom) and based on groups of derived character states. As in table 9.1, ancestral (plesiomorphic) character states are signified by 0, and derived (apomorphic) states are indicated by 1. Across the top, characters are numbered as in table 9.2, where they are described.

Taxon	Character												
	1	2	3	4	5	6	7	8	9	10	11	12	13
Hermosilla (Kyphosidae)	0	0	0	0	0	0	0	0	0	0	0	0	0
Amphistichus	1	0	0	0	0	0	0	0	0	1	1	0	0
Hyperprosopon	1	0	0	0	0	1	0	1	0	1	1	0	0
Embiotoca	1	1	1	0	0	0	0	0	0	0	0	1	0
Hypsurus	1	1	1	0	0	0	0	0	0	0	0	1	0
Rhacochilus	1	1	1	1	1	0	0	0	0	0	0	0	1
Damalichthys	1	1	1	1	1	0	0	0	0	0	0	0	1
Phanerodon	1	1	1	1	1	0	0	0	0	0	0	0	0
Cymatogaster	1	1	1	1	1	1	0	0	0	0	0	0	0
Zalembius	1	1	1	1	1	1	1	1	0	0	0	0	0
Brachyistius	1	1	1	1	1	1	1	1	1	0	0	0	0
Micrometrus	1	1	1	1	1	1	1	1	1	0	0	0	0

group of fish taxa. We provide the taxa and transformation series of shared characters. Just proceed by drawing branches and marking steps to yield the fewest extra steps, using the information supplied in a character matrix.

Taxa for this exercise are 11 genera of marine fishes in the viviparous surfperch family Embiotocidae, whose females give birth to relatively well-developed young, resembling miniature adults in shape, color, and general behavior. For out-group comparisons, we provide a typical representative of the presumed sister family of rudderfishes, Kyphosidae. All genera (fig. 9.2) live in sandy and reef habitats along coastal California. (To simplify the analysis, the two Japanese genera of surfperches and the single freshwater genus are not included.) Data are mostly from the Tarp (1952) monograph of the family.

Characters (table 9.1) were selected from the Tarp (1952) taxonomic monograph on the Embiotocidae. Character states in the rudderfish representative (*Hermosilla*) provide out-group comparisons for determining transformation series of the 13 characters used. The mostly tropical rudderfishes are all oviparous and are more likely to resemble the common ancestor of both families. Since most fish are egg layers, viviparity is probably a phylogenetically derived condition.

To start you on the cladogram assembly line, we have conveniently arranged the character matrix with genera having smallest blocks of derived character states (1) at the top following the out-group representative (table 9.2). Now, working from left to right on graph paper, assemble the cladogram. Use alternative X in figure 9.1 as a model if you like. It is convenient to start with characters 10, 11 and 2, 3

to define two primary sister groups of the family, one including *Amphistichus* and *Hyperprosopon* on a branch to the left, the other with all other surfperches on a branch to the right. Tarp and others consider these groups to be sub-families: Amphistichinae and Embiotocinae. Mark steps and number characters used as synapomorphies, adding no more extra steps than necessary. You should end up with no more than 13 steps of synapomorphies and 2 extra steps of autapomorphies[2] as well, for a total of 15.

If you have time for a much more ambitious exercise, classify familiar taxa by using your previous results from measuring "common morphological characters" (chap. 6, table 6.1) to construct a cladogram. First decide on a list of "informative" characters likely to provide synapomorphies. Then calculate average values per character per species (or other taxon). Arrange the results by shifting species averages about so that characters diagnostic of subsets of species emerge, just as you did for finding key characters (chap. 6). To the list of characters, you might add others suggested by some authority. Determine transformation series by comparing with descriptions of species in what are thought to be more ancestral out-groups.

---

2. Note here that autapomorphy is relative to the genus being the taxonomic unit of analysis. If species were units, the autapomorphies would be synapomorphies shared by species within the genus.

References and Suggested Readings for Section Two

Atz, J. W. 1971. *Dean bibliography of fishes 1968.* 512 pp. New York: American Museum of Natural History.

___. 1973. *Dean bibliography of fishes 1969.* 853 pp. New York: American Museum of Natural History.

Barlow, G. W. 1961a. Intra- and interspecific differences in rate of oxygen consumption in the gobiid fishes of the genus *Gillichthys. Biol. Bull.* 121:209–29.

___. 1961b. Gobies of the genus *Gillichthys*, with comments on the sensory canals as a taxonomic tool. *Copeia* 1961:423–37.

___. 1963. Species structure of the gobiid fish *Gillichthys mirabilis* from coastal sloughs of the eastern Pacific. *Pacific Sci.* 17:47–72.

Bohlke, J. E., and Chaplin, C.C.G. 1968. 771 pp. *Fishes of the Bahamas and adjacent tropical waters.* Wynnewood, Pa.: Academy of Natural Sciences of Philadelphia, Livingston Publishing.

Bond, C. E. 1979. *The biology of fishes.* 514 pp. Philadelphia, Pa.: W. B. Saunders.

Busack, C. A.; Thorgaard, G. H.; Bannon, M. P.; and Gall, G.A.E. 1980. An electrophoretic, karyotypic and meristic characterization of the Eagle Lake trout, *Salmo gairdneri aquilarum. Copeia* 1980:418–24.

Buth, D. G.; Burr, B. M.; and Schenck, J. R. 1980. Electrophoretic evidence for relationships and differentiation among members of the percid subgenus *Microperca. Biochem. Syst. Ecol.* 8:297–304.

Buth, D. G., and Mayden, R. L. 1981. Taxonomic status and relationships among populations of *Notropis pilsbri* and *N. zonatus* (Cypriniformes: Cyprinidae) as shown by the glucosephosphate isomerase, lactate dehydrogenase and phosphoglucomutase enzyme systems. *Copeia* 1981:583–90.

Camin, J. H., and Sokal, R. R. 1965. A method for deducing branching sequences in phylogeny. *Evolution* 19:311–26.

Cohen, D. M., and Russo, J. L. 1979. Variation in the fourbeard rockling, *Enchelyopus cimbrius*, a North Atlantic gadid fish, with comments on the genus of rocklings. *Fish. Bull.*, U.S. 77:91–102.

Collette, B. B.; Russo, J. L.; and Zavala-Camin, L. A. 1978. *Scomberomorus brasiliensis*, a new species of Spanish mackerel from the western Atlantic. *Fish. Bull.*, U.S. 76:273–80.

Dean, B. 1916–1923. *A bibliography of fishes.* 3 vols. New York: American Museum of Natural History.

Ebeling, A. W., and Weed, W. H., III. 1963. Melamphaidae III. Systematics and distribution of the species in the bathypelagic fish genus *Scopelogadus Vaillant.* Dana-Report no. 60 (Copenhagen). 58 pp.

Emery, A. R., and Smith-Vaniz, W. F. 1982. Geographic variation and redescription of the western Atlantic damselfish *Chromis enchrysura* Jordan and Gilbert (Pisces: Pomacentridae). *Bull. Mar. Sci.* 32:151–65.

Eschmeyer, W. N.; Herald, E. S.; and Hammann, H. 1983. *A field guide to Pacific Coast fishes of North America.* 336 pp. Boston: Houghton Mifflin.

Felsenstein, J. 1982. Numerical methods for inferring evolutionary trees. *Quart. Rev. Biol.* 57:379–404.

Gibbs, R. H., Jr. 1961. Cyprinid fishes of the subgenus *Cyprinella* of *Notropis*, IV: The *Notropis galacturus-camurus* complex. *Am. Midland Nat.* 66:337–54.

Gold, J. 1979. Cytogenetics. In *Fish physiology*, vol. 8, ed. W. S. Hoar and D. J. Randall. New York: Academic Press.

Hart, J. L. 1971. *Pacific fishes of Canada.* Bulletin 180. 740 pp. Toronto: Fisheries Research Board of Canada.

Hennig, W. 1966. *Phylogenetic systematics.* 263 pp. Urbana: University of Illinois Press.

Hildebrand, S. F., and Schroeder, W. C. 1972. *Fishes of Chesapeake Bay.* Reprint. Smithsonian Institution. 388 pp. Neptune, N.J.: T.F.H. Publications.

Hubbs, C. L., and Lagler, K. F. 1958. *Fishes of the Great Lakes region.* 213 pp. Ann Arbor: University of Michigan Press.

Keenleyside, M.H.A. 1979. *Diversity and adaptation in fish behavior.* 208 pp. Berlin: Springer-Verlag.

Lagler, K. E.; Bardach, J. E.; Miller, R. R.; and Passino, D.R.M. 1977. *Ichthyology.* 2d ed. 506 pp. New York: Wiley.

Liem, A. H., and Scott, W. B. 1966. *Fishes of the Atlantic Coast of Canada.* Bulletin 155. 485 pp. Toronto: Fisheries Research Board of Canada.

Marr, J. C. 1955. The use of morphometric data in systematic, racial and relative growth studies in fishes. *Copeia* 1955(1):23–31.

Matthews, W. J.; Jenkins, R. E.; and Styron, J. T., Jr. 1982. Systematics of two forms of blacknose dace, *Rhinichthys atratulus* (Pisces: Cyprinidae) in a zone of syntopy, with a review of the species group. *Copeia* 1982:902–20.

Miller, D. J., and Lea, R. N. 1972. *Guide to the coastal marine fishes of California.* California Department of Fish and Game Fish Bulletin 157. 249 pp. Berkeley: Publications Division of Agricultural Sciences, University of California.

Moyle, P. B. 1976. *Inland fishes of California.* 405 pp. Berkeley: University of California Press.

Moyle, P. B., and Cech, J. J., Jr. 1982. *Fishes: An introduction to ichthyology.* 593 pp. Englewood Cliffs, N.J.: Prentice-Hall.

Neave, S. A., ed. 1939–40. *Nomenclator zoologicus: A list of the names of genera and subgenera in zoology from the tenth edition of Linnaeus 1758 to the end of 1935.* 4 vols. London: Zoological Society of London.

Page, L. M. 1977. The lateralis system of darters (Etheostomatini). *Copeia* 1977:472–75.

Randall, J. E. 1963. Notes on the systematics of parrotfishes (Scaridae), with emphasis on sexual dicromatism. *Copeia* 1963:225–37.

Robins, C. R.; Bailey, R. M.; Bond, C. E.; Brooker, J. R.; Lachner, E. A.; Lea, R. N.; and Scott, W. B. 1980. *A list of common and scientific names of fishes from the United States and Canada.* 4th ed. American Fisheries Society Special Publication no. 12:1–174. Bethesda, Md.: American Fisheries Society.

Rohlf, F. J., and Sokal, R. R. 1981. *Statistical tables.* 2d ed. 253 pp. New York: W. H. Freeman.

Simpson, G. G.; Roe, A.; and Lewontin, R. C. 1960. *Quantitative zoology.* Rev. ed. 400 pp. New York: Harcourt Brace Jovanovich.

Sokal, R. R., and Rohlf, F. J. 1981. *Biometry.* 2d ed. 859 pp. New York: W. H. Freeman.

Sterba, G. 1962. *Freshwater fishes of the world.* 877 pp. London: Longacre Press.

Tarp, F. H. 1952. *A revision of the family Embiotocidae (the surfperches).* Fish Bulletin 88. 99 pp. Sacramento: California Department of Fish and Game.

Thomson, D. A.; Findley, L. T.; and Kerstitch, A. N. 1979. *Reef fishes of the Sea of Cortez.* 302 pp. New York: Wiley.

Trautman, M. B. 1957. *The fishes of Ohio.* 683 pp. Columbus: Ohio State University Press.

Wiley, E. O. 1981. *Phylogenetics: The theory and practice of phylogenetic systematics.* 439 pp. New York: Wiley.

Zoological Society of London. 1864–date. *The Zoological Record.*

SECTION THREE
NATURAL HISTORY OF FISHES

Significant recent ichthyological research involves studying and describing the life histories of fishes and investigating the interactions among fishes themselves and between them and their animate and inanimate environments. This section is designed to introduce you to the basic approaches you can take to understand the natural history of the fishes in your area better. First, we review the ways in which fishes can be collected and describe the best ways to process and store the specimens. We present guidelines for determining the ages of fish and characterizing their growth patterns in chapter 12. Chapters 13 and 14, respectively, describe various approaches to studying the feeding habits of fishes and methods for determining their reproductive characteristics, such as their maturity and fecundity and the seasonality of their reproductive activities. Following this, chapter 15 covers the parasites commonly found on or in fish hosts and some information about them to provide a better understanding of parasite-host interactions. Finally, chapter 16 offers a brief description of the morphological anomalies often found in fishes, especially those living where environmental conditions allow or stimulate such anomalies.

Chapter 10
Habitats: Collecting and Survey Techniques

Fish specimens must be collected for many studies, such as taxonomy, growth rates, respiration, or even stock assessment (see Gulland 1983). Thus a knowledge of sampling is important before beginning any such study because most capture methods are selective as to species and size class, and they therefore sample only a small part of the entire fish population. The size of hook or net mesh, for instance, can affect which individuals will be caught. Moreover, sampling methods vary in how they affect different species or size classes. This chapter describes some of the most common collecting methods ichthyologists use and discusses the advantages and disadvantages of these methods.

Before conducting any sampling, contact your state wildlife conservation or fish and game agencies, as virtually all states have restrictions on sampling methods, bag limits, and open seasons. Sampling permits are often needed, and local wardens may have to be notified before you make a collection.

UNDERWATER DIVER SURVEYS

Not all survey techniques require fish collection. As an example, where water visibility is good, underwater diver surveys may be an effective, nondisruptive way to enumerate taxa. Traditionally, diver surveys involved divers swimming a transect (either fixed or randomized), counting fishes as they swam and recording the counts on a waterproof slate (Brock 1954, DeMartini and Roberts 1982). Some recent surveys have recorded the transect on film, using a motion picture camera in an underwater housing (Ebeling et al. 1980). Counts are then made from the developed film and screened in the laboratory. Though more expensive, this variation allows workers to count massive fish aggregations as the film can be slowed down, stopped, and repeatedly viewed, yielding more accurate estimates. In any case, care must be taken to consider the problems of overlooking cryptic or nocturnal species, or missing fleeing, alert species (see Russell et al. 1978).

Although usually considered a technique for marine or lake habitats, Northcote and Wilkie (1963) described an underwater method for making a census of stream fish pop-

ulations. As an example, in one study, divers were stationed at 10-foot intervals on a marked rope across a stream with the first diver 10 feet from the riverbank. The team began upstream and swam downstream, with divers counting only those fish between themselves and the diver on the right.

ANAESTHETICS AND PISCICIDES

Many compounds kill or render fishes unconscious (Frey 1951, McFarland 1960, Bell 1967, McFarland and Klontz 1969). Fish poisons and anaesthetics are very effective methods of sampling small, enclosed bodies of water, such as tide pools. Secretive or cryptic species, not easily taken by other means, are particularly susceptible to this approach. Due to the effectiveness of these methods, many state regulations severely limit the use of these chemicals. It is essential for you to check with local fish and game agencies about rules governing the use of fish anaesthetics and poisons. Also, you need not poison large bodies of water to secure representative samples. Even small treatments should be conducted carefully and used only when absolutely necessary.

The fish-killing properties of certain plant products have been known for hundreds of years. Peoples all over the world have used these plants to harvest fish from poisoned waters. Rotenone, derived from the root of several species of the South American plant *Derris*, is the most widely used plant-derived piscicide. Rotenone is a vasoconstrictor and prevents gill respiration so the poisoned fish soon suffocates. Interestingly, several temperate-world plants, such as the wild cucumber, *Marah macrocarpus*, and buckeye, *Aesculus californica*, are also potent piscicides.

Anaesthetics, such as quinaldine and MS-222 (tricaine methanesulfonate) can also be useful and in many cases are preferable to rotenone, particularly if small pools are to be sampled (Gibson 1967, Marking 1969, Moring 1970, Blasiola 1977). Quinaldine can kill fishes, but it does so at higher dosages and over a longer time period than rotenone. Most narcotized fish soon revive when placed in uncontaminated and aerated water. However, quinaldine can cause severe allergic reactions and is considered by some to be carcinogenic to humans—it should be handled with caution and perhaps it would be wise to wear rubber gloves. It is usually mixed with isopropanol before use (often in proportions of ten to one, isopropanol to quinaldine). On the other hand, MS-222 is considered relatively safe and is actually registered for food fish by the Environmental Protection Agency (Meyer et al. 1976). It is used more often in live fish physiology experiments rather than field application due to its cost.

A third anaesthetic, etomidate, a nonbarbiturate hypnotic used previously on other animals, has proven to be "an effective and safe anesthetic for several fish species" (Limsuwan et al. 1983). This new anaesthetic has been used and tested to overcome some of the disadvantages of quinaldine and MS-222: low safety indices, ineffectiveness for prolonged periods of sedation, effects of water chemistry on efficiencies, and the modification of reflexes for more than just the anaesthetic periods (Limsuwan et al. 1983). Since it has only been used in laboratory or aquarium situations, we do not propose that it be used yet in field applications.

For field applications we still recommend quinaldine, but because its effectiveness depends on several environmental factors, such as water temperature and current strength, this agent does not have precise dosage rates, although some guidelines may be found in Gibson (1967) and Moring (1970). Generally, larger quantities applied for longer times are required in water of lower temperature and greater motion. Quiet, isolated habitats, such as tidepools and small embayments are good study sites because they limit chemical dispersion, and specimens are less likely to drift away.

Application is quite simple. Place the agent in plastic bags or squeeze bottles and release on the bottom throughout the site. Bottom release helps ensure proper mixing throughout the water column. Apply only on slack and incoming tides (or when water movement is at a minimum), thus keeping the chemicals within the study site and preventing specimens from floating outward. Squeeze bottles are particularly effective when you are selectively collecting specimens from small areas, such as algal mats or coral heads.

Long-handled dip nets are very useful for retrieving specimens, particularly in deep pools where wading is difficult. If any current is expected, place a fine mesh net (a gill net is excellent) down current from the site to gather drifting individuals. Snorkling or scuba diving can be used to recover fish that sink or hide. It is important to have collectors ready as soon as the chemicals are distributed. Although it may take considerable time for the chemical to take effect, generally some fish are relatively sensitive and succumb quickly.

Chemical collectors are useful in certain specific circumstances. When live fishes are required, quinaldine is often a rapid and effective collecting tool. Small and cryptic species often missed by other methods are usually susceptible to this method. Chemicals may be more effective in such habitats as crevices or algal mats that are difficult to sample by other techniques. Lastly, chemicals are often an excellent way to make a survey of all the fishes in an area. Often a very large number of specimens, of virtually every species present, can be collected quickly for relatively little cost.

The major disadvantage to these chemicals is that they are nonselective, often killing or stunning virtually all fishes (and sometimes many invertebrates) in a treated area. Further, some poisons may have long-lasting effects, completely destroying the ability of a water body to support life for years. Thus, if you want only one or a few species, chemicals are probably not appropriate.

Using carbon dioxide to collect fish may circumvent some of the long-lasting negative effects of poisons. Carbon dioxide has long been used to sedate hatchery fish during transport (Leitritz and Lewis 1976). Carbon dioxide can be an effective collecting agent under certain conditions, particularly in small, enclosed habitats. Carbon dioxide gas can be bubbled into a study site from a CO_2 cylinder, using a pressure regulator to control the flow rate. Gas is dispersed throughout the habitat using tubes attached to air stones, set on the bottom. This is a relatively new technique, and we do not yet know optimal flow rates for all habitats. Application time will vary with water volume, flow rate, and so on, which means as much as 20 minutes may be required for complete anaesthesia within a site. Affected fish usually rise toward the surface. An advantage of carbon dioxide is that most fish will recover within minutes of removal to oxygenated water. Additionally, carbon dioxide is quickly removed from a system, with no long-term effects.

Another related method, using carbonic acid, is effective in sedating fish in aquaria and holding tanks. It may work for collecting purposes as well (Fish 1942, Post 1979).

HOOK AND LINE

Most hook-and-line devices (reviewed in Scofield 1947 and Browning 1980) employ a large number of hooks (often thousands) attached to lines that may stretch for miles. **Drop lines** (fig. 10.1) are relatively short lines, fished vertically; **long lines** (fig. 10.2), such as set lines, line trawls, and trot lines, are laid out horizontally, either on or above the bottom.

Drop lines are composed of a **main line**, secured by rod and reel, hand, or buoy, from which leaders (**gangings, gangions**) extend. A ganging is composed of a swivel and length of line and hook. At the bottom, a sinker (often a sash weight, lead weight, or small anchor) holds the line in place.

For long lines, vertical end lines are anchored to buoys to support the long, horizontal, hook-laden (main or

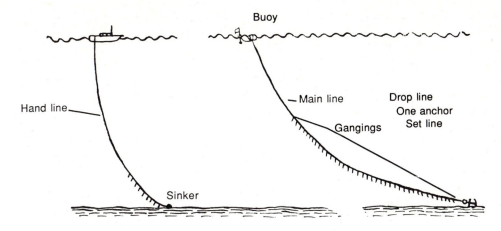

Figure 10.1 Diagram showing deployment of drop lines for catching fishes. (Scofield 1947)

ground) line. Buoys may be kegs, corks, plastic bottles, and the like, often with flags, lights, or radar reflectors attached. A series of gangings with hooks dangles from the main line. As the main line is payed out, usually from the stern of a moving vessel, additional gangings with hooks are added. Before setting, hooks may be coiled in tubs, baskets, or on deck. If only a few hooks are set on the main line, they can be hung along a length of dowling and slid into the water as the vessel moves ahead.

Hooks are baited before reaching the sampling site. Tough baits such as squid or salted fish stay on hooks well, though some sought-after fish prefer fresh bait. Make sure that all obstacles are masked or removed from the deck because they may snag hooks as they are being set.

Once baited and assembled aboard the vessel, gear is set in two ways. For drop lines, the vessel is positioned over the sampling site, and the assembly is lowered into the water. Long-line gear is set somewhat like a gill net—with buoy and anchor first, followed by the main line, hooks, and the end anchor and buoy. If the lines are very long, additional buoys or anchors may be added at intermediate lengths. Ideally, the anchor should hit bottom before the hooks are set. This will help prevent the hooks from flying out at an uncontrollable rate.

Fishing time for the gear depends on location. For instance, bottom sets made off much of the Pacific Coast must be retrieved after only a few hours, as hagfish, *Eptatretus stoutii*, crabs, seals, and sea lions quickly attack hooked individuals. In tropical water, sharks may destroy the catch even sooner. At the maximum, lines should be checked once every 24 hours.

Retrieving your gear is relatively simple. As the lines are pulled in, fish are removed and hooks replaced on or in their containers. Though retrieval can be a one-person operation, heavy currents or winds, causing drag on the line, usually require a second pair of hands.

Hook-and-line fishing, depending on needs, may or may not be advantageous. Fish can often be captured alive, par-

ticularly if hooks are only fished for brief periods. Equipment costs, including both initial purchase and later repair, are lower than for some other methods. Collecting by hook and line is more selective than by most other methods. Hook size and bait type will limit species and size ranges taken. Hence, the number of unwanted species caught can be reduced. Lastly, some large strong species, such as oceanic sharks, are difficult to catch by other methods.

However, catching a fish by hook and line depends on the fish's willingness to bite. If fish are not feeding (or cannot otherwise be induced to strike), they are not caught. Thus the selectivity of hook-and-line fishing makes it a poor single choice for surveys to determine fish diversity in an area.

NETS

Fishing with nets can be effective (reviewed by Browning 1980). There are various types of nets, each designed for a different purpose. Generally, nets act in one of two ways, entangling or impounding. Entangling nets are laid out for specific periods and then retrieved. Impounding nets are set around specific fish aggregations.

Nets have certain features in common. All are constructed of webbing—usually knotted fabric—that acts to impound or entangle. Webbing is now most often made of multistrand nylon or monofilament (particularly in experimental gill nets), though cotton, linen, or hemp are still occasionally used. Mesh size in webbing is commonly measured as the distance between two diagonally opposite knots of a mesh, when the mesh is pulled tight ("stretch size," fig. 10.3). It may also be measured as "square mesh," and this is usually about one half the stretch-mesh dimensions. In most nets, the upper edge of the webbing is hung from a **cork line** (head rope, head line), along which floats—cork, plastic, or glass—are hung. Polyethylene line, which is buoyant, may also be used. The lower edge of webbing is attached to

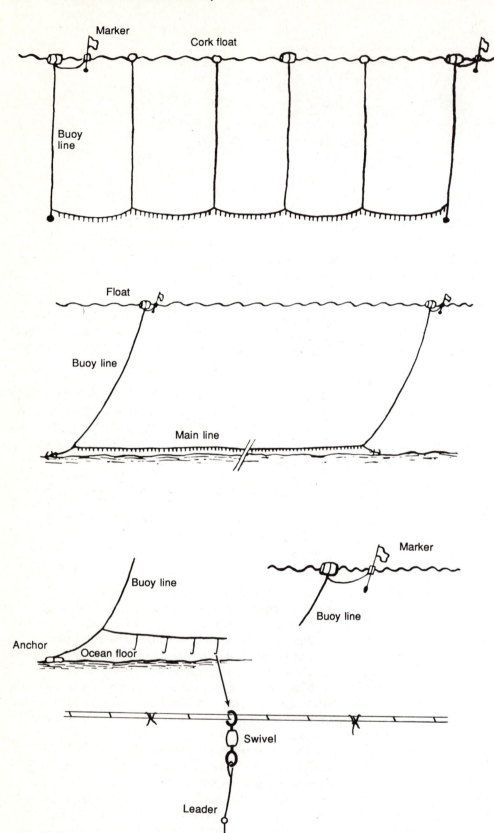

Figure 10.2 Diagrams showing various ways of deploying long lines. (Scofield 1947)

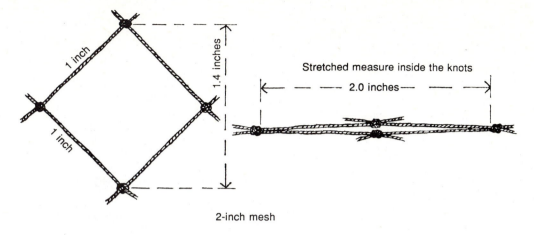

Figure 10.3 Configuration of mesh used in many kinds of fishing nets. Note that the mesh can be measured in its "square" form (left) and "stretched" form (right). (Scofield 1948)

a **lead line** (foot line, ground line) that can be lead cored or have lead weights or chains attached. Cork lines prevent the webbing from collapsing downward, and lead lines keep the nets from riding upward.

Entangling Nets

Gill and **trammel nets** capture fish by entanglement (fig. 10.4). The gill net is a single mesh wall, with cork and lead lines keeping the net upright. A trammel net is a wall formed by three parallel pieces of mesh, the outer two of a wide mesh, the inner finer. Gill nets capture fish that swim into and partially through the mesh. Fish swim into a tram-

mel net and carry the finer meshed inner net through the adjacent wider mesh. Except when the nets are drifted, anchors and buoys are attached to each end. Drifting nets may have buoys and are lightly weighted.

Nets are generally made of nylon or monofilament and are designed to fish while floating at the surface, suspended at mid-depths, or resting on the bottom. Gill nets are usually set with their length paralleling the bottom, but occasionally they are hung vertically. Because gill nets are passive (nonmoving), they can be set over both smooth and rocky bottoms.

Gill and trammel nets are highly selective (Hanley 1975), the size of the specimens taken depending on mesh size and fish behavior. Many scientific collecting nets are

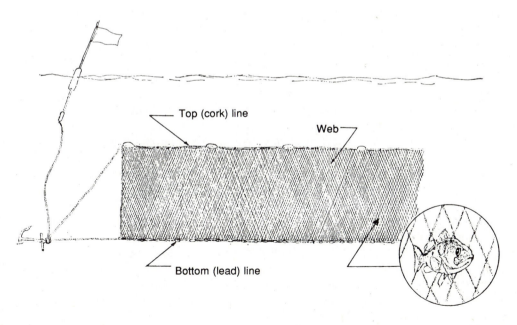

Figure 10.4 General configuration and arrangement of gill net set on the bottom to entangle fish. (Lagler 1978)

made of a series of panels, each one of a different-sized mesh.

The efficiency and selectivity of these nets depend on the amount that fish move about in the area. Hence, variation in a number of factors, such as barometric pressure, temperature, and light levels, may cause differences in catches. You can stimulate fish movement by copper sulphate, light, noise, electrical fields, or bubble screens. A series of nets is preferable for comprehensive sampling. Nets should be checked frequently, as many enmeshed fish may be attacked by larger species. However, the duration the net is set depends on local conditions and needs. If live fishes are required, nets must be tended frequently, as many species quickly die once entangled.

Both gill and trammel nets can be set from vessels, by divers, or, in shallow waters, by waders. When setting a net from a boat, it is very important to prepare the anchors, buoys, and nets carefully. The net is stacked in layers, lead lines on one side and cork lines on the other. Buoys and anchors should be placed away from the net to prevent the possibilities of tangling during setting. You can set nets from stern, sides, or bow. With outboard-driven vessels, bow setting will prevent the net from becoming entangled in the boat's propeller.

After the boat is underway, the buoy is set out, followed by the anchor. Ideally, the anchor should hit bottom *before* the net is payed out. This eliminates the possibility of the dropping anchor pulling the net along with it, distorting the net's shape. Therefore, the distance between anchor and net should be greater than the water depth. Because the anchor may be some distance from the net, make sure the net is set in the sampling area. That is, if the sampling area is small, you might have to drop the first anchor before the sampling site is reached. After the first anchor hits bottom, pay the net out and set the second anchor and buoy.

Setting these nets with divers can be very efficient. Nets may be situated precisely where desired, and you eliminate the risk of net fouling during setting. Moreover, divers can pick out enmeshed specimens without having to pull the net out of the water. If live fish are needed, divers can retrieve trapped specimens rapidly. Note, however, that these nets are very cumbersome to maneuver underwater, and it takes extreme care to keep divers from becoming entangled in them.

Once the net is pulled aboard, picking out enmeshed specimens can be very time consuming, as multiple layers of webbing often catch on the fishes' opercula, spines, and so on. Time spent removing specimens may be reduced by using a small piece of wood to which a bent, flattened nail has been attached (fig. 10.5). This device, resembling a shoehorn, helps pry webbing and fish apart.

Entangling nets are excellent for survey work. By setting nets with several mesh sizes, you can take a wide range of species and size intervals. You can set from small vessels or from shore with limited personnel (one person can set and

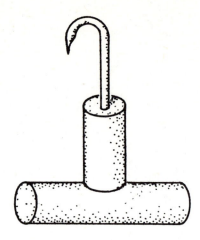

Figure 10.5 Device designed to help pull fish out of entangling nets with webbing.

retrieve). Often, you can capture fish alive if they are plucked quickly from the nets, especially by divers before the fish emerge.

Unless monitored by divers, gill and trammel nets are difficult to use over rocky or rough bottoms as they are apt to catch and tear. The nets' effectiveness may also depend on water visibility, time of day, or weather patterns. For instance, incoming weather fronts may affect catches, perhaps because they increase fish movement.

Impounding Nets

Beach seines are impounding nets, typically set by skiffs parallel to the shoreline. Then they are pulled to the beach by means of hauling lines, trapping fishes onshore. These nets are generally set close to shore, the maximum distance limited by the length of the haul lines, the depth of both the net and water, and the workers available to pull! They are excellent for sampling shallow, sandy, and smooth bottom environments (sand beaches, lagoons). Rocky bottoms, debris, high waves, or strong currents that lift the net off the bottom will lower fishing performance.

Beach seines (fig. 10.6) normally range from 60 to 100 feet in length (and occasionally up to 300 feet). **Bridles** at each end of the net attach to the haul lines. At the net center, a finer meshed section, the **bag**, concentrates the impounded fishes.

Because currents, wave action, and wind may move both net and boat, it is most important that lines and net are stacked to facilitate rapid sets. The longer the process lasts, the more likely it is that the net will be lifted from the bottom or otherwise deformed.

Though beach seines may be set from various types of vessels, they are best set from small skiffs. Stack the skiff's

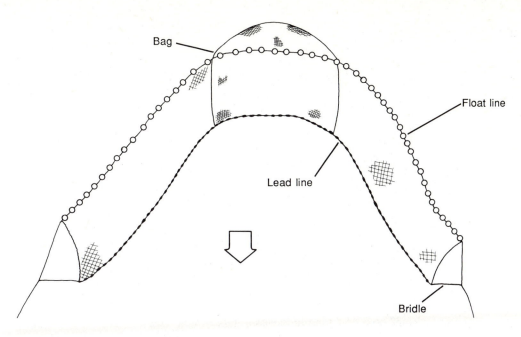

Figure 10.6 Diagram showing deployment of a large beach seine from the shore. Note the arrow, which depicts the direction to pull the net.

stern, preferably in a holder or on a plank (Giger and Williams 1972); if a motor is used, stack the net in the bow, away from the propeller. You must remove or mask all rivets, nails, or other protrusions to prevent the webbing from catching during setting. Place one of the two lines in the boat before the net is stacked. Draping the line loosely in the bottom of the boat seems to produce fewer tangles than coiling.

The net is stacked in layers, lead lines on one side and cork lines on the other. Periodically pack the net down to reduce volume. Place the bridle and the second line on top of the net (fig. 10.7). They should be draped so that it will pay out smoothly as the boat is rowed (or motored) offshore.

Though one person can both control the boat and set the net, having two people, one to set and one to propel the vessel, works better.

Before leaving shore, make sure the end of the top line is either held or properly secured on shore. Allow the line to pay out as the vessel moves offshore (fig. 10.8). When the line end is reached, turn the boat parallel to shore into the current, if any, and begin to set the net. It is important to set the net smoothly. Frequent stops for untangling often result in the net bunching in the water. If this occurs, hold the net and continue moving, straightening it. When the net is set, head toward the nearest point on shore, paying out the second line. This will help ensure that this line will be sufficiently long to reach shore.

Pull lines in slowly and steadily. Rapid or erratic pulling causes the lead lines to rise off the bottom. Both lines should be pulled at equal rates. Lead lines also tend to rise

when they enter the turbulent surf zone. If possible, keep them down by wading out and pushing them down with feet or hands. As the net is pulled in close to shore, some haulers should work their way down and inside the net, keeping the lead lines down and making sure the floats are not submerged.

After the net is out of the water, quickly place the captured fishes in water-filled containers prepared and placed in position beforehand. Many fishes, if pulled out of the net promptly, will survive, and you can release them after observation.

The beach seine is a very effective, nonselective method for sampling shallow, inshore waters. The net is easily set and retrieved (especially with an entire class), and fishes may be captured alive if quickly removed from the beached net.

The **haul seine** (also called a common-sense or two-person seine) is a very small beach seine, with a pole attached to each end of it. The nets are held by poles and walked either parallel to shore or offshore to onshore. Poles are held at about a 45-degree angle away from the direction of movement. After a collection is made, both collectors walk ashore and purse the net together. The lead lines are pulled up on shore immediately to prevent escape. In another method, the net is moved in an arclike fashion, with one end held against shore and the other swung from one side to the other.

The haul seine is most effective in shallow, sandy environments, as rocks or weeds allow the lead line to rise up off the bottom. You can get the best results in water no deeper than two-thirds the height of the net. Haul seines are

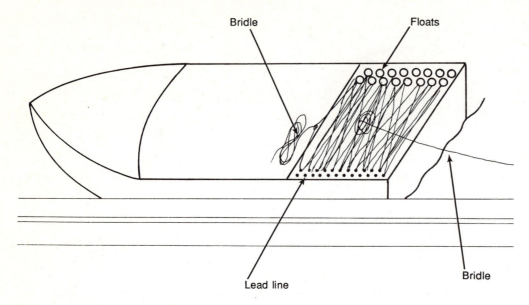

Figure 10.7 Rack arrangement on the stern of a small boat designed to facilitate deployment of a beach seine.

selective, in that swiftly moving species may escape entrapment.

Otter trawls (shrimp trawls, semiballoon trawls) are baglike nets towed along the bottom or in midwater (Scofield 1948, Knake 1956, Rupp and DeRoche 1960). As a bottom trawl, the otter trawl is most efficient over flat, sandy bottoms relatively free of debris and rocks. Recently, however, special trawls, outfitted with large rollers or wheels, have made rocky-bottom trawling feasible.

Otter trawls are widely used in biological surveys. Though they are relatively selective (because fast-swimming species avoid capture), they are useful in surveying many of the slower smooth-bottom fauna. These nets are usually not suitable for collecting fish for live studies, especially in deep water. Buffeting during capture often kills or weakens specimens.

A generalized otter trawl is pictured in figure 10.9. The net is bag-shaped with cork or float lines and lead lines to keep the mouth open vertically. **Otter boards** (constructed of wood or metal or both) are placed in front of the net mouth, where water motion during towing keeps the boards flared outward, opening the net and pulling it down laterally. Trapped fish are shunted back to a finer mesh bag—the **cod end.** At the posterior of the cod end is an opening tied off by a rope. To release the catch, the rope is untied and the cod end allowed to open.

Before setting the net, lay it out on the stern deck, the cod end nearest the stern. As the vessel moves forward, trail the cod end over the stern. (If an outboard motor drives the vessel, release the net over one of the sides, away from the propeller.) After paying the net out, place the otter boards in the water. Be careful because the boards often move quickly over the stern, potentially injuring someone or the boat. Two persons, one on each board, should lower the otter boards into the water. Once the boards are submerged, stop paying out line and allow the net to fill out behind the

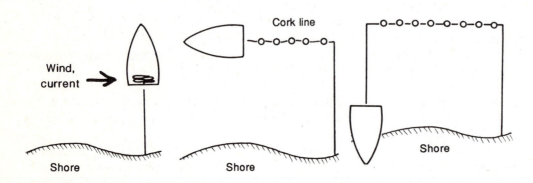

Figure 10.8 Suggested method of deploying a beach seine from shore using a small boat.

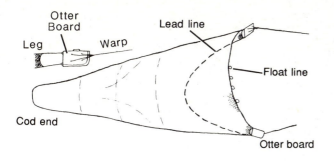

Figure 10.9 Diagram showing a generalized otter trawl, useful for collecting bottom fishes from a small boat or research vessel. (Scofield 1948)

vessel. Check that the otter-board lines are not twisted and that the net mouth is open. After inspection, begin paying out line or cable. In shallow water (less than about 100 meters), allow about three to five times as much line out as the trawling depth (i.e., a bottom depth of 30 meters equals 90 to 150 meters of line or cable). In water deeper than 100 meters, two-to-one ratios are acceptable.

Otter trawls are commonly towed at 1.5–3.0 knots. Slower speeds increase fish escape, and higher speeds can pull the net off the bottom.

Nets are towed for varying periods, depending on bottom conditions, currents, and so on. For instance, with large amounts of bottom-drift algae that can clog the net, trawling time would be relatively short. Generally 10 to 30 minutes will yield an adequate sample.

During retrieval, a slow, steady pull will prevent net deformation. When the otter boards reach the surface, pull them on board immediately to help close the mouth.

When the net is on deck, untie the cod end and shake the contents into a fish box or water-filled container. Do not grope blindly through the trawl contents, as scorpionfish, electric rays, or the like may be hidden by other fishes and algae.

Roundhaul Nets

Roundhaul nets (fig. 10.10) are used to encircle fish aggregations (Scofield 1951). The nets are continuous and wall-like, with corks along the top and leads along the bottom. The net is piled on the stern of the vessel, lead lines on one side and cork lines on the other. The end of the net is attached by a short rope to a buoy or skiff, which is often towed behind the vessel.

When a school of fish is sighted, release the buoy or skiff into the water and set the net across the path of the fish. Set the net in a complete circle, pick up the buoy or skiff, and the school is effectively sealed off. **Lampara nets** are closed off by pulling the lead lines first, thus closing off the bottom. **Purse seines** have a drawstring running the length of the lead line, which is pulled tight after the set.

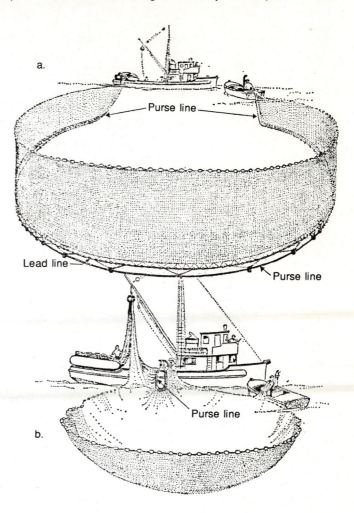

Figure 10.10 Diagram of a roundhaul net (purse seine) being deployed from a fishing vessel: (a) the general shape of the net after deployment; (b) the pursing action and retrieval of the catch. (Lagler 1978)

Roundhaul nets are most useful in sampling fishes that form large aggregations over deep water or smooth bottoms. They are also useful when collecting smaller species, such as anchovies, or swift forms, such as tuna. Such fishes are often difficult to take by other methods. In survey work, roundhauls are usually set around already located schools, whereas gill nets or otter trawls are often used more or less blindly. Roundhauls can capture fish in excellent condition, making this a good technique for taking fish alive.

They are not, however, useful over shallow rough bottoms, where they tend to hang up. The time and effort involved in setting and retrieving roundhauls mean that these nets are not particularly cost effective unless the species sought form large aggregations.

MAZE GEAR

Maze gear is designed to lead fish into enclosures from which escape is difficult.

a.

b.

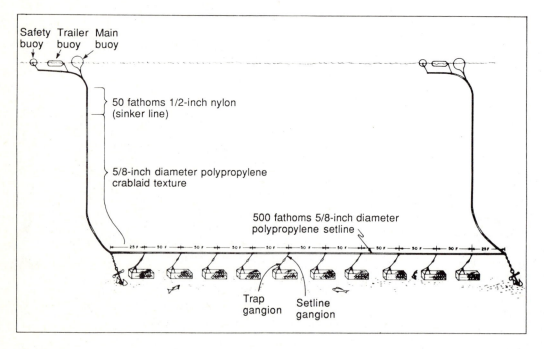

c.

Figure 10.11 Diagrams of fish traps, used with bait to attract fish through a one-way funnel. The traps in (a) and (b) are used for sablefish off the west coast of the United States (DeWees 1980); (c) shows a string of sablefish traps.

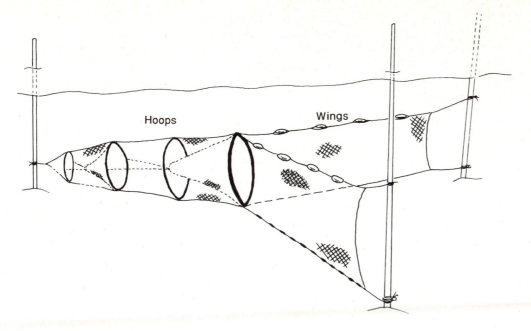

Figure 10.12 A diagram depicting the structure and deployment of a fyke net. (U.S. Fish and Wildlife Service, Commercial Fisheries Circular 48)

Fish Traps (Pot Gear)

These are relatively small rectangular or cylindrical cages (fig. 10.11) that are set on bottom or in midwater. They are constructed of metal, wood, or plastic framing, with wire, net, or plastic walling attached. Larger traps use bricks, concrete, or metal pieces as weights. The traps have openings that become smaller toward the inside. Fish find it more difficult to leave the traps than to enter because of the smaller interior diameter of the cones. Traps are attached by lines to a buoy or, if set from shore, to a structure on the bank. To prevent theft, lines of traps set from shore should be hidden. A small buoy is sometimes placed above the trap to help prevent the line from cutting on the bottom. To increase efficiency, commercial fisherman often string a series of traps on one line, allowing more traps to be set and pulled in a given time. Traps may or may not be baited. Bait is usually placed in a small separate compartment inside the trap, safe from most predators and scavengers. Fish traps are useful in habitats difficult to sample by other means, such as deep-water rocky areas or in collecting small secretive species.

Fyke Nets

The **fyke net** (fig. 10.12) exemplifies a number of nets that trap fish by conducting them (by deflectors) into an impounding enclosure. Escape is made difficult by funnels or V-shaped baffles or cones that extend inward at the mouths. Though the nets can be set directly from a vessel, divers can position the wings and hoops more accurately. These nets are usually fished on the bottom, though occasionally they are placed in midwater.

These devices are often extremely effective when placed along existing fish swimways, such as jetties and sand-rock interfaces. By placement of one wing across the swimway, fish are directed into the net.

ELECTROFISHING

Electrofishing, the use of electricity for fish capture, is a very popular method of estimating species composition and abundance in freshwater systems, particularly streams. In electrofishing, current is passed between two submerged electrodes. Alternating current (AC) stuns (but rarely kills) fish, whereas direct current (DC) causes fish to move toward the positive electrode.

Price (1982) described an efficient electrofishing method for small streams. A 30-meter stream section is walled off by vertical nets to prevent fish movement into or out of the sample area. A backpack electroshocker with two hand-held poles is used. Three people seems a good minimum number for this sampling, a "shocker" and two "netters," carrying dip nets to capture stunned fish. All crew members wear waterproof rubber gloves and waders.

The shocker starts at the downstream net and samples upstream to the second net. The netters stay alongside or slightly behind the shocker. Captured fish are placed in water-filled buckets.

Electrofishing is not, however, the perfect sampling method (Mahon 1980). (If, in fact, we knew the perfect method, we would be both rich and famous.) Species vary in their susceptibility to electrical current. For instance, catostomids (suckers) are very easily influenced, whereas freshwater perches—particularly some species of *Etheostoma*—are not. A species' behavior and habitat may also influence how easily members are caught. Cryptic species, such as sculpins, may lodge in rocks after being stunned, making them less easily captured.

Chapter 11
Care and Handling of Specimens

PRESERVATIVES AND STORAGE

Fish specimens are more valuable when they are carefully preserved and well cared for. Freshly collected specimens may be frozen for a time, but eventually they should be fixed—so that tissues are hardened and resist decomposition—in a solution of nine parts formalin to one part freshwater or seawater. Since the resulting 10 percent formalin solution tends to become progressively acidic, it should be buffered by adding calcium carbonate to saturation. While very small specimens may be fixed by simply placing them in formalin, larger specimens should have their body cavities perforated and perhaps small incisions made into their flanks, but only on the right side so systematic work can still be done.

Fixation time depends on temperature and specimen size. However, most fish will be fixed within four or five days. After fixing, wash the specimens and store permanently in a solution of either 45 percent isopropanol or 70 percent ethanol. These preservatives are preferable to buffered formalin, which is a noxious liquid, quite poisonous and irritating to the skin. A complete discussion of fixatives and fixation procedures is found in *A Report on Current Supplies and Practices Used in Curation of Ichthyological Collections*, available from Dr. Leslie Knapp, Smithsonian Oceanographic Sorting Center, Smithsonian Institution, Washington, DC 20560.

Specimens should be stored in glass jars or buckets, preferably with gasket-tight lids of glass or other durable and nonrusting material. Canning jars with clamp-down glass lids fitted with rubber gaskets are best because they minimize preservative evaporation. You can also use other less costly jars with plastic lids or metal lids with plastic liners. Large fishes may be stored in metal drums, either enameled on the inside or fitted with plastic liners, and secured with clamp-down lids. If at all possible, the preserved fish collection should be housed in a dark room because light causes the colors and markings on fish to fade rapidly. The level of preservative should be checked regularly because even the tightest container allows some evaporation. Because alcohol is more volatile than water, it evaporates first, leaving the preservative diluted. Therefore,

if the fluid levels are simply brought back to brim full by adding more preservative solution, the preservative will eventually become too dilute. It is better to pour all the old preservative from the specimen jars into a large mixing jar, then add pure alcohol until you have brought the percentage back to normal. Correct concentrations of preservative can be easily checked with an alcohol hydrometer.

Specimens left in formalin or placed in isopropanol or ethanol soon lose skin color due to oxidation and the high solubility of skin pigments in alcohol. Several antioxidants may retard color loss: erythorbic acid (Miles Chemical) and Ional CP-40 (Shell Chemical), both 1 percent in 10 percent formalin. Erythorbic acid maintains reds, oranges, yellows, and greens, and Ional is sometimes effective with reds and oranges.

LABELS AND CATALOGUES

Place all specimens of one species collected together at the same time and date in the same jar and label. Labels should be cut from high-quality rag paper that can be placed inside the jar and not deteriorate. Print necessary information in indelible ink (that will neither fade nor run in the liquid). Essential information includes species name, family, determiner (the person who identified the fish), the collector of the fish, and the date and exact locality specimens were collected (fig. 11.1b, 11.1c). Also, add a collection or catalogue number to reference the specimens to a collection data sheet or set of field notes made out at the time of collection (fig. 11.1a). Large fish may be tagged with stiff labels attached to the jaws or through the mouth and operculum or tail with tough cord or thread. Then to save space, specimens of different species can be stored together in a single large drum or other oversized container.

Locating specimens in a large collection is time consuming. A system that indexes specimens makes retrieval and replacement easier. The system we present (table 11.1) assigns group numbers to all fish families and orders. These numbers are placed on the collection cards in the species jars, on the jar tops and slides, and on shelves in the collec-

Table 11.1 Lists of orders, families, and family numbers of fishes. (Spellings conform to rulings by the International Commission on Zoological Nomenclature.)

Myxiniformes
1   Myxinidae
Petromyzontiformes
2   Petromyzontidae
Chimaeriformes
3   Callorhynchidae
4   Chimaeridae
5   Rhinochimaeridae
Hexanchiformes
6   Chlamydoselachidae
7   Hexanchidae
Heterodontiformes
8   Heterodontidae
Lamniformes
9   Rhincodontidae
10   Orectolobidae
11   Odontaspididae
12   Lamnidae
13   Scyliorhinidae
14   Carcharhinidae
15   Sphyrnidae
Squaliformes
16   Squalidae
17   Pristiophoridae
18   Squatinidae
Rajiformes
19   Pristidae
20   Torpedinidae
21   Rhinobatidae
22   Rajidae
23   Dasyatidae
24   Potamotrygonidae
25   Hexatrygonidae
26   Myliobatididae
27   Mobulidae
Ceratodontiformes
28   Ceratodontidae
Lepidosireniformes
29   Lepidosirenidae
30   Protopteridae
Coelacanthiformes
31   Latimeriidae
Polypteriformes
32   Polypteridae
Acipenseriformes
33   Acipenseridae
34   Polyodontidae
Lepisosteiformes
35   Lepisosteidae
Amiiformes
36   Amiidae
Osteoglossiformes
37   Osteoglossidae
38   Pantodontidae
39   Hiodontidae
40   Notopteridae
41   Mormyridae
42   Gymnarchidae
Elopiformes
43   Elopidae
44   Megalopidae
45   Albulidae
46   Halosauridae
47   Notacanthidae
48   Lipogenyidae

Anguilliformes
49   Anguillidae
50   Heterenchelyidae
51   Moringuidae
52   Xenocongridae
53   Myrocongridae
54   Muraenidae
55   Nemichthyidae
56   Cyematidae
57   Synaphobranchidae
58   Ophichthidae
59   Nettastomatidae
60   Colocongridae
61   Macrocephenchelyidae
62   Congridae
63   Derichthyidae
64   Serrivomeridae
65   Saccopharyngidae
66   Eurypharyngidae
67   Monognathidae
Clupeiformes
68   Denticipitidae
69   Clupeidae
70   Engraulididae
71   Chirocentridae
Gonorynchiformes
72   Chanidae
73   Gonorynchidae
74   Kneriidae
75   Phractolaemidae
Cypriniformes
76   Cyprinidae
77   Psilorhynchidae
78   Homalopteridae
79   Cobitididae
80   Gyrinocheilidae
81   Catostomidae
Characiformes
82   Citharinidae
83   Hemidontidae
84   Curimatidae
85   Anostomidae
86   Erythrinidae
87   Lebiasinidae
88   Gasteropelecidae
89   Ctenoluciidae
90   Hepsetidae
91   Characidae
Siluriformes
92   Diplomystidae
93   Ictaluridae
94   Bagridae
95   Cranoglanididae
96   Siluridae
97   Schilbidae
98   Pangasiidae
99   Amblycipitidae
100 Amphiliidae
101 Akysidae
102 Sisoridae
103 Clariidae
104 Heteropneustidae
105 Chacidae
106 Olyridae
107 Malapteruridae

108 Ariidae
109 Plotosidae
110 Mochokidae
111 Doradidae
112 Auchenipteridae
113 Pimelodidae
114 Ageneiosidae
115 Helogenidae
116 Cetopsidae
117 Hypophthalmidae
118 Aspredinidae
119 Trichomycteridae
120 Callichthyidae
121 Loricariidae
122 Astroblepidae
Gymnotiformes
123 Sternopygidae
124 Rhamphichthyidae
125 Hypopomidae
126 Apteronotidae
127 Gymnotidae
128 Electrophoridae
Salmoniformes
129 Esocidae
130 Umbridae
131 Argentinidae
132 Bathylagidae
133 Opisthoproctidae
134 Alepocephalidae
135 Searsiidae
136 Lepidogalaxiidae
137 Osmeridae
138 Plecoglossidae
139 Salangidae
140 Sundasalangidae
141 Retropinnidae
142 Galaxiidae
143 Salmonidae
Stomiiformes
144 Gonostomatidae
145 Sternoptychidae
146 Photichthyidae
147 Chauliodontidae
148 Stomiidae
149 Astronesthidae
150 Melanostomiidae
151 Malacosteidae
152 Idiacanthidae
Aulopiformes
153 Aulopididae
154 Chlorophthalmidae
155 Scopelarchidae
156 Notosudidae
157 Synodontidae
158 Giganturidae
159 Paralepididae
160 Anotopteridae
161 Evermannellidae
162 Omosudidae
163 Alepisauridae
164 Pseudotrichonotidae
Myctophiformes
165 Neoscopelidae
166 Myctophidae

Percopsiformes
167 Percopsidae
168 Aphredoderidae
169 Amblyopsidae
Gadiformes
170 Muraenolepididae
171 Moridae
172 Melanonidae
173 Bregmacerotidae
174 Gadidae
175 Merlucciidae
176 Macrouridae
Ophidiiformes
177 Ophidiidae
178 Carapidae
179 Bythitidae
180 Aphyonidae
Batrachoidiformes
181 Batrachoididae
182 Lophiidae
183 Antennariidae
184 Brachionichthyidae
185 Chaunacidae
186 Ogcocephalidae
187 Caulophrynidae
188 Ceratiidae
189 Gigantactinidae
190 Neoceratiidae
191 Linophrynidae
192 Oneirodidae
193 Thaumatichthyidae
194 Centrophrynidae
195 Diceratiidae
196 Himantolophidae
197 Melanocetidae
Gobiesociformes
198 Gobiesocidae
199 Alabetidae
Cyprinodontiformes
200 Exocoetidae
201 Hemiramphidae
202 Belonidae
203 Scomberesocidae
204 Oryziidae
205 Adrianichthyidae
206 Horaichthyidae
207 Aplocheilidae
208 Cyprinodontidae
209 Goodeidae
210 Anablepidae
211 Jenynsiidae
212 Poeciliidae
Atheriniformes
213 Atherinidae
214 Isonidae
215 Melanotaeniidae
216 Neostethidae
217 Phallostethidae
Lampriformes
218 Lampridae
219 Veliferidae
220 Lophotidae
221 Radiicephalidae
222 Trachipteridae
223 Regalecidae

Table 11.1 *Continued*

224	Stylephoridae	280	Agonidae	344	Cichlidae	409	Acanthuridae
225	Ateleopodidae	281	Cyclopteridae	345	Embiotocidae	410	Siganidae
226	Mirapinnidae	*Perciformes*		346	Pomacentridae	411	Scombrolabracidae
227	Eutaeniophoridae	282	Centropomidae	347	Gadopsidae	412	Gempylidae
228	Megalomycteridae	283	Percichthyidae	348	Cirrhitidae	413	Trichiuridae
Beryciformes		284	Serranidae	349	Chironemidae	414	Scombridae
229	Monocentrididae	285	Grammistidae	350	Aplodactylidae	415	Xiphiidae
230	Trachichthyidae	286	Pseudochromidae	351	Cheilodactylidae	416	Luvaridae
231	Anomalopidae	287	Grammidae	352	Latrididae	417	Istiophoridae
232	Diretmidae	288	Plesiopidae	353	Owstoniidae	418	Amarsipidae
233	Anoplogastridae	289	Acanthoclinidae	354	Cepolidae	419	Centrolophidae
234	Berycidae	290	Glaucosomatidae	355	Mugilidae	420	Nomeidae
235	Holocentridae	291	Teraponidae	356	Sphyraenidae	421	Ariommatidae
236	Polymixidae	292	Banjosidae	357	Polynemidae	422	Tetragonuridae
237	Stephanoberycidae	293	Kuhliidae	358	Labridae	423	Stromateidae
238	Melamphaidae	294	Centrarchidae	359	Odacidae	424	Anabantidae
239	Gibberichthyidae	295	Percidae	360	Scaridae	425	Belontiidae
240	Rondeletiidae	296	Priacanthidae	361	Bathymasteridae	426	Helostomatidae
241	Barbourisiidae	297	Apogonidae	362	Zoarcidae	427	Osphronemidae
242	Cetomimidae	298	Dinolestidae	363	Stichaeidae	428	Luciocephalidae
Zeiformes		299	Sillaginidae	364	Cryptacanthodidae	429	Channidae
243	Parazenidae	300	Malacanthidae	365	Pholididae	430	Mastacembelidae
244	Macrurocyttidae	301	Labracoglossidae	366	Anarhichadidae	431	Chaudhuriidae
245	Zeidae	302	Lactariidae	367	Ptilichthyidae	*Pleuronectiformes*	
246	Oreosomatidae	303	Pomatomidae	368	Zaproridae	432	Psettodidae
247	Grammicolepididae	304	Rachycentridae	369	Scytalinidae	433	Citharidae
248	Caproidae	305	Echeneididae	370	Bovichthyidae	434	Bothidae
Gasterosteiformes		306	Carangidae	371	Nototheniidae	435	Pleuronectidae
249	Hypoptychidae	307	Nematistiidae	372	Harpagiferidae	436	Cynoglossidae
250	Aulorhynchidae	308	Coryphaenidae	373	Bathydraconidae	437	Soleidae
251	Gasterosteidae	309	Apolectidae	374	Channichthyidae	*Tetraodontiformes*	
Indostomiformes		310	Menidae	375	Opistognathidae	438	Triacanthodidae
252	Indostomidae	311	Lefognathidae	376	Congrogadidae	439	Triacanthidae
Pegasiformes		312	Bramidae	377	Chiasmodontidae	440	Balistidae
253	Pegasidae	313	Caristiidad	378	Champsodontidae	441	Ostraciidae
Syngnathiformes		314	Arripidae	379	Notograptidae	442	Triodontidae
254	Aulostomidae	315	Emmelichthyidae	380	Pholidichthyidae	443	Tetraodontidae
255	Fistulariidae	316	Lutjanidae	381	Trichodontidae	444	Diodontidae
256	Macrorhamphosidae	317	Caesionidae	382	Trachinidae	445	Molidae
257	Centriscidae	318	Lobotidae	383	Uranoscopidae		
258	Solenostomidae	319	Gerreidae	384	Trichonotidae		
259	Syngnathidae	320	Haemulidae	385	Creediidae		
Dactylopteriformes		321	Inermiidae	386	Leptoscopidae		
260	Dactylopteridae	322	Sparidae	387	Percophidae		
Synbranchiformes		323	Centracanthidae	388	Mugiloididae		
261	Synbranchidae	324	Lethrinidae	389	Cheimarrhichthyidae		
Scorpaeniformes		325	Nemipteridae	390	Tripterygiidae		
262	Scorpaenidae	326	Sciaenidae	391	Dactyloscopidae		
263	Synanceiidae	327	Mullidae	392	Labrisomidae		
264	Caracanthidae	328	Monodactylidae	393	Clinidae		
265	Aploactinidae	329	Pewpheridiidae	394	Chaenopsidae		
266	Pataecidae	330	Leptobramidae	395	Blenniidae		
267	Congiopodidae	331	Bathyclupeidae	396	Icosteidae		
268	Triglidae	332	Toxotidae	397	Schindleriidae		
269	Platycephalidae	333	Coracinidae	398	Ammodytidae		
270	Hoplichthyidae	334	Kyphosidae	399	Callionymidae		
271	Anoplopomatidae	335	Ephippididae	400	Draconettidae		
272	Hexagrammidae	336	Scatophagidae	401	Rhyacichthyidae		
273	Zaniolepididae	337	Rhinoprenidae	402	Eleotrididae		
274	Normanichthyidae	338	Chaetodontidae	403	Gobiidae		
275	Ereuniidae	339	Pomacanthidae	404	Gobioididae		
276	Cottidae	340	Enoplosidae	405	Trypauchenidae		
277	Cottocomephoridae	341	Pentacerotidae	406	Kraemeriidae		
278	Comephoridae	342	Nandidae	407	Microdesmidae		
279	Psychrolutidae	343	Oplegnathidae	408	Kurtidae		

Source: *Newsletter of Systematic Ichthyology,* Department of Ichthyology, California Academy of Sciences, Golden Gate Park, San Francisco, California 94118, sponsored in part by the American Society of Ichthyologists and Herpetologists. Follows Nelson (1984).

MOSS LANDING MARINE LABORATORIES - FIELD JOURNAL

General Location_____ Date_____
_____ Time_____
County_____ Field No._____
Lat_____ ON; Long._____ OW
Map_____ Weather:_____%cover;Air Temp._____
Wind Dir. & Force_____
Sal._____% Water Temp._____OC Turbidity_____
Tide_____Sea Cond._____Surface current_____
Dist.Offshore_____Preservative_____
Collected By:_____
Method of Capture:_____
Depth of Capture:_____
Misc. observations:_____
_____
Total # species _____Total # individuals_____
Species list:_____
_____
_____
_____   _____   _____   ____
___   ___   ___

a.

MUSEUM, MOSS LANDING MARINE LABORATORIES

Name _____ Cat. No. _____

Collector _____ Det. by _____

Date, Collected _____ Preserved _____

Location _____

_____

_____

Size _____ Depth _____ Substrate _____

Preservative _____ Fixative _____ Relaxant _____

No. Specimens _____Method of Capture _____

Remarks _____

_____

b. _____

MUSEUM, MOSS LANDING MARINE LABORATORIES

Name _____

Date _____ Acc. No. _____

Location _____

Lat._____ Long. _____

Depth _____ No. Spec. _____

c.   Coll. by _____ Det. by _____

Figure 11.1 Typical field journal (a) and museum labels (b) and (c) used when collecting and preserving fishes.

tion room. Then you arrange the specimens starting with the lowest numbers and continue serially.

When examining preserved specimens, take care to avoid breaking or destroying any parts. Fragile fin rays, for example, are often important characters that distinguish species. Parts removed for counting, such as pharyngeal teeth or gill arches, should be replaced in the specimens. Specimens should never be allowed to dry out. Place the fish in a tray of water while examining them. And, of course, the jars containing alcohol preservative should be kept covered while working to prevent evaporation.

Chapter 12
Age and Growth

Throughout history, human beings have engaged in a multitude of fisheries and have persistently managed to overfish a good number of populations. In the nineteenth century, the magnitude of this problem led to the beginnings of systematic fishery investigations. Age, length, and weight data are important tools in fishery biology since details of species growth and mortality rates, age at maturity, and life span can be calculated from such information (Ricker 1975, Gulland 1983). So important have age determinations been to fishery science that generations of fishery biologists have managed to pay off mortgages and have their children's teeth straightened doing little else but estimating the age, or aging, of fish.

AGE DETERMINATION AND VERIFICATION

Although numerous methods have been used to age fishes (see Nielsen and Johnson 1983), three general methods predominate. The first is recovering marked fish of a known age, which requires the capture, release, and recapture of fish. This is expensive and time-consuming and will not be discussed here. The second, called the Peterson method, involves comparisons of length-frequency distributions of fish population samples (Ricker 1975). This method requires measuring the lengths of a large number of fish in a population, and it is based on the supposition that the lengths of fish in a particular year-class will distribute normally around a mean (see chap. 8). Thus when such data are plotted, a series of normal curves for each age group will become apparent (fig. 12.1). Though often useful, this method is most reliable in younger year classes because they are easier to sample; older fish grow in length more slowly, and variation among individuals tends to obscure variation between year classes (Westrheim and Ricker 1978). Because many fish populations in tropical waters spawn throughout the year, distinct year classes are difficult to recognize in such settings. Therefore, the Peterson method is best limited to studies of temperate species with seasonal spawning activities that can be adequately sampled. The third method is to count marks that develop periodically in various hard parts of fishes. Due to its practicality and widespread applicability, we cover this method in the remainder of this chapter.

Several kinds of hard parts in fishes can be useful in determining age (Nielsen and Johnson 1983). Otoliths and scales are the hard parts most often used, but in elasmobranchs and some other bony fishes, rings or bands in the vertebrae have been studied as well. Also, bony fish opercula, fin rays, and other hard (calcified) structures may show annual marks (Six and Horton 1977) and could be useful for certain species if the more commonly used structures do not work out. Though concentrating here on otoliths and scales, we also present some methodology using fin rays and vertebrae. Should you wish to use other structures, such as operculi, clean them by soaking them in hot water (a little detergent may help) for about 20 minutes and remove remaining flesh with forceps and scalpel. Rings, if any, usually show up as the structure dries. If not, try immersion in one of the agents suggested for cleaning otoliths. For additional information on age determination in fishes, consult Bagenal (1973), Chilton and Beamish (1982), and Nielsen and Johnson (1983), for comprehensive reviews of the subject.

It is useful at this point to discuss what concentric marks in fish hard parts might represent. Although the exact process is unknown for many species, fish biologists have reached some consensus on species that have been extensively studied. In many species, these marks represent seasonal variations (usually winter-summer) in somatic growth rates. For some of the fine-scale marks seen, the time frame may be smaller, including monthly, daily, and even hourly deposition periods. These marks may also be strongly influenced by the amount and quality of food; physical factors such as temperature, salinity, or oxygen; and the physiological condition of the fish being studied. Of course, these factors may also vary seasonally or dielly. In general, the more extreme the temperature difference between summer and winter, the greater the differences will be in seasonal growth rates and hence the more obvious the annual marks will be. Fishes from areas of rapidly fluctuating temperatures may develop several marks per year. Tropical fishes often do not show much annual mark-

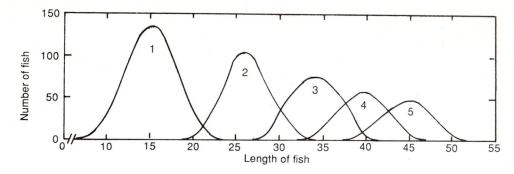

Figure 12.1 A typical size frequency curve indicating five size (age) classes in a sample of fish from a population.

ing, apparently because they live in a seasonally stable climate. However, this does not appear to be true for deep-sea fishes, which live in constant cold conditions. There may be a "biological clock" operating to deposit seasonal growth marks, even where seasonal fluctuations are minimal.

Because of this uncertainty about the cause or the time frame involved in deposition of annuli or concentric rings or bands on the hard parts of fishes, one must be cautious in interpreting their number and dimensions (Van Oosten 1929, Beamish and MacFarlane 1983, Casselman 1983). Various ways have been proposed and used to verify the time frame of deposition of these marks. These include the Peterson method of following size modes through time (especially of young age classes). You can also tag and recapture both laboratory-reared and field-caught individuals (using tetracycline to mark that hard part at the time it is depositing calcium) and then recapture or sacrifice the fish at a later time. These and other approaches are reviewed in Cailliet et al. (1983) for elasmobranchs, and in Casselman (1983) for bony fishes, but these principles apply to all fishes.

Another point is that the source and quantity of specimens used in age-determination studies are extremely important. First, specimens must be obtained from all size classes and should represent at least a one-year interval so that the progression and pattern of annulus formation is apparent for the species in question. Often the examination of numerous size classes, including juvenile and subadult forms, will reduce confusion and will ensure more accurate (and hopefully precise) age determination.

A word of encouragement and warning seems appropriate here. In many cases, annual marks are only imperfectly set down in bony or calcified material. It will soon become apparent that aging fishes is only part science; art and even metaphysics also play a role. You may find, after examining a number of scales or otoliths, that you develop impressions of what is a true annulus or a false one. We suggest you pay attention to these feelings, for herein lies the art of this field. In any case, as long as you are consistent and can instruct others in how to be consistent in exactly the same way, you will be able to come up with some meaningful age estimates and growth information for your fish species.

Another caution is necessary at the outset of this discussion. In the voluminous literature on age and growth of fishes, many terms have been used to describe the periodic marks on hard parts of fishes, and a whole other set of terms has been used to designate their meaning. For example, in the previous paragraph, we used the word *annulus* and distinguished true from false annuli. The intention here might be interpreted that the word *annulus* (or its plural form, annuli) implies a yearly pattern of deposition. However, annulus does not linguistically mean yearly, although the term *annual* does. The term *annual* or *annual mark* actually should be defined as a structural feature that correlates with a yearly event. An **annulus** is a concentric zone, band, or mark that is either a ridge, valley, or translucent or opaque zone. It does not necessarily imply a unit passage of time, despite the fact that it has been traditionally designated as a yearly mark (Chilton and Beamish 1982, Wilson et al. 1983). A recent publication of the *Proceedings of the International Workshop on Age Determination of Oceanic Pelagic Fishes: Tunas, Billfishes, Sharks* (Prince and Pulos 1983) has a glossary at the end that you should consult for accepted definitions of these and other commonly used terms in age determination of fishes (Wilson et al. 1983).

Otoliths

Otoliths are hard, calcareous bodies in the paired labyrinth systems of teleosts, located in the cranial bones near the brain. In most teleosts, the sagitta is by far the largest otolith and is usually used in aging studies. Figure 5.2, p. 61 illustrates a teleost sagitta, showing the terminology for various structures.

Sagittae viewed on a dark background by reflected light exhibit a series of dark and light rings. Otoliths are composed of calcium carbonate crystals embedded in an organic matrix. The organic material consists of layers of concentric shells. There is evidence that the variations in the amount and thickness of shells are responsible for ring formation. With some exceptions, opaque zones are laid down during summer, and translucent (hyaline) zones are formed during winter (see Casselman 1983 for a discussion of this). Translucent rings appear dark and opaque rings light when viewed by reflected light against a black background. We emphasize these conditions because vast confusion exists over the terminology of the rings. For instance, zones viewed by reflected light appear the reverse of those seen through transmitted light. Otoliths are usually examined on dark backgrounds with reflected light in an aqueous medium.

Otolith Removal

Fresh or frozen specimens are best for otolith studies, as nonneutralized formalin decalcifies otoliths, making them unfit for study. The way in which otoliths are removed depends on the type of fish, the permissible amount of allowable damage, and the personality of the dissector.

For least damage to the specimen, cut away the gill arches and remove the sagitta through the capsular otic bulla the base of the skull (fig. 12.2a). The bones of the bulla are relatively thin and may be cut or broken with blunt forceps or a scalpel.

It is also possible to cleave the head with a cleaver or strong knife in a sagittal (longitudinal) direction or to lift off the top of the skull, exposing the otoliths (fig. 12.2b). A cut across the head, somewhat behind the eyes, also exposes the otoliths. These methods involve a greater chance of damaging the otoliths, but once learned they are rapid techniques, particularly useful when large samples must be processed. Similarly, for flatfish, a cut above the upper eye into the skull (fig. 12.2c) will expose the otoliths.

Storage

The simplest way to store otoliths is to clean and dry them, then place them in small envelopes (such as coin envelopes). Small otoliths can be mounted on slides. If the otoliths are to be kept wet, they are stored in screw-top vials or plastic storage trays, in water, ethanol, or water and glycerine (often in 50-50 mixtures). Formalin should not be used. With water or water-glycerin storage, 0.5 percent thymol is added to inhibit fungus development.

Various otoliths respond differently to the same storage medium. Thus periodic inspections should be made. In particular, note if changes are occurring in surface or ring characteristics. For instance, otoliths stored in water will often develop a chalky coating, thus increasing surface opacity and making surface aging more difficult. This can be removed by dipping the sagitta into weak hydrochloric acid (20 percent), then rinsing it in water. However, this does wear away some of the otolith, possibly causing the loss of some bands. Also, ethanol or glycerin solutions clear otoliths to some degree.

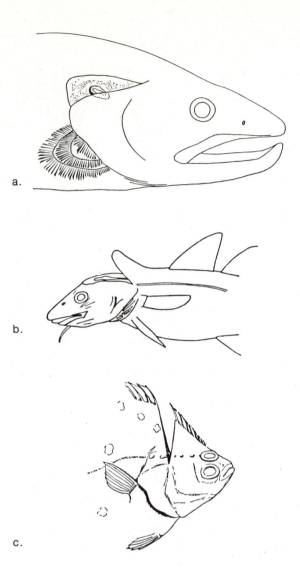

a.

b.

c.

Figure 12.2 Three methods of otolith extraction: (a) via the operculum above the gills; (b) by slicing the top of the skull off; and (c) by a vertical skull cut in flatfishes. (Tesch 1971)

Preparation and Viewing

The simplest way to view otoliths is to place the whole otolith in water on a dark-backed dish illuminated from above. This technique is very effective with thin, clear sagitta of young fish. When reading otoliths, compare the estimated age from both otoliths. Often one of the two has more distinct markings. Otoliths may have surface bands that are not annual (checks), particularly in the first few rings where growth is very rapid. Because these bands usually disappear when viewed from a different perspective, be sure to tilt the otolith in various ways to verify that the rings are spatially consistent.

Improving Ring Resolution

Whole Otolith Techniques. Thick otoliths are often quite opaque. These can often be cleared by immersing them in

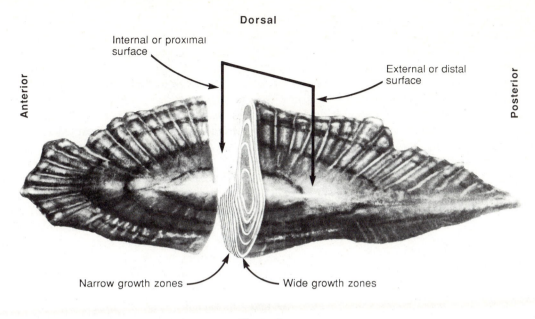

Dorsal

Internal or proximal surface

External or distal surface

Anterior

Posterior

Narrow growth zones

Wide growth zones

Ventral

Figure 12.3 Drawing of a Pacific hake otolith showing the relation between annuli visible on the surface and from sections. Note the smaller growth zones as the fish grows older. (Beamish 1979; Chilton and Beamish 1982)

various oils (such as anise, clove, or cedar), glycerin, xylol, or cresol for periods of a few days to a few months. Care should be taken, as the otoliths will continue to clear, sometimes completely clearing away the rings. Otoliths cleared in oil should be viewed in the same medium.

In many species, the outermost rings become very thin as growth slows, and these rings are often hard or impossible to see on whole otoliths. In fact, many species cease to lay down rings on the external surface; instead, growth and ring formation continue on the internal side (fig. 12.3). These sagittae can be sectioned to expose the additional rings. However you halve the otolith, it is always necessary to break the sagitta through the nucleus. If you miss the nucleus, you will also miss the record of the first year.

It has been demonstrated that sectioning the otolith (either by breaking or the thin-section method) is necessary to more accurately determine ages for longer-lived and more difficult-to-read species. We therefore recommend that you make initial careful comparisons of ages using both surface and section methods to decide at what age, if any, it becomes necessary to section the otolith. In making this decision, give consideration to the early natural history of each species, particularly the age at reproductive maturity. For all species, the use of surface aging as a supplement to section aging is beneficial in identifying the first several age zones in difficult specimens.

Burned and Dyed Section Techniques. Otoliths may be sectioned in several ways. One simple technique involves breaking the otolith by placing your thumbs on either side

of the nucleus and snapping it. Trivial as it sounds, this method has been commonly used. The sections are then mounted in plasticine—broken end up and horizontal—and examined under a dissecting microscope (fig. 12.4). Each piece is then illuminated from the side, keeping the broken surface in shadow (see Chilton and Beamish 1982 for more details). The otoliths can also be broken using forceps, or they can require deep scoring prior to breaking. This can be done with a handsaw or an Isomet low-speed saw. The broken surface may require some grinding.

In some species—notably some soles, rockfishes, carps, and eels—otolith rings are indistinct or invisible. There are several methods that might augment their visibility.

Burning (Christensen 1964, Chilton and Beamish 1982)

1. After removing adhering tissue and cleaning it in alcohol, heat the otolith over a very low alcohol or gas flame. Heating time will vary, but whole otoliths may take 10-30 seconds and sections perhaps 5-8 seconds. Heat the surfaces evenly, passing the broken surface back and forth through the yellow portions of the flame until a brown color is attained. Too much heat will cause the otolith to crumble; too little will not char sufficiently. After gentle heating, the translucent rings will darken, and false annuli will be less dark. Less burning time may be necessary for younger fish.

2. On the burned surfaces of both whole and younger sectioned sagittae, brush on cooking oil to bring out additional detail. With sectioned otoliths in particular,

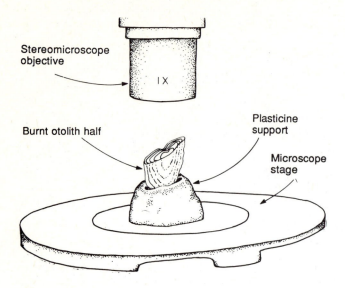

Figure 12.4 Drawing of a broken and burnt otolith positioned in Plasticine under a microscope. (Chilton and Beamish 1982)

cooking oil brushed on the broken surface may be sufficient, and heating may not be necessary. Cool for approximately 15 seconds.

3. Store burned otoliths dry. The dark color will fade with time but can be returned by additional heating.

Dyeing (Albrechtsen 1968)

1. Dissolve 0.05 gr methyl violet B to 30 ml distilled water and add 1 ml concentrated hydrochloric acid, stirring continuously. The solution should be used within a few hours.
2. Apply a thin covering of the dye to the otolith surface. The dye will effervesce and leave the organic membranes slightly protruding. After 20-40 seconds, the calcium carbonate from the otolith neutralizes the acid.
3. When the fluid changes from almost colorless to a light violet, dyeing of the membranes begins and continues until the water has evaporated. If the result is unsatisfactory, apply more dye by touching a brush to the edge of the otolith. Do not touch the surface of the protruding membrane. After dyeing the otolith, clean the specimen by dipping it in water for a short time.

Thin-Section Techniques. In some species, the otoliths require that a section be removed from the nucleus in order to produce readable growth zones. In this technique, the otoliths are embedded in epoxy on small wooden cubes or on thin pieces of plastic, and then they are cut from exterior to interior through the otolith center, using two diamond-impregnated blades on a lapidary saw. The thickness of the wafer is equal to the distance between the blades, typically 0.5 mm. Either a Buehler Isomet low-speed saw or Bron-

will high-speed sectioning machine may be used. With the resin-embedding method, you can also use a jeweler's saw. Polishing sections may be desired and accomplished using very fine grade wet-dry sandpaper (400-600 grit carborundum) or jeweler's rouge. High-quality optics—either compound or dissection microscopes could be required—are critical to achieve precision in otolith section reading. This promising technique is further explained by Beamish (1979) and Chilton and Beamish (1982).

Year-Class Assignment

Though both the opaque and translucent zones have been used as annual marks, a completed annual ring is often defined as the interface between an inner translucent and outer opaque zone. As the new opaque zone is just being formed, it can be quite difficult to see. This could lead to its being overlooked, and the fish assigned to an incorrect year class. For this and other reasons (detailed by Collins and Spratt 1969 and Chilton and Beamish 1982), an agreed-upon birth date is often given to a species. This date generally coincides with the period when an annual band is formed. January 1 is widely used (Chilton and Beamish 1982), though other dates (such as June 1—Collins and Spratt 1969) have been assigned, depending on species.

Let us assume a January 1 birth date and give an example of how this might work. Examine the otolith in figure 12.5. It has three visible opaque zones (white) and three translucent ones (dark). As far as the eye can ascertain, the outer margin is hyaline. If the fish were taken in December, it must be assumed, by definition, that no opaque outer margin is present. Thus the fish is age 2. If taken in January, an opaque band is assumed to be visible on the outer margin. Then this fish is age 3.

Scales

Scales in teleosts are composed of two layers: the outer one ridged and calcified, and the inner flat and fibrous (Van Oosten 1957). A number of structures can occur on the scales (see chap.1, fig. 1.19). The innermost section, inside the first **circulus**, is the **focus**. Circuli are ridges (often concentric around the focus) on the outer scale surface. When body growth is rapid, these ridges are laid down farther apart than during slower growth, when crowded fine circuli appear. Circuli may not be concentric. On herring scales, for example, most circuli run dorsoventrally; only scales from the caudal fin show the concentric pattern.

A scale **annulus**, used to denote a year's growth (Chilton and Beamish 1982), is generally produced during slow-growth winter periods (fig. 12.6). It may be identified in various ways. Commonly, annuli are zones of crowded circuli that can often be followed around the scale. Annuli are sometimes typified by groups of circuli that appear to be broken or to cross over one another. Not all zones of

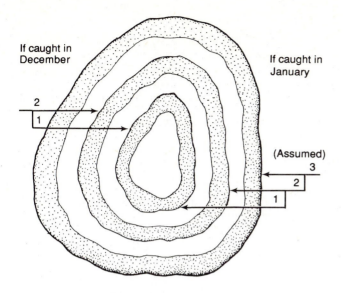

Figure 12.5 An example using an otolith of assigning a year class and/or birth date, using information on the time of year in which it was collected.

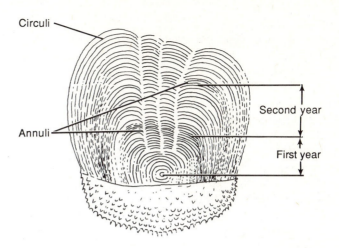

Figure 12.6 A typical ctenoid scale, showing groups of concentric rings that can be classified into annuli and interpreted as seasonal growth marks.

crowded circuli are annual. They may represent accessory rings, indicating reduced growth not associated with low temperatures (such as spawning).

Two types of scales, **ctenoid** and **cycloid**, are most commonly used in age determination. Cycloid scales occur principally on soft-rayed fish. They are circular, and the focus is near the scale center and is surrounded by more or less concentric circuli. Ctenoid scales are found principally on spiny-rayed fish, and they show unequal growth around the scale center.

Scale Removal

Scales taken for age studies are usually plucked from the middle of the body, often from the flanks at the tip of the pectoral fins. However, the sites of useful scales may vary among species. Sample a number of areas before making a decision. When comparing ages of individual fish, take scales from the same area. Scales that are large and symmetrical are most useful. Lateral-line scales, because of structural barriers to ring formation, are not normally used. Regenerated scales—indicated by a very large focus—are not useful in age determination because they lack some or all circuli. Fish of some species, particularly older individuals, may have more than two-thirds of their scales regenerated.

Wash the fish under cold running water and rub the body lightly in a head-to-tail direction. This removes loose scales that could have come from other fish. Using forceps (and a scalpel if the scales are deeply embedded), loosen and remove a few scales. You will feel a slight resistance if the scale is embedded in the sample fish. Clean the scales by dipping them in fresh water and rubbing them between the thumb and fingers. Alternatively, place the scales under a few drops of water and remove adhering tissue while viewing them under a dissecting microscope.

Storage

As with otoliths, scales can be stored in small coin envelopes. But, as scales tend to curl when dry, they store better when mounted between two glass slides held together with clear tape. This is also a satisfactory way to view and age scales.

Viewing

The simplest way to read scales is to place them on a glass slide, cover them with a few drops of water, and examine them under a microscope. Microprojectors, which project an image of the scale onto a screen, are also commonly used (Chilton and Beamish 1982).

Another technique involves making scale impressions on acetate. The scale is pressed into the acetate under high pressure and elevated temperature. These impressions are then placed in a projector and viewed on a screen.

Fin-Ray Sections

Fin-ray cross sections (Beamish 1981, Chilton and Beamish 1982) have been used to age fishes, notably pelagic fishes, such as billfishes and tunas (Prince and Pulos 1983). This technique has certain distinct advantages. Fish with small otoliths (tunas) or with no other hard parts (such as spiny dogfish and sturgeon) have previously been difficult to age. In addition, use of this method means specimens need not be killed. Pectoral fin rays have been used to age sturgeon (Kohlhorst et al. 1980).

Procedure

Some experimentation is called for in using fin rays. All fins should be initially sectioned. Though dorsal, pectoral, and pelvic rays are most commonly used, any fin spine or ray may be optimal.

Cut four to six rays at their bases. These can be frozen for later preparation or air dried immediately. The cut base of the fin should be perpendicular to the longitudinal axis of the rays. Mount the dried fin ray, embedded in epoxy, on wooden blocks. Completely embed small fins in epoxy. Section using the sectioning techniques described under Otoliths. Beamish (1981) found that sections 0.5-0.8 mm thick were optimal. After sectioning is complete, fin sections may be mounted on glass slides in mounting medium or stored in envelopes.

Elasmobranch Age Determination

Traditionally, aging elasmobranchs has presented problems. Conventional age determination methods used in bony fishes were not applicable to sharks, skates, and rays because they lack the commonly used calcareous otoliths and other skeletal hard parts. Vertebral centra have proved useful in age determinations in several elasmobranch species (Cailliet et al. 1983). In most elasmobranch species studied, there are two kinds of concentric marks on the vertebral centra (fig. 12.7). A **ring** is defined as the narrowest kind of concentric mark observed, and a **band** as wider concentric marks composed of a group of rings. Wider bands contain widely spaced rings; narrow bands have rings that are more tightly spaced. These bands are thought to be annual in many species (Holden and Vince 1973, Stevens 1975, Jones and Geen 1977), but validation studies are few (Cailliet et al. 1983).

Centrum Cleaning

It is important to use the larger, more anterior centra for age studies, as smaller centra from the caudal region may lack some bands (Cailliet et al. 1983). All aging techniques require centra free of tissue. First remove the neural and haemal arches. Tissue-removal techniques vary with species. For many, soaking the centrum in distilled water for 5 minutes followed by air drying allows the connective tissue to be peeled away. Soaking in bleach may be required for other species. Bleaching time is proportional to centrum size and ranges from 5 to 30 minutes. After bleaching, rinse the centrum thoroughly in water.

Centrum Staining

In this technique (a modification of Stevens 1975), calcium salts in the centrum bands are replaced with silver, which become dark upon ultraviolet illumination. Therefore, the narrow bands, with more tightly spaced rings, appear darker than broad ones. Fresh specimens and those preserved in 70 percent isopropanol can be used.

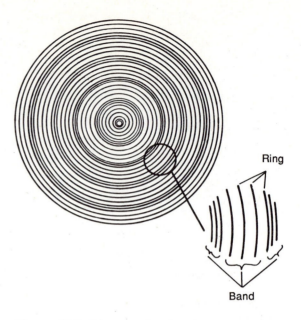

Figure 12.7 Diagram showing the two kinds of concentric marks on the vertebral centrum of elasmobranchs.

1. Soak the cleaned centrum in concentrated (88 percent) formic acid for 2-4 minutes to remove any traces of bleach and to etch its surface.
2. Soak the centrum in distilled water for about 15 minutes.
3. Place centrum in 1 percent silver nitrate solution and immediately place in a chamber illuminated by ultraviolet light. Illuminate for 3-15 minutes, depending upon species and centrum size.
4. Rinse centrum in distilled water to remove excess silver nitrate.
5. To remove excess silver and fix the chemical substitution, soak centrum in 5 percent sodium thiosulfate solution for 2-3 minutes. This fixation often eradicates very narrow rings (but not the bands). Therefore, if counting narrow rings is desired, make these counts before fixation.
6. Store centrum in 70 percent isopropanol.

To read the centrum, examine under a dissecting microscope with transmitted light focused laterally on the centrum.

Two other useful techniques require sectioning the cleaned centrum (either transversely or longitudinally, fig. 12.8), particularly when the centra have relatively deep cones. Large vertebrae may be secured in a vise and cut with a small circular saw attachment on a jeweler's drill. For smaller specimens, half of the centrum can be worn away with aluminum oxide wheel points and fine sandpaper attachments for the same tool (Cailliet et al. 1983).

The second technique involves taking x-radiographs of half-centra. This technique was suggested in Miller and

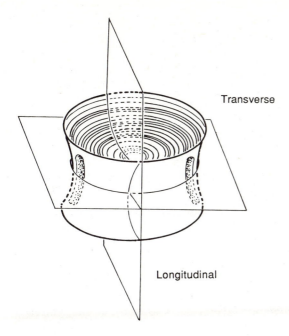

Figure 12.8 The shape of an elasmobranch vertebral centrum and two planes of sectioning that are often useful in aiding ring and band counting.

Tucker (1979). The x-radiographs can be viewed through dissecting or compound microscopes using transmitted or reflected light.

A third technique involves applying oil to the face of the centrum, which increases the clarity of the bands by eliminating superficial irregularities. Scraping the centrum face with a scalpel frequently enhances the clarity of finer bands. Though cedarwood oil has been used for this process, other oils, including cooking oil, might prove effective. View centra prepared with oil under a dissecting microscope over a dark background with light transmitted both vertically and horizontally.

Further discussion of elasmobranch aging is found in Cailliet et al. (1983).

Back-Calculated Lengths

It is possible to estimate the length at each year of life of each of the specimens examined, using **back-calculation** (Nielsen and Johnson 1983). The technique involves measuring the diameters of whatever structure was used to age the fishes and using these measurements to estimate lengths at given ages. For example, let's assume we have used otoliths for age determination:

1. Choose one axis of the otolith and measure the diameters of all otoliths used and record the data. Attempt to use otoliths of all size classes of fish in your study. After measuring, plot otolith diameter against

fish length. Calculate the linear regression ($y = ax + b$) of the relationship (see Sokal and Rohlf 1981).

2. With each otolith, measure the diameters of the outer edge of each opaque ring. Each ring can be converted to a length by placing its diameter into the regression equation. For instance, in the formula

$$y = ax + b$$

y = annual ring diameter, a = slope, b = y-intercept, and x = the unknown length at that ring diameter. We know a and b from 1 and we have just measured y. Thus we can solve for x. Here we are assuming that the completion of each opaque ring is an annual event. This may not be true for all fishes or all hard parts studied.

3. Calculate the mean lengths at each back-calculated "age" for all specimens. As an example, let us assume we have 14 specimens, of ages 1-7, with 2 specimens for each year. A table of values might look like table 12.1. For this example, we have included the two back-calculated lengths per age. Normally, only the means would be shown, and sample sizes would need to be considerably larger.

We now have an estimate for back-calculated lengths at age. If the age at capture was 6, for instance, we have calculated that the mean lengths at ages 1-5 were 39.5, 59.5, 70.5, 79, and 87, respectively (table 12.1).

Note that larger fish were smaller at each back-calculated age. For example, at back-calculated age 1, 7-year-olds were 36.5, whereas 4-year-olds were 41.5. This is Rosa Lee's phenomenon, which notes that larger fish in a year class often have a different (usually greater) mortality rate from smaller ones (Ricker 1975).

• What other reasons could account for the differences in back-calculated sizes at given ages? See Ricker (1975) for some guidance in answering this question.

Growth Curves

A major goal of fishery biologists is fishery management. To construct the necessary yield models, one needs to know the growth rates of individuals. A number of growth curve models (von Bertalanffy, Gompertz, and logistic, summarized in Ricker 1975) are available. Because the von Bertalanffy is widely used, we employ it here as an example.

The von Bertalanffy growth equation is expressed as

$$l_t = L_\infty(1 - e^{-K(t - t_0)})$$

where

l_t = predicted length at time t
L_∞ = maximum length predicted by the equation

Table 12.1 Table of values estimating lengths.

Age at Capture	Calculated Lengths at Successive Completed Rings												
	1	x	2	x	3	x	4	x	5	x	6	x	7	x
1	56,58	57												
2	50,54	52	75,76	75.5										
3	41,43	42	67,66	66.5	88,89	88.5								
4	41,42	41.5	65,64	64.5	80,80	80	88,86	87						
5	40,42	41	61,61	61	75,75	75	84,82	83	91,90	90.5				
6	39,40	39.5	59,60	59.5	71,70	70.5	80,78	79	88,86	87	88,90	89		
7	36,37	36.5	55,56	55.5	65,67	66	80,78	79	83,85	84	83,83	83	88,86	87

e = base of the natural log

t = time

t_0 = the size at which the organism would theoretically have been age 0

K = the growth coefficient (instantaneous rate)

If the mean lengths at various ages of a species are known, it is possible to estimate the parameters L_∞, K, and t_0. There are many computer programs that will quickly yield these parameters (see, for example, Pauly 1984). However, they may also be obtained graphically, and doing it manually will help you understand the pros and cons of using this model.

Below, we give an example of how to estimate these parameters graphically, using a Walford plot. You can find a full exposition of each step in Ricker (1975), Everhart and Youngs (1981), and Gulland (1983). The data for this example come from Manooch and Barans (1982).

1. List age and mean length as in columns 1 and 2 in table 12.2.
2. Plot mean length at age 1 against mean length at age 2. Continue plotting age 2 against age 3, and so on (fig. 12.9).
3. We can determine L_∞ in two ways.
   a. Draw a line best approximating a regression through the data points. Since there will often be some scatter, the regression equation should be calculated (see Sokal and Rohlf 1981). The intersection of this line with a 45-degree line drawn from the axis is an estimate of L_∞. In our example, our first approximation was L_∞ = 300 mm (fig. 12.9).
   b. Alternatively, L_∞ may also be obtained by solving the equation:

$$L_\infty = \frac{y - \text{intercept}}{(1 - k)}$$

   where k = slope of the line in figure 12.9.

The parameter K = $-\log_e$ slope. From our graph, we estimated a slope of .87, thus K = $-\log_e 87$ = .14.

5. These are, however, only first approximations of the most accurate L_∞ and K. We can improve our accuracy by selecting several L_∞'s around our first estimate (300) and plotting ($L_\infty - l_t$) against each age. The L_∞ giving the straightest line is the best approximation of L_∞ and K. In this new plot (fig. 12.10), K is equal to the slope of the line.

We have selected three L_∞'s (295, 300, and 310). The mean lengths at age were subtracted from the trial L_∞'s (columns 3, 4, 5—table 12.2), and the points were plotted in figure 12.10. It is apparent that 310 mm is the best approximation of L_∞. The new improved K = .24.

6. To find t_0, we use the equation

$$t_0 = \frac{y - \text{intercept} - \log_e L_\infty}{K}$$

where all values were taken from figure 12.10. Thus

$$t_0 = \frac{5.45 - 5.70}{.24} = \frac{-.25}{.24} = -1.04$$

Thus the von Bertalanffy equation is

$$l_t = 310 \, (1 - e^{-.24(t+1.04)})$$

For this example, we have used only graphical techniques. Of course, any calculator-assisted regression analysis can also give y-intercepts and slopes (see Pauly 1984).

LENGTH AND WEIGHT

Fisheries biologists often find it useful to be able to ascertain the weight of a fish when only the length is known (and vice versa). If, for example, fish are not marketable until 1

Table 12.2 Example of von Bertalanffy parameters.

Column 1	Column 2	Column 3		Column 4		Column 5	
Estimated Age	Mean Length (mm)	Trial $L_\infty = 295$ $(L_\infty - l_t)$	$\log_e (L_\infty - l_t)$	Trial $L_\infty = 300$ $(L_\infty - l_t)$	$\log_e (L_\infty - l_t)$	Trial $L_\infty = 310$ $(L_\infty - l_t)$	$\log_e (L_\infty - l_t)$
1	135.4	159.6	5.1	164.4	5.1	174.6	5.2
2	181.9	113.1	4.7	118.1	4.8	128.1	4.9
3	203.0	92.0	4.5	97.0	4.6	107.0	4.7
4	220.0	75.0	4.3	80.0	4.4	90.0	4.5
5	234.5	60.5	4.1	65.5	4.2	75.5	4.3
6	255.7	39.3	3.7	44.3	3.8	54.3	4.0
7	265.8	29.2	3.4	34.2	3.5	44.2	3.8
8	277.0	18.0	2.9	23.0	3.1	33.0	3.5
9	286.7	8.3	2.1	13.3	2.6	23.3	3.2

Source: Manooch and Barans 1982.

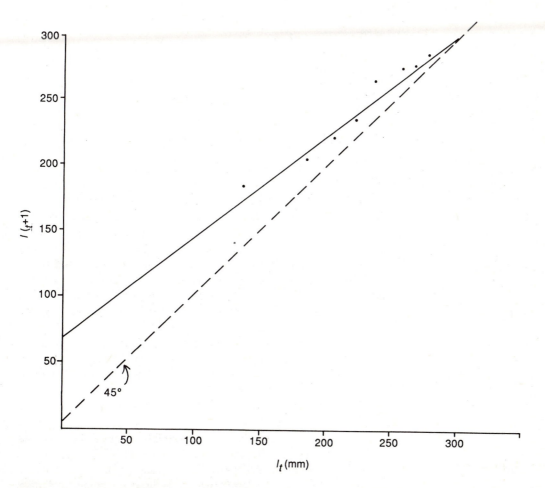

Figure 12.9 Ford-Walford plot of adjacent, successive lengths to estimate values for L_∞ and K in the von Bertalanffy growth model.

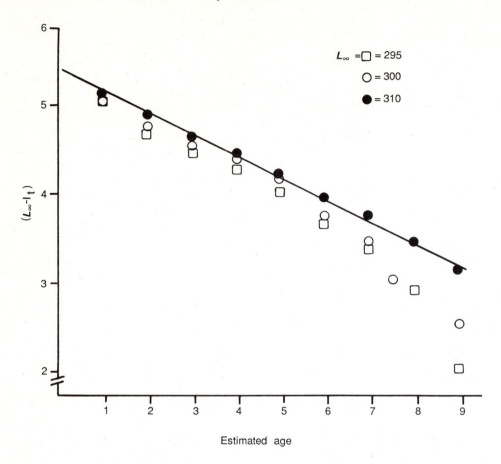

Figure 12.10 Iterative method of solving for $L∞$ and K in the von Bertalanffy growth model.

kg or more, mesh size of commercial nets may be regulated to allow smaller individuals to escape if the length-weight relationship is known.

The relationship between length and weight is often well described by the formula for a parabola:

$$W = aL^b$$

where W = weight, L = length, and a and b are constants. This relationship can also be described as

$$W = \log a + b \log L$$

This is a transformation often used by fishery biologists. Many computer programs are available to evaluate this relationship, and a number of pocket calculators also perform the calculations.

EXERCISE: FISH GROWTH

To compute the age-length and length-weight relationships for a species, you will need numerous specimens representing the entire size range in the population. In general,

the more specimens available for measurement and age determination, the more accurate the relationship you will obtain. Also, as large a sample of each size category as possible is important to adequately represent the age and weight characteristics of all sizes of fish. If large numbers of specimens cannot be captured by field sampling, they may be available as filleted carcasses, which would otherwise be discarded from fish markets and processing houses. Although there will not be any weight information from such specimens, the length can be measured, and you can also obtain hard parts such as otoliths.

Record the following data on a data sheet such as shown in table 12.3: species, fish length (total, standard, or fork, as convenient, but be consistent; see sect. 2) to the nearest millimeter, weight to the nearest 0.1 gram, sex, state of maturity (see tables 14.1, 14.2 in chap. 14 for criteria), and gonad weight. If the gonads are to be used in a later laboratory exercise on reproduction, preserve them as described in chapter 11, or freeze them if only eggs are to be counted before the gonads are discarded.

Remove the hard parts to be used for aging, including otoliths (sagittae), scales, opercles, fin rays, and vertebrae if possible. Prepare these structures as described previously, and read them for estimated ages. Enter your estimates on

Table 12.3 Data sheet.

Species	Length	Weight	Sex	Gonad State	Gonad Weight	Age				
						Otoliths	Scales	Vertebrae	Opercula	Other

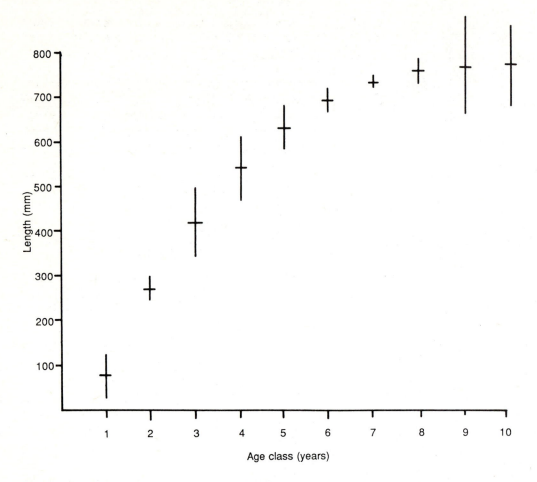

Figure 12.11 Age-length growth curve showing mean sizes, plus and minus one standard deviation, for each age class.

the data sheet. Discard structures that are unreadable or difficult to read; limited quality data are better than abundant poor data.

Once all size classes are represented, assemble the data and perform the following tasks:

1. Calculate the mean length, variance, standard deviation, and standard error of the lengths in each age group (methods for computing these statistics are described in section 2, pp. 108–114).
   a.   For each sex separately
   b.   For combined sexes
2. Plot the mean lengths and their 95 percent confidence limits against ages on a graph similar to figure 12.11.

   • Did males and females grow at different rates?
   • Is there an inflection (steep bend) in the growth curve or a rapid leveling off toward the end? If so, what might these inflection points represent?

3. Using the data available, calculate the von Bertalanffy growth model parameters L_∞, K, and t_0, and use these

in the equation to generate a von Bertalanffy growth curve. Plot the predicted lengths at each age from this model on the same graph, and compare these theoretical lengths with the means of the observed ones.

   • Do the two approaches to plotting growth differ? If so, what do you think most contributed to these differences?

4. If you estimated ages using different structures, compare the readings on a fish-by-fish basis. Another way to compare them is to repeat the procedures in steps 1-3 above for each of the structures aged and compare the growth curves that result.

   • How would you measure the relative precision of two different methods of determining age using rings in hard parts? Can you conceive of a quantitative measure of precision amenable to statistical analysis?
   • Do you think that the growth curves that resulted from your analysis would differ from curves resulting from the work of others? Consider the various reasons that interreader differences could significantly alter a growth curve.

5. For purposes of back-calculations, measure the diameter of all rings (completed opaque rings, for example, if you are aging otoliths) from several individuals of each age (size) class. Using a regression of hard-part diameter against length of the fish, assign each ring-diameter measurement a total length estimate, and use the pooled information to calculate:
   a.   An average calculated length for each age group
   b.   Age- or size-specific growth increments
   Plot a growth curve based on these back-calculated lengths and compare it with the curve you generated in 2 and 3 above.

   • Do these methods give different estimates of growth? If so, why do you suppose this occurred?

   • Is there much difference in incremental growth characteristics between the two methods? If so, what do you think contributed the most to these differences?

6. Using the length and weight data, compute the constants a and b in the formula $W = aL^b$. If enough data are available, compute separate constants for each sex and for both sexes combined. Using weights to replace lengths, replot your growth curves.

   • Do the curves of weight versus age differ much from the curve of length versus age? If so, why?

Chapter 13
Feeding

There is increasing interest in the study of community ecology—the relationships between organisms and their environment. Food-habit studies can contribute to an understanding of the interactions between members of a community. In addition, knowledge of prey selection enables mapping of energy, nutrient, and, occasionally, pollutant flow.

The feeding methods and food habits of fishes are strongly correlated with external and internal (alimentary tract) morphology (Keenleyside 1979). For example, body, fin, and mouth shape, fin and tooth placement, and jaw protrusibility can all affect how a fish feeds and what it eats (see chap.5, pp. 62–68).

At one extreme, swift and continuously swimming fishes that eat swift-moving prey have fusiform bodies, with somewhat rounded cross sections and long falcate pectoral and forked caudal fins. At the other, fish that cannot swim for extended periods but are agile and stable have gibbose or laterally compressed bodies, wide pectoral fins, and truncated or rounded tails (see fig. 1.9, chap. 1, for illustrations). Many gibbose fish live in complex habitats, such as among kelp and algae or coral heads, and they prey on small food items. There are, of course, many variations on these themes (Keast and Webb 1966). Similarly, a fish's internal morphology—its tooth shape, number, and placement; its gill raker size and shape; its gut length and pyloric caeca number, and so on—are also related to diet and feeding behavior.

A number of schemes have been used to classify fishes by their food habits and foraging strategies. Generally, these schemes fall into two categories: **foraging guilds** and **foraging methods** (Keenleyside 1979). A guild is a group of species coexisting in a community and sharing the same resource base. Foraging methods—the ways in which a species captures prey—may differ within a guild; the resource may be exploited in a number of different ways in terms of method, space, or time. A species may occupy different guilds in its lifetime. For instance, young fish may be midwater planktivores and then become demersal mesocarnivores as they mature. Some species may occupy two guilds, switching from one to another as various alternative prey become available (Love and Ebeling 1978).

FORAGING GUILDS

Demersal planktivores are primarily tropical fishes that are usually territorial and switch from herbivory to planktivory. Many damselfishes (Pomacentridae) are members of this guild.

Demersal microcarnivores may be grazing or browsing species that feed on benthic invertebrates. Typical microcarnivores include suckers (Catostomidae), freshwater basses (Centrarchidae), minnows (Cyprinidae), surfperches (Embiotocidae), wrasses (Labridae), parrotfishes (Scaridae), and croakers (Sciaenidae).

Demersal mesocarnivores are often stalkers and ambushers that sit in wait for larger moving prey such as fish and mobile invertebrates. Many mesocarnivores are nocturnal or forage during the crepuscular periods. Examples include freshwater basses, predatory catfishes (Ictaluridae), snapper (Lutjanidae), scorpionfishes (Scorpaenidae), and marine basses (Serranidae).

Plant-cropping omnivores are specialized forms that bite off pieces of algae but probably mostly assimilate the sessile animals living thereon. Plant croppers include opaleyes (Girellidae) and rudderfishes (Kyphosidae).

Herbivores eat and assimilate algae or other plant material and are most abundant in tropical marine waters and temperate freshwaters. Examples include minnows, damselfishes, and parrotfishes.

Midwater planktivores are diurnal or nocturnal fishes that eat plankton. Juveniles whose parents belong to other guilds are often planktivorous. Adult planktivores include topsmelt (Atherinidae), freshwater basses, herrings (Clupeidae), anchovies (Engraulidae), and damselfishes.

Midwater microcarnivores feed by picking or plucking small invertebrates from surfaces of plants or even other fishes in the water column. They can also pick plankton when the occasion arises. Many juveniles feed in this manner. Many adult wrasses are microcarnivores. In temperate waters they can browse or pick prey off the surfaces of giant algae, but in the tropics, which lack such kelp forests, small wrasses often "clean"; they pick ectoparasites from the bodies of larger "host" species.

Midwater mesocarnivores are larger predatory fishes

that feed on smaller fishes, squids, or other nektonic prey in midwater. Many large, pelagic fishes are members of this guild. Examples include pikes (Esocidae), billfishes (Istiophoridae), oceanic sharks (Lamnidae), and tunas (Scombridae).

Megacarnivores are the very largest piscivores, such as giant groupers (Serranidae) and large oceanic sharks that feed on other large fishes.

FORAGING METHODS

Pursuers are continuous fast swimmers that actively pursue their prey. They are often pelagic forms, with fusiform bodies and forked or lunate caudal fins. Examples include many oceanic sharks (Lamnidae) and tunas.

Stalkers often swim slowly or hover, then dart after prey in short bursts. They commonly have elongate bodies. Examples include freshwater basses, pikes, barracudas (Sphyraenidae), and marine basses (Serranidae).

Ambushers are usually benthic and cryptically colored and seize prey with quick lunges from hiding places. Their eyes are often oriented dorsally, and the mouth is large and frequently upturned. Typical ambushers include anglerfishes (Lophiidae) and scorpionfishes and rockfishes (Scorpaenidae).

Strainers usually swim continuously and have streamlined, fusiform bodies. Lacking strong jaws or teeth, they strain food out of the water through their large mouths by numerous long and close-set gill rakers. Their guts are often quite long. Strainers include the giant whale (Rhincodontidae) and basking sharks (Cetorhinidae), herrings, and anchovies.

Pickers hover and dart about, selecting small prey from the substrate or water column. They have short, gibbose, maneuverable bodies, highly protrusible mouths (often upturned), and small, numerous teeth. Typical pickers include topsmelt and wrasses.

Browsers crop tips off plants and sessile animals. **Grazers** indiscriminately engulf mouthfuls of substrate (sand, mud, pebbles, turf), then winnow or digest out food items. Their bodies are often short and compressed. Their teeth are quite variable: Some species have teeth fused into plates, others have small and numerous teeth, and still others lack teeth altogether. Examples include minnows, mullets (Mugilidae), and parrotfishes.

COLLECTION AND DATA ANALYSIS

Most collection methods bias the results of fish-feeding studies in one way or another. For example, fish caught by hook and line often have a higher-than-average proportion of empty stomachs because hungry fish are most apt to strike at bait. Fish collected by poisoning often glut themselves on organisms that die before the fish succumb. Specimens taken by spear and brought up from deep water often regurgitate their stomach contents. Fish must be collected somehow though. As long as the drawbacks of each collecting method are known and taken into consideration during data analysis, the results can still be valuable.

Fish should be preserved soon after capture to prevent continued digestion. Fish digestive tracts can be extracted and placed in 4–10 percent buffered formalin immediately after capture, the digestive tracts injected with formalin, or the entire fish preserved. If the whole fish is preserved, open the coelom to admit the formalin, or inject formalin into the body cavity. Do not place living fish directly into formalin because they will usually regurgitate their meal. Though formalin quickly halts digestion, it may also cause the food mass to solidify, making prey identification difficult. Sometimes it helps to transfer the solid preserved mass to 70 percent ethanol; then shake to dislodge food items. After the tissue has been fixed (one to three days), rinse it in fresh water for a few hours to remove the formalin and store in alcohol (50–70 percent ethanol, isopropanol, or methanol).

Some investigators chill newly captured specimens on ice, freezing them soon after. However, chilling may only slow down digestion. Dry ice can be used to freeze specimens (particularly small ones) in the field. Then, the specimens are thawed, their guts removed, and the gut contents preserved in 70 percent ethanol. The ethanol dissolves any mucus that binds the food. Shaking the gut contents in alcohol and then decanting the residue separates the food items nicely for identification.

Several different ways of measuring prey use and analyzing feeding habits have been proposed and used, but little agreement exists that would enable uniformity in analyzing food habit data. This is primarily due to differences in objectives; in the type, size, and digestibility of prey; and in the way different fish predators process their food. Most methods use one or more of the following three measures: (1) **frequency of occurrence**—the proportion or percent of fish guts in which a particular food item was found; (2) **numerical abundance**—the number of individuals of a particular food item found in each gut or the percent of all gut contents combined that the prey type comprised; (3) **volumetric (weight) importance**—the quantity of each item measured either by water displacement (usually in a graduated cylinder) or scale (after the item is blotted dry), or the percent by volume or weight that a given prey type comprised of the total volume of all gut contents. Any one of these measures can be ranked, creating **rank-hierarchy lists**, as done for predator A (table 13.1). Here, food items (prey species) are ranked by percent number and percent volume measures.

Any single measure by itself can, however, be potentially misleading in some way. For example, relative

Table 13.1 Feeding-habit data of two hypothetical fish predators. Prey importance is listed by number, volume, frequency, and the index of relative importance (I.R.I.).

	Predator A					Predator B			
Prey Species	Number (percent)	Volume (percent)	Frequency (percent)	I.R.I.	Prey Species	Number (percent)	Volume (percent)	Frequency (percent)	I.R.I.
1	30	25	20	1100	1	50	45	30	2850
2	18	22	25	1000	2	10	20	10	300
3	18	18	30	1080	3	9	10	5	95
4	15	16	10	310	4	8	11	7	133
5	8	10	12	216	5	7	2	12	108
6	6	5	18	198	6	9	10	50	950
7	5	5	32	320	7	7	2	11	99

number of each food item reflects how many of a particular item were consumed but is highly correlated with food size. It is therefore biased toward smaller food items, which, if commonly used by a fish predator, must be more numerous than large food items. On the other hand, volumetric or weight measures are often biased toward larger items, which may take longer to digest. However, this measure may also better reflect the amount of biomass that each prey item is contributing to the diet of a fish predator. Frequency of occurrence information is useful in that it represents what proportion of fish predators sampled consumed at least some of a particular item, but it may be biased toward relatively scarce food items that occur often but do not contribute very much either in number or volume.

For these reasons, some combination of the above three measures (number and frequency, volume and frequency, or all three together) is often used to classify fish diets as a whole or to estimate "overall importance" of particular food items. Employing such combination indices, we can then use various measures of prey ranks, species composition, trophic diversity, evenness, and dominance—and even prey preference—in ecological studies of fish-feeding habits. For instance, does one kind of food item predominate, by number, by volume, or by frequency of occurrence in a fish's diet, or does the fish prey on a wide spectrum of food items? Using the data presented in table 13.1, we will demonstrate how these measures can be used to answer such questions.

We should now consider sample size. For example, if we are characterizing the feeding habits of stream fishes, we need to know if our sample represents all the fishes in the community and their forage base. One can envision the problem, say, of using only samples taken near some underwater shrubbery for diet analysis, when it is very possible that a large portion of the population of a given species hangs out in the middle of the stream and consumes primarily benthic invertebrates. If our sample only considered one portion of this stream fish population, it would not adequately describe the feeding habits of the entire population.

Several approaches can avoid this kind of bias problem. First, attempt to sample your fish from throughout its geographic range and over as many time periods as possible. If a fish feeds nocturnally, then sampling it in late afternoon might result in an overly high proportion of empty guts and a misrepresentation not only of stomach fullness and digestive state but also of prey importance. Second, to assess whether you have a sufficient sample size for gut analysis, it is useful to plot the cumulative number of prey types (or even prey diversity indices if you wish—see Hurtubia 1973, and pp. 161–163) against the cumulative number of guts analyzed. The point at which this curve begins to level indicates that the number of guts (samples) analyzed is sufficient to represent the entire food array for that fish predator at that time and place (Hurtubia 1973, Cailliet 1977).

Measures of Prey Importance

Combinations of the three separate measures (frequency, number, volume) of prey importance may allow a more representative feeding-habit data summary yet still allow each measure to be evaluated individually. The most commonly used measure, the Pinkas et al. (1971) **Index of Relative Importance (I.R.I.)**, combines all three measures, allows the prey items to be ranked by this combined index, and can be graphically represented (fig. 13.1). Yet it allows each separate food-importance measure to be visualized. This can be done by pooling the contents of all guts in a group (by location, sex, time of day, or the like) and calculating the percent by number (percent N) percent by volume or weight (percent V), and the proportion of guts in that category containing each kind of prey item (percent F). It can also be done by calculating percent N and percent V for each gut, then taking the mean percent N and V values and combining these with the overall percent F value to produce the I.R.I. The second method is more time consuming but allows one to evaluate the variability of number and volume values for specific prey items.

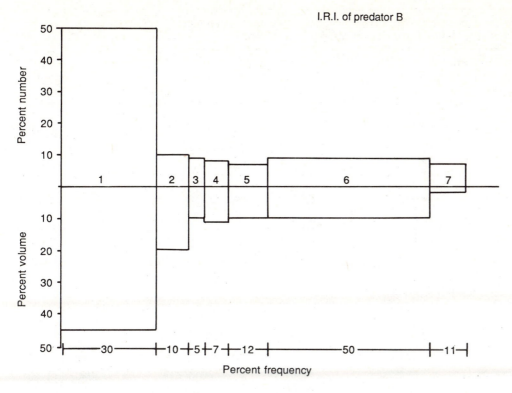

Figure 13.1 An I.R.I. diagram of the prey items and their numerical, volumetric, and frequency of occurrence values. Prey items are not ranked but are in the order of prey items of predator A. The percent frequency occurrence axis is rezeroed for each prey.

Either way these three measures are calculated, the index of relative importance is then calculated using the following equation:

$$I.R.I. = (\% N + \% V)(\% F)$$

Since each of the three individual measures can range from 0 to 100 percent, the minimum I.R.I. is 0, and the maximum would be 20,000, in which all items were of the same type in all the guts examined. Species A and B (table 13.1) appear to have similar diets based on percent number, but their prey rankings using I.R.I. values lead to a different conclusion, probably based in part on differences in volumetric and frequency-of-occurrence importance measures. Therefore, considering all importance measures, their dietary differences might be more substantial.

As stated earlier, the I.R.I. values for each prey species can be graphically represented (see fig. 13.1 for the I.R.I. diagrams for predator B). Here, a rectangle, with the vertical axis comprised of percent N and percent V and the horizontal axis, rezeroed for each prey, representing percent F, indicates the prey's importance as a food item. Again, they can be ranked by their respective I.R.I. values, but the relative contribution of percent N, percent V, and percent F can also be visualized. A predator that consumes many small prey items would have its prey exhibit an I.R.I. diagram similar to prey items 5 and 7; whereas one that

consumed fewer, more voluminous prey items would be more like prey items 2, 3, and 4. Prey items 1 and 6 were equally important numerically and volumetrically but dominated in terms of frequency of occurrence among the population sampled.

Measures of Trophic Diversity

Many indices measure diversity or breadth of diet and most are derived from community studies. Each of these indices has its own assumptions, limitations, and applicability. Generally, such indices combine the importance of the number of different prey types (prey species richness) with how evenly the numbers of prey individuals are distributed among these types (prey species equitability or dominance). A species with both many prey types in its diet and an even distribution of numbers or volume among these types will have the highest trophic diversity or diet breadth. Here we will present only those most commonly used diversity indices. For further information, consult Hurtubia (1973), Cailliet (1977), and Hyslop (1980).

Prey Diversity

The most commonly used measure of diversity is the Shannon-Wiener Information Measure (H) (Wilson and Bossert 1971). It is calculated using the following equation:

Table 13.2 Calculation of trophic diversity for predators A and B using the Shannon-Wiener information measure on both the numerical and volumetric prey importance values.

Prey Volume

Prey Species	p_i	$\ln p_i$	$p_i \ln p_i$	Prey Species	p_i	$\ln p_i$	$p_i \ln p_i$
		A				B	
$i=1$	.25	−1.39	−.35	$i=1$	.45	−7.99	-3.60
$i=2$	.22	−1.51	−.33	$i=2$	.20	−1.61	−.32
$i=3$	.18	−1.71	−.31	$i=3$	.10	−2.30	−.23
$i=4$	.16	−1.83	−.29	$i=4$	.11	−2.21	−.24
$i=5$	.10	−2.30	−.23	$i=5$	.02	−3.91	−.08
$i=6$	.05	−3.00	−.15	$i=6$	.10	−2.30	−.23
$i=7$	.05	−3.00	−.15	$i=7$	.02	−3.91	−.08
			$\Sigma = -1.81$				$\Sigma = -4.78$
			$H = 1.81$				$H = 4.78$

Prey Numbers

Prey Species	p_i	$\ln p_i$	$p_i \ln p_i$	Prey Species	p_i	$\ln p_i$	$p_i \ln p_i$
		A				B	
$i=1$	.30	−1.2	−.36	$i=1$	.50	−.69	−.35
$i=2$	.18	−1.7	−.31	$i=2$	.10	−2.3	−.23
$i=3$	.18	−1.7	−.31	$i=3$	.09	−2.4	−.22
$i=4$	.15	−1.9	−.29	$i=4$	.08	−2.5	−.20
$i=5$	.08	−2.5	−.20	$i=5$	.07	−2.7	−.19
$i=6$	.06	−2.8	−.17	$i=6$	.09	−2.4	−.22
$i=7$	.05	−3.0	−.15	$i=7$	.07	−2.7	−.19
			$\Sigma p_i \ln p_i = -1.79$				$\Sigma p_i \ln p_i = -1.6$
			$H = 1.79$				$H = 1.6$

$$H = -\sum_{i=1}^{S} (p_i)\, ln(p_i)$$

where p_i = the proportion of each different food item (which may be either relative number, volume, or frequency of occurrence), contributing to the whole diet (table 13.2).

In assessing trophic diversity measures for predators A and B, one arrives at different conclusions when using numerical prey importance values versus volumetric values (table 13.2). Note that H values for predator A are quite similar for number and volume, but for predator B, the tropic diversity is much higher when prey are assessed volumetrically than by number.

• By looking at the relative numerical and volumetric numbers, can you tell why such a large difference should occur? (Remember that the Shannon-Wiener index measures both richness and evenness.)

An alternative measure of dietary diversity is diet breadth (B), which is merely the inverse of the dominance index (described in the following section, Prey Evenness). Dietary diversity is calculated using the following equation:

$$B = 1 \left/ \sum_{i=1}^{N} (p_i)^2 \right.$$

where p_i is the proportion of the ith of N items in the diet, the same value used in calculating the Shannon-Wiener index. This index is more sensitive to abundant items and tends to deemphasize relatively rare prey items.

• Using the values of p_i in table 13.3, what are the dietary diversity values (B) that result? Do your conclusions differ with those derived from using Shannon-Wiener (H) values? Why or why not?

Prey Evenness

As mentioned earlier, most diversity indices are sensitive both to species richness and the evenness with which their abundances are distributed among species. Therefore, an

Table 13.3 Calculation of percent dominance (d) using numerical prey proportion (p_i) information, for predators A and B.

		Percent Volume			
	A			B	
Prey Species	p_i	$(p_i)^2$	Prey Species	p_i	$(p_i)^2$
$i=1$	.25	.0625	$i=1$	.45	.2025
$i=2$	.22	.0484	$i=2$	.20	.0400
$i=3$	.18	.0324	$i=3$	.10	.0100
$i=4$	.16	.0256	$i=4$	.11	.0120
$i=5$	.10	.0100	$i=5$	.02	.0004
$i=6$	.05	.0025	$i=6$	.10	.0100
$i=7$	.05	.0025	$i=7$	.02	.0004

$\Sigma(p_i)^2 = .1839$ $\Sigma(p_i)^2 = .2753$

additional measure is necessary to separate out these two components.

The first measure (e) assesses diversity relative to the maximum possible diversity if all items were represented equally, and therefore it measures how evenly the prey species are distributed in the diet. It is calculated as follows:

$$e = \frac{H}{H_{max}}$$

where $H_{max} = ln\ S$ and $ln\ S$ = the natural log of the number of food types. This value ranges from 0 to 1.0, with the higher number indicating the maximum evenness, given the number of prey species involved.

Another measure would be B/S, which measures evenness by emphasizing the contribution of predominant items. It is maximum (close to 1.0) when all prey items are equally abundant.

A third measure is dominance (d), which measures the extent to which one or a few species dominate the diet, and it can be expressed simply as the denominator in the equation to calculate B, or

$$d = \sum_{i=1}^{N} (p_i)^2$$

An example of how to calculate d is given in table 13.3. Note here that predator B has a diet that is more dominated by one prey type than predator A, at least numerically.

• Would dominance values using volumetric prey importance give you the same result as in table 13.3? Why not just calculate them and see?

• Do the conclusions from evenness (e) and dominance (d) measures agree with those from diversity (H) and diet breadth (B)?

Measures of Association or Overlap

Certain indices can be used to determine whether two species of fish have similar or different diets. Assuming that you have analyzed sufficient samples to characterize the diet and that you have used proper methods to describe the array of prey, you can apply methods of measuring overlap. These measures are quite varied and numerous, but several stand out as simple to calculate and relatively unbiased (Cailliet and Barry 1978, Hurlburt 1978). The simplest measures use only presence or absence data and compare joint occurrences of prey items; the more elaborate overlap measures use relative proportions of the different dietary items as well as their presence or absence. For these measures, there is no statistically sound cutoff, but general guidelines have been proposed. To further explore the statistical ramifications of overlap measures, we would have to look in detail at techniques such as nonparametric correlation coefficients, which is beyond the scope of this volume. Briefly, these are rank correlation tests, where prey items from each group are ranked by importance (volumes, numbers, frequency, or I.R.I.'s). Since these tests are somewhat complicated, we suggest consulting the following references for suggestions: Horn (1966), Hurtubia (1973), Bray and Ebeling (1975), Silver (1975), Cailliet and Barry (1978), Hurlburt (1978), Hyslop (1980), and Wallace (1981).

Index of Similarity

This index (Barbour et al. 1973) uses presence or absence and joint occurrence of food items but provides no indication of the importance of relative abundance of prey items in the two diets.

$$S = \frac{2c}{A + B}$$

Where A, B = number of different prey items in predators A, B; C = number of joint prey items shared by predators A, B; and S ranges from 0 to 1.0.

Index of Affinity

This index (Silver 1975) is based on the similarity in proportions of items in two diets.

$$I = \sum_{i = 1}^{s} \text{Min } p_i$$

where I (percent similarity) is derived by summing up all of the smallest proportion of each item (Min p_i) in the two lists of prey items (table 13.4). Silver (1975) assumed that 80 percent was significant for phytoplankton, but there is no absolute cutoff level.

EXERCISE: FEEDING MORPHOLOGY AND FOOD-HABIT ANALYSIS

Morphology

1. Using a fish of the species to be studied, examine and sketch its general body shape (side and transverse views) and the shape and placement of its pectoral, pelvic, and caudal fins (see sect. 1 for guidance).
2. Examine and sketch the mouth parts.

   - Are there any noticeable sensory structures such as barbels or papillae on or near the fish's lips?
   - What are the lips like? Are they thin or thick?
   - Is the mouth large or small?
   - Are the jaws protrusible or nonprotrusible?
   - Is the mouth terminal, superior, or inferior?

Table 13.4 Calculation of prey species similarity (I) indices for predator A and B.

Prey Species	Predator A	Predator B	Min p_i
1	0.30	0.50	0.30
2	0.18	0.10	0.10
3	0.18	0.09	0.09
4	0.15	0.08	0.08
5	0.08	0.07	0.07
6	0.06	0.09	0.06
7	0.05	0.07	0.05

$I = \sum = 0.75 = 75$ percent similarity

3. Size and protrusibility of the mouth and jaws are important indicators of food items as they limit the type of prey that the fish can ingest. Open the oropharyngeal cavity by making a vertical cut through the head. Sketch and describe the teeth on jaws, tongue, vomer, pharynx, and so on.

   - What type of teeth are they? (See examples in chap.1, fig. 1.17.)
   - Are all the teeth in the mouth and pharynx similar in shape?

4. Examine the gill rakers.

   - Are they long or short, many or few, toothed or smooth?

5. Open the body cavity by cutting away the body wall. Remove the digestive tract by cutting just behind the pharynx and at the anus. Stretch the digestive tract so it is laid out on a tray, and measure and record its length. Count the pyloric caeca (if present). Open the various sections of the tract and sketch the interior surface of each.

   - Are there any differences between sections?
   - Do some sections have little or no food?

Table 13.5 Data sheet for feeding morphology analysis.

Species _____

Date _____ Time _____

Capture location _____

SL _____ Sex _____

Morphology:

Lips _____

Jaw/mouth configuration _____

Teeth:

   Location _____

   Kind _____

Gill rakers:

   Number _____   Length _____

   Spacing _____   Shape _____

Length of digestive tract _____

Number of pyloric caeca _____

Number of stomachs _____

Fullness of stomach (0 = empty to 4 = full) _____

Stage of digestion (1 = digested to 4 = undigested) _____

Table 13.6 Data sheet for prey analysis.

	Volume (percent)	Frequency (percent)	Number (percent)	I.R.I.
Primary planktonic (sum =)				
Chaetognaths	_____	_____	_____	_____
Cladocerans	_____	_____	_____	_____
Copepods	_____	_____	_____	_____
Euphausiids	_____	_____	_____	_____
Fish larvae	_____	_____	_____	_____
Megalops larvae	_____	_____	_____	_____
Ostracods	_____	_____	_____	_____
Tunicates	_____	_____	_____	_____
Zoea larvae	_____	_____	_____	_____
Other _____	_____	_____	_____	_____
_____	_____	_____	_____	_____
Primarily nektonic (sum =)				
Fish	_____	_____	_____	_____
Squid	_____	_____	_____	_____
Other _____	_____	_____	_____	_____
_____	_____	_____	_____	_____
Primarily substrate oriented (sum =)				
Free-moving animals	_____	_____	_____	_____
Caprellid amphipods	_____	_____	_____	_____
Crabs	_____	_____	_____	_____
Fishes	_____	_____	_____	_____
Gammarid amphipods	_____	_____	_____	_____
Hyperiid amphipods	_____	_____	_____	_____
Isopods	_____	_____	_____	_____
Mysids	_____	_____	_____	_____
Octopi	_____	_____	_____	_____
Polychaete worms	_____	_____	_____	_____
Shrimps	_____	_____	_____	_____
Snails	_____	_____	_____	_____

Continued

Table 13.6 *Continued*

	Volume (percent)	Frequency (percent)	Number (percent)	I.R.I.
Sessile or burrowing forms (sum =)				
Algae	_____	_____	_____	_____
Barnacles	_____	_____	_____	_____
Clams	_____	_____	_____	_____
Hydroids	_____	_____	_____	_____
Mussels	_____	_____	_____	_____
Polychaete worms	_____	_____	_____	_____

Total volume (weight) of food items _____

Total number of empty tracts _____

Total number of specimens examined _____

• Can you evaluate the state of digestion of the prey items in the different portions of the digestive tract?

When you have completed your sketches, enter the data on table 13.5. Then try to deduce the feeding habits of the fish from its morphology. For instance, does it have large teeth and a grasping-type mouth to hold onto large mobile prey? Does it have small, widely set gill rakers because it needs to retain small prey? Does it have a relatively short gut for digesting large prey of high food quality, such as small fish? If so, the fish is probably a piscivore or consumer of large, mobile invertebrates. On the other hand, if the fish's body is gibbose in shape and its mouth is small and protrusible with large lips and weak teeth, it is probably a microcarnivore. It picks out and sucks up relatively small prey from midwater or bottom surfaces. Its gill rakers are predictably long and close set to bar exit of the small food items through its gill opening as it breathes.

Food Habits

1. Remove the food material. Place the material from each section on a separate petri dish or watch glass. If the specimens have been preserved, place a small amount of alcohol over the tract contents to prevent drying.
2. Food material becomes more difficult to identify as it is digested and passes along the tract. Most food studies emphasize the content of only the stomach or anterior part of the gut, where items are least digested. Often only the stomach, if present, is examined. If a stomach is absent, examine the first third or half of the tract.

Before analyzing food material, decide how much of the tract you will examine for each species.
3. Record data from each specimen on a data sheet similar to tables 13.5 and 13.6.
4. For each species, pool the following data:
   a. Number of empty tracts
   b. Food item frequency of occurrence
   c. Numbers of food items
   d. Volume (or weight) of food items
   If enough specimens are available, separate fish into size classes and pool data. Record pooled data.

   • Does the feeding habit you guessed at from your examination of the fish's alimentary morphology match that determined directly by observing the gut contents?

5. Compute and graph the I.R.I. for each food item.
6. Compute and compare trophic diversity, evenness, and so on, for each species (or size class) based on pooled data. Using one of the association measures, compare the food habits of the various species.

   • Do there appear to be any differences?
   • Are there differences between species in the percent of empty guts? Can this be correlated with differences in capture time of day or year? Are differences associated with sex of predator, location of capture, or differences in diet? How?
   • Compute the ratio of digestive tract length to fish length, and find the mean value for each species. Also calculate the mean count of pyloric caeca. Do the mean values vary between fishes from different feeding guilds?

Chapter 14
Reproduction

The study of how fish reproduce forms a basic part of the biology of fishes, especially those that support important fisheries. Knowledge of the sex ratio and the state of maturity of individuals in a population is useful, and estimates of fecundity (the number of eggs in the ovary that will mature before spawning) are considerably important in studies of population dynamics, productivity, or population estimates (Scott 1979, Wootton 1979).

For this exercise, you will need data on length, weight, and age for each specimen. You can use fish dissected during the age-growth lab if you wish to combine age and growth information with reproductive condition. To save time and effort, you can split the exercise in two: dissections and preservation of eggs one day, and fecundity estimates the second.

SEX DETERMINATION

Sex determination in adult fishes is usually straightforward. In some species, such as cichlids (color morphs), some cottids (gonopodia), and elasmobranchs (claspers), sexually dimorphic characters are external. In many flatfish, adult females have longer body cavities (extending farther posterior) than males. Sex determination in these fishes is a matter of holding a specimen against a light or up to the sun.

If examination of the gonads is necessary, mature ovaries and testes are simple to distinguish. Ovaries are tubular and normally pink, yellow, or orange. Ovaries seem to be surrounded by a clear bag. This can be determined by picking at them with forceps. Testes are flattened, often crinkly at the margins, and usually white during spawning season and brownish at other times. Normally, sexes of even older immature fishes can be distinguished using these criteria, though ovaries may be clear and testes stringlike rather than flattened and ribbonlike. Very young, immature fishes, where gonads are extremely small, often must be examined histologically.

MATURITY STAGES

Fish biologists are an eccentric group. As an example of this, they spend much of their lives either seasick on a heaving deck or passed out below, overcome with formalin fumes. This eccentricity can be the only explanation for their misuse of the term *maturity stage*. Maturity stage refers to the degree of ripeness (that is, how close an individual is to spawning) of the ovaries and testes of a fish. The term *first maturity* is used to describe a fish spawning for the first time. The term *spawning stage* rather than maturity stage would perhaps be more appropriate, but we will use maturity stage since it is so pervasive.

Fishes are either total (isochronal) or multiple (heterochronal) spawners. Total spawners release eggs or sperm all at once or over a week or so. They generally have short, distinct breeding seasons. A majority of temperate species are total spawners. Multiple spawners (such as cyprinids and sciaenids) spawn over a longer period. In fact, some, such as tropical wrasses, spawn throughout the year (Thresher 1984). In these species, eggs in varying stages of development exist in a single ovary. Staging is most clearcut with total spawners. Multiple spawners may have ovaries that fit two or more stages.

Often in fisheries work, the goal is to examine large numbers of fish to gain an accurate picture of the maturity stage(s) of a population. Thus, though histological examination may be more elegant, routine staging uses characters that can be differentiated by eye. We present two classification schemes of total spawners for oviparous (table 14.1) and ovoviviparous (table 14.2) species. A further discussion of multiple spawners is found in Holden and Raitt (1974).

GONAD INDICES

Gonad indices are tools for statistically and graphically comparing gonadal states (as between seasons and size

Table 14.1 The seven stages of maturity in oviparous fishes.

I. Immature: Young individuals that have not yet engaged in reproduction; gonads are very small.

II. Resting stage: Sexual products have not yet begun to develop; gonads are of very small size; eggs are not distinguishable to the naked eye.

III. Maturation: Eggs are distinguishable to the naked eye; a very rapid increase in weight of the gonads is in progress; testes change from transparent to a pale rose color.

IV. Maturity: Sexual products are ripe; gonads have achieved their maximum weight, but the sexual products are still not extruded when light pressure is applied.

V. Reproduction: Sexual products are extruded in response to very light pressure on the belly; weight of the gonads decreases rapidly from the start of spawning to its completion.

VI. Spent condition: The sexual products have been discharged; the genital aperture is inflamed; gonads have the appearance of deflated sacs; the ovaries usually contain a few leftover eggs and the testes some residual sperm.

VII. Resting stage: Sexual products have been discharged; inflammation around the genital aperture has subsided; gonads are of very small size; eggs are not distinguishable to the naked eye.

Source: Nikolsky 1963.

Table 14.2 Stages of maturity for ovoviviparous fishes.

Condition	Description
	Males
Immature	Stringlike, translucent
Maturing	Stringlike, slight swelling, translucent white
Mature:	
Resting	Ribbonlike, small, brown
Developing	Ribbonlike, swelling, brown-white
Developed	Large, white, easily broken
	Females
Immature	Small, translucent
Maturing	Small, yellow, translucent or opaque
Mature	Large, yellow, opaque
Fertilized	Large, orange-yellow, translucent
Ripe	Large, translucent yellow or gray, with black dots (contain embryos or larvae)
Spent	Large, flaccid, red; a few larvae may be present
Resting	Moderate size, firm, red-gray, some with black blotches

Source: Westrheim 1975.

classes). Several types of indices can be used, and three are listed below:

1. Gonad index (GI) = $\dfrac{W}{L^3} \times 10^8$

2. Gonosomatic index (GSI) = $\dfrac{W}{B} \times 100$

where W is the weight of both gonads, B is the weight of the fish, and L is the length of the fish.

There is some evidence that care should be taken in the choice of indices used. For instance, the best expression of a gonadal index in the fluffy sculpin, *Oligocottus snyderi*, is log ovarian weight divided by log standard length. DeVlaming et al. (1982), Grossman and DeVlaming (1984), and Erickson et al. (1985) discuss this problem at length. Their major concern is that gonadal growth is often allometric. Thus gonadal weight (W) is related to body size (S) as

$$W = \alpha_i \, S^{\beta_i}$$

where α_i and β_i are parameters to be estimated for gonadal developmental stage i (Erickson et al. 1985). Then, α_i and β_i can be estimated by using a linear least-squares regression for the log-transformed model

$$(W) \; \beta_i \; ln \, (S) + ln \, (\alpha_i)$$

where i is the slope and $ln \, (\alpha_i)$ is the intercept. Then a third gonadal index can be calculated (Erickson et al. 1985):

3. Relative gonadal index (RGI) = $\dfrac{\alpha_i \, W}{S^{\beta_i}}$

FECUNDITY

Fecundity is the number of eggs in the ovaries that will mature during a particular spawning season. Fecundity data are used to calculate the reproductive potential of a population. This, in turn, leads to estimates of the minimum adult population needed to maintain recruitment. It may also be used (along with the adult sex ratio) to estimate stock size.

Egg Preservation

Though it is possible to count eggs from unpreserved ovaries, it is difficult and perhaps not too accurate. Most fecundity studies utilize hardened, preserved eggs that are easier to count.

Formalin (5 percent) has the advantage of fixing eggs relatively quickly, often within 24–48 hours. However, eggs will occasionally become fixed into a very hard aggregate. Drain off the formalin and rinse repeatedly in freshwater before counting the eggs.

Gilson's Fluid is a very popular egg preservative. It does not cause overhardening of the eggs and will, in fact, loosen them from the surrounding ovarian tissue. However, Gilson's may require several days to a few weeks to harden eggs sufficiently. Gilson's is composed of equal parts of glacial acetic acid, chloroform, and 60 percent ethanol.

Procedure

Remove the ovaries from the fish, split longitudinally, and turn inside out. Place in labeled jar and cover with preservative. Use preservative liberally as the eggs will not harden if too little is used. Shake well and let stand for at least 24 hours. Gentle heating in an oven may hasten the fixation process. Periodic shaking helps loosen eggs. Before counting eggs, replace the preservative with water. Wash the eggs repeatedly, decanting off the supernatant.

Fecundity Estimation

I. Total counts. The most accurate estimate of fecundity is by total count of eggs in a fish. As this can be tedious and time consuming, most fecundity estimates are based on subsampling.

II. Subsampling of eggs

   A. Volumetric method

     1. On a paper towel, air dry the entire lot of eggs for a few minutes and obtain the total volume in a finely graduated cylinder or burette by water displacement.

     2. Take a sample(s) of the ovary. Blot or dry excess moisture and obtain the volume as in 1.

     3. Count the number of eggs in the sample(s).

     4. To obtain the total number of eggs in the unknown volume, use the formula

$$\frac{X}{n} = \frac{V}{v}$$

       where X = unknown total number of eggs in the lot

       n = number counted in sample

       V = total displaced volume of all eggs

       v = volume of the sample

   B. Egg/volume method

     1. Count out 100 eggs and measure the volume of water displaced.

     2. Measure the total displacement of the entire lot, including the sample, and calculate as above—n now will be equal to 100.

   C. Gravimetric method

     1. Weigh a known number of eggs or a standard subsample following removal of moisture.

     2. Find the total weight of the entire lot similarly dried, and compute the total number by using a ratio similar to that in A4 above.

   D. Wet subsample method. The wet subsample method (Bagenal and Braum 1968) has been widely touted, but its accuracy is debated by some workers.

     1. Place all the eggs in a beaker of water of known volume. Stir the contents using a magnetic stirrer.

     2. Using a pipette, take four to six subsamples and count the eggs in each.

     3. Estimate fecundity by multiplying the mean number of eggs per milliliter of sample by the volume of water and eggs from which the subsamples were drawn. For example, if all the eggs were placed in 1000 ml of water, fecundity equals 1000 n, where n = the mean number of eggs per milliliter in the subsamples.

Fecundity Estimation: Multiple Spawners

The previous methods are most useful for total spawners. There are other, somewhat more complicated, techniques for multiple spawners. In some species, egg measurements made early in the spawning season show ova with two or more size (diameter) modes. The larger mode(s) will indicate those eggs that will be spawned during the current season. However, these counts must be made early in the season before any mature eggs are spawned. Another approach has been to count all yolked ova, assuming that these are all that will be spawned that season. Unfortunately, all yolked eggs may not be shed. Also, unyolked ova could mature later in the same season. Mackay and Mann (1969) and Macer (1974) discuss these problems further.

Fish biologists, virtual wellsprings of creativity, have tried several new techniques for estimating fecundity. These are based on the assumption that the fecundity of a female multiple spawner is equal to her number of spawning events per season multiplied by the number of eggs shed per spawning. Several methods of deriving this estimate have been suggested (Hunter and Goldberg 1980, DeMartini and Fountain 1981).

In one procedure, repeated samples of a population are made to indicate the percentage of females with hydrated eggs on any particular day during spawning season. Females hydrate eggs before spawning. By repeated sampling of the population, the length of the spawning season can be approximated. Batch fecundity (the number of eggs spawned per event) is estimated by counting the hydrated eggs per female.

As an example, let us suppose that 10 percent of the mature females collected per day carry hydrated eggs. Thus, a typical female would spawn once per 10 days. If the

Table 14.3 Data sheet for reproduction analysis.

| | Specimen Number | | | | | |
	1		2		3	
Species						
SL (L: mm)						
Weight (B: g)						
Age						
Females	Right	Left	Right	Left	Right	Left
Ovary (side)						
Length (mm)						
Weight (W: g)						
State of maturity						
Volume (cc)						
Subsample						
Weight (g)						
Volume (cc)						
Number of eggs						
Weight 100 eggs						
Egg diameters						
Range						
Mean						
Size peaks						
Both ovaries						
Weight (W)						
Fecundity estimate*						
Volumetric						
Egg/volume						
Gravimetric						
Males						
Gonad weight						
Gonad volume						
Gonad index						
Gonosomatic index						

*If total egg count is possible, ignore other fecundity estimates.

spawning season lasted 90 days, the female would spawn 9 times. If batch fecundity for a particular size class had a mean of 10,000, then a typical female in that size class would spawn 90,000 eggs in a spawning season.

EXERCISE: FECUNDITY ANALYSIS

For each specimen, record the following and list in table 14.3: species, length (total, standard, or fork) to the nearest millimeter, weight (to the nearest 0.1 gr.), age (from otoliths and so forth), and state of maturity. Remove the gonads (separating right and left), weigh, and measure. Preserve ovaries as described above, keeping left and right separated.

After preservation, make fecundity estimates using the various methods listed above. Using an ocular micrometer in a dissecting microscope, measure the diameters of 100 eggs taken at random from throughout the ovaries. Record all data in table 14.3. Pool data from all fish examined by the class.

1. Plot fecundity against length (fecundity on y-axis, length on x-axis).

   • What form does the relationship assume?

2. Compare estimates derived from various methods.

   • Do any give relatively high or low estimates? If so, why?
   • Is there asymmetry in ovary egg numbers?

3. Plot percent mature and immature fish against length (and, if possible, age).

   • At what size and age does the species mature?

4. Plot gonad and gonosomatic indices (y-axis) against length (x-axis).

   • Does your conclusion about size or age at maturity differ with that above? Why?

5. Graph the diameter of eggs against percent of all eggs measured.

   • Are distinct peaks present?

Chapter 15
Parasites

Parasitism may be defined as a close association between two organisms in which one, the parasite, is metabolically dependent on the other, the host. Inherent in the relationship is a mutual exchange of chemical substances. Parasites are normally either **ectoparasitic** (found on the exterior of the body) or **endoparasitic** (found within the body).

Parasites have infected fish for millions of years, and virtually every fish species carries one or more parasites during some part of its life. At any one time, individual fish may have four, five, or more parasite species (its parasite mix) on and in its body, often numbering (if protozoa are included) in the millions.

With few exceptions, parasites rarely seem to harm their hosts; that is, few are **pathogenic**. It is quite common to find a seemingly healthy fish with hundreds of monogenetic trematodes on its gills or tens of digenetic trematodes in its stomach. Occasionally, however, some parasites (particularly protozoa) will cause extensive harm, even leading to death. A few species are major problems in fish hatcheries.

• What selective forces might operate to reduce pathogenicity of parasites?

Parasites exhibit one of two types of life cycles. Species with a **direct cycle** infect only one host during their lifetime. Many fish parasites, particularly worms, must pass through two or more hosts before maturing, and so these have an **indirect life cycle**. Animals parasitized by a larval stage are **intermediate hosts**; **final hosts** harbor the adult. It is quite possible for a fish to be both a final host to some parasites and an intermediate host to the larval stages of others.

Good overviews of parasite ecology can be found in Cheng (1973), Kennedy (1975), and Noble and Noble (1982). In this chapter we present a brief summary of fish parasites, describe ways to examine hosts for these parasites, and discuss other parasite-related studies that you can carry out if time permits.

PARASITE GROUPS

Protozoa
Thousands of protozoa (figs. 15.1 and 15.2) are known to be parasites on fish, and they may infect virtually every organ and tissue system. Protozoa may live singly (particularly inside organs such as the gall bladder) or in large groups in cystlike structures (often in muscles or under the skin). Jahn et al. (1979) have illustrations and keys to most protozoan groups.

Monogenetic Trematoda
These worms (fig. 15.3) are normally ectoparasitic, though some inhabit gill chambers and gills, mouth cavities, and so on. Monogenes have a direct life cycle. The animals are normally flattened and have suckers or hooks at one or both ends of the body. Yamaguti (1963b) and Schell (1970) have keys and illustrations to most genera.

Digenetic Trematoda
As adults, digenes (fig. 15.4) are endoparasitic. Every organ in some host will harbor some digene or another. Digenes have an indirect life cycle, and the larval stages may be found encysted in any part of the host's body. Schell (1970) and Yamaguti (1971) have keys and illustrations to most genera.

Cestoda (Tapeworms)
As adults, these long ribbonlike endoparasites (fig. 15.5) infect the intestine of bony fish and the spiral valve of

Figure 15.1 Myxosporida (*Ceratomyxa*). (Jahn et al. 1979)

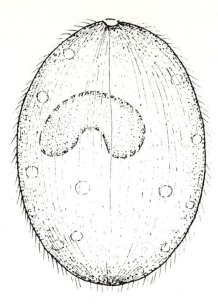

Figure 15.2 Protozoan in the family Holophryidae, genus *Ichthyophthirius.* (Jahn et al. 1979)

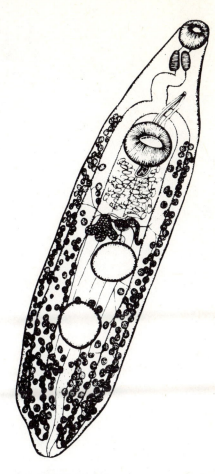

Figure 15.4 Digenetic trematode. (Yamaguti 1971)

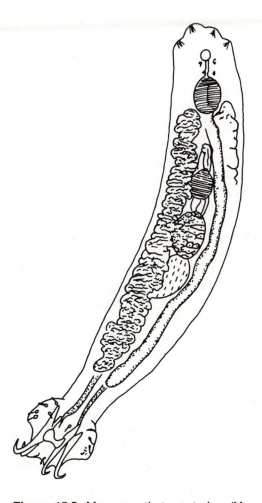

Figure 15.3 Monogenetic trematode. (Yamaguti 1963b)

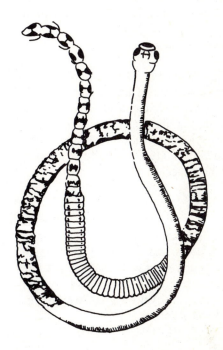

Figure 15.5 A cestode, or tapeworm. (Yamaguti 1959)

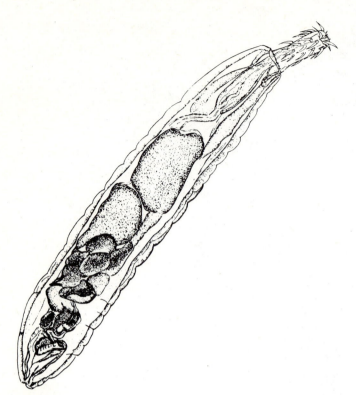

Figure 15.6 A spinyheaded worm, Acanthocephala. (Yamaguti 1963c)

Figure 15.7 General morphology of a hypothetical female nematode. (Yamaguti 1961)

sharks and rays. Tapeworms have an indirect life cycle, and the larval stages are usually small cystlike structures attached to the outside wall of the stomach, pyloric caeca, intestine or mesentery, or the muscle. A few larval stages are elongate and wormlike, often filling up the body cavity of the host. Yamaguti (1959) and Schmidt (1970) have keys and illustrations to most genera.

Acanthocephala (Spinyheaded Worms)

These are common endoparasites of fish (fig. 15.6). They have an indirect life cycle, with the adult inhabiting the intestines and larvae attaching themselves on the outside of the stomach, intestine, pyloric caeca, or in the mesentery. Yamaguti (1963c) and Golvan (1969) have keys and illustrations to genera and most species.

Nematoda

The nematodes (fig. 15.7), particularly the larval stages, are extremely common in fish. Adult worms are found in the muscles or digestive systems, and the larvae live virtually throughout the body (though most commonly in the muscles and around the outside of the digestive system). Nematodes have an indirect life cycle. Yamaguti (1961) has keys and illustrations to most genera.

Hirudinea (Leeches)

The leeches (fig. 15.8) are ectoparasites found most commonly on freshwater fish. They have a direct life cycle.

Copepoda

Copepods (figs. 15.9 and 15.10) infect most fish species. Primarily ectoparasites, some species are endoparasitic and may be found in the gut cavity, musculature, and so on. Though most species are readily identifiable as crustacea (fig. 15.9), some species have evolved most unusual shapes, often having no external evidence of legs or hooks (fig. 15.10). An informal rule of parasitology is, "If you don't know what it is, it's probably a copepod." Yamaguti (1963a) has keys to genera and some illustrations.

Isopoda

Isopods (fig. 15.11) are found on a number of fish species, though not nearly as commonly as copepods. They are primarily gill parasites, though some species are found in the mouth and on the body surface. They have a direct life cycle. Schultz (1969) has keys to species and illustrations.

DISSECTION

The following equipment will be useful in dissection: scalpel, scissors, fine paintbrush, dropper, forceps, petri dish, saline solution, jars, dissecting and compound microscopes.

Large, freshly caught fish are best for dissections. Larger fish are more easily dissected and tend to have more parasites. Fresh fish usually have live parasites that show their

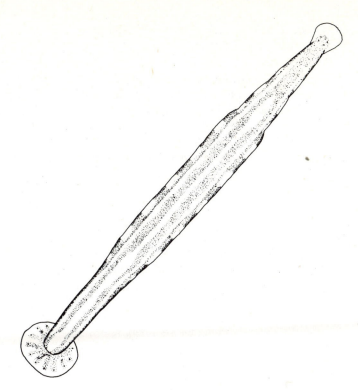

Figure 15.8 A leech, Hirudinea. (Burreson 1977)

Figure 15.10 Parasitic copepod, *Sarcotaces arcticus.* (Yamaguti 1963a)

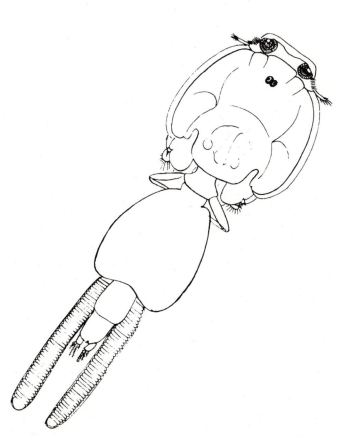

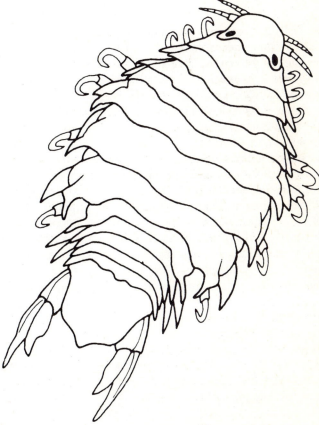

Figure 15.9 Parasitic copepod, *Caligus mutabilis.* (Yamaguti 1963a)

Figure 15.11 Parasitic isopod, *Nerocila.* (Schultz 1969)

normal color, shape, and so on. If fresh specimens are not available, frozen ones are also good. Freezing specimens is often more convenient and may allow for a wider diversity of hosts. Preserved hosts can also be used, though they are distinctly inferior, as the parasites are often quite distorted in appearance and the hosts more difficult to dissect.

Because parasites are generally quite delicate, pick them up with a pipette or fine brush. Larger or tougher individuals can be transferred with a pipette. List all parasites found using the data sheet (table 15.1) provided.

Body Surface

Protozoa, leeches, copepods, monogenes, and occasionally isopods may be found on the body surface, or as in some protozoa, in cysts or lesions under the skin.

Place the host fish on a tray, and examine it under a strong light. Many of the parasites are small and relatively colorless so close examination is necessary. Examine the entire body, paying particular attention to areas between the fin rays, under the pectoral and pelvic fins, and inside the nares. If cysts and lesions are present, carefully cut into them and examine some of the contents under a compound microscope. If the parasites are alive and seem to be firmly attached to the host tissue, you may have to remove some host tissue along with the parasite.

Oral and Gill Cavities, Gills

Examine the inside of the mouth and the gill cavity. The roof of the mouth and the inside of the operculum are particularly good areas for copepods, monogenes, and isopods.

Cut the gills out with scissors; place one gill on a petri dish, and examine its filaments under a dissecting microscope. Many gill parasites are small, cryptic, and difficult to separate from the surrounding tissue. Try different light angles and light intensities to make some of these animals visible. Cysts should be opened and smears of the contents examined under a compound microscope. If the parasites are dead and do not adhere to the filaments (if, for instance, the host has been frozen), a shortcut method is possible: Place the gills in a jar of water and shake vigorously. Most of the parasites will be washed off the gills into the water. Remove the gills and let the heavier material, containing the parasites, settle out. Remove the supernatant fluid and examine the sediment, a little at a time, in a petri dish through a dissecting microscope. This technique does not work as well if the parasites are alive, as they tend to cling to the gill surface.

Muscles

Adult and larval nematodes, larval tapeworms, and protozoa are often found in muscle tissue. Fillet the fish, running a scalpel along the backbone, starting along the dorsal region and working the blade down to the ventral area. Cut the muscle into thin slices, paying particular attention to any differences in texture or color. Larval helminths are often

darker colored and easy to spot, whereas protozoan cysts may be cream colored or whitish.

Body Cavity and Mesentery

Larval acanthocephala, nematodes, digenes, and tapeworms are often found loose in the body cavity or encysted in the mesentery. Open the body cavity by cutting the belly from anus to gill isthmus with scissors. Cut a flap out of the ribs, exposing the body cavity. Examine the mesentery, body cavity, and external parts of the stomach, intestine, and pyloric caeca.

Stomach

Nematodes and digenes are normal stomach parasites. Cut the stomach away from the body, place on a petri dish, and slit open. Remove the contents and examine under a dissection microscope. Often some parasites are left in the stomach after the food is removed. Place the opened stomach (emptied of food) in a jar of water and shake vigorously, as you did the gills. Examine the sediment after removing the supernatant.

Intestine

Nematodes, digenes, tapeworms, acanthocephala, and occasionally protozoa are found in the intestine. Remove the intestine and slit it lengthwise. Remove the contents (a curved forceps works best) and examine them on a petri dish under a dissecting microscope. Scrape a little material from the intestine wall, place on a slide, and examine for protozoa under a compound microscope.

Gallbladder

Digenes and protozoa are common in gallbladders. Remove the bladder and examine it under a dissecting microscope. Digenes are often visible through the transparent walls. Place a few drops of bladder fluid on a slide and examine for protozoa.

Kidney and Urinary Bladder

Protozoa are quite common in these organs. Place samples of tissue and fluid on slides and examine under a compound microscope.

Heart

Digenes, nematodes, and a few protozoa are found in the heart. Remove the heart and open the ventricle and atrium. Examine the contents under a dissecting microscope. Place a drop of blood on a slide and examine it under a compound microscope.

ADDITIONAL PROJECTS

To begin any project, identify the parasite. Because there are often only slight differences between many parasite

Table 15.1 Data sheet for parasite analysis.

Host species _____

Size _____

Sex _____

Parasite (species, genus, and so on)

External site

  Fins

    Dorsal _____

    Anal _____

    Caudal _____

    Pectoral _____

    Pelvic _____

  Skin

    Head _____

    Body _____

  Muscles _____

Internal site

  Branchial cavity _____

  Mouth _____

  Gill cavity _____

  Gill arches 1. _____

         2. _____

         3. _____

  Body cavity, mesentery _____

  Alimentary tract _____

    Stomach _____

    Intestine _____

    Pyloric caeca _____

  Gall bladder _____

  Kidney _____

    Urinary bladder _____

  Heart _____

Total _____

species, close examination of microscopic structures is often necessary. Parasites must often be fixed and stained before they can be identified adequately.

Fixing and Staining

Many fixatives and stains are available, and methods for their use are legion. We suggest Galigher and Kozloff (1971) or Pritchard and Kruse (1982) for a complete discussion on the subject.

Here we employ a standard fixative, AFA, useful for most parasites, and a good simple stain, Van Cleave's Hematoxylin, suitable for monogenes and digenes. Copepods and isopods are rarely stained. Consult Galigher and Kozloff (1971) or Pritchard and Kruse (1982) for staining acanthocephala, cestoda, nematoda, and protozoa.

Fixing the Parasite

Some parasites must be relaxed or straightened before they can be observed, fixed, and stored. This is particularly true for some cestodes, nematodes, and trematodes. Worms will relax in warm AFA or refrigerated saline. Nematodes, which occasionally do not respond to the above, will relax in concentrated glacial acetic acid or hot 70 percent ethanol.

AFA (10 parts formalin, 50 parts 95 percent ethanol, 2 parts glacial acetic acid, and 40 parts distilled water) is a most common parasite preservative. Below we have listed methods for fixing and preserving various parasites.

Copepods and Isopods
Place in AFA for a few minutes. Then transfer to 70 percent ethanol.

Monogenes and Digenes
Place the specimen on a glass slide in a drop of saline and cover with a cover slip. Place a few drops of AFA next to the cover slip, simultaneously withdrawing water from the opposite side using a piece of paper towel. AFA will be drawn under the slip and over the specimen. Ideally, let the worm harden for 10–30 minutes, adding more AFA as it evaporates. Then transfer the worm to a vial filled with AFA. After 12–24 hours, replace the AFA with 70 percent ethanol. If time is limited, adequate fixation will normally occur after only the initial 10–30 minutes of preparation.

Cestodes
Place the worm in a small amount of tap water. Quickly add several times as much AFA and continue swirling. Remove the worm after about 10 minutes and place in 70 percent ethanol for permanent storage.

Acanthocephala
If you have not already done so, evert the specimen's proboscis, as it is an important taxonomic character. This is done by placing the worm in distilled water or by pressing on it with a cover slip. Fix by immersing in AFA for 10–30 minutes; store in 70 percent ethanol.

Nematoda
Fix in concentrated glacial acetic acid for 5 to 10 minutes, AFA for 30 minutes, or hot 70 percent ethanol for 10 minutes. Store in 70 percent ethanol.

Staining, Clearing, and Mounting

This procedure involves several steps:

1. Hydration. After fixation, parasites are normally stored in 70 percent ethanol (occasionally isopropanol). Van Cleave's stain is effective only in water; therefore, the specimen must be transferred from alcohol to distilled water.
2. Staining.
3. Dehydration. The specimen must now be transferred back to 100 percent ethanol, as the clearing and mounting media do not function in water. If dehydration is not 100 percent effective, the parasite will not clear completely. *Both dehydration and hydration must be carried out slowly.* If this is not done, the specimen can shrivel, burst, or not clear properly.
4. Clearing. Most worms are opaque after staining, so clearing agents should be used to allow observation of internal structure.
5. Mounting. Various viscous substances are used to permanently attach worms to slides.

Hydration
1. Place the specimen, now in 70 percent ethanol, in a watch glass. Remove about one-third of the alcohol and replace with distilled water. Wait 10 minutes.
2. Remove about half the liquid, replace with distilled water. Wait 10 minutes.
3. Repeat step 2.
4. Remove all liquid, replace with distilled water. Wait 10 minutes.
5. Repeat step 4.

Staining
The specimen is now in distilled water, ready for staining. We suggest Van Cleave's Hematoxylin stain, as it is highly selective and stains only cell nuclei. Cuticular structures, ducts, and so on, are left clear. It is inexpensive, simple to use, requires little application, and bears no risk of overstaining.

Prepare Van Cleave's Hematoxylin by mixing 100 parts 6 percent potassium alum, 1 part Delafield's Hematoxylin, and 1 part Ehrlich's Hematoxylin.

Staining is best done in a small shallow container such as a watch glass or shell vial. Remove most of the water, leaving enough to cover the worm. Add enough stain to brightly color the water, but not so much as to obscure the specimen (about one-sixth the total liquid volume). Cover the container and let it stand at least two hours but preferably overnight.

Dehydration
This is essentially the reverse of the hydration process. The schedule is:

30 percent ethanol: 10 minutes
50 percent ethanol: 10 minutes
80 percent ethanol: 10 minutes
95 percent ethanol: 10 minutes
100 percent ethanol: 10 minutes
100 percent ethanol: 10 minutes

This schedule is a conservative one, and, in most cases, the lower alcohol steps may be skipped. The specimen should remain longest in the 95 percent and 100 percent ethanol to remove any last traces of water that may remain.

Clearing
A number of agents, such as xylene and beechwood creosote, are effective for clearing worms. We suggest beechwood creosote because, though it acts more slowly than xylene, it does not leave the specimens as brittle. Add a few drops of the creosote to the ethanol-immersed worm. Ten minutes or more is needed to clear helminths.

Mounting
A number of adequate mounting compounds are available. Permount, for instance, is readily obtainable and gives satisfactory results. Mix a bit of Permount in with the cleared worm and alcohol. Stir or swirl briefly, then add more Permount. When the liquid is viscous, pull the specimen up with a dropper and place it on a slide. Cover carefully with a cover slip, avoiding air bubbles. The medium will harden most quickly if the slide is placed on a slide warmer. For thick helminths, a slight weight may be necessary on the cover slip to compress the specimen. The medium hardens completely only after a number of days or weeks.

Possible group projects include studying such aspects of the ecology of parasitism as seasonal, geographic, and host-size variability in parasite-mix and infection rates.

Seasonality
The infection rates of many parasites are seasonal. Changes in host behavior, availability of intermediate hosts, and so on, can all influence infection rates. If possible, collect specimens from the same host species during several seasons; then compare parasite diversity, abundance, and rate of infection. Take care to compare similar-size hosts. Noble (1957), Hopkins (1959), Kennedy (1969 and 1975), and Amin (1975) discuss various aspects of the phenomena.

Geographic Variation
Fish from different areas often exhibit variable parasite mixes or rates of infection. A parasite's intermediate host might not be present in one area. Environmental factors such as salinity or temperature could be outside the parasite's physiological tolerances. Or a host population could be isolated from others and never become exposed to the parasite. If available, compare hosts from widely separated locations. To reduce variability, make the collections during the same seasons and use similar-size hosts.

It has been suggested that stressed hosts will have more parasites than those not stressed. To test this, compare parasite mixes and loads in fish from disturbed areas, such as hot water effluent, sewage outfalls, and chemical dumping grounds, with fish from undisturbed areas. Kabata (1963) and Noble and Noble (1982) review geographic variation in parasite infections.

Host Size
Parasite mix may change with host size. Some parasites infect fish for relatively brief periods during the host's life. A host may change its behavior (such as breeding or food habits), which removes it from contact with the parasites, or the host may change physically, which can prevent infection or reinfection.

In general, larger individuals are more heavily infected and have a greater parasite diversity. The chances of acquiring certain parasites may be greater for larger individuals, as these hosts have greater surface area, consume more potentially parasite-laden food, and have lived longer than smaller individuals. Compare parasite mixes and numbers in hosts of various sizes. Dogiel (1961) and Noble and Noble (1982) discuss host size versus parasite mix.

Chapter 16
Anomalous Fishes

Anomalies and disease conditions in fishes have been recognized and reported since the year 1555. And realization that world fish production from natural stocks has finite limits has prompted growing interest in factors such as disease that may affect population size. Furthermore, there is now great interest in the possible effects of increasing pollution on fish stocks. Some fish diseases may be associated with environmental degradation by various kinds of contaminants. Some symptoms are obvious, so they can be easily recorded to provide more comprehensive knowledge about distribution and prevalence of fin erosion, ulcers, tumors, skeletal anomalies, and the like.

DISEASES AND TUMORS

A number of "disease states" are found in fish, some of which have been linked to or associated with degraded waters. **Fin erosion** (fig. 16.1), the flaking and breaking of fin rays, is commonly found in fishes from polluted waters. Two forms are recognized: one found in bottom fishes (particularly flatfishes), in which the fins that touch the substrate are effected. Another is found in midwater or pelagic species, in which erosion is typically (but not exclusively) in the caudal fin. It has been suggested that various pollutants, including PCB's and heavy metals, may remove or modify the mucous covering, exposing tissues to pollutants and microbes.

Ulcers (fig. 16.2) and **lymphocystis** are apparently caused by microorganisms. Ulcers (open sores found on the exterior surface) are a common abnormality in fishes from polluted waters. Though not always implicated, the bacterium *Vibrio anguillarum* is often associated with ulcerations. Lymphocystis, a viral disease causing extreme cell enlargement, may also be linked to pollutants; several studies (summarized by Sindermann 1979) report higher infection rates in some polluted waters. Though the connection is unclear, it is thought that environmental stress from pollutants may increase susceptibility to microbial disease.

Similarly, there is strong circumstantial evidence associating some forms of fish **tumors** (particularly epidermal papillomas) with environmental pollution. Fishes (such as flatfish) that contact polluted substrate or are benthic feeders seem particularly vulnerable.

STRUCTURAL AND PIGMENT ANOMALIES

Spinal and **vertebral** anomalies include: (1) spinal curvature (lordosis), a dorsal-ventral shifting, causing humping; (2) scoliosis (fig. 16.3), lateral shifts in vertebrae that cause lateral flexures and body humps; and (3) kyphosis, a backward curvature of the spine.

Pugheadedness (fig. 16.4) may be of varying severity. In many cases only a somewhat steep forehead is present. At its most extreme, it is characterized by (1) a very steep bulging forehead, (2) no upper jaw and associated structures, (3) projection of the lower jaw past the upper, (4) a smaller gape and incomplete closure of the mouth, (5) tongue and gill arches partially exposed, (6) the tongue and lower oral cavity partially pigmented, (7) the tongue partly scaled, and (8) abnormal protrusion of the eyeballs as a result of changes in the skull, or exophthalmia (Hickey 1972).

Fins may show anomalies including: (1) missing fins, (2) bent fin rays, (3) additional or missing rays, (4) shortened fins, and (5) partial or complete loss of the pelvic girdle.

Though heredity and environmental factors (such as temperature, salinity, and oxygen) can cause skeletal and fin deformities, anomalies have been induced by exposing fish to heavy metals (such as zinc, cadmium, and lead) and pesticides (toxaphene, malathion, kepone, and so on).

Asymmetry, differences between the right and left sides of a bilateral character (such as pectoral fin rays or gill rakers), also occurs in many species and could be genetically or environmentally induced. Some ichthyologists be-

Figure 16.1 Fin erosion. (Sindermann 1979, p. 721)

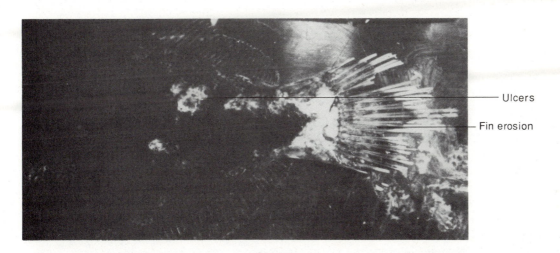

Figure 16.2 Ulcers and fin erosion. (Sindermann 1979, p. 723)

lieve that some sort of index of asymmetry might be a sensitive indicator of environmental stress.

Ambicoloration, or anomalous pigmentation, can occur in flatfish, which occasionally have dark pigment on their normally white, blind side. Anomalous pigmentation may be partial (where only part of the blind side is pigmented) or complete. Entirely pigmented flatfish, colored on both sides, usually have incomplete eye migration (indicated by a "hook" in the anterior dorsal region) and a number of other structural abnormalities. Partially ambicolored individuals are normal in other aspects.

Other pigment variations, such as albinism, melanism, and xanthocroism (which produces a gold or orange color) are occasionally seen in many fishes.

Internal organ size may also vary between populations and this, too, may be linked to pollution. Sherwood (1977) found significantly higher ratios of liver weight to body weight in dover sole (*Microstomus pacificus*) from a relatively polluted habitat. Dover sole from the polluted area also do not mature; the gonads remain small.

EXERCISE: ANOMALOUS FISHES

Ideally, compare fish samples from a potentially stressed environment—sewer outfalls, power plant waste-heat plumes, industrial waste dump sites, and so on—with samples taken from a relatively unpolluted site. An interesting variant is to compare a sample of fish collected in the past with those taken more recently.

1. List species, length, weight, sex, and capture location of the specimen and record on a data sheet.

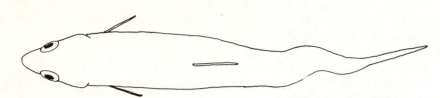

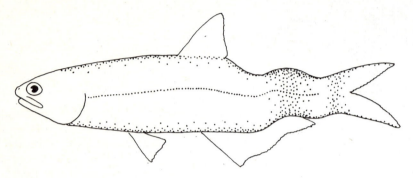

Figure 16.3 Scoliosis.

Figure 16.4 Pugheadedness. (a) is a normal longspine combfish; (b) is a pugheaded specimen; (c) and (d) are x-radiographs of the heads of (a) and (b), respectively. (Talent 1975)

2. Examine the specimen for both external (tumors, fin erosion, and so on) and internal (i.e., vertebrae, neural, and hemal-spine) abnormalities, using, if possible, a radiograph of the specimen.

3. To determine the presence of asymmetry, count pectoral fin rays and gill rakers on each side of the fish. Count the number of pectoral rays in each fin as close to the fin base as possible. Remove the gill arches to count rakers. Count first-arch rakers only if those on successive arches are rudimentary.

4. Remove and weigh the liver.

   • Compare the presence of internal or external abnormalities in fish between sites. Are there any that seem to predominate?

To compute the amount of overall asymmetry, use the formula

$$\frac{100\,(l + r)}{N}$$

where l and r represent counts that are higher on the left and right side, respectively, and N is the total number of specimens in the sample.

To compare the amount of asymmetry between sites, time periods, or size classes, subtract the left side count from the right side to obtain the signed difference. Calculate the standard deviation of the signed differences (S_{r-1}) for the entire sample (that is, for all fish from the same site, time period, or size class). Calculate the mean of the character ($\bar{x}_{r+1}$) by pooling and summing the absolute value from both sides and dividing by the sample size. Then the squared coefficient of asymmetry variation (CV^2_a) for each sample is

$$CV^2{}_a = \left(\frac{S_{r-1} \times 100}{\bar{x}_{r+1}} \right)^2$$

To test for significant differences in asymmetry between samples, assume that the CV^2's are variances (see sect. 2) and test by the F test (Sokal and Rohlf 1981), which is a ratio of the variances.

To compare the liver weights, first compute the liver-somatic indices (ratio of wet liver weight to wet body weight multiplied by 100) of each individual, and then compute the mean, variance, standard deviation, and 95 percent confidence limits of the summed values (see sect. 2).

Other detailed accounts of anomalies include Rosenthal and Rosenthal (1950), Mansueti (1958), Eisler (1963), Dahlberg (1970), Kroger and Guthrie (1971), Nelson (1971), and Valentine et al. (1973).

References and Suggested Readings for Section Three

Albrechtsen, K. 1968. A dyeing technique for otolith age reading. *J. Cons.* 32:278–80.

Amin, O. M. 1975. Host and seasonal association of *Acanthocephalus parksidei* Amin, 1974 (Acanthocephala: Echinorhynchidae) in Wisconsin fishes. *J. Parasit.* 61:318–29.

Bagenal, T. B., ed. 1973. The ageing of fish. 234 pp. Proc. Int. Symp. London: Unwin.

Bagenal, T. B., and Braum, E. 1968. Eggs and early life history. In *Methods for assessment of fish production in fresh waters*, ed. W. E. Ricker, pp. 159–81. Oxford: Blackwell Scientific Publications.

Barbour, M. G.; Craig, R. B.; Drysdale, F. R.; and Ghiselen, M. T. 1973. *Coastal ecology of Bodega Head.* 338 pp. Berkeley: University of California Press.

Beamish, R. J. 1979. Differences in the age of Pacific hake (*Merluccius productus*) using whole otoliths and sections of otoliths. *J. Fish. Res. Bd. Can.* 36:141–51.

___. 1981. Use of fin-ray sections to age walleye pollock, Pacific cod, and albacore, and the importance of this method. *Trans. Am. Fish. Soc.* 110:287–99.

Beamish, R. J., and Chilton, D. E. 1982. Preliminary evaluation of methods to determine the age of sablefish (*Anoplopoma fimbria*). *Can. J. Fish. Aquat. Sci.* 39:277–87.

Beamish, R. J., and McFarlane, G. A. 1983. Validation of age determination estimates: The forgotten requirement. *Trans. Am. Fish. Soc.* 112:735–43.

Bell, G. R. 1967. *A guide to the properties, characteristics, and uses of some general anaesthetics for fish.* Bulletin 148. 9 pp. Toronto: Fisheries Reserve Board of Canada.

Blasiola, G. C., Jr. 1977. Quinaldine sulphate, a new anaesthetic formulation for tropical marine fishes. *J. Fish. Biol.* 10:13–19.

Bray, R. N., and Ebeling, A. W. 1975. Food, activity and habitat of three "picker-type" microcarnivorous fishes in the kelp forests off Santa Barbara, California. *Fish. Bull., U.S.* 73(4):815–29.

Brock, W. E. 1954. A preliminary report on a method of estimating reef fish populations. *J. Wildl. Management.* 18:297–308.

Browning, R. J. 1980. *Fisheries of the north Pacific.* 423 pp. Anchorage: Alaska Northwest Publishing.

Burreson, E. M. 1977. Two new species of *Malmiama* (Hirudinea; Piscicolidae) from Oregon coastal waters. *J. Parasit.* 63(1):130–36.

Cailliet, G. M. 1977. Several approaches to the feeding ecology of fishes. In *Fish food habits studies*, ed. C. Simenstad and S. Lipovsky, pp. 1–13. Proceedings of the First Pacific Northwest Technical Workshop, WSG-WO 77-2.

Cailliet, G. M., and Barry, J. P. 1978. Comparison of food array overlap measures useful in fish feeding habit analyses. In *Fish food habits study*, ed. S. Lipovski and C. Simenstad, pp. 67–79. Proceedings of the Second Pacific Northwest Technical Workshop, WSG-WO79-1.

Cailliet, G. M.; Martin, L. K.; Kusher, D.; Wolf, P.; and Welden, B. 1983. Techniques for enhancing vertebral bands in age estimation of California elasmobranchs. In *Proceedings of the international workshop on age determination of oceanic pelagic fishes: Tunas, billfishes, sharks,* ed. E. Prince and L. Pulos, pp. 157–65. NOAA Technical Report/National Marine Fisheries Service 8.

Casselman, J. M. 1983. Age and growth assessment of fish from their calcified structures—Techniques and tools. In *Proceedings of the international workshop on age determination of oceanic pelagic fishes: Tunas, billfishes, sharks,* ed. E. Prince and L. Pulos, pp. 1–17. NOAA Technical Report/National Marine Fisheries Service 8.

Cheng, T. C. 1973. *General parasitology.* 965 pp. New York: Academic Press.

Chilton, D. E., and Beamish, R. J. 1982. *Age determination methods for fishes studied by the groundfish program at the Pacific Biological Station.* 102 pp. Can. Spec. Publ. Fish. Aquat. Sci. no. 60.

Christensen, J. M. 1964. Burning of otoliths, a technique for age determination of soles and other fish. *J. Cons.* 29:73–81.

Collins, R. A., and Spratt, J. D. 1969. Age determination of northern anchovies, *Engraulis mordax,* from otoliths. *California Department of Fish and Game, Fish Bulletin* 147:39–55.

Dahlberg, M. D. 1970. Frequencies of abnormalities in Georgia estuarine fishes. *Trans. Am. Fish. Soc.* 99(1):95–97.

DeMartini, E. E., and Fountain, R. K. 1981. Ovarian cycling frequency and batch fecundity in the queenfish, *Seriphus politus:* Attributes representative of serial spawning fishes. *Fish. Bull.,* U.S. 79:547–60.

DeMartini, E. E., and Roberts, D. 1982. An empirical test of biases in the rapid visual technique for species-time censuses of reef fish assemblages. *Mar. Biol.* 70:129–34.

DeVlaming, V.; Grossman, G.; and Chapman, F. 1982. On the use of the gonosomatic index. *Comp. Biochem. Physiol.* 73A:31–39.

DeVrees, C. M. 1980. *The sablefish fishery.* Leaflet 21155. 10 pp. Davis: Division of Agricultural Science, University of California, Davis.

Dogiel, V. A. 1961. Ecology of the parasites of freshwater fishes. In *Parasitology of fishes,* ed. V. A. Dogiel, G. K. Petrushevski, and Yu. I. Polyanski, pp. 1–47. London: Oliver and Boyd.

Ebeling, A. W.; Larson, R. J.; Alevizon, W. S.; and Bray, R. N. 1980. Annual variability of reef-fish assemblages in kelp forests off Santa Barbara, California. *Fish. Bull.,* U.S. 78:361–77.

Eisler, R. 1963. Partial albinism and ambicoloration in winter flounder, *Pseudopleuronectes americanus. Copeia* 1963(2):275–77.

Erickson, D.; Hightower, J.; and Grossman, G. D. 1985. The relative gonadal index: An alternative index for the quantification of reproductive condition. *Comp. Biochem. Physiol.* 81A:117–20.

Everhart, W. H., and Youngs, W. D. 1981. *Principles of fishery science.* 349 pp. Ithaca, N.Y.: Cornell University Press.

Fish, F. F. 1942. The anaesthesia of fish by high carbon dioxide concentrations. *Trans. Am. Fish. Soc.* 72:25–29.

Frey, D. G. 1951. The use of sea cucumbers in poisoning fishes. *Copeia* 1951(2):175–76.

Galigher, A. E., and Kozloff, E. N. 1971. *Essentials of practical microtechniques.* 531 pp. Philadelphia: Lea and Febiger.

Gibson, R. N. 1967. The use of the anaesthetic quinaldine in fish ecology. *J. Anim. Ecol.* 36(2):295–301.

Giger, R. D., and Williams, D. A. 1972. A net-board for setting beach seines from small boats. *Trans. Am. Fish. Soc.* 101(1):133–35.

Golvan, Y. J. 1969. *Systematique des Acanthocephales. Premiere partie. L'ordre des Palaeacanthocephala Meyer* 1931. *Premier fascicule. La super-famille des Echinorhynchoidea* (Cobbold 1876) *Golvan et Houin* 1963. *Mem. Mus. Nat. Hist. Nat. Paris Ser. A* 57:1–373.

Grossman, G. D., and deVlaming, V. 1984. Reproductive ecology of female *Oligocottus snyderi* Greeley: A North American intertidal sculpin. *J. Fish Biol.* 25:231–40.

Gulland, J. A. 1983. *Fish stock assessment: A manual of basic methods.* 223 pp. New York: Wiley.

Hanley, J. M. 1975. Review of gill net selectivity. *J. Fish. Res. Bd. Can.* 32(11):1943–69.

Hickey, C. R., Jr. 1972. *Common abnormalities in fishes, their causes and effects.* 21 pp. N.Y. Ocean Sci. Lab. Tech. Rep. no. 0013.

Holden, M. J., and Raitt, D.F.S. 1974. *Manual of fisheries science.* Pt. 2: *Methods of resource investigation and their application.* 214 pp. F.A.O. Fisheries Investigation Tech. Paper no. 115, rev. 1.

Holden, M. J., and Vince, M. R. 1973. Age validation studies on the centra of *Raja clavata* using tetracycline. *J. Cons.* 35:13–17.

Hopkins, C. A. 1959. Seasonal variation in the incidence and development of the cestode *Proteocephalus filicollis* (Rud. 1810) in *Gasterosteus aculeatus* (L. 1766). *Parasitology* 49:529–42.

Horn, H. S. 1966. Measurement of "overlap" in comparative ecological studies. *Am. Nat.* 100:419–24.

Hunter, J. R., and Goldberg, S. R. 1980. Spawning incidence and batch fecundity in northern anchovy, *Engraulis mordax. Fish. Bull.,* U.S. 77:641–52.

Hurlburt, S. H. 1978. The measurement of niche overlap and some relations. *Ecology* 59(1):67–77.

Hurtubia, J. 1973. Trophic diversity measurement in sympatric predatory species. *Ecology* 54(4):855–90.

Hyslop, E. J. 1980. Stomach content analysis, a review of methods and their application. *J. Fish Biol.* 17:411–30.

Jahn, T.; Bovee, E.; and Jahn, T. F. 1979. *How to know the protozoa.* 279 pp. Dubuque, Iowa: W. C. Brown.

Jones, B. C., and Geen, G. H. 1977. Age determination of an elasmobranch (*Squalus acanthias*) by x-ray spectrometry. *J. Fish. Res. Bd. Can.* 34:44–48.

Kabata, Z. 1963. Parasites as biological tags. *Int. Comm. Northwest Atlantic Fish.,* Spec. Publ. no. 4:31–37.

Keast, A., and Webb, D. 1966. Mouth and body form relative to feeding ecology in the fish fauna of a small lake, Lake Opinicon, Ontario. *J. Fish. Res. Bd. Can.* 23(12):1845–74.

Keenleyside, M.H.A. 1979. Diversity and adaptation in fish behavior. *Zoophysiology.* Vol. 11. 208 pp. New York: Springer-Verlag.

Kennedy, C. R. 1969. Seasonal incidence and development of the cestode *Caryophyllaeus laticeps* (Pallas) in the River Anon. *Parasitology* 59:783–94.

___. 1975. *Ecological animal parasitology.* 474 pp. New York: Wiley.

Knake, B. O. 1956. *Assembly methods for otter trawl nets.* 17 pp. Fishery Leaflet, U.S. Fish and Wildlife Service, no. 241.

Kohlhorst, D. W.; Mella, L. W.; and Orsi, J. J. 1980. Age and growth of white sturgeon collected in the Sacramento-San Joaquin Estuary, California, 1965–1970 and 1973–1976. *Calif. Fish and Game* 66(2):83–95.

Kroger, R. L., and Guthrie, J. F. 1971. Incidence of crooked vertebral columns in juvenile Atlantic menhaden, *Brevoortia tyrannus. Chesapeake Science* 12(4):276–78.

Lagler, K. F. 1978. Capture, sampling and examination of fishes. In *Methods for assessment of fish production in fresh waters,* ed. T. Bagenal, pp. 7–47. London: Blackwell Science Publications.

Leitritz, E., and Lewis, R. C. 1976. *Trout and salmon culture (hatchery methods).* Fish Bulletin 164. 197 pp. Sacramento: California Department of Fish and Game.

Limsuwan, C.; Grizzle, J. M.; and Plumb, J. A. 1983. Etomidate as an anaesthetic for fish: Its toxicity and efficacy. *Trans. Am. Fish. Soc.* 112:544–50.

Love, M. S., and Ebeling, A. W. 1978. Food and habitat of three switch-feeding fishes in the kelp forests off Santa Barbara, California. *Fish. Bull.,* U.S. 76(1):257–71.

Macer, C. T. 1974. The reproductive biology of the horse mackerel *Trachurus trachurus* (L.) in the North Sea and English Channel. *J. Fish Biol.* 6:415–43.

McFarland, W. N. 1960. The use of anaesthetics for handling and transportation of fish. *Calif. Fish and Game* 46:407–32.

McFarland, W. N., and Klontz, G. W. 1969. Anesthesia in fishes. In *Federation of American societies for experimental biology proceedings* 28:1535–40.

Mackay, I., and Mann, K. H. 1969. Fecundity of two cyprinid fishes in the River Thames, Reading, England. *J. Fish. Res. Bd. Can.* 26:2795–805.

Mahon, R. 1980. Accuracy of catch-effort methods for estimating fish density and biomass in streams. *Env. Biol. Fish.* 5:343–60.

Manooch, C. S., III, and Barans, C. A. 1982. Distribution, abundance, and age and growth of the tomtate, *Haemulon aurolineatum,* along the southeastern United States coast. *Fish. Bull.,* U.S. 80:1–20.

Mansueti, R. 1958. Eggs, larvae and young of the striped bass, *Roccus saxatilis. Maryland Dep. Res. Educ., Contrib.* 112:1–35.

Marking, L. L. 1969. *Investigations in fish control: 23. Toxicity of quinaldine to selected fishes.* 10 pp. U.S. Bureau of Sportfishing and Wildlife.

Meyer, F. P.; Schnick, R. A.; and Cumming, K. B. 1976. The registration status of fisheries chemicals. *Progr. Fish-Cult.* 38:3–7.

Miller, J. M., and Tucker, J. W. 1979. X-radiography of larval and juvenile fishes. *Copeia* 1979(4):535–38.

Moring, J. R. 1970. Use of the anaesthetic quinaldine for handling Pacific coast intertidal fish. *Trans. Am. Fish. Soc.* (4):802–5.

Nelson, J. S. 1971. Absence of the pelvic complex in ninespine sticklebacks, *Pungitius pungitius* collected in Ireland and Wood Buffalo National Park Region, Canada, with notes on meristic variation. *Copeia* 1971(4):707–17.

___. 1984. *Fishes of the world.* 2d ed. 522 pp. New York: Wiley.

Nielsen, L. A., and Johnson, D. L., eds. 1983. *Fisheries techniques.* 496 pp. Bethesda, Md.: American Fisheries Society.

Nikolsky, G. V. 1963. *The ecology of fishes.* 352 pp. New York: Academic Press.

Noble, E. R. 1957. Seasonal variation in host-parasite relations between fish and two protozoa. *J. mar. biol. Ass. U.K.* 36:143–55.

Noble, E. R., and Noble, G. A. 1982. *Parasitology.* 522 pp. Philadelphia: Lea and Febiger.

Northcote, T. G., and Wilkie, D. W. 1963. Underwater census of stream fish populations. *Trans. Am. Fish. Soc.* 92:146–51.

Pauly, D. 1984. *Fish population dynamics in tropical waters: A manual for use with programmable calculators.* ICLARM Studies and Reviews 8:1–325. Manila, Philippines: International Center for Living Aquatic Resources Management.

Pinkas, L.; Oliphant, M. S.; and Iverson, I.L.R. 1971. *Food habits of albacore, bluefin tuna, and bonito in California waters.* Fish Bulletin 152. 139 p. Sacramento: California Department of Fish and Game.

Post, G. 1979. Carbonic acid anesthesia for aquatic organisms. *Prog. Fish-Cult.* 41:142–44.

Price, D. G. 1982. *A fishery resource sampling methodology for small streams.* Pacific Gas and Electric Report 420–81.141. 49 pp.

Prince, E., and Pulos, L., eds. 1983. *Proceedings of the international workshop on age determination of oceanic pelagic fishes: Tunas, billfishes, sharks.* NOAA Technical Report/National Marine Fisheries Service 8:1–211.

Pritchard, M. H., and Kruse, G.O.W. 1982. *The collection and preservation of animal parasites.* 141 pp. Lincoln: University of Nebraska.

Ricker, W. E. 1975. Computation and interpretation of biological statistics of fish populations. *Bull. Fish. Res. Bd. Can.* 191:1–382.

Rosenthal, H. L., and Rosenthal, R. S. 1950. Lordosis, a mutation in the guppy. *J. Heredity* 41:217–18.

Rupp, R. S., and DeRoche, S. E. 1960. Use of a small otter trawl to sample deep-water fishes in Maine lakes. *Prog. Fish-Cult.* 22(3):134–37.

Russell, B. C.; Talbot, F. H.; Anderson, G.R.V.; and Goldman, B. 1978. Collection and sampling of reef fishes. In *Coral reefs: Research methods,* ed. D. R. Stoddart and R. E. Johannes, pp. 329–43. UNESCO. Norwich, England: Page Bros.

Schell, S. 1970. *How to know the trematodes.* 355 pp. Dubuque, Iowa: W. C. Brown.

Schmidt, G. D. 1970. *How to know the tapeworms.* 266 pp. Dubuque, Iowa: W. C. Brown.

Schultz, G. A. 1969. *How to know the isopods.* 359 pp. Dubuque, Iowa: W. C. Brown.

Scofield, W. L. 1947. *Drift and set line fishing gear in California.* Fish Bulletin 66. 41 pp. Sacramento: California Department of Fish and Game.

___. 1948. *Trawling gear in California.* Fish Bulletin 72. 63 pp. Sacramento: California Department of Fish and Game.

___. 1951. *Purse seines and other roundhaul nets in California.* Fish Bulletin 81. 87 pp. Sacramento: California Department of Fish and Game.

Scott, D.B.C. 1979. Environmental timing and the control of reproduction in teleost fish. *Symp. Zool. Soc. Lon.* 44:105–32.

Sherwood, M. J. 1977. Fin erosion disease and liver chemistry: Los Angeles and Seattle. In *Southern California Coastal Water Research Project, Annual Report*, pp. 213–19.

Silver, M. W. 1975. The habitat of *Salpa fusiformis* in the California current as defined by indicator assemblages. *Limnol. Oceanogr.* 20(2):230–37.

Sindermann, C. J. 1979. Pollution-associated diseases and abnormalities of fish and shellfish: A review. *Fish. Bull.*, U.S. 76(4):717–50.

Six, L. D., and Horton, H. F. 1977. Analysis of age determination methods for yellowtail rockfish, canary rockfish, and black rockfish off Oregon. *Fish. Bull.*, U.S. 75:405–14.

Sokal, R. R., and Rohlf, F. J. 1981. *Biometry.* 2d ed. 859 pp. New York: W. H. Freeman.

Southwood, T.R.E. 1978. *Ecological methods.* 524 pp. New York: Wiley.

Stevens, J. D. 1975. Vertebral rings as a means of age determination in the blue shark (*Prionace glauca* L.). *J. mar. biol. Ass. U.K.* 55:657–65.

Talent, L. G. 1975. Pugheadedness in the longspine combfish, *Zaniolepis latipinnis*, from Monterey Bay, California. *Calif. Fish and Game* 61(3):160–162.

Tesch, F. W. 1971. Age and growth. In *Methods for assessment of fish production in fresh waters*, ed. W. E. Ricker, pp. 98–130. London: Blackwell Scientific Publications.

Thresher, R. E. 1984. *Reproduction in reef fishes.* 399 pp. Neptune City, N.J.: TFH Publications.

Valentine, D. W.; Soule, M. E.; and Samollow, P. 1973. Asymmetry analysis in fishes: A possible statistical indicator of environmental stress. *Fish. Bull.*, U.S. 71(2):357–70.

Van Oosten, J. 1929. Life history of the lake herring (*Leucichthys artedi* Le Sueur) of Lake Huron as revealed by its scales; with a critique of the scale method. *Bull. U.S. Bur. Fisheries* 44 (1053):265–428.

___. 1957. The skin and scales. In *The physiology of fishes*, vol. 1, *Metabolism*, ed. M. E. Brown, pp. 207–44. New York: Academic Press.

Wallace, R. K., Jr. 1981. An assessment of diet-overlap indices. *Trans. Am. Fish. Soc.* 110:72–76.

Westrheim, S. J., and Ricker, W. E. 1978. Bias in using an age-length key to estimate age-frequency distributions. *J. Fish. Res. Bd. Can.* 35:184–89.

Wilson, C. A.; Brothers, E. B.; Casselman, J. M.; Lavette Smith, C.; and Wild, A. 1983. Glossary. In *Proceedings of the international workshop on age determination of oceanic pelagic fishes: Tunas, billfishes, and sharks*, ed. E. Prince and L. Pulos, pp. 207–8. NOAA Technical Report/National Marine Fisheries Service 8.

Wilson, E. O., and Bossert, W. H. 1971. *A primer of population biology.* 192 pp. Sunderland, Mass.: Sinauer.

Wootton, R. J. 1979. Energy costs of egg production and environmental determinants of fecundity in teleost fishes. *Symp. Zool. Soc. London* 44:133–59.

Yamaguti, S. 1959. Systema Helminthum. Vol. 2. *The cestodes of vertebrates.* 860 pp. New York: Interscience.

___. 1961. Systema Helminthum. Vol. 3. *The nematodes of vertebrates.* Parts 1 and 2. 679 pp. New York: Wiley Interscience.

___. 1963a. *Parasitic copepoda and branchiura of fishes.* 1104 pp. New York: Wiley Interscience.

___. 1963b. Systema Helminthum. Vol. 4. *Monogenea and Aspidocotylea.* 287 pp. New York: Wiley Interscience.

___. 1963c. Systema Helminthum. Vol. 5. *Acanthocephala.* 423 pp. New York: Wiley Interscience.

___. 1971. *Synopsis of digenetic trematodes of vertebrates.* Vols. 1, 2. 980 pp. Tokyo: Keigaku Publishing Co.

Index